Gushing with enthusiasm and admiration, Beahm's compendium of Harry Potter trivia and essays should tide over fans waiting for book [seven] to come out. . . . Throughout, Beahm pitches the prose just right; it's both sophisticated enough to interest adults and lively enough to keep younger fans engaged.

—*Publishers Weekly*

Beahm offers a plethora of information, opinions, and facts that revolve around Harry Potter and the likes of J. K. Rowling. This general-interest guidebook includes sections on [four] movie adaptations, [six] books, merchandise and collectibles, and Harry Potter websites. . . . A 16-page centerfold of full-color photos as well as black-and-white photographs and illustrations throughout enliven the well-written, interesting text.

—*School Library Journal*

Books by George Beahm

The Vaughn Bode Index (Heresy Press, 1975)

Kirk's Works (Heresy Press, 1977)

How to Sell Woodstoves (George Beahm, Publisher, 1980)

How to Buy a Woodstove—and Not Get Burned (George Beahm, Publisher, 1980)

Notes from Elam (editor) (George Beahm, Publisher, 1983)

How to Publish and Sell Your Cookbook: A Guide for Fundraisers (GB Publishing, 1985)

Write to the Top: How to Complain & Get Results—Fast! (The Donning Company, 1988)

The Stephen King Companion (Andrews McMeel Publishing, 1989)

The Stephen King Story (Andrews McMeel Publishing, 1990)

War of Words: The Censorship Debate (Andrews McMeel Publishing, 1993)

Michael Jordan: Shooting Star (Andrews McMeel Publishing, 1994)

The Stephen King Companion (Rev.) (Andrews McMeel Publishing, 1995)

The Unauthorized Anne Rice Companion (Andrews McMeel Publishing, 1995)

Stephen King: America's Best-Loved Boogeyman (Andrews McMeel Publishing, 1998)

Stephen King from A to Z (Andrews McMeel Publishing, 1998)

Stephen King Country (Running Press, 1999)

Stephen King Collectibles (Betts Bookstore, 2000)

The Unofficial Patricia Cornwell Companion (St. Martin's Press, 2002)

The Essential J. R. R. Tolkien Sourcebook (New Page Books, 2003)

How to Protect Yourself & Your Family against Terrorism (Brasseys, 2003)

Fact, Fiction, and Folklore in Harry Potter's World: An Unofficial Guide (Hampton Roads, 2005)

Passport to Narnia: A Newcomer's Guide (Hampton Roads, 2005)

Caribbean Pirates: A Treasure Chest of Fact, Fiction, and Folklore (Hampton Roads, 2007)

The Whimsic Alley Book of Spells (with Stanley Goldin; Hampton Roads, 2007)

Stephen King: American Storyteller (Flights of Imagination, 2007)

Philip Pullman's Dark Materials: The Golden Compass and Other Stories (Hampton Roads, 2007)

MUGGLES AND MAGIC

— Revised and Expanded —

3rd Edition

An Unofficial Guide
to J. K. Rowling
and the Harry Potter Phenomenon

George Beahm

Illustrations by Tim Kirk

HAMPTON ROADS
PUBLISHING COMPANY, INC.

To the memory of my mother-in-law,
Mildred "Lib" Bryant,
and her magical grandchildren:
Courtney, Melissa, Patrick, and Kevin.

"You'll never make any money out of children's books, Jo."
—Barry Cunningham, then co-partner of the Christopher Little Literary
    Agency, who pointed out to Joanne Rowling prior to the publication of
    her first book that, for the most part, most children's book authors
    make very little money.

Gringotts Bank

Contents

A Note to the Reader

This book is intended as a general interest, albeit unofficial, companion guide to J. K. Rowling and her most famous fictional creation, Harry Potter.

Though there are dozens of books about Rowling, Muggles, and the wizarding world in print, the biographies tend to be hagiographies, uncritical and gushing with praise; and the critical texts are written for academicians—students and scholars who perhaps hope to stake a literary claim. What used to be virgin territory is now well trod, as the fields of academe have yielded a bumper crop of books about Harry Potter, exploring every conceivable topic.

In my opinion, the publication of this book corrects a glaring omission in that line-up of books: one written for the general fan who simply enjoys the stories but wants to know more. In other words, it's a book for the rest of us.

Written especially for new Harry Potter fans—the ones who come to the books after seeing one of the film adaptations—this book necessarily covers a lot of ground. Organized by topic, it's designed to be dipped into, not read straight through, so there's some necessary repetition.

A Muggle's guide to the wizarding world and its most famous citizen, this book is your train ticket, as it were, to Platform Nine and Three-Quarters and the enchantment that lies beyond.

Tim Kirk

Acknowledgments

Writing a book is a solitary activity, but publishing it is a team effort. The following people deserve to take a bow:

Stephen McGinty, a Scottish journalist from the *Scotsman* who allowed me to reprint his biographical piece on J. K. Rowling.

Thomas N. Thornton, COO of Andrews McMeel Publishing, who encouraged me to write this book, championed it, and urged its publication. I am privileged to know him and to have books published by his house.

Tim Kirk, who graciously allowed me to reprint his art to grace the pages of this book. His works add the right touch throughout.

Ned Brooks, who served as my research assistant on matters both large and small. Drawing from his considerable knowledge of fantasy and, especially, children's literature, Ned was indispensable.

I am also indebted to **Catherine Collins,** who not only provided a Harry Potter fan trip report, but more than two dozen photographs as well. She went out of her way, time and again, to assist me at the eleventh hour; her presence in this book measurably improves it.

My friends at Hampton Roads Publishing, who believed in me and this book: **Robert S. Friedman,** an old friend from when we both worked at the Donning Company, a book publisher he founded in southeast Virginia; **Richard Leviton,** a senior editor at HRP, whose eagle eyes took my raw manuscript and improved it immeasurably; **Sarah Hilfer** and **Tania Seymour,** who cared for my manuscript in-house; and the artful **Jane Hagaman**.

For timely and much-appreciated assistance on rights and permissions, I'd like to thank **Gary Ink** of *Publishers Weekly*; **Bill Bradley, Kerry Black,** and **Stephen McGinty** of *The Scotsman* in Edinburgh, Scotland; and **Tom Courtney** of Tonner Doll Company.

Mary, my wife, who gave encouragement and support, and was an indispensable source of editorial input. Thanks, too, to **Britton McDaniel,** a treasured friend. And our niece **Courtney Bryant,** who introduced me to the Harry Potter books, for which I am eternally grateful.

Thank you, one and all.

Introduction

We're Off to See the Wizards!

Time magazine cover story

Harry Potter fans will long remember 2007, not only because it's the year that marks a decade of Harry Potter in print, but because it's the year that marks the end of the most popular and best-loved book series in the history of the world.

It was 1997 when "the boy who lived" made his unheralded appearance: a young boy who lived in obscurity with his perfectly dreadful uncle, aunt, and cousin until he discovered he was a wizard. Not only a wizard, as it turned out, but a world-class wizard who would go on to make an indelible mark in the magical world that Joanne Rowling imagined, painstakingly constructed, and recorded in seven novels.

It's now 2007 and, with the publication of the seventh and last Harry Potter novel, it's time to look back down the yellow brick road; we cannot look forward, unfortunately, because there will be (alas!) no more Harry Potter tales from the pen of J. K. Rowling.

Looking back, the fact that strikes me most obviously is that Rowling accomplished a rare and wonderful thing in writing this enchanting series.

Yes, it's great that she got kids to pick up her increasingly longer novels and put aside the electronic toys that diverted but did not spark their imaginations. Yes, it's great that her publishers and film company made so many galleons that the wizard bank Gringotts will have to build more tunnels beneath London to store the wealth in cavernous bank vaults. And, yes, it's wonderful that fans gathered together for the last few books to celebrate with parties and conferences. But what's really important is that Rowling reaffirmed in a very real and important way that reading is fundamental. That, in a world increasingly filled with the noise of cell phones, PDAs, Blackberries, laptops, and other electronic distractions, not to mention soundtracks and the admittedly wonderful and colorful films, there's a timeless quality to the quiet power of the printed word on a page that cannot be equaled. Storytelling begins with the printed word and it is all about the power of imagination.

In my mind, that's what's worth celebrating.

Rowling, who is frequently asked by interviewers what her books are about, wisely avoids rehashing plot summaries because that's not what the books are *about*. They are *about* the transformational power of imagination. They are *about* values worth celebrating—friendship, honor, duty, bravery, and above all, sacrifice, the noblest virtue of them all. They are *about* our relationships not only with others but the world we live in as well, with the sure knowledge that we are short-lived custodians and passersby in an infinite universe filled with wonder. The books are *about* children learning, growing, and becoming responsible adults, and how they must have the courage to realize their potentials by engaging their imaginations and daring to look beyond the obvious—to dare to dream.

Most of all, it's *about* the power of love in all of its magical manifestations. It is what has saved Harry time and again, and it's what will possibly save him in his final confrontation with You-Know-Who, a creature filled with self-destructive qualities, festering hate, loathing for others (especially Muggles), and who must (I hope) ultimately fail in his quest for immortality.

For it is Harry Potter that will live on in our hearts and minds, but the seemingly powerful dark wizard, Lord Voldemort, will live on only in infamy. And isn't that how it should be?

In the past ten years, we've been off to see the wizards, the wonderful wizards of Hogwarts, of Hogsmeade, and the rest of the wizarding world. We've come to love the timeless wisdom of Dumbledore, the stern but loving Professor McGonagall, and all the other faculty members at Hogwarts. We've come to bear witness to the familial love exhibited by the Weasleys, and we've seen how love can be twisted and warped by the Malfoys.

We've seen everything that Rowling has carefully and lovingly put down on paper about the wizarding world, but we shall see no more: All good things come to an end, and so, too, must the tales of Harry and company.

Don't mourn for what you won't get—more novels—but celebrate what you have forever: seven enchanting novels that you can read and reread whenever you wish, and later share with your kids and your grandchildren in turn.

Here's to ten years of celebrating Harry Potter and the magical writer who brought him and his world so vividly to life. Thank you, Joanne Rowling, for sharing with us the gifts of your imagination and, by doing so, illuminating the lives of millions of readers worldwide.

George Beahm
Williamsburg, VA
January 2007

Part One:
The Real World of
Joanne Rowling

Tim Kirk

I would have been crazy to have expected what has happened to Harry. The most exciting moment for me, against very stiff competition, was when I found out Harry was going to be published. It was my life's ambition to see a book I had written on a shelf in a bookshop. Everything that has happened since has been extraordinary and wonderful, but the mere fact of being able to say I was a published author was the fulfillment of a dream I had had since I was a very small child.

—*J. K. Rowling, quoted in Kidsreads.com*

Chronology

1965   March 14: Pete Rowling and Anne Volant marry at All Saints Parish Church.

        July 31: Joanne Rowling is born at Chipping Sodbury general Hospital (Gloucestershire, England).

1967   June 28: Her only sibling, a sister named Dianne, is born.

1970   At age five, she attends St. Michael's Church of England Primary School. Family friends include the Potter family. The Rowlings live in a town called Yate.

1971   The family moves to Winterbourne (near Bristol).

1974   When Joanne is seven, the family moves to Tutshill, near Chepstow in Wales.

        She attends Tutshill Church of England Primary School.

1975   She becomes a Brownie and joins the Second Tidenham (St. Mary's) Brownie Pack.

1976   She attends Wyedean Comprehensive in Sedbury.

1980   Her mother, Anne, is diagnosed with multiple sclerosis.

1982   She is selected as Head Girl at Wyedean Comprehensive.

1983   Her mother, suffering from multiple sclerosis, makes her will.

        Turned down for Oxford, she attends the University of Exeter.

1985   Joanne spends time in Paris.

1987   She graduates from the University of Exeter with a degree in French and the classics, moves to an apartment in Clapham (South London), and spends free time during lunch and after hours writing two adult novels (both unpublished).

1990   June: On a train ride between Manchester and London, she dreams up Harry Potter.

December 30: Her mother, Anne, dies at age 45.

1991   She takes a job teaching English at Encounter English Schools in Porto, Portugal.

1992   October 16: She marries TV journalist Jorge Arantes at the civil register office in Porto.

1993   April 2: Her father, Pete Rowling, remarries; his new wife is his former secretary, Janet Gallivan.

July 27: Joanne's daughter, Jessica, is born.

November 17: Joanne's husband throws her out of their house, but she goes back in to get Jessica; she makes plans to leave for England with her daughter in tow.

December 21: Settled in Scotland, she applies for public assistance from the Department of Social Security in Edinburgh.

1994   March 15: After discovering that Jorge Arantes is in Edinburgh and looking for her, she starts proceedings to get a temporary restraining order against her husband.

November 23: She renews the temporary restraining order against Arantes.

1995   June 26: The restraining order against Arantes becomes permanent; she is officially divorced from him.

She finishes writing the first Harry Potter novel and begins submitting it to agents for literary representation.

1996   February: She signs on with the Christopher Little Literary Agency.

July: She receives certification to teach, a Postgraduate Certificate of Education, and begins teaching French at Leigh Academy, in Edinburgh.

1997   February: Receives £8,000 from the Scottish Arts Council. She uses most of the money to buy a word processor, replacing her £40 typewriter.

June 26: The first Harry Potter novel, *Harry Potter and the Philosopher's Stone*, is published in the U.K., with a print run of 500. She splurges, spending £100, on a jacket to wear when meeting the press.

September: Scholastic buys the book for the U.S. market for $100,000, with plans for a first printing of 50,000 copies.

She quits teaching to become a full-time writer.

She moves from a rented apartment in South Lorne Place to a new residence at Hazelbank Terrace, which she buys.

1998   July 2: *Harry Potter and the Chamber of Secrets* is published in the U.K.

October: *Harry Potter and the Sorcerer's Stone* is published in the U.S.

1999   June: *Harry Potter and the Chamber of Secrets* is published in the U.S.

July: *Harry Potter and the Prisoner of Azkaban* is published in the U.K.

September: *Harry Potter and the Prisoner of Azkaban* is published in the U.S.

She signs a major movie deal with Warner Bros.

2000   July 8: *Harry Potter and the Goblet of Fire* is published simultaneously in the U.K. and the U.S.

September: She accepts a post as an ambassador for a charity, the National Council for One Parent Families.

2001   April: A patron of the Multiple Sclerosis Society in Scotland, she attends the opening of one of its resource centers in Aberdeen.

She publishes two books, *Quidditch Through the Ages* and *Fantastic Beasts and Where to Find Them,* the proceeds of which benefit Comic Relief.

November: *Harry Potter and the Sorcerer's Stone* is released as a movie.

December 26: She marries Dr. Neil Murray.

2002   September: A U.S. judge dismisses the lawsuit filed by Nancy Stouffer against Rowling.

Hagrid holding Norbert the Dragon

November: *Harry Potter and the Chamber of Secrets* is released as a movie.

2003 March 23: Their son, David, is born.

June 21: *Harry Potter and the Order of the Phoenix* is published in the U.K. and the U.S.

June 26: She appears at the Royal Albert Hall in London for a reading.

November: The sales of Harry Potter novels reach 250 million, according to Christopher Little.

2004 June: *Harry Potter and the Prisoner of Azkaban* is released as a movie.

2005 January 24: Their daughter, Mackenzie Jean, is born.

July 16: *Harry Potter and the Half-Blood Prince* is published.

November 18: The movie *Harry Potter and the Goblet of Fire,* directed by Mike Newell, is released.

2007 July 13: The movie *Harry Potter and the Order of the Phoenix* is scheduled for release.

July 21: Publication of *Harry Potter and the Deathly Hallows,* the seventh Harry Potter novel.

2008 November 21: The movie *Harry Potter and the Half-Blood Prince* is scheduled for release.

2009 The movie of *Harry Potter and the Deathly Hallows* is scheduled to be released (projected).

The J. K. Rowling Story
by Stephen McGinty

Before Harry Potter, before the novels, before the films, before the millions and millions of pounds, there was a little girl who liked to play witches and wizards. During the sleepy summer months, in the English town of Winterbourne, a half-hour journey by car from Bristol, Joanne Rowling, then six years old, first encountered a wizard called Potter. The game of Let's Pretend was played out in the front garden of number 35 Nicholls Lane, one of a row of grey brick, three-bedroom houses, into which Pete and Anne Rowling and their two young daughters had recently moved.

The game was Joanne's idea and involved raiding her mother's cupboard for costumes, the neighbours' garages for brooms, and corralling the children next door to make up the numbers. Joanne, her younger sister, Dianne, and friend Vikki were all witches while the solitary wizard was five-year-old Ian Potter. As he recalled almost 30 years later: "I used to wear my Dad's long coat back to front to look like a wizard. I think there were a pair of joke specs in the box as well—a bit like Harry's."

The life of J. K. Rowling began with the meeting of two strangers on a train in 1964. Pete Rowling was an 18-year-old soldier when he met Anne Volant, a WREN (Women's Royal Navy Service), also 18, on the train from King's Cross bound for the headquarters of 45 Commando in Arbroath. Introductions across the seated compartment led to a long conversation and stolen kisses beneath duffel coats. By the time they alighted in Scotland, Pete and Anne were a confirmed couple.

A few months into their courtship Anne became pregnant with her first child (Joanne). The young lovers decided to discard their uniforms to marry on 14 March 1965 before setting up home in Yate, ten miles outside Bristol. Four months later, on 31 July 1965, their daughter was born at the Cottage Hospital, in the more affluent suburb of Chipping Sodbury, where Rowling would later claim her family lived. While her father secured employment as an apprentice engineer at a Bristol factory, her mother cared for Joanne and her sister, Dianne, born two years later on 28 June 1967. A year later the family moved to the larger house at Winterbourne, where Joanne first discovered the magical world of books and created her own adventures in the front garden.

A childhood bout of measles, at the age of four, provided the author's earliest memory of books, when her father raised her spirits by reading aloud to his bed-bound daughter the adventures of Toad of Toad Hall, from *The Wind in the Willows*. Books were spread around the house, crammed in every room, and although young Joanne had little interest in the adventures of the Famous Five, she would later praise the work of Richard Scarry, whose anthropomorphic work inspired her earliest work of fiction: a story called "Rabbit" written at the age of six. By this time she was a happy pupil at St. Michael's Church of England Primary School, five minutes' walk from the family home. But another move was afoot. In 1974 her parents purchased an old stone cottage in Tutshill, on the Welsh border, close to the Forest of Dean, which would become a blueprint for Harry Potter's Forbidden Forest, just as it had inspired the work of another local author, the late Dennis Potter.

The idyllic Church Cottage, which had a flagstone floor and a covered well, was just a goblin's throw from the local graveyard and was surrounded by countryside in which the Rowling sisters would enact their adventures. But for the young J. K. Rowling, the first day at Tutshill Church of England Primary School in September 1974 was not a success. She scored only half a mark out of ten in a test that led to her being positioned on the less intellectual side of the class. Her natural ability soon shone through and she was promoted, but as she explained: "The promotion was at a cost . . . Mrs Morgan made me swap seats with my best friend." The teacher, Mrs Sylvia Morgan, was a strict, intimidating woman, who frightened Joanne as a child and whose presence would work its way into the less sympathetic masters of Hogwarts. By the age of ten, Joanne was a keen Brownie, a voracious reader, and a serious student who raced to get her hand up first. "I was the epitome of a bookish child, short and squat, thick National Health glasses, living in a world of complete daydreams."

When she made the move to secondary school, Joanne found herself accompanied by her mother. After 12 years of bringing up her daughters, Anne Rowling secured the position of laboratory technician at Wyedean

Comprehensive under the supervision of John Nettleship, the school's head of science. Nettleship remembers Joanne, whom he taught, as a bright but quiet girl and considers himself an early inspiration for Professor Snape. "I think chemistry maybe made the most impact on her because I did teach her about the philosopher's stone, the alchemist's stone. Possibly she knew about it already, but I did include it in my lessons and explained how it turned things to gold." He then chuckles before adding: "It seems to have worked for her, hasn't it?" Although bright, she was not the most enthusiastic student, as Nettleship, who is now retired, recalls: "Her attitude in the science lessons was more like Harry's in the potions class rather than Hermione's."

Anne Rowling, meanwhile, was delighted to be around the beakers and chemicals and working once again after such a long absence. "She was absolutely brilliant, a sparkling character, totally reliable, very interested in words and stories and things like that. Although her job was on the technical side, she was also very imaginative," says Nettleship.

A brief encounter with bullying led Joanne to spend her break walking to the science block to collect her dinner money rather than face the intimidating atmosphere of the playground. A larger girl in her own year picked a fight with her. "I didn't have a choice. It was hit back or lie down and play dead," recalls the author. "For a few days I was quite famous because she hadn't managed to flatten me. The truth was, my locker was right behind me and it held me up."

Throughout her teens Rowling honed her taste in reading material. It is unsurprising that she was greatly influenced by J. R. R. Tolkien's *The Lord of the Rings*, but she also loved Jane Austen, whose work *Emma* she has read more than 20 times. Another seminal influence was Jessica Mitford, whom she adopted as a personal heroine, and whose autobiography, *Hons and Rebels*, became a significant text for Rowling.

But as with all teenagers, Rowling became more and more interested in pop music. It was the early 1980s and so she was inspired by the Smiths and Siouxsie Sioux, whose look she adopted early on and maintained for many years; when she began university, she still sported startling back-combed hair and heavy black eyeliner.

At this point Rowling's home was a happy and stable environment. Her father, Pete, was now an executive engineer at the Rolls Royce plant and her mother was working in a job she adored. But things were about to change dramatically, casting a shadow over Rowling's life and tearing apart her close-knit family.

The spectre of her illness first appeared to Anne Rowling in 1978 when her hand began to tremble while she was pouring tea. At first the symptoms were fleeting and she dismissed them with a shrug but over the next two years her loss of physical control intensified. She began breaking beakers at work and often dissolved in tears of frustration. On a good day she could still play guitar, but the bad days began to mount up. When Joanne was 15, her mother was diagnosed with multiple sclerosis. The disease was triggered by the lack of a certain protein in her spinal column, which served to scramble the signals from her brain and resulted in a loss of control of her limbs. Anne was brokenhearted at having to give up her lab technician's job, but busied herself by volunteering to clean the local church.

Rowling could only watch helplessly as her mother succumbed to this destructive disease. In an article the author wrote, published in *Scotland on Sunday,* she described how at one point her mother was reduced to crawling upstairs. The "galloping" progression of the illness meant that within a few years Anne Rowling moved from walking with difficulty to using a walking frame and then a wheelchair.

A depression settled over Church Cottage, leaving Rowling feeling trapped and miserable. Escape came in the form of a new pupil at Wyedean Comprehensive, Séan Harris, who quickly became a firm friend. In 1982 he drew up outside the family home in his blue Ford Anglia and whisked her away from the grim stillness of Tutshill to the concerts and bars of Bristol. He would park under the Severn Bridge and together the pair dreamt up better futures for each other. Harris's blue Ford Anglia would become immortalised in Rowling's fiction as Ron Weasley's family car and he would be described in the dedication in her second book as "getaway driver and foul weather friend."

Joanne's academic achievements led to her being appointed Head Girl at Wyedean and her ambition was to study languages at Oxford. Her A-levels in English, French, and German (two A's and a B) were good enough on paper to secure an Oxbridge place, but she wasn't accepted. Her teachers were surprised, believing she was the victim of institutional prejudice against comprehensive pupils. The dreamed-of spires of Oxford were instead replaced by the red-brick halls of residence at the University of Exeter.

Lecturers remember Rowling as nervous and insecure, but a fellow student, Yvette Cowles, told Sean Smith, her unofficial biographer, that she was popular and striking. "She wore long skirts and used to have this blue denim jacket she liked to wear. Jo was very shapely and she had this big hair, kind of back-combed and lacquered, and lots of heavy eyeliner. I think she was quite popular with the guys."

In her first year she signed up for French and classics, but an attitude to academia best described as minimum work, maximum fun led to her abandoning classics after she failed to register properly for an exam. Her third year was spent teaching in a school in Paris and sharing a flat with an Italian, a Russian, and a Spaniard. She found the Italian disagreeable and would avoid him by spending whole days in her room reading. During this time she read Charles Dickens's *A Tale of Two Cities*, a literary discovery that may have influenced her alleged intention to kill off Harry Potter at the end of book seven. The death of Charles Darnay, sacrificing his life for a friend, and his moving last words—"It is a far, far better thing that I do than I have ever done; it is a far, far better rest that I go to than I have ever known."—had a major impact on Rowling.

Anne Rowling attended her daughter's graduation in 1987 in a wheelchair and watched with pride as she was awarded a 2:2 in French. The next four years were to see her daughter work through a variety of temporary jobs including posts with Amnesty International and the Manchester Chamber of Commerce, a post so brief there is no record of her ever being there. During this time she began a parallel life as a writer, toiling over two adult novels, which were never published, and developing a passion for classical music.

It was while Rowling drifted aimlessly through these years that the most important moment of her life occurred. In the summer of 1990, Rowling's boyfriend had moved to Manchester and she found herself returning to London by train after a weekend spent flat-hunting with him. Quite spontaneously during that trip an idea took shape: "All of a sudden the idea for Harry just appeared in my mind's eye. I can't tell you why or what triggered it. But I saw the idea of Harry and the wizard school very plainly. I suddenly had this basic idea of a boy who didn't know who he was, who didn't know he was a wizard until he got his invitation to wizard school. I have never been so excited by an idea."

The birth of Harry Potter was followed six months later by the death of her mother. Anne Rowling passed away on 30 December 1990 at 45. Joanne had visited home six days earlier but had not realised the seriousness of her mother's illness. "She was extremely thin and looked exhausted. I don't know how I didn't realise how ill she was, except that I had watched her deteriorate for so long that the change, at the time, didn't seem so dramatic." The death of her mother sent Rowling into a tailspin. Within months her relationship ended, she moved into a hotel and would soon leave the country altogether.

An advert in the *Guardian* for English teachers in Portugal held out the promise of warmth and a fresh start. Rowling was soon living in the bustling city of Porto in a shared flat with Aine Kiely, from Cork, and an English girl, Jill Prewett. Between 5 P.M. and 10 P.M. the trio taught classes at the Encounter English School before heading out to Swing, the town's largest nightclub. Rowling spent her days in local cafés, sipping strong coffee and writing in longhand the first draft of the first Harry Potter. Maria Ines Augiar was the school's assistant director and became a close friend, remembering Rowling as a "very nervous person, anxious" and one who was "desperate for love." Only after she had been resident in the country for 18 months did Rowling find love, albeit briefly, with Jorge Arantes, a dashing journalism student three years her junior.

Arantes was drinking with friends in Meia Cava, a downstairs bar, when, as he recalled: "This girl with the most amazing blue eyes walked in." He approached her, they began to chat in English and found they were both fans of Jane Austen. The night ended with an exchange of kisses and phone numbers and within a couple of days they were sleeping together. But if Arantes, who had an abundance of Latin machismo, thought he could treat her in a casual manner, he was mistaken, as his new girlfriend made clear when he began chatting to other girls while they were on a date. Rowling approached him and whispered in his ear that it was her or them. She won that contest, but a volatile passion came to exist between the pair. Against the odds their relationship continued, with Rowling providing money through her work, which Arantes spent while looking for employment he never seemed to find.

The couple had been together for only a few months when Rowling became pregnant, just as Arantes embarked on eight months' national service. They agreed that Rowling would move in with Arantes's mother, who lived in a small two-bedroom apartment on the rua Duque de Saldanha, and await his return. Unfortunately, the pregnancy ended in miscarriage. The disappointment brought Rowling and Arantes closer together and on 28 August 1992 he proposed. Friends in Portugal were taken aback when Rowling accepted.

Maria Ines Augiar believed Jorge to be both possessive and jealous, while Steve Cassidy, who ran the school where Rowling worked, viewed him as rough and untrustworthy. His perception was not altered by an incident at the language school prior to their wedding. The couple had been drinking coffee in a café across the street when an argument broke out during which Jorge violently pushed his fiancée. Rowling burst into tears and ran back to the school, but the intensity of Jorge's outburst led one onlooker to inform the police, who arrived to find a large crowd surrounding Arantes as he cried, "Joanne, forgive me, I love you." According to Maria Ines Augiar, Rowling was soon shouting back, "I love you, Jorge."

The marriage lasted 13 months and one day. Later, when Rowling was writing *Harry Potter and the Prisoner of Azkaban,* she had one character, Professor Trelawney, inform a pupil that the thing she was most fearful of would take place on 16 October—the date of her wedding in 1992. The ceremony took place in Porto's registry office and was attended by Rowling's sister, Dianne, and her boyfriend. Photographs suggest a subdued affair with Rowling in black holding a bunch of deep red flowers. The girls' father did not attend. The speed of Pete Rowling's decision to move in with his secretary after his wife's death distressed both sisters and a fault line now separated them from their father.

The marital home remained that of Arantes's mother and was far from happy. Two months after the ceremony Rowling found herself pregnant once again. She continued her job and, worryingly, discovered she was losing weight due to the stress of arguments with Arantes. Prior to the birth of her daughter, Jessica, named after Jessica Mitford, on 27 July 1993, Rowling's friends were urging her to leave her husband, but she was determined to make her marriage work. Arantes's behaviour made this impossible. Rowling has never spoken publicly about her marriage, except to dismiss her former husband's claims to have helped shape the first Potter novel, with the withering line: "He had as much input into Harry Potter as I had in *A Tale of Two Cities.*"

But Arantes has described his shameful and violent behaviour. The extent of the domestic violence Rowling endured is not known, but Arantes admits slapping her "very hard" early in the morning on 17 November 1993 and throwing her out of the house without her daughter. When Rowling returned the following day with Maria Ines Augiar, a policeman accompanied them and it did not take long before Jessica was handed over.

For two weeks Joanne and Jessica stayed in hiding with friends whom Arantes did not know. Then she boarded a flight to Britain and flew from Arantes and his terrifying temper. Her precious cargo included a cherished daughter and three chapters about Harry Potter, her surrogate son.

Trains run through J. K. Rowling's life with timetabled frequency. Her parents met on a train, the idea for Harry Potter was first conceived on a train, and now, in the winter of 1993, a train carried both mother and daughter north toward a new life in Scotland. After arriving back in Britain, Rowling had nowhere else to turn. Her father had married Janet Gallivan, his secretary, and relations were strained, but Dianne had recently married in Edinburgh and swung open her door. Despite her sister's hospitality, the next few years were to be Rowling's nadir. Although never quite as bad as the press has painted in terms of poverty—she always had food and clothes, heat and light—Rowling did endure a deep depression brought about by circumstance and frustration.

For the first few weeks Rowling and her daughter stayed with her sister Dianne and restaurateur brother-in-law, Roger Moore, in their home in Marchmont Road, but it was an arrangement that could not continue indefinitely. Social services organised a small flat at 28 Gardner's Crescent. So began Rowling's experience of government bureaucracy as she was forced to fill in endless forms and attend demeaning interviews in order to secure a weekly allowance of £69. A Christmas present she received, REM's new album *Automatic for the People,* only added to the gloom. The album was viewed by critics as REM's nihilistic best and Rowling seized on the spirit-sapping track "Everybody Hurts," which she began to play incessantly.

The new year brought with it a new flat, but her depression deepened. Shortly after her return to Britain her old friend Séan Harris had offered to lend her money, but she refused. By midwinter she was so unhappy in Gardner's Crescent that she changed her mind and borrowed £600 from him to use as a deposit on a rented flat. Finding one was more difficult than she thought and it was only after enduring rejection after rejection from owners unwilling to rent to an unemployed single mother that she secured the keys to a flat in South Lorne Place. It was a pebbled and brick-faced four-story flat, furnished thanks to contributions from friends.

It was here that Rowling was overcome by a feeling of hopelessness. Her despair was compounded by the arrival in March 1994 of her estranged husband in search of his wife and daughter. Since Rowling's departure from Porto, Arantes had succumbed to drug abuse and his wife was so concerned for the safety of herself and her daughter that she was forced to obtain an Action of Interdict, an order of restraint that prevented Arantes from "molesting, abusing her verbally, threatening her or putting her in a state of fear and alarm by using violence toward her anywhere within the sheriffdom of Edinburgh." Arantes returned to Portugal and Rowling filed for divorce in August 1994.

The sense that she was failing her daughter was unbearable to Rowling. Whenever she visited the homes of other mothers, Rowling gazed covetously at their children's bright bundles of toys. Her own daughter's toys could fit comfortably in a shoe box. Yet when an insensitive, if well-meaning, health visitor brought around a raggedy teddy bear and a small plastic phone, she junked them in a fit of shame.

Only after a period of counselling was she able to tackle her depression and begin writing again. But once she did, it was the writing that elevated her self-worth. The first three chapters of *Harry Potter and the Philosopher's Stone* had made her sister laugh, a reaction that kindled hope in Rowling. In the long evenings at home, with little else to do, she set about working on further chapters. In the mythology of J. K. Rowling, Nicolson's restaurant is where the majority of Harry Potter was written. Yet the brightly coloured restaurant has now gone, long since replaced by a Chinese restaurant, King's Buffet. The new owner, Winnie Yau, still receives pilgrims from all over the world, asking about the building's most famous customer.

Rowling went to Nicolson's either as a respite from a freezing flat or through a passion for good coffee, depending on which version you believe. Nicolson's was scarcely convenient, half a mile from her flat and at the top of 20 steps, quite a hike for a mother with a young child in a push-chair, but it was owned by her brother-in-law, which allowed her to draw out a single coffee over a few hours, and the primary colours in which it was painted couldn't help but lift the spirits of even the most despondent visitor. A second establishment she visited regularly was the Elephant House, on George

IV bridge, whose much patronised back room has windows overlooking Greyfriars cemetery. A sign at the entrance now reads: "Experience the same atmosphere that J. K. Rowling did as she mulled over a coffee, writing the first Harry Potter novel."

The writing of *Harry Potter and the Philosopher's Stone* was slow. Rowling wrote in longhand then typed up the finished work on a secondhand manual typewriter. In the meantime she needed a job. At first she took on secretarial work for a few hours each week, but a full-time job was a necessity. She wanted a career, not just a means to make money, and so applied to study for a Postgraduate Certificate of Education in modern languages at Moray House, now part of Edinburgh University. A generous friend supplemented a small grant and in August 1995 she became a student once again. Staff at St. David's High School on Dalkeith Road and Leith Academy, where she taught as part of her teaching training, remember her as keen and well-organised. She graduated in June 1996, around which time she heard the news that Harry Potter was to be published at last.

In early 1996, with the manuscript of *Harry Potter and the Philosopher's Stone* complete, Rowling visited Edinburgh Central Library to look up the *Writers' and Artists' Year Book* in search of a literary agent. Her first approach had been unsuccessful: a brief rejection letter. She then posted a sample of three chapters and a cover letter to the Christopher Little Literary Agency, based in Fulham. It was here that a young reader, Bryony Evans, read the first chapter and laughed. Evans passed the chapters to Fleur Howle, a freelance reader, who agreed with her assessment and together they persuaded Little to sign up Rowling. A few days later Rowling received a letter asking for the remainder of the manuscript. The agency sent Rowling's 200-page manuscript to 12 publishers, all of whom, to their eternal regret, turned down the book. HarperCollins showed interest but was too slow in formulating a bid and so the first book by the most lucrative writer in the world was picked up by Bloomsbury for an advance of £1,500.

When Barry Cunningham, head of children's fiction at Bloomsbury, invited Rowling to lunch in London, he praised her book but told her to be prepared as there was no financial reward in children's books. Rowling did not care. To hold a hardback copy in her hand was reward enough.

Anxious to finish the second novel, *Harry Potter and the Chamber of Secrets,* Rowling applied for a grant from the Scottish Arts Council and was awarded £8,000, which allowed her to purchase a word processor and steady her turbulent finances. The publication date for *Harry Potter and the Philosopher's Stone* was set at 26 June 1997 and Joanne Rowling was rechristened J. K. Rowling. Christopher Little had discovered that boys were unlikely to read a book written by a woman and so pushed for Bloomsbury to use the ambiguous initials in order to attract both sexes.

But before Harry Potter and Hagrid, Hermione and Ron Weasley, Professors Albus Dumbledore and Severus Snape could bewitch the children of Britain, they had cast a collective spell over an American publisher. Arthur Levine, the editorial director of Scholastic, a large American publishing house, first read the novel at 36,000 feet as he flew over the Atlantic to attend the Bologna Book Fair. He became so engrossed that he had no wish to land. Little had organised an auction for the American publishing rights to Harry Potter and Levine became determined to be the highest bidder. Three days after the British publication date, Rowling received a call from her agent to say that Scholastic had bid $100,000—an unprecedented sum—for a children's book that already had the makings of a phenomenon.

In the Eye of the Storm

In the autumn of 1999 J. K. Rowling arrived in America for yet another nationwide tour. *The Prisoner of Azkaban*, her third novel in as many years, had just been released three months after its British edition, a delay that had caused thousands of eager Americans to order Bloomsbury editions over the Internet. Her American publishers, Scholastic, were anxious to develop Rowling's profile with a series of book-signing sessions. Previous tours in 1997 and 1998 had seen the number of excited children and patient parents rise from dozens to a few hundred. No one expected to see thousands.

When Rowling's black Lincoln arrived at Politics and Prose, a popular bookstore in Washington, D.C., and Rowling saw a queue that snaked out the door and two blocks back, she assumed there was some kind of sale. On that visit she managed to sign 1,400 copies before her handlers dragged her on to the next event. The same delighted crowds of children and, for the first time, unaccompanied adults, met her at every city on the tour. Chat-show hosts such as Katie Couric of the *Today Show* and Rosie O'Donnell were delighted to share their sofas with the hottest author in America.

In the season of Halloween, Harry Potter reached critical mass and exploded. Across the country six giant printing presses were spinning 24 hours a day to maintain demand for his three adventures. The *New York Times* had J. K. Rowling at the first three slots on their best-seller lists and would eventually have to a create a new children's book list in order to evict her. *Time* magazine placed the boy wizard in the company of world leaders when it granted him a cover story. When embarking on the writer's life, the height of Rowling's ambition was for a sales assistant to recognise her name off her credit card and declare herself a fan. "In my wildest fantasy I could not have imagined anything like this," she told Katie Couric on the *Today Show* that autumn. "I could not even come close."

In Britain the books had been a slow steady burn. *Harry Potter and the*

Philosopher's Stone had a first print run of 500 copies, but Bloomsbury knew they had a hit when new orders began to arrive and the book ran into reprint after reprint. British sales had been assisted through the publicity generated by her $100,000 advance from the American publisher. Although in later years Rowling would have cause to regret her portrayal as "poverty-stricken single mum makes good," those stories gave her a profile most first-time authors could only dream about. Yet all the hype and publicity would have faded like the steam off a cauldron if children had not grasped the books as their own. Teachers and parents who presented the novel to their children could almost hear an audible "click." They got Harry Potter and they wouldn't let him go. The first Harry Potter sold 70,000 copies in the first year and won the Smarties Prize for Children's Literature.

The advance from Scholastic for the American rights had allowed Rowling to purchase a two-bedroom flat in Hazelbank Terrace. Jessica soon settled into Craiglockhart Primary School and a nanny was hired to allow Rowling extra time to write and attend signings and readings. While Rowling remained nervous and unsure around adults and particularly during interviews, she adored visiting schools and attending children's events. By the time her second novel, *Harry Potter and the Chamber of Secrets*, was released in July 1998, an anxious audience was already waiting. The book became a number one best-seller and the hype continued to build, this time infecting adults who overcame their embarrassment to lose themselves in a pacy, humorous read. In order to lasso a wider audience and spare the blushes of commuters, Bloomsbury released the books with moody adult covers.

Rowling's ambition was to release one book a year for seven years, taking young Harry up to graduation and no further. By the time the *Prisoner of Azkaban* was released in July 1999 Rowling was on the verge of her first million and had maintained her tight writing schedule. She had also taken the next step toward ensuring her creation's global dominance—a film deal with Warner Bros. had finally been agreed upon. An executive at Heyday Films, Tania Seqhatchian, had read the first Potter book, spotted its potential, and passed it onto her boss, David Heyman, an experienced producer who was representing the Hollywood studio in Britain.

Christopher Little, Rowling's agent, was aware of the tremendous potential in the film rights and urged a slow, cautious approach, while the author herself was highly protective. "I would do everything to prevent Harry Potter from turning up on fast-food boxes," explained Rowling. "That would be my worst nightmare." The deal Rowling finally consented to gave her unprecedented powers for an author, who is usually handed a cheque with one hand and shown to the door with the other. Under the deal she took a lower fee, said to be around $1 million, but had veto on the director, the script, and merchandising ideas.

Rowling showed she shared the pluck of Harry Potter when she disagreed with Steven Spielberg, who took an interest in directing the film. The director of *ET* and *Raiders of the Lost Ark* wished to merge the plots of the first two books and cast Haley Joel Osment, the American child actor who starred in *The Sixth Sense,* as Harry Potter. Rowling insisted each film tackle one book and that Harry had to be British. Spielberg walked away.

The Harry Potter phenomenon was to be driven by America, where 55 percent of all Rowling books are sold, and it was there, at the buckle of the Bible Belt, that the backlash began. In autumn 1999 the board of education in South Carolina agreed to review whether the novels should be available in schools after receiving complaints from parents. One outraged mother criticised them for possessing "a serious tone of death, hate, lack of respect, and sheer evil." A few Christian schools in Australia banned them on account of their tone, but the Catholic Church later rode to their defence and praised them for instructing children on good and evil.

For the feminist academic Dr. Elizabeth Heilman, the trouble was not broomsticks, but boys. The males were forever rescuing the females, who, she believed, were "giggly, emotional, gossipy and anti-intellectual." It was a charge Rowling dismissed out of hand. The more serious charge of plagiarism levelled by Nancy Stouffer required the judgment of the American courts.

Stouffer was the author of *The Legend of Rah and the Muggles,* a children's book published in 1984 that featured a hero called Larry Potter, who also had black hair with glasses. In her book Muggles were imps; in Rowling's work it is a term given to ordinary non-magic folk—but still Stouffer believed she was the inspiration for a now multimillion-dollar success story. Rowling defended the case through the courts and was vindicated in September 2002.

By the time *Harry Potter and the Goblet of Fire* was published in July 2000, Rowling was struggling to cope with her new status. The pressure to complete her longest novel to date had been intense, compounded by a plotting error that forced her to rip up chapters and begin again. The manuscript was delivered in March and so concerned were her publishers about plot leaks that it was placed in a safe. Bloomsbury's marketing campaign meant no copy was available to anyone prior to the publication date, 8 July, and even the title was a closely guarded secret, to be revealed as part of a slow press campaign. The book sold one million copies in Britain and more than five million in America.

The success of her books had made Rowling inaccessible to fans. Book signings were increasingly difficult due to the volume of demand. When Bloomsbury converted King's Cross into Platform Nine and Three-Quarters from which the Hogwarts Express departs in her books, Rowling was unable to meet the children who had gathered because of the press scrum and could only shout an apology out the window as the antique train hired for the event steamed off. She had greater success at communicating her message at the University of Exeter, where she returned that summer to collect an honorary degree, urging the students never to fear failure.

Rowling's success in cash terms was staggering. The *Sunday Times* Rich List of 2001 estimated her wealth at £65 million, a sum Rowling used to insulate herself from the world. The small flat in Hazelbank Terrace was donated to a close friend, a fellow single mother, while Rowling and Jessica moved into a Georgian mansion in Merchiston whose nine-foot-high wall would deter even the most intrusive snooper. She also paid £4.5 million for a second home in London's Kensington, complete with indoor swimming pool. A country house on the banks of the River Tay called Killiechassie was added to her property portfolio in 2001. In previous years Rowling was regularly spotted around Edinburgh in cafés and restaurants, but her success restricted her movements to dinner parties with friends. When Giles Gordon, the literary agent, announced in his column in the *Edinburgh Evening News* that the author regularly frequented Margiotta, the popular city deli, Rowling never returned.

The next stage of the Potter phenomenon was triggered by the success of the first film, *Harry Potter and the Philosopher's Stone*. Rowling approved Chris Columbus as director and was delighted by the casting of Daniel Radcliffe as Harry and pleased that Robbie Coltrane had accepted the role of Hagrid. Writing on the next book was set aside as she discussed set designs and script notes, and watched rushes on what would become the second-highest-grossing film of all time (after *Titanic*), grossing $926 million and creating millions of new readers. Escorting Rowling to the premieres in London and Edinburgh was Dr. Neil Murray, an anesthesiologist whom she had met at a friend's dinner party. Murray, then separated from the wife whom he later divorced, brought love and a new balance into Rowling's life.

The couple married on Boxing Day 2001 in a private ceremony at Killiechassie, attended by close friends and family including her father, with whom relations had thawed, and his second wife. The couple's first child, a boy, was born in March 2003 and the world breathed a sigh of relief when it was announced he would be christened David and not Harry.

There are now only four days to endure before the publication of *Harry Potter and the Order of the Phoenix* and Rowling can gaze with considerable pride on what her work has achieved. In just six years more than 160 million Harry Potter books have been sold in more than 100 countries, and both films have achieved box office records. Harry Potter licensing deals have been struck with the biggest companies in the world, with Coca-Cola bidding £65 million for the rights. Next week Rowling will become the first artist since Madonna to participate in a live webcast at the Albert Hall, at which 4,000 children will have the chance to ask her questions as Stephen Fry tries to contain them. Even Prince Charles has swooned in her presence, commenting, "I'm staggered that someone can write so beautifully."

The tragedy for fans is that they are one book closer to the end. The final chapter has already been written and is tucked in a yellow folder in an anonymous safety deposit box. We may think we're experiencing a literary phenomenon—but just wait until that box is unlocked. . . .

The Legacy of Harry

It was, she later said, "the best moment" in "one of the best weeks of my life." It was the summer of 1998, and J. K. Rowling was touring the country reading extracts from her second book, *Harry Potter and the Chamber of Secrets*. She had just finished a reading and the children had begun to drift away when a mother approached her for a quiet word. She explained that her nine-year-old son was dyslexic and Harry Potter was the first book he had ever managed to finish on his own. "She said she'd burst into tears when she found him reading it in bed the morning after she'd read the first two chapters aloud to him," Rowling recalled. "I'm not sure I managed to convey to her what a wonderful thing that was to hear, because I thought I was going to cry too."

That scene has since been repeated in bookshops, libraries, and schoolrooms around the globe, as the adventures of Harry Potter have drawn an entire generation, previously bewitched by television and computer games, back to the traditional comfort of a book. Rowling's Harry Potter novels have been a godsend to teachers and parents who feared they could not open a book in front of a child without evoking a yawn. This love of reading in young children is part of a long legacy spawned by the Harry Potter books and by Rowling herself. It has been noted, too, that Harry Potter has become a trusted guide through the difficulties of childhood, tackling fears, death, and disappointment in a most admirable manner.

"We cannot sing the praises of Rowling high enough," says Charlie Griffiths, director of the National Literacy Association. "Anyone who can persuade children to read should be treasured and what she's given us in Harry Potter is little short of miraculous. To see children queuing outside a store, not for concert tickets or computer games, but for a book, is brilliant."

Griffiths says that the books themselves rise above the massive publicity campaigns that now surround the release of a new Harry Potter book.

"I know people will insist it's all down to clever marketing, but if there is not a story that a child wants to read then no amount of marketing will persuade them. Her novels have created positive peer pressure in favour of reading. A child might not have that great an interest in reading but he wants to keep up with his friends and so he'll get sucked in. She's also helped shine a light on other wonderful children's writers."

The works of Jacqueline Wilson, Philip Pullman, Lemony Snicket, and Eoin Colfer have all been given a boost by young readers who, having torn through the four Potter novels, are anxious to kill time before the release of the fifth. In an unprecedented reversal, Harry Potter has also been responsible for the swelling hordes of adults reading children's literature. It is unlikely, for example, that Sir Tom Stoppard would be scripting an adaptation of Pullman's *Northern Lights* trilogy were it not for the interest in children's fiction triggered by Rowling. Children remain her principal audience, though, and there is no way to quantify the sheer delight and happiness she has brought to their lives. As one Scottish mother explained it: "She's made bedtime less of a struggle than it once was and for that alone I'm grateful."

But Rowling is determined that her legacy will encompass more than book sales and pencil cases. It will be to make a difference in the lives of those who struggle. She's determined to reduce the stigma attached to single mothers, ease the pain borne by multiple sclerosis sufferers, and simultaneously raise their standard of care. She has said she will not be satisfied until Scotland has a chain of centres designed to comfort and support those with cancer. She has invested her publicity, time, and generosity in issues she can relate to, rather than adopting a scattergun approach. Today she is a patron of three charities: the National Council for One Parent Families, the MS Society of Scotland, and Maggie's Centre.

To One Parent Families she donated £500,000 and in September 2000 accepted an offer to become their ambassador, a role she has taken to heart. Far more valuable than her money is her time and the attention she can draw to an issue often neglected. An article she wrote for the *Sun* newspaper attacked the public perception of single parents as careless teenagers, pointing out that 60 percent are separated, divorced, or bereaved. "We are all doing two people's jobs single-handed before we even start looking for paid work and, as I found out the hard way, we have to fight twice as hard to get half as far," she wrote.

When Ann Widdecombe had the temerity to suggest that married couples were the norm, Rowling retaliated in a speech at a charities conference attended by Gordon Brown. "We may not be some people's preferred norm but we are here," she declared, before adding: "We should judge how civilised a society is not by what it prefers to call normal but by how it treats its most vulnerable members." The author has continued to support the organisation even though her second marriage means she no longer falls in the category of single parent.

Personal experience of the assistance Edinburgh's Maggie's Centre provided to a friend with breast cancer led her to offer her patronage to the organisation. The aim of Maggie's Centre is to provide cancer sufferers a place where they can receive information and support. Situated close to hospitals that provide treatment, plans are currently afoot to build another six across Scotland. By attending charity functions and organising readings, Rowling has helped raise thousands of pounds for Maggie's. Marie McQuade, the charity's fundraiser, says her backing is invaluable. "Her endorsement has raised awareness and we're delighted with her support." As Rowling declares in the centre's annual report, "I saw with my own eyes the difference that Maggie's Centre made to a very good friend of mine."

The charity to which she has the strongest bond, however, is the Multiple Sclerosis Society of Scotland. It is a cause close to her heart. Rowling's mother was crippled by the disease and it eventually killed her. Rowling donated a large sum to help fund a senior fellowship in multiple sclerosis (MS) research at Aberdeen University, and last year she hosted a Halloween ball at Stirling Castle, which raised £280,000.

Of deep concern to Rowling is the fact that Scotland has the highest MS rate in the world, twice that of England and Wales, for entirely unknown reasons. There is no national standard of care, with treatment varying wildly across the country, and a crucial drug, beta-interferon, is underprescribed. "She's in it for the long haul," says Mark Hazelwood, director of MS Scotland. "She has a deep and personal concern about MS because she has experienced how it affected her mother. She may attract press and publicity when she visits our centres, but when the media have moved on she stays for a few hours just talking to people and I think that says a lot."

Rowling's legacy stretches to the cinema, too. The Harry Potter movies could yet be the most successful series of films in history. If Warner Bros. continue to produce a film for each book, the result could be $5 billion in box office receipts and billions more in merchandise and DVD sales. Daniel Radcliffe, the actor who plays Harry, is set to bow out after the fourth film, but a substitute will be secured and the magic will roll on. The Harry Potter film franchise is a gravy train that will not be derailed.

This level of success in film and literature is unparalleled. J. R. R. Tolkien was dead for decades before the *Lord of the Rings* trilogy was released, and Ian Fleming saw only *Dr. No* before he died, while other best-selling authors such as Stephen King have seen adaptations of their work flop at the box office. In a decade's time a boxed set of all seven films is sure to be a feature in many homes, as traditional at Christmas as *The Wizard of Oz* or *It's a Wonderful Life*.

It now looks likely that Rowling will live to see her net worth surpass £1 billion, the first author ever to do so. But she is grounded enough to know that her most personal legacy remains her two children. Her success in shielding her daughter, Jessica, whom no one has ever legitimately photographed—

those who did so illicitly were rapped by the Press Complaints Council—looks set to be repeated with her son, David. Meanwhile, the incredible wealth the books have generated allows Rowling to focus on what remains her primary purposes, her family and her writing.

The final chapter of Harry Potter's saga lies written, locked in a safety deposit box. For the next few years Rowling will work toward reaching that chapter in adventures that will span two more books. The question remains, what then? There are two things to consider. One is the reaction of children around the globe if the long rumoured climax is true and Harry, as children sometimes do, actually dies. The collective sadness of an entire generation would be palpable and who could judge the consequences of an authorial execution? It is this that spurs fans' confidence that she will stay her hand, entwining Harry instead in a romantic ending with Hermione.

Whichever veil Rowling chooses to draw over her multi-book saga, readers will never forget the boy with the lightning-bolt scar.

Bryony Evens on Submitting HARRY POTTER

"Then I started sending the book out. Twelve publishers, including Penguin, turned it down, and then Bloomsbury said yes. They paid Jo about £1,500—very little, but quite normal for a children's book at that time.

"I thought the book would sell, because I was convinced children would love it. It has all the elements of a children's classic—an orphaned child, boarding schools, magic, a secret world. Everything is in there. But I can't say I believed it would be a best-seller."

—Bryony Evens quoted by Tracey Lawson in "Spellbound," News.Scotsman.com (June 14, 2003)

Cover by Gahan Wilson for *Realms of Fantasy*: Gandalf and the Wizard of Oz stand in line to get their Potter books signed

This, in turn, will cast a long shadow over any adult books that flow from her pen. One challenge will be whether she can resist the temptation to return to the ivy-draped cloisters of Hogwarts or to trace Harry's adult adventures. Whether her success will be replicated in the world of adult fiction, something she has expressed an interest in trying when she has finished the Potter canon, remains to be seen.

The ultimate legacy of J. K. Rowling is to create a character that will be read long after she is gone and will sit in the same company as Bilbo Baggins, Peter Pan, and Alice in Wonderland. An immortal wizard is how Harry Potter will be remembered, one who had the power to charm the world.

Stephen McGinty is a senior feature writer with the *Scotsman* newspaper.

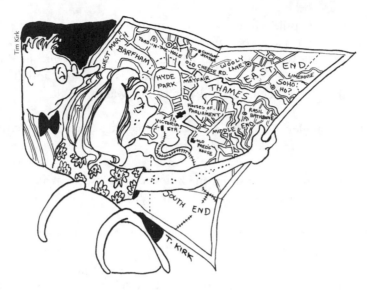

Novel Places: The Literary Landscape of J. K. Rowling

In an Internet interview, a young American reader asked if there would be any students from the United States attending Hogwarts as a foreign exchange student. No, Rowling answered firmly, Hogwarts is British and will always remain that way.

For non-British readers, that is part of the essential charm of the Rowling novels: a Muggles world similar to our own but with a different culture, and a magical world set against the backdrop of a school for witches and wizards.

For that reason, those in the United States who want to explore the literary landscape of J. K. Rowling, personally and professionally, will have to go across the pond, as they say, to England.

The Guided Tour

Though not officially endorsed by Rowling, Bloomsbury, or Warner Bros., private companies are offering tours themed to Harry Potter, focusing on the film tie-ins. British Tours, for instance, offers tours to several key places that served as film settings:

1. London: The Reptile House at the London Zoo, where Harry speaks Parseltongue to a snake; the Australia House on the Strand, which served as Gringotts, the Wizard Bank; and King's Cross station, with its dual significance as the place where Rowling's parents first met and the place where Harry Potter begins his journey to Hogwarts.

2. Black Park, Langley, Berkshire, a 600-acre park that served as the setting for the Forbidden Forest skirting Hogwarts.

3. Picket Post Close, Martin's Heron, Bracknell, Berkshire, which served as the fictional Privet Drive where the Dursleys live.

4. Lacock, Wiltshire, the location of Lacock Abbey, a former monastery. Harry's classroom friends were filmed here.

5. Oxford University, Oxfordshire, where the Bodeleian Library served as the Hogwarts library, and where Oxford's hospital served as the Hogwarts hospital. Its Duke Humfrey's Library and its Divinity School also served as locations for interior shots.

6. Gloucester Cathedral, Gloucester, the cloisters of which served as the setting for ghost scenes.

7. Alnwick Castle, Northumberland, used for the exterior of Hogwarts, the Quidditch games, and the broomstick lesson from the first film. (The second-largest occupied castle in England—the first is Windsor—it has been the home of the Percy family's earls and dukes of Northumberland since 1309.)

8. Durham Cathedral, in which can be found one of the classrooms at Hogwarts. Also, its cloisters served as hallways for Hogwarts students.

9. Goathland Station, North Yorkshire, which served as the train station for Hogwarts.

For more information, go to http://london-tour.conciergedesk.co.uk/private-guide-tour-harry-potter.htm.

For those with a more adventurous bent, a self-tour using maps provided by the British Tourist Authority offers more flexibility, allowing you to linger at favorite places instead of being on a forced march with a planned itinerary. This also allows stops at non-film-related sites and personal sites as well, if you know where to look, which is important because Rowling's novels draw heavily on a sense of place.

A good place to start is the British Tourist Authority (www.visit england.com), which is the official government office that provides both Web and print-based resources. Though incomplete—owing to restrictions placed on the number of places Warner Bros. would allow to be cited—a free map, "Discovering the Magic of Britain," with Harry Potter on the front, is available. The map has been hugely successful, with 340,000 copies in print, in six languages, in all 26 countries where the British Tourist Authority maintains offices. (The U.S. office can be reached by telephone at 866-4HEDWIG.)

In documentaries filmed for British release, Rowling has gone back to her childhood homes and schools, but understandably the tourism bureau declines to highlight these, since they are not only off the beaten path but, in the cases of the homes, private residences not currently owned by Rowling or her family. Similarly, the schools she attended, all of which have approached her to celebrate the affiliation, are not set up to handle tours.

Here then are the highlights for a personally guided tour, depending on the extent of your interest:

Personal

- Chipping Sodbury, Gloucestershire: Rowling's birthplace.

- 35 Nicholls Lane, Winterbourne: Childhood home.

- 108 Sunridge Park, Yate: Childhood home.

- Tutshill, Gloucestershire: She grew up as a young girl here, in a quaint stone cottage.

- 28 Gardner's Crescent: Temporary quarters until she could get situated, the first apartment she rented after leaving Portugal was in this building.

- 7 South Lorne Place in Leith, Edinburgh, Scotland: She rented an unfurnished one-bedroom apartment in this building after borrowing money from Séan Harris to afford the move.

- 19 Hazelbank Terrace in Edinburgh, Scotland: Her first home, purchased with the proceeds of the U.S. sale of the first Harry Potter book.

- Edinburgh, Scotland: After returning from Portugal, she rented an apartment here; after Scholastic bought the U.S. rights to the first Harry Potter novel, she bought her first house here, which she subsequently gave away to a single mother who befriended her in those early years; and after becoming successful on a big scale, she bought a larger house, her current residence. She maintains two other residences: a Georgian mansion in London's Kensington, and another Georgian mansion, Killiechassie House, in Aberfeldy, Scotland.

Educational

• Tutshill Church of England Primary School: This was her childhood school in Tutshill, Gloucestershire.

• Wyedean Comprehensive: She attended this school in Sedbury after primary school.

• University of Exeter: She graduated with a degree in French.

• Moray House: She obtained her postgraduate Certificate of Education here.

• St. David's Roman Catholic High School in Dalkeith: She student-taught here.

• Leith Academy: She taught French here to get her teaching certification, and was subsequently posted here.

• Porto, Portugal: She taught English as a Second Language at Encounter English Schools.

Miscellaneous Sites

• Nicolson's in Edinburgh, Scotland: The café is no more—it's now King's Buffet, a Chinese restaurant. This was where, at a corner table overlooking the street, Rowling nursed cups of coffee while she wrote in longhand and her daughter Jessica slept in a baby carriage.

• A train ride from Manchester to London. On such a train ride, during an unexpected prolonged stop at an undisclosed location, Rowling dreamed up the beginnings of the Harry Potter universe. (Who knows what *you* might dream up on such a ride? There could be magic in the air!)

• Bloomsbury Publishing in London. Obviously, there are no tours of Rowling's publishing house, but the city's many bookstores, new and used, make it a delight for any bibliophile.

• Severn Bridge in Tutshill, Gloucestershire, a favorite hangout of Rowling and Séan Harris, a model for Ron Weasley, Harry Potter's best friend.

Making Your Way around Jolly Old England

Before flying off to England, take a cybertrip to the official U.K. tourism website (www.visitbritain.com), where you'll find a wealth of information.

The second stop is your local bookstore, where you'll need to decide which guidebooks to buy. There are many to choose from, but all share the same basic information; beyond that, you must decide whether you want a full-featured book (usually thick and large) or a portable and necessarily slimmer version (usually thin and long). All, of course, have maps, though those in the books are traditionally bound in, which may make map-reading challenging, since you'd likely be outside and not necessarily in agreeable weather.

My preference would be to buy a full-featured book that covers the entire U.K., and a second one (a portable edition) for the local area you intend to visit. This way, you get the overview and a localized view, as well.

Finally, you will need good maps. These, too, come in two flavors: the traditional, full-featured, detailed map that unfolds to approximately 36 x 46 inches, or a portable map that gives an overview with selected highlights.

My preference, always, is for the larger, more detailed map, which can be refolded to a handheld size.

Cautionary note: Unlike other kinds of books, guidebooks are very much a personal preference and, thus, require a personal inspection. Though you can buy them from an online bookseller, your local store is a better bet because books are organized by topic, which means browsing all the available titles can be accomplished in a single trip.

Remember, whatever you buy will be your primary guide, so take your time and make a proper selection.

If all else fails, keep in mind that although you'll be in a foreign country, the English essentially speak the same language and are always glad to help out their cousins from across the pond.

- Platforms 4 and 5 at King's Cross station, where Harry Potter catches the train to Hogwarts in the film version.

- Waterloo and City line at King's Cross station, which served as backdrops in the first two Harry Potter films.

- The North Yorkshire Moors Railway at the moorland village of Goathland, North Yorkshire: This served as the terminus for the train line from King's Cross station to Hogwarts—Hogsmeade Station in the Harry Potter films.

- The Dining Hall at Christ Church College in Oxford, which was used as the Hogwarts Great Hall.

In the United States, there are no specific sites of interest; however, the New York bookstore of Scholastic is worth a visit, since it is the best place to see a wide array of Potter products, from books to toys for girls and boys. Its address: 557 Broadway, New York, NY 10012; 212-343-6166.

Frequently Asked Questions (FAQs): General Things People Need to Know about J. K. Rowling

Most authors' websites have a FAQs (Frequently Asked Questions) page because it saves them the trouble of answering general questions their readers are likely to ask. Because Rowling does not have a FAQs section on any websites with which she's affiliated, I have answered the questions most commonly asked by her readers and the media, drawn from interviews.

Why does she use initials instead of her full name on her novels?
Because her British publisher was concerned that boys would not read a children's book written by a woman—an ungrounded fear, as it turned out.

What does J. K. Rowling stand for?
Joanne Kathleen Rowling. Her middle name comes from her grandmother on her mother's side.

Is there an official J. K. Rowling fan club?

No. Nor is one in the works. Sometimes, as with *The Lord of the Rings*, the film studio licenses an official fan club, mostly to promote the film and tie-in merchandising. But Warner Bros. has not done so, and is not likely to do so.

How can I get a signed copy of one of Rowling's novels?

Rowling has estimated that she's signed "tens of thousands" of books, mostly U.K. editions, and mostly earlier books, some of which are offered by auction houses, antiquarian (rare book) dealers, and eBay.

Keep in mind that in recent years, she has signed very few books because she's attended so few public functions, and most of them have been U.K. functions.

Here's what you need to know:

1. Do *not* write to her publishers asking for a signed book. Because of the high volume of mail she receives, they must screen her mail and forward only those that they feel she may be interested in reading. Neither her publishers nor Rowling herself has the time to arrange for you to get a signed book directly.

2. Indirectly, a logical source is eBay, but unfortunately there's no way to verify a signature's authenticity, so unscrupulous sellers simply forge her distinctive signature and write ad copy to make it appear that the book was obtained at one of her public functions.

Rowling herself has cautioned her fans against buying from eBay, saying on her website that "as far as I could tell on the day I dropped in, only one of the signatures on offer appeared genuine. There seems to be a lot of people out there trying to con Harry Potter fans."

Like me, she recommends that you buy from antiquarian booksellers.

What's the best way to reach J. K. Rowling?

By regular mail sent to her U.S. or U.K. publishers. Despite the volume of mail, she does read what she can and, occasionally, even answers mail. Obviously, with millions of readers, it's impossible for her to be your pen pal, so be forewarned that a response is unlikely.

Her U.S. publisher: J. K. Rowling, c/o Scholastic, 557 Broadway, New York, NY 10012, USA.

Her U.K. publisher: J. K. Rowling, c/o Bloomsbury Publishing, 38 Soho Square, London, W1V 5DF, UK.

Does she have an e-mail address?

Yes, but even if I knew it—and I don't—I wouldn't share it with anyone. In fact, it's a secret more closely guarded than what's in vault #713 at Gringotts, so if you know what's good for you, you won't even ask.

What are the official websites?

The principal sites include: (1) www.harrypotter.com, the Warner Bros. site; (2) www.scholastic.com, her U.S. publisher's general book site; (3) www.blooms bury.com, her U.K. publisher's website; and (4) www.jkrowling.com, her personal website.

What's the title of book seven and when is it due out?

Harry Potter and the Deathly Hallows, due out July 21, 2007.

Will Rowling write any more books about Harry Potter?

No. She has repeatedly said that she planned a seven-book series. Though readers would love to read about Harry Potter after he graduates from Hogwarts and (presumably) becomes an Auror (a wizard from the Ministry of Magic who goes after dark wizards), Rowling has no intention of writing more Potter novels. If you absolutely *cannot live* without stories about a post-Hogwarts Harry, then check out the fan fiction on the Internet—a wide body of work, running the gamut from bad to pretty good.

What does Rowling plan to write after she finishes the seventh Harry Potter novel?

At a press conference in August 2006 in NYC, Rowling said that she's nearly finished with a children's book aimed at a younger audience than those who read Harry Potter.

In interviews given over the years, she's also said that she plans to write a nonfiction book drawing on her extensive notes and back stories about Hogwarts and the wizarding world, an encyclopedia with all proceeds going to benefit charity.

How do I become an extra in one of the Harry Potter movies?

With great difficulty. For one thing, Rowling is adamant about keeping Harry Potter true to form, which means (among other things) that the film director and casting director draw from the talent pool in the United Kingdom. Typically, a general announcement is made in the media, since it's not always a requirement that one be a professional actor; Rupert Grint (playing Ron Weasley), after all, had no prior acting experience. But be warned that the turnout will be large and the chances of actually landing a character role are *very* slim. Recently, for instance, an open casting call went out for Luna Lovegood, for *Harry Potter and the Order of the Phoenix.* The casting call drew nearly 15,000 girls, out of which 400 were called back. Fourteen-year-old Evanna Lynch eventually got the coveted role.

Can J. K. Rowling recommend a literary agent to me?

No. If you want to write and get published, do what she did and go to the library to consult the standard writers' directories, which provide detailed information on what publishers and literary agencies are looking for and how to contact them. Then put together a first-class presentation for an agent. Remember, you won't get a second chance to make a first impression.

Also, if you can't, or won't, do your own research, writing is probably not the vocation for you: It's all paperwork.

Can J. K. Rowling read my work and tell me what she thinks?

No. Best-selling authors are frequently asked to do this, but as any attorney will tell you, it inevitably leads to unwanted lawsuits. It's always an amateur who claims his idea was stolen by the pro. It's insulting because Rowling doesn't *need* to steal ideas from anyone, since she comes up with some pretty good ones on her own.

Can J. K. Rowling make an appearance at my house/store/business/school?

No. Again, one writer cannot personally serve the needs of millions of people, all of whom want a personal connection. She's had requests to attend children's birthday parties, charity functions, school events—you name it. Rowling can best serve everyone by producing more work, instead of spending valuable time meeting far fewer people at private functions.

Will Rowling attend our fan convention as the Guest of Honor?

Rowling has never attended a major convention of any kind, much less one specifically devoted to her and her work. It is not likely she will ever do so.

In the few instances where she's made a public appearance, it's been at a large venue where as many fans as possible may see, but not meet, her.

Is it possible to become a writer if you're not a reader?

No. End of discussion.

I've written a screenplay. Can she help me get it in front of a major film studio?

No. Film agents exist for that purpose and can be reached via addresses published in standard directories. Without exception, film studios return, unopened, any unsolicited submission to its sender, because they want to avoid even the suspicion of theft.

I've read about J. K. Rowling or her representatives suing to protect their interests. What are justifiable grounds for her lawsuits?

Rowling, like most creators, prefers spending her valuable and irreplaceable time writing, not suing. But sue she must if she wants to protect what is unarguably the most valuable literary franchise of our time. In addition to defending herself against charges of theft (e.g., the case brought against her by Nancy Stouffer), she's had to bring suit twice, against a Chinese publisher and a Russian publisher; they both issued books that constituted literary plundering, with the Harry Potter characters stolen outright or minimally changed. Unfortunately, Rowling had no option but to sue because if she as a creator does not protect her copyrights, she runs the real risk of losing them forever.

Don't I have the right to take pictures of Rowling in public or ask her for an autograph? After all, as a reader, I'm the reason she's successful. Without me, she'd be nowhere.

Being rich, famous, and a public figure means that Rowling gives up some of her privacy in public, but common sense must prevail. Unless she's in a public venue like a bookstore signing or at a public appearance, she should be considered a private person and treated accordingly. She has the right, for instance, to shop at her favorite stores without being interrupted by well-intentioned fans who want a personal moment or memento in the form of an autograph. She has the right to sit in a café and write without interruptions and not have to endure press stories in which someone gleefully reports a "Rowling sighting." As to her success and its relationship to you: She writes a book, you buy it, and it's a fair exchange.

A Concordance: The People, Places, and Things in Joanne Rowling's Life

7, South Lorne Place, Leith, in Edinburgh, Scotland: An unfurnished, ground-floor apartment Rowling rented while on social welfare.

£2800: The total amount in royalties Rowling received from her first year's worth of sales. (Note: A book advance is in essence a loan from the publisher to the author on contract signing; it's an advance against future royalties.)

Amnesty International: A human rights organization for which Rowling worked as a research assistant after graduating from college.

Arantes, Jorge: Rowling's first husband, a Portuguese journalist with whom she had their daughter, Jessica. After a heated argument between Rowling and Arantes in November 1993, he threw her out of the house, but she later returned to get her daughter; two weeks later, mother and daughter left Porto, Portugal, behind and headed to Edinburgh, Scotland. Subsequently, when Arantes traveled to Edinburgh to see her, she obtained a temporary restraining order; on the day the order became permanent, she also obtained a divorce from him. Arantes later attempted to sell his story to the British tabloids, which ran stories headlined "Lost Love Who First Saw Harry Potter" and "Why I threw my wife out of our home five months after our baby was born and waved goodbye forever to our marriage and my daughter."

Austen, Jane: Rowling's favorite novelist (1775–1817) who wrote six novels, including *Emma* and *Pride and Prejudice*, set in the English countryside.

Bloomsbury Publishing: Rowling's publisher in the United Kingdom, who was the first to take a chance on her work.

Book eight: Since the Harry Potter series are chronologically published, they are often referred to as book one, book two, and so forth. If she were to write book eight, Rowling said in an interview, it would not be a novel but a work of nonfiction, *The Harry Potter Encyclopedia*, which would be a concordance of people, places, and things, with all proceeds going to charity. Like most authors, she knows more about her fictional universe than the readers do, because she has to. If published, this eighth book is where the history of Hogwarts and other miscellany might eventually see the light of day.

Brewer's Dictionary of Phrase and Fable: Originally published in 1989, this dictionary contains 18,000 words with "tales to tell." Rowling uses it as a sourcebook for ideas and names.

Cartoonist: Rowling is a skilled cartoonist who enjoys doodling. A preview of her artwork, shown on a BBC documentary, makes one wish she had illustrated her own books. (Like Tolkien and Pullman, Rowling downplays her skill as an illustrator.)

Chipping Sodbury, England: Birthplace of Rowling.

Columbus, Chris: Film director whose credits include *Home Alone, Mrs. Doubtfire, The Goonies, The Young Sherlock Holmes,* and *Gremlins.* He directed the first two film adaptations: *Harry Potter and the Sorcerer's Stone* and *Harry Potter and the Chamber of Secrets.*

Comic Relief: A charitable organization established in 1985 to end poverty and social injustice in the United Kingdom. At the behest of U.S. literary agent Richard Curtis, Rowling agreed to write two books (*Fantastic Beasts and Where to Find Them,* and *Quidditch Through the Ages*), with all royalties going to this organization. He originally asked for a short story for an anthology, but she offered the books as an alternative. "You will do real magic by buying these books," she later told a child interviewer, in a video clip posted on the Comic Relief website, at www.comicrelief/harrysbooks. The two books raised an estimated $27 million for the charity.

Cuarón, Alfonso: Director of the third Harry Potter movie, *Harry Potter and the Prisoner of Azkaban.*

Dale, Jim: Celebrated audiobook reader of the Harry Potter books in the U.S. editions (www.jim-dale.com).

Department of Social Security: The social welfare system, to which Rowling applied for benefits after leaving Portugal. It was a humiliating and demeaning experience for Rowling, through which she received approximately $100 a week in benefits.

Doctor of Letters: Rowling was honored by her alma mater, the University of Exeter, with an honorary doctorate degree 13 years after her graduation.

Dunn, Alfred: The headmaster at St. Michael's Church of England School when Rowling attended its junior school.

Edinburgh, Scotland: After a failed marriage in Portugal, Rowling and her daughter moved to this city, because her sister lived there. Rowling's principal residence is in this town; she has two other homes, in Kensington and in the Scottish Highlands.

Elephant House: Like Nicolson's, a café where Rowling sought refuge to write fiction.

Evens, Bryony: A "first reader" of unsolicited manuscripts at the Christopher Little Literary Agency, Evens championed Rowling's submission, the first Harry Potter novel, accompanied by her illustrations. (Mindful of Evens's role in Rowling's career, in a copy of *Harry Potter and the Goblet of Fire*, Rowling wrote, "To Bryony—who really did discover Harry Potter.")

Fraser, Lindsey: The executive director of Scottish Book Trust, Fraser interviewed Rowling for *Conversations with J. K. Rowling* (Scholastic, 2001). It's not a biography, despite what Scholastic or Rowling has stated. Yes, it *does* have biographical information, but it's an interview followed by an overview and not (as one might be led to believe) a full-fledged biography.

Fry, Stephen: Celebrated audiobook reader of the Harry Potter books in the U.K. editions.

Gallivan, Janet: Pete Rowling's second wife, whom he married less than two and a half years after Anne Rowling's death. Some believe this marriage created a temporary rift between Rowling and her father, since the dedication of the first Harry Potter novel acknowledges everyone in her family except him—a curious but understandable omission.

Getty, Coleman: Rowling's publicist (www.colmangettypr.co.uk).

Goudge, Elizabeth: Author of *The Little White Horse*, Rowling's favorite book, which she credits as a big influence on the Harry Potter novels.

Gray, Francesca: Author of the first fan letter Rowling ever received. Like most others at that time, Gray had no idea Rowling was a woman, and addressed the letter with the salutation "Dear Sir."

Guinea pig: Rowling owns one, named Jasmine (the name given by her previous owner).

Harris, Séan: One of Rowling's best friends. He owned a turquoise Ford Anglia which they used to get away from the rural community of Tutshill. He is generally considered to be an inspiration for the fictional character Ron Weasley, Harry Potter's best friend.

Hazelbank Terrace: After the sale of her first novel through Little's agency to Scholastic, Rowling left South Lorne Place and bought an apartment here, near her sister's apartment. After she became wealthy, she gave this apartment to a single mother who befriended her in those early years.

Heyman, David: Formerly with Warner Bros., he moved to England and set up Heyday Films to act as a talent scout for Warner Bros. for potential film properties from the United Kingdom. This association eventually resulted in Rowling signing with Warner Bros., whose first two Potter films grossed $1.9 billion worldwide.

Howle, Fleur: A freelance reader who screened unsolicited manuscripts at the Christopher Little Literary Agency. With Bryony Evens, Howle championed Rowling's submission, the first Harry Potter novel.

June 26, 1997: The official publication date of *Harry Potter and the Philosopher's Stone* in England.

Kensington (London, England): The location of one of three homes owned by Rowling, in a suburb of London. A Georgian-style house costing nearly $7 million, this is her home away from home when she goes to see her publisher or literary agent on business. (Previously, she would have to stay in hotels when in town.)

Killiechassie: A residence of Rowling's, this house, within two hours of Edinburgh, is two miles from the nearest town, Aberfeldy. Originally constructed in 1864, this stone house has among its virtues not only the square footage necessary to accommodate a growing family but, more importantly, the seclusion necessary to shield Rowling from prying eyes—journalists, of whom she is not fond, and the general public, which treats her as if she's a public commodity.

Leith Academy: Rowling student-taught here in preparation for her teaching certificate; after obtaining her Postgraduate Certificate of Education, she subsequently taught at this school.

Levine, Arthur A.: An editorial director at Scholastic (U.S.), who secured the U.S. publishing rights for the Potter novels.

Little, Christopher: Literary agent who represents Rowling.

The Little White Horse: Novel by Elizabeth Goudge, which Rowling admired. "I absolutely adored *The Little White Horse*," blurbed Rowling for an edition reprinted in 2000. A careful reading of the book shows it to be an influence on the Harry Potter novels.

Matthewson, Emma: The editor of all the Harry Potter novels.

McDonald, Natalie (Gryffindor): A nine-year-old girl who is mentioned on page 159 of the U.S. edition of *Harry Potter and the Goblet of Fire,* she is the only real person whose name appears in any of the Potter novels. A big Harry Potter fan, the child died before Rowling could respond to family correspondence about her, so Rowling gave her literary immortality by making her a student at Hogwarts; and as long as there are Potter fans reading the books, her name will live in print.

Merchiston (Edinburgh, Scotland): A residence of Rowling's, this Georgian mansion features enhanced security measures—a nine-foot-high wall with a security panel—to ward off journalists and the general public, to the dismay of her neighbors, who felt it was not in keeping with the "look" of the neighborhood.

Misty: Family dog when Rowling was in her mid-teens.

Mitford, Jessica: American writer whom Rowling credits as the most influential on her work. Jessica, Rowling's daughter, is named after Mitford.

Moray House: The postgraduate school that Rowling attended to obtain a teaching certificate, which she got in July 1996.

Murray, David Gordon Rowling: The son of Joanne Rowling and Dr. Neil Murray, born March 23, 2003.

Murray, Dr. Neil: Rowling's second husband, whom she married in a ceremony at her Perthshire home in Scotland on December 26, 2002. Only 15 guests, mostly members of the immediate family, were invited.

Murray, Mackenzie Jean Rowling: The daughter of Joanne Rowling and Dr. Neil Murray, born January 23, 2005.

Newell, Mike: Director (*Mona Lisa Smile, Donnie Brasco,* and *Enchanted April*) of the fourth Harry Potter movie, *Harry Potter and the Goblet of Fire,* released in 2005.

Nicolson's: A restaurant in Edinburgh, where Rowling, nursing coffee, wrote fiction. The family connection: It was half-owned by her brother-in-law, Roger Moore.

Porto, Portugal: After graduation from the University of Exeter, Rowling moved here to teach at Encounter English School. While in Porto, she met Jorge Arantes, whom she married and subsequently divorced.

Postgraduate Certificate in Education: Obtained by Rowling so she could teach school.

Rabbit: Rowling's first attempt at fiction at age six, a novel influenced by the fiction of Richard Scarry. She later got a large black rabbit, which her daughter named Jemima.

Rowling, Anne: Rowling's mother who died in December 1990 at age 45 from complications resulting from multiple sclerosis.

Rowling, Dianne: Rowling's only sibling, born at home on June 28, 1967, at 109 Sundridge Park. Her family nickname is "Di."

Rowling, Jessica: Daughter of Joanne Rowling and Jorge Arantes, born July 27, 1993.

Rowling, Kathleen: Rowling's grandmother on her father's side, who died from a heart attack at age 52. After her death, Joanne Rowling adopted her grandmother's first name as her middle name, thus: Joanne Kathleen Rowling.

Rowling, Pete: Rowling's father who met his first wife-to-be, Anne Volant, at King's Cross station in London.

Scamander, Newt: Pen name Rowling used as the author of _Fantastic Beasts and Where to Find Them,_ the proceeds of which went to charity.

Scottish Arts Council: Organization that supported the arts with grants. After submitting her proposal, which discussed her plans for the Harry Potter novels, Rowling obtained a grant for £8,000, the council's maximum allowable amount to a single person.

Second Tidenham (St. Mary's) Brownie Pack: In September 1975, Rowling became a Brownie scout.

Shepherd, Lucy: Secondary school teacher who taught English; Rowling credits her as an early, lasting influence.

Spiders: Rowling has arachnophobia, a fear of spiders.

St. David's Roman Catholic High School (Dalkeith, Scotland): Rowling student-taught here in preparation for a teaching certificate.

St. Michael's Church of England Primary School: The first school she attended, at age five.

Stouffer, Nancy: American writer who unsuccessfully sued Rowling for copyright infringement, claiming that her 1984 book, *The Legend of Rah and the Muggles,* was ripped off by Rowling, an assertion that, predictably, drew a lot of media attention to Stouffer and her books. In the end Rowling prevailed and Stouffer not only lost the suit, but was also fined $50,000. According to U.S. District Judge Allen G. Schwartz, "the court finds, by clear and convincing evidence, that Stouffer has perpetuated a fraud . . . through her submission of fraudulent documents as well as through her untruthful testimony." End of case, end of story.

Though Rowling emerged triumphant in the courts, she found herself distracted by the legal brouhaha, one of several matters that may have had a bearing on the three-year interval between book four *(Harry Potter and the Goblet of Fire)* and book five (*Harry Potter and the Order of the Phoenix* published in 2003).

Thumper: Family dog when Rowling was a small child.

Tutshill: Rural community in South Wales where Rowling grew up.

Tutshill Church of England Primary School: Rowling attended this school beginning in 1974.

University of Exeter: After failing to get into Oxford, Rowling applied for and was accepted to this university.

Warner Bros.: Film studio that wooed Rowling and secured the film and merchandising rights to the Harry Potter franchise.

Whisp, Kennilworthy: Pen name Rowling used as the author of *Quidditch Through the Ages,* the proceeds of which went to charity.

Wyedean Comprehensive: Rowling was a head girl at this school, which she attended after Tutshill School. (A head girl or boy is a senior student assigned to monitor duties.)

Yates, David: Director of the fifth Harry Potter movie, *Harry Potter and the Order of the Phoenix.*

Give a Hoot! No Owls for Pets!

If you give a hoot about real owls, here's my advice, echoed by animal trainers and animal conservancy groups: *Don't give your child a snowy owl for a pet.*

Not surprisingly, when children read the Harry Potter novels and, especially, see the film adaptations, the mistaken impression they get is that owls are wonderful pets: beautiful to look at, cuddly (especially the snowy owl), and responsive to human interaction.

Nothing could be further from the truth.

In a BBC news story (December 18, 2001), Lucy Clark, a spokesperson for the Royal Society for the

Pepe Lulu, an adult Barn Owl

Prevention of Cruelty to Animals, stated, "We are concerned by the surge in demand for owls because we don't think they make suitable pets. By their nature they are shy and reclusive birds, preferring to spend time in secluded places."

Here are a few facts about the owl that you probably didn't know, according to Clark, as quoted by the BBC:

1. It is large. Up to two feet tall with a six-foot wingspan, it can weigh up to eight pounds.

2. It is noisy, especially at night.

3. It is expensive, if you can find one. (In Europe, you can buy one, but there are strict laws governing their ownership. In the United States, you *cannot* own one, unless you have a special license.)

4. It has very sharp talons and can inflict deep wounds.

5. It requires a regular supply of food.

6. It requires a flight aviary and specialist veterinary care.

7. It lives up to 20 years, which means owning one is a commitment. (When children tire of their pet cats and dogs, it's off to the animal shelter with the pets.)

The BBC story also quoted Campbell Murn, of the Hawk Conservancy in England: "Unless they are trained properly they are not going to sit on a perch or a fist."

An article in the *Washington Post* (November 28, 2001) pointed out that the gentle hooting associated with owls isn't necessarily the sound emitted by *all* owls. As *Post* staff writer Don Oldenburg humorously observed, "[N]ot all owls give a hoot. Instead of the resonant muffled 'whoot' associated with the great horned owl, the screech owl makes a quavering down-scale whistle and the barn owl lets out a chilling hissing scream. . . ." Oldenburg added that during mating season female snowy owls "make odd guttural noises and doglike barks, cackles, shrieks, and hissing. Hey, it's a jungle out there."

In other words, the image of a cuddly, affectionate owl who is going to hoot appreciatively and give you a gentle nip with its beak is a fantasy, which belongs, properly, in the pages of the Harry Potter novels and not in your child's life.

If that's not enough to discourage you, the prospects of owning an owl in the United States are slim to none, for it requires a wildlife or falconry permit, which most people can't get. The same article in the *Washington Post* quoted Patricia Fisher, a spokeswoman for the U.S. Fish and Wildlife Service, who bluntly said, "The deal is, you are not going to get one. You are not going to find one for sale by a legitimate pet dealer."

If you're a parent, chances are good that after every popular movie featuring potential pets—Dalmatians *(101 Dalmatians),* clown fish *(Finding*

Nemo), and more horses than you can whinny at—your child will clamor for one "just like the one in the movie." Be thankful, perhaps, that your child doesn't want a shark (Bruce, in *Finding Nemo)*; but after all is said and done, if your child still cannot live without an owl, two recommendations come to mind.

First, adopt an owl being protected by an organization. Raptor Education Group will gladly accept your donation to adopt a bird. An owl, for instance, costs $100 to adopt. And what, you ask, do you get for your money? You get a chance to make a real difference and help protect a species, some of which are on endangered lists. On its website (www.raptoreducationgroup.org), the Raptor Education Group encourages contributions:

> Wildlife does not have health insurance. Expenses, i.e., veterinary and pharmacy costs, can add up to many hundreds of dollars for treatments for a single bird. Food and housing costs significantly increase these numbers. By joining our adopt a bird program, you can contribute financially to the annual support of one of our avian residents.
>
> Please choose the level at which you would like to contribute and send this form, along with your adoption donation, to: Raptor Education Group, Inc., P.O. Box 481, Antigo, WI 54409. (Special adoption requests may be submitted.) In return, we will send you a photo of the bird you are supporting, as well as information about that bird's history and a certificate suitable for framing. Your involvement is priceless to the future of these wild birds. We truly appreciate your support of the Raptor Education Group.

The other alternative—and one that will fit your budget and be cute and cuddly—is to buy the licensed plush doll, a replica of Harry's owl, Hedwig, which costs $14.95, available in toy stores nationwide.

Hedwig plush doll

Footprints on the Heart:
Catie Hoch and Joanne Rowling

T his is all TOP SECRET, so you are allowed to tell [some close friends] and your Mum, but no one else or you'll be getting an owl from the Ministry of Magic. It is clear to me . . . that you are an extremely brave person and a true Gryffindor. With lots of love, J. K. Rowling (Jo to anybody in Gryffindor).

—in an e-mail (January 2000) from Rowling to Catie Hoch

Joanne Rowling has, through her novels, touched millions of lives, most of whom she can never, and will never, meet.

One reader in particular—a brave little girl named Catie Hoch—counted herself among those millions, but with a difference: Rowling had planned to meet her because of a special bond that existed between them. Sadly, the two never met because Hoch, who had suffered from a malignant form of cancer that afflicts children, died at the age of nine.

Her death, as Rowling so poignantly put it, left "footprints on my heart."

With Catie having so much to live for but so little time, her parents tried to give her everything they could, to make her last few years as comfortable as possible under the circumstances. Like other children, she was a big Harry Potter fan and asked that all the Potter novels be read to her.

Her mother, Gina Peca, sat down to do just that, and in due course finished reading aloud the first three, which were in print; the fourth, unfortunately, could not be read because it was still being written. So her mother did what any other parent would do. She sent an e-mail to Rowling's publisher to ask when the fourth book would be released, and spoke of the joy the Potter novels had brought into her daughter's life, a life that would not likely see the publication of the fourth Potter novel.

Rowling's fan mail is, as you might expect, voluminous. I'm sure Catie's mother would have understood, though she would have been disappointed, if no response were forthcoming. Realistically, her mother probably thought the best she could hope for was a firm publication date, so she could, in a race against time, buy the book and read it to her dying daughter.

Rowling's publisher realized the uniqueness of the letter and forwarded it to Rowling, who, to the surprise and delight of mother and daughter, replied with news about the next novel, *Harry Potter and the Goblet of Fire.*

And so began an extraordinary, special friendship.

Rowling followed up with a toy owl, Pigwidgeon. Putting on a brave face, Rowling likely wrote through her tears as she wrote the note that accompanied it: "I'm so glad Pigwidgeon got there all right because (as you find out in book four) he's not a very reliable owl—a bit overenthusiastic."

Rowling has often said that she writes for an audience of one—herself. But in this special circumstance, she also wrote for one other—a brave child who, facing a certain and premature death, was determined to fight until the end.

As Catie and Rowling exchanged e-mails, their friendship blossomed, but there would be no fairy tale ending in this real-life story.

Rowling was there for Catie, with encouragement, by e-mail; and when Catie was too ill to answer e-mail, the author was there with phone calls, reading the work in progress, knowing—like Catie's mother—that it was a losing race against time.

Even toward the end, the child was a tiny figure of strength. "Catie never complained or asked 'Why me?' She was a ray of sunshine," her mother quietly affirmed.

Catie Hoch died on May 18, 2000. The long-planned get-together between Hoch and Rowling would never happen. But what did happen was that, as Rowling put it, the brave little girl touched her deeply. As Rowling wrote to Catie's parents, "I consider myself privileged to have had contact with Catie. I can only aspire to being the sort of parents both of you have been to Catie during her illness. I am crying so hard as I type. She left footprints on my heart. With much love, Jo."

After her daughter passed away, Catie's mother agreed to give an interview to a British newspaper to publicize a memorial fund that she had set up to help other ill children, and the process of asking for donations began.

Out of the blue, Rowling, who had read of the foundation, sent a $100,000 check accompanied by a heartfelt letter as well. Her unselfish actions speak volumes about her generous heart, about the power of the

The Catie Hoch Foundation

The Foundation gratefully accepts donations. (Foreign donors are urged to buy an international bank check.) The address to mail checks:

The Catie Hoch Foundation
27 Southwood Drive
Ballston Lake, NY 12019
Phone: 518-877-7539
e-mail:
gina@catiehochfoundation.org

written word to touch and inspire us, and, most of all, about what Rowling considers *real* magic—the enduring power of love and the human heart.

NOTE: Several newspapers and magazines have run stories about Catie Hoch, most drawing on articles published in the *London Sunday Telegraph* and the *Times Union*. These two newspapers, *Newsweek,* and the official Catie Hoch website (www.catie hochfoundation.org) are my sources for this article.

One-Parent Families and
J. K. Rowling

A single parent herself, Rowling went through an all-too-familiar and painful experience that many other women face every day. Knowing full well the difficulties involved, Rowling became an Ambassador for One Parent Families (a registered charity in England; website: www.oneparentfamilies.org.uk), using her visibility to bring attention to this worthy cause. She has also made a sizable donation to assist the organization, which actively solicits contributions through its website or through the mail.

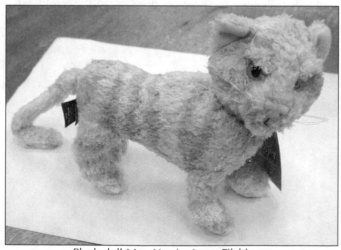

Plush doll Mrs. Norris, Argus Filch's cat

On October 4, 2000, the organization launched its official website and at a press conference to publicize the event Joanne Rowling not only showed up but spoke eloquently, demolishing the myths of single parenting and hammering home the facts that most people don't know, or don't care to know.

At the press conference, Rowling concluded:

> I am very proud to be the new Ambassador for the National Council for One Parent Families, proud to help work toward a fairer deal for a group of people who need to be supported, not stigmatized. Seven years after becoming a lone parent myself, I feel qualified to look anyone in the eye and say that bringing up children single-handedly deserves congratulation, not condemnation. We do two people's jobs single-handedly even before we take on paid work. I would like to think that the day will come when the phrase "single mother" and the word "penniless" do not go together quite as easily as they do now and that there will be much less surprise the next time one of us turns up in the newspapers as a success story.

J. K. Rowling on Being a Single Parent

Do you have any advice for struggling single mothers?

Rowling: "I am never very comfortable giving other single mothers 'words of advice.' Nobody knows better than I do that I was very lucky—I didn't need money to exercise the talent I had—all I needed was a [pen] and some paper. Nor do other single mothers need to be reminded that they are already doing the most demanding job in the world, which isn't sufficiently recognized for my liking."

—quoted by Margaret Weir in
"Of Magic and Single Motherhood,"
Salon.com (March 31, 1999)

Multiple Sclerosis and J. K. Rowling

Beyond the obvious, there are two good things about being wealthy and famous: The former allows you the financial freedom to give back to the community, and the latter allows you to lend your name to publicize any cause you endorse.

For Rowling, that cause is the Multiple Sclerosis Society of Scotland, for which she is a patron, currently spearheading a nationwide effort to fight the

Plush doll Fluffy, Hagrid's pet

disease on several fronts: by educating the public, by pushing for much-needed and long overdue legislation, and by soliciting tax-deductible donations.

Like most people, the disease was the furthest thing from Rowling's mind until it hit home. Her mother, diagnosed with it at age 35, lived a scant ten more years. Then, on December 31, 1990, for Rowling, what is normally a time of celebration became a time forever fixed in pain. Her father called and said her mother had died the night before. Multiple sclerosis (MS) finally took its toll and claimed another victim, this time striking at her heart's center.

If you have never lost a parent suddenly, unexpectedly, you cannot begin to understand the extent of the pain. For the parent who has passed away, the suffering has ended; but for you, it has just begun, and you will carry it to the end of your days.

As you go through life and celebrate its most poignant moments, you want to share them with those closest to you, but you can't: Your mother or father is gone, and your heart breaks, time and again.

Rowling's infinite regret is underscored by her sure knowledge that if a national standard of care had existed in Scotland for those afflicted with MS, her mother might still be here, or would have suffered less.

Love, of course, and infinite regret.

In *Harry Potter and the Sorcerer's Stone,* Harry Potter looks into the Mirror of Erised (*desire* spelled backwards) and sees what he wants the most. He sees his parents and reaches out to try and touch them, but he can't. He feels happiness and profound sadness at the same time, for seeing them brings joy, but knowing he will never know them brings a profound sadness.

This one brief scene of Harry Potter reaching out to his parents is Rowling the writer at her most poignant. She can write about it with such clarity because she knows what Harry Potter is going through. She knows all too well what the young wizard-to-be feels because she's been there.

Rowling, like everyone else, looks back and tortures herself with "what if" questions, the kind you ask yourself regarding a frustrating situation.

Back then Rowling could do nothing but rage against the darkness of the night. Now she can use her visibility to draw attention to the disease, and as a patron of the MS Society of Scotland she has become its most visible spokesperson, championing its cause.

Way too much has been written about Rowling and the essentially inconsequential: the number of books sold, the dollars earned in merchandised Potter products, the box-office receipts of her movies, and her personal holdings and wealth, which put her in a financial position that exceeds that of English royalty.

Far less has been written about her advocacy of the Multiple Sclerosis

Society of Scotland. Though news-worthy, it's a depressing subject that journalists would rather gloss over or ignore. More's the shame, since Rowling has worked and will continue to work tirelessly to pro-mote the organization, to bring the disease to public awareness, even as journalists trip over them-selves to report every little upward tick in her personal fortune.

When basketball star Michael Jordan's grandmother died, he carried the grief privately, and no one knew just how much she meant to him until he put it in terms everyone could understand. When asked if he had any regrets in life, he said that he'd give anything just to have five more minutes to spend with his grand-mother. Tragically, a few years later, his father would be sense-lessly murdered and Jordan would grieve again. Being rich and famous, as Rowling would readily admit, doesn't insulate you from the kind of never-ending sorrow that visits when you lose someone close to you. Your life is irrevocably changed and all you can do is pick up the pieces and move forward.

> ## J. K. Rowling on Multiple Sclerosis
>
> "Would a national standard of care have made much difference to my mother? I am convinced that it would have done. Visits from a spe-cialist nurse, proper support from social services, physiotherapy when appropriate: all would have improved her quality of life dra-matically. . . . I cannot give her my time anymore, but I see being patron of the MS Society as my continuing tribute to her, to all she did for me and my sister, Di, and to how much we loved her. I know she would have cared deeply that noth-ing much has improved for people with MS in over a decade. It now remains to be seen whether the people in Scotland with the power to change that situation care enough to make the difference."
>
> —*from an op-ed piece in the* Sunday Herald *(November 16, 2003)*

Rowling has done just that. By being involved in a prominent way with the Multiple Sclerosis Society of Scotland, she does her most important work. Her books may entertain, but her work for that organization illumi-nates a greater cause.

J. K. Rowling at the Royal Albert Hall in London: One Author and 4,000 Children

Rowling has a cold place in her heart for journalists, but a warm one for children. In an increasingly media-centric world, the press is courted by book publishers anxious to get the word out. What the press wants, the press usually gets, unless it's an audience with Rowling, who acknowledges that its members have a job to do but often pursue it too vigorously. No wonder she parodied the press in her caricature of a pushy newspaper reporter, Rita Skeeter, whose insectlike name is rather apt. (A "skeeter" is a "mosquito," about which *The American Heritage Dictionary* notes that "the female of most species is distinguished by a long proboscis for sucking blood." That certainly sums Rita up, doesn't it?)

Instead of the media onslaught of interviews that usually presages the appearance of a new book, Rowling's interviews for book five were restricted to a handful: notably, one with U.S. television anchorwoman Katie Couric and, in Rowling's own backyard, a long interview with the BBC. All other requests for interviews were politely declined.

Journalists, though, were invited to cover what turned out to be the media event of the year in the book trade. On June 26, 2003, Rowling appeared at the Royal Albert Hall, her only major public appearance.

Most of the 4,000 tickets sold were available on a school lottery basis to teachers in Britain and Ireland. (Ten were set aside for children from the United States, who were encouraged to write short essays on the question: "If you could have one special power taught at Hogwarts, what would it be and why?")

For the rest of the world, the event seemed off-limits, until a real-time webcast was set up so that everyone could enjoy what promised to be a unique event.

For those lucky enough to attend, it turned out to be a picture perfect day, sunny and warm. Thousands of excited schoolchildren converged on the grounds of the Royal Albert Hall. Considering the crush of the crowd, no one would have faulted Rowling for slipping in unseen through a back entrance, but she obviously didn't want to disappoint her young fans who wanted to see her, not from a distance, but up close and personal, and close enough to get a book signed, if possible.

When Rowling arrived in the late afternoon, pandemonium ensued. The press immediately surged forward, shouting to get her attention. She made a beeline for the American children, however, the contest winners who waited with books in hand for signing.

She stopped to make a brief statement to the press, but it wasn't enough. The media shouted even

Scholastic Essay Contest Winners

Initially, American students had no hope of getting a ticket to the Royal Albert Hall appearance of Rowling, until Scholastic arranged for a group of handpicked schoolchildren to get tickets by writing a 300-word essay on "If you could have one special power taught at Hogwarts, what would it be and why?" Students put on their thinking caps and took pen to paper, writing a total of 12,000 entries, from which ten were chosen.

Those lucky ten not only got to see the event, but were able to attend free of cost, with an all-expenses-paid trip courtesy of Scholastic. On top of that, Rowling signed copies of their books as well.

According to one of the contest judges, Scholastic's Editorial Director Arthur A. Levine, "Reading these essays was a wonderful reminder of the deep connection Rowling's books make with her readers, how her stories tweak the imagination and speak to our deep yearning for the power to make our lives better and to leave an impact on this world."

The children ranged in age from 8 to 16:

Sudipta Bandyopadhyay (Somerset, NJ)

Daniel Boyce (Camarillo, CA)

Marty Cain (Marlboro, VT)

Nancy Chen (Tulsa, OK)

David Dawson (St. Petersburg, FL)

Louisa George (Rexburg, ID)

Brittany Hawkrigg (Bohemia, NY)

Emily Grayson (Brownsburg, IN)

Thomas Pardee (Modesto, CA)

Angela Wyse (Tecumseh, MI)

more loudly to get her attention, but she turned away from them and refocused her attention on the kids, signed more books, and then went inside.

No expense was spared to make this a special event for the attendees. The Royal Albert Hall was transformed into Hogwarts, with everyone involved playing a part, including the ushers dressed as Hogwarts students. On stage, a set recalled the common room of a Hogwarts house, complete with an overstuffed sofa, framed portraits on the wall, and a crackling fireplace.

With the audience divided into four sections—one for each Hogwarts house—students felt as if, for those few hours, they *were* at Hogwarts, trappings and all, with two special guests: Rowling herself and Stephen Fry, who reads her Potter novels on audiotape for the books-on-tape market.

Fry made his grand entrance via Floo Powder in the fireplace and wasted no time in making it clear why he was present. "Can I introduce J. K. Rowling, the most famous and most popular author in the whole wide world?"

He could and did, and the hall rocked with the collective enthusiasm of thousands of young Harry Potter fans who surely had counted down the days to this special event, just as they had done for the appearance of the fifth Potter novel, which had appeared only five days previous.

After a conversational interview conducted by Fry, a precarious dangling Ford Anglia descended from the ceiling and took a position behind Rowling. It was time for Rowling to read, which she does with considerable skill. (Clearly, she could, if she wanted, read her own books instead of relying on others.) She read from page 583 of the British edition of *Harry Potter and the Order of the Phoenix*, encouraging those who had brought a copy of the book to read along.

She finished the reading and closed the book. The children gave her a standing ovation. She thanked the crowd and—poof!—she was gone, leaving behind an auditorium filled with excited children.

The Art of Illustration:
Mary GrandPré

A lice was beginning to get very tired of sitting by her sister on the bank and of having nothing to do: once or twice she had peeped into the book her sister was reading, but it had no pictures or conversations in it, "and what is the use of a book," thought Alice, "without pictures or conversations?"

—*Lewis Carroll,* Alice's Adventures in Wonderland

Mary GrandPré

Painting vivid word pictures in our collective minds' eye, Rowling's prose hardly needs illustrations—or so I thought,

Welcome to the visionary world of Mary GrandPre. The portfolio is divided into two sections; Gallery and Children's books to simplify your browsing. Please take your time and enjoy!

Screenshot of marygrandpre.com

until I bought American editions of the Potter novels with art by Mary GrandPré. Unlike the British editions, the American editions are wonderfully, delightfully,

It's about TIME: Harry Potter's Cover Story

The best portrait ever done of Harry Potter, drawn by Mary GrandPré for a *Time* magazine cover story on Harry Potter ("The Magic of Harry Potter," September 20, 1999), is available as an inexpensive miniposter from Time, Inc. The print (alas, with type overlaid) is available in two sizes. It is available online from the webstore Barewalls (www.barewalls.com). Type "Harry Potter" in its search engine, which will yield movie posters and two versions of the *Time* cover: an 8 x 10-inch print for $15.95, and the 11 x 14-inch print for $19.95 (plus a $6.50 flat rate for shipping).

Time magazine cover with art by Mary GrandPré

and appropriately illustrated with her charming work. In fact, I can't imagine reading a Potter novel without her enchanting illustrations that adorn the chapter heads.

With deft skill and the right humorous touch, GrandPré's illustrations are perfect examples of how the right art can serve not as mere decoration but can also illuminate the text. Take, for instance, the illustration for chapter one from the first novel: Swaddled in blankets, the infant Harry Potter is asleep under a sky of stars. All looks normal, but looks can be deceiving. What, one asks, is that curious mark on Harry's forehead? Another example: The illustration for chapter two from the same book shows Dudley Dursley surrounded by a mountain of birthday gifts. The look on his face suggests his sense of entitlement and an air of disdain for his cousin, Harry Potter.

I could go on for pages, pointing out one delightful illustration after another, from all five of the Potter novels, but I won't. After all, you are best advised to go to the source and see for yourself—GrandPré's art is magical.

Mary GrandPré's involvement with Scholastic began with an unexpected phone call when its art director asked if she'd be interested in illustrating the first Harry Potter book, of which she knew nothing.

"It sounded like a nice job," reflected GrandPré in a profile for *Communication Arts,* "so I said 'sure.' I presented three cover sketches, they chose one, and I was pretty happy with everything. They were great to work with, and I think I remember them saying there might be more. At the time, it just seemed like another job."

It was anything *but* just another job. As with Cliff Alexander (the British cover artist for the first Potter novel), Mary GrandPré suddenly found herself in the limelight, principally because of her high visibility Harry Potter–related assignments, including book covers and interior illustrations for the subsequent four books, a portrait of Harry Potter for a *Time* magazine cover story, and art for the official Rowling websites.

So, you ask, how good is Mary GrandPré? She is, simply, the best. In fact, Rowling herself has in several interviews stated that although many artists have illustrated her work, she ranks GrandPré's art first—no small compliment from a writer who is a talented cartoonist in her own right.

As GrandPré discovered, being an integral part of the Harry Potter book world translates to instant fame. In demand at schools and bookstores, GrandPré is probably a bit surprised at the overwhelming response to her art. After all, although she's got an impressive resume, all that most people see is her Harry Potter art, the most visible of her output.

As GrandPré told *Communication Arts*, "Harry Potter is the most popular part of my work. But it's a very small part."

It may be a small part of her output, but it's a big deal to millions of American readers who take delight not only in the Harry Potter stories but in their illustrations from the talented pen of Mary GrandPré.

Framing Harry Potter

Harry Potter—along with other children's book favorites—rates the front page of *Publishers Weekly*.

For fans who want an original drawing by Mary GrandPré of anything in the Harry Potter universe—sorry, you're out of luck. The rights belong to Warner Bros., and no originals from the books have ever been offered to the general public.

Fortunately, two options exist for the fan who would understandably prefer not to tear apart his copies of the Harry Potter books to frame Harry Potter and put him up on the wall.

The first option is to buy a calendar with GrandPré's art, beautifully reproduced and printed in an oversized format by Andrews McMeel Publishing. The 2005 and 2006 wall calendars measured approximately 11 x 13 inches. The art and the printing justify taking the calendar apart to frame individual pages. (A mini-calendar was also issued for 2006.)

The second option, if you have a few Galleons set aside, is to invest in a giclee print. Oversized, printed in full color, and limited in number, these are high-fidelity reproductions that are reasonably priced, especially when compared to the cost of GrandPré's original art, which can run up to $3,000 each.

The giclees range from $150 to $300, with most averaging $225.

Muggles Visit the Wizarding World: HP Fan Trips

If you want to explore the real world of Harry Potter and aren't native to England, consider going on a guided tour sponsored by HP Fan Trips (www.hpfantrips.com), a tour company that tailors your Harry Potter experience in three excursions covering London/Oxford, Scotland, or Science in a Wizarding World. Ranging from inexpensive weekend packages to seven and eight day packages, these itineraries offer several advantages: by saving time, money, and frustration in trying to locate these places on their own, tourists can maximize their traveling experience. The added bonus: You will be in the company of other Potter fans and will surely have a lot to talk about and share.

Sightseeing in London: the York Minister Cathedral in Yorkshire

The brainchild of three Potter fans—editor Jeff Guillaume of www.hpana.com, Heidi Tandy of FictionAlley, and Jeannie Barresi (co-owner of Beyond Boundaries Travel)—HP Fan Trips provides a great way to experience

Catherine Collins

The Hogwarts Express, Engine #5972

the real world of Muggles as depicted in Rowling's novels and get a taste of the wizarding world as well, since the tours include the sights and sites that have become famous through the film adaptations.

The London Tour

For the new Harry Potter fan, especially for one who has never been to England before, this is the package of choice. It's a good way to get your feet wet, so to speak, before immersing yourself in the Scotland tour.

Day one: Arrive in London and transfer to Oxford for a city tour. Called the City of Dreaming Spires, it's not only the backdrop for many scenes in the Harry Potter movies but has significant ties to other writers, including J. R. R. Tolkien, C. S. Lewis, and Philip Pullman. In the evening, loosen your belts for the Hogwarts-style dinner. It will, as hobbits from Middle-earth say, rain food and drink!

Day two: Take the Hogwarts Express to the Lake District for shopping. While on the train, there will be games, divination classes, and stories told (and retold), all with a Harry Potter theme. This is, of course, the actual train used to transport students to Hogwarts in the films.

Day three: Visit Christ Church College and other locations seen in the making of the Potter films, fly a broomstick via virtual reality and try to catch the golden rings, and then hear Oxford lecturer Robin Briggs talk about the witch trials in England. It's also the opportunity to visit the Museum of Oxford, where *Alice in Wonderland* memorabilia is on display and, in the gift store, sold. Note to Tolkien fans: Take the opportunity to pay your respects to J. R. R. Tolkien when in town. For anyone who loves fantasy, no trip to Oxford is complete until you have visited The Master.

Day four: The first half of the day is spent on a sightseeing tour of London: Buckingham Palace, Westminster Abbey, Big Ben, the Houses of Parliament, and other places of interest. The afternoon is open so you can explore London, a city replete with literary connections, from Sherlock Holmes to the world of Charles Dickens.

Day five: Visit the British Museum or the Museum of Science to learn more about the history of England. Take the afternoon off to do your own shopping and visit some of the favorite tourist destinations like the London Dungeon (where they probably keep the chains oiled, just as the anticipatory Argus Filch does at Hogwarts), Madame Tussaud's, and Westminster Abbey.

Day six: Put on your Sherlock Holmes hunting cap and search throughout London for treasure at Harry Potter film locations. You will be furnished with clues, maps, and travel cards, and (if you are reasonably adept at navigation) will find yourself at Platform Nine and Three-Quarters, Gringotts Bank (real world: Australia House), and Diagon Alley (real world: Leadenhall Market). The fourth clue will take you to The Leaky Cauldron (or similar pub) where you can unwind, lubricating your throat with robust ale and chowing down on all manner of fish and fowl. Make sure to take plenty of photos with the provided disposable camera to collect "evidence." Dinner is included at the end of this long but rewarding day.

Day seven: Head to Heathrow airport to go home. Take a long break and recover your strength, so that you can return next year to take the Scotland tour.

Scotland Tour

The heart of England may be in London, but for Harry Potter fans, the soul of that book series can be found in Edinburgh, Scotland, which is home to J. K. Rowling. So it makes sense that a trip to Scotland is, for Potter fans, inevitable; and, if so, why not go with an experienced tour company?

Day one: Arrive in London and go on a sightseeing tour to see film locations from the Potter films. Dinner will be a Hogwarts-style banquet, with more food than you can imagine (literally) at one sitting. *Accio*, desserts!

Day two: Take the Hogwarts Express to the Lake District for shopping and dining. A full schedule of activities is planned en route, including games, divination classes, and storytelling. Of course, socializing with fellow Potter fans is par for the course.

Day three: Visit Christ Church College and other

The Holdenby House, where fans watched a falconry demonstration and potted plants in a herbology class

Catherine Collins

The Holdenby House's greenhouse, where herbology class was held

locations used as settings for the Harry Potter films. And try your hand as well at testing your flying skills on a virtual reality ride—mount your broomstick, push off, and head to the clouds. (Watch out for Muggles looking skyward, since they're not used to seeing witches and wizards flying through the skies.)

Take in an informative lecture on witch hunting by Oxford lecturer Robin Briggs. Take the time, too, to visit the Museum of Oxford and make a pilgrimage—a must!—to see J. R. R. Tolkien's gravesite.

The evening is free for personal time. Rest and recuperate because you'll need it for day four.

Day four: Take the Hogwarts Express to Newcastle. Take in a falconry demonstration. See the weaponry at Leeds Royal Armouries Museum, which has five galleries of exhibits and demonstrations, as well. At Newcastle, enjoy a sumptuous dinner and rest up for day five.

Day five: Visit Alnwick Castle and Alnwick Gardens. The castle is where, on the grounds outside, flying lessons were taught in the first Harry Potter film. Also, in the Gardens, a herbology class will be taught. (Bring earmuffs in case you have to uproot mandrakes.) After lunch, try your hand at a land-based version of Quidditch. Dinner will be served in the Great Hall of Alnwick Castle.

Day six: Spend the day in Edinburgh, which is where J. K. Rowling calls home. Enjoy the Edinburgh Festival. Check out the now-abandoned underground vaults. And enjoy a leisurely dinner.

Day seven: Take a trip on the train to Harry Potter film locations, crossing over the

Catherine Collins

Potting mandrake plants at the Holdenby House

Glenfinna Viaduct which has been used in several of the Potter films, notably *Harry Potter and the Prisoner of Azkaban,* during which the Hogwarts Express stops to allow boarding by Dementors. See the Scottish countryside—the same views Harry and his fellow students took in as they rode to the train station at Hogsmeade Village—and, finally, return to Edinburgh for a tour of the city and a stop at its most prominent landmark, Edinburgh Castle.

Day eight: Head home and rest up, so you can return next year to take in a specialized tour, Science in a Wizarding World.

Catherine Collins, wand in hand, standing in front of Platform Nine and Three-Quarters at King's Cross Station

Science in a Wizarding World

"This itinerary," it states on the website, "has been specially designed for fans wanting to delve deeper into the scientific concepts presented in the Harry Potter books. From alchemy and potions, post-delivering owls, illusion, witches, real magical creatures, and flying on a broomstick, you will enjoy the thrill of discovery through the eyes of Harry Potter, Alice in Wonderland, ghosts, goblins, and legends of this land which have inspired writers for centuries."

Day one: Arrive in London and take a coach to Oxford for a city tour. Enjoy the sights, but rest up for the sumptuous Hogwarts-style feast in which there will be food and drink aplenty.

Day two: Take Locomotive #5972 (better known to Harry Potter fans as the Hogwarts Express) to the Lake District for an

A welcome respite: a trellis outside the Merchant's Adventurer's Hall

65

Catherine Collins

The Head Table at the Great Feast in the
Painted Hall of the Old Royal Naval College

afternoon of shopping and dining. Do stay awake for the ride, since there will be plenty of activities to pass the time: games, divination classes, stories, and lots of time to socialize and meet fellow Potter fans.

Day three: Visit the Museum of Natural History, the Pitt Rivers museum, and Christ Church College, and take in a lecture about witch hunts by Oxford historian Robin Briggs. In the afternoon, mount your brooms; a virtual reality experience will convince you that Muggles can fly. (Just watch out for splinters.)

Day four: Explore the world of pagans (no, I'm not talking about Muggles like the Dursleys). Visit ancient Stonehenge and Avebury. In the early evening, visit the Hawk Conservancy for a rare opportunity to hold owls, to watch them fly, and to learn more about their nocturnal habits.

Day five: In London, visit the Chelsea Physic Garden and the Old Operating Theatre. Learn about potion-making and alchemy. Learn about the real Nicholas Flamel and take in a discussion about mandrakes. After lunch, visit the Science Museum. With the spare time before dinner, take in some of the more popular sights in town: The British Museum, Westminster Abbey, Harrod's, Madame Tussaud's, or The London Dungeon.

Day six: Go on a treasure hunt in the streets of London, searching for Harry Potter film locations. Use the clues and maps to find them and photograph them with a provided disposable camera. See the famous Platform Nine and Three-Quarters (though *don't* try running through the barrier!), see Gringotts Bank (cleverly disguised as a Muggle bank, Australia House), and walk straight through Diagon Alley (cleverly disguised as Leadenhall Market). A buffet lunch, of course, will be at The Leaky Cauldron, or its equivalent.

A farewell dinner concludes this educational trip.

Day seven: Head to Heathrow to catch a flight home. Rest up, though, so that you can return next year and explore London and Scotland on your own.

Mischief managed!

A sailing ship moored on the Thames River

Harry Potter Fan Trip 2004
by Catherine Collins

In the Beginning

On Tuesday, June 1, 2004, the very first HP Fan Trip began. This spectacular event, spanning five magical days in York and London, England, took excited Harry Potter fans into the boy wizard's very own world.

A chance meeting at Nimbus 2003, the first-ever Harry Potter symposium, led to the birth of HP Fan Trips. It is the brainchild of Jeff Guillaume, webmaster of HPANA; Heidi Tandy, editor at The Leaky Cauldron and cofounder of FictionAlley; and Jeannie Barresi, managing director of the travel company Beyond Boundaries. All three wanted to give Harry Potter fans an opportunity to experience the world J. K. Rowling created within the pages of her books. The idea is to allow fans to step into Harry's shoes for a few

The Hogwarts Express steam engine (#5972) used in the Harry Potter films

A wizard's duel: Eric of Mugglenet.com and
Wirda square off, wands at the ready

days and to live his life: attend herbology class, play Quidditch, and ride on the Hogwarts Express. The goal is to have them come away feeling closer to Harry and knowing him a bit better. In addition to that, participants learn about the rich history of British literature and experience the culture that inspired great works of art.

According to Jeannie Barresi:

> The trip has always had the vision of integrating the myths and legends of England into the Harry Potter experience. These myths and legends inspired J. K. Rowling and many other fantasy writers. We wouldn't have Harry, for example, without the legend of Merlin, Padfoot, the Hand of Glory, Tolkien's world, the Loch Ness Monster, and all sorts of mythical creatures and characters. So the point is to see the culture, history, landscape, and stories of this culture filtered through the eyes of a literary character. This makes for a richer experience in that we all share a common language, all the phrases and stories in the Harry Potter books, and can then leap from the pages of the book to the reality/historical fantasy in which the character was conceived.*

Jeff Guillaume of HPANA, Eric Scull of MuggleNet, and Catherine Collins of HarryPotterFanZone and TheDarkLord.net joined forces to document the fan trip with daily videos, a photo gallery, and reportage.

---

*For more information on the folklore, myths, and legends found in the Harry Potter novels, consult *Fact, Fiction, and Folklore: An Unofficial Guide* by George Beahm.

Pre-Trip: The Build-Up

Planning this trip took close to a year. Jeff worked tirelessly with Jeannie and Heidi to create an unforgettable Harry Potter fan's dream vacation. Midway through the planning, I jumped on board to help organize the chaperone program for teenage guests traveling without a guardian. Eric joined to create promotional material for the travel company. For the participants' enjoyment, Eric created in-depth trivia questions.

In mid-March, Beyond Boundaries set up a message board to give those already signed up for the trip an opportunity to get to know one another.

Catherine Collins

The front of Australia House, used as Gringotts Bank in a Harry Potter movie

Many took advantage of this, and by the time we were ready to depart for the trip, more than a thousand messages had been posted. Participants discussed everything from finding a roommate, to traveling tips, to who would be bringing robes.

The last couple of weeks were spent finalizing trip details. At last, May 31 arrived and it was time to leave for the airport. Eric and I would be traveling together, and we planned to meet Jeff in London. Everything went smoothly and our plane took off at eight in the evening. For fun, we played about twenty games of Harry Potter Uno. We could barely contain our excitement by the time our six-hour flight was over. We couldn't wait to exit the plane and begin the trip!

The Magic Begins

We landed at London's Heathrow Airport at 8:00 A.M. on June 1. Most of the trip's participants were arriving by way of Heathrow. We met trip representatives after exiting customs. From there it was a short shuttle ride to the Novotel London Heathrow Hotel, where we would be meeting the other travelers throughout the morning. It was so much fun to get to know everyone. There were more than ninety participants on the trip, and ages ranged from under ten to over sixty. Many were from the United States, but we met people from all over the world, including Australia, Malaysia, and Taiwan. We

Harry Potter fans in front of Alnwick Castle in Northumberland, England

had whole families, groups of friends, and fans over eighteen traveling solo. We even met the staff of Contra Veritas, an HP website dedicated to Draco and Hermione. No one was alone for long, though, because it was very easy to strike up a conversation. All of us had at least one very important thing in common, our love of Harry Potter.

Around 2:00 P.M. there was a formal welcome meeting, and we were introduced to our guides for the journey. Sean and Marcus would take us through the York and London sites. They were both great sources of information and had us rolling with laughter as they went over the guidelines for the tour. Amy, the storyteller, mesmerized us with tales and riddles.

After the meeting, we were escorted to our coaches, referred to as "The Knight Buses." Prior to boarding, we were each handed a toothbrush and a cup of hot chocolate. Then it was off to our first Harry Potter adventure.

Our first stop was Holdenby House located in Northhamptonshire. Built in 1583 by Sir Christopher Hatton to honor Queen Elizabeth I, its estate is home to legendary gardens and the Falconry Centre. We began with a British afternoon tea. From there it was on to our first herbology class, where we received a lesson on the properties and uses of lavender, wormwood, and saponaria. Most exciting was learning about the very famous mandrake plant. We were given real mandrake roots to repot. They were not the exact versions Professor Sprout grows in Greenhouse Three, for that would have been too risky for us Muggles.

Then we headed off to learn about falconry, training hawks to hunt in cooperation with humans. A falconer gave us a demonstration. We watched, fascinated, as a falcon swooped in to snatch meat out of his hand.

After our adventure, we boarded the coaches and headed for York. A buffet dinner was waiting for us when we arrived at our hotel, the Holiday Inn York. It was a great opportunity to continue to mingle. After supper, we had the pleasure of receiving our very own Alivan's wand, designed specially in honor of the trip. I'd venture to say most of us tried to cast a spell or two.

What Does It Feel Like to Be Professor McGonagall?

We spent our third day traveling from York to London. On the way, we stopped at St. Hugh's College in Oxford for a lecture on witchcraft by Professor Robin Briggs, author of *Witches and Neighbors: The Social and Cultural Context of European Witchcraft.* Professor Briggs amused us by comparing his talk to one Harry might receive in his History of Magic class from Professor Binns. He hoped we would enjoy his more. Needless to say, we all remained open-eyed as he spoke about the history and myths of witchcraft.

From there we took a walking tour of Oxford. This historic city has been a source of inspiration to many great writers such as C. S. Lewis, J. R. R. Tolkien, and Lewis Carroll. It houses the legendary University of Oxford, which has been teaching students since the thirteenth century. The university encompasses thirty-nine colleges, five museums, and three parks, all sprawled throughout the city. Its rich architecture spans every period from medieval to the present.

The place that everyone wanted to see was Christ Church College. We toured its Great Hall, the inspiration for Hogwarts own Great Hall. The cloisters, built a thousand years ago, are where Harry first sees the plaque engraved with his father's name in the *Philosopher's Stone* movie. Its halls are the same ones seen in the films.

The most anticipated site was the famous sixteenth-century staircase that leads to the Great Hall. This is where Professor McGonagall greets the first year students. Many took turns tapping their fingers on the marble banister with stern looks on their faces. This is also where Filch catches Harry and Ron sneaking into school in the *Chamber of Secrets* movie and where Tom Riddle stood while speaking to Dumbledore inside the diary memory.

Another famous Harry

Catherine Collins

A terrestrial Quidditch match played on the grounds of the Old Royal Naval College in Greenwich

Potter location in Oxford is the Divinity School, which serves as the hospital wing of Hogwarts. We wanted to sneak into the Bodleian Library where Harry snooped around the Restricted Section, but, unlike him, we left our Invisibility Cloaks back home.

A Hogwarts-style feast in the Painted Hall at the Old Royal Naval College

From here, it was on to London. We arrived at our hotel, the London Marriott Hotel Regents Park, in the evening. Participants who couldn't wait to explore the city headed out. Eric, Jeff, and I met with Jamie of MuggleNet and Jenna, webmistress of DanRadcliffe.com. We had a great time!

At Last, Prisoner of Azkaban!

This was another fun-filled day packed with activities. We started with the HP Treasure Hunt, a scavenger-type event that would take us throughout the city. We all met in the lobby of our hotel and were divided into eleven teams. Each team was given a bag containing one-day travel passes, maps, an instant disposable camera, marked sealed envelopes, and a clue. The rules of the hunt: We were given a clue that would lead us to a place where we would find one of the tour guides and pick up our next clue. At each location, we had to take a group picture with the camera to prove we had been there. Each group was judged according to how quickly they finished and how creative their pictures and team name were. If we could not figure out a clue, a matching sealed envelope provided the answer, but envelopes returned opened reduced the chance of winning.

The Treasure Hunt was a lot of fun, but not easy. The very talented Galadriel Waters, author of the *Ultimate Unofficial Guide to the Mysteries of Harry Potter*, wrote the clues. Each clue contained hints we had to decipher to determine the exact location. One was to look for a place "down under." Our group thought it was so easy. We figured it *had* to be a train station. After a frustrating half-hour of searching, we realized we were quite wrong. It turned out that "down under" referred to Australia Bank, whose lobby was the backdrop for Gringotts Bank. We definitely lived up to our team name, The Aloho-Morons, lovingly given to us by Eric. (For those of you who are wondering, The Aloho-Morons did not win the Treasure Hunt. In fact, we never came close!)

Each clue led to somewhere in London where filming for the Harry Potter movies took place. We saw Leadenhall Market where Hagrid walks with Harry on the way to Diagon Alley. There is even a shop there called Oliviers. Some of us could have sworn for a brief moment the sign actually read Ollivanders. We stood in front of the Glass House, the entrance to The Leaky Cauldron in the first film. Other exciting places included St. Pancras Station, a famous spot for seeing a flying Ford Anglia. At Octopus House is

another entrance to The Leaky Cauldron, seen in the third film. Along the way, we even had a chance to visit the famous Tower of London.

King's Cross was the fans' favorite. It actually has a sign marking the entrance to Platform Nine and Three-Quarters. Naturally, visiting here would not be complete with-

Wipeout! Eric of Mugglenet.com fails to pass through the barrier at Platform Nine and Three-Quarters.

out a trolley crash re-enactment. Yes, we had quite a crowd laughing at us as Eric sprawled on the floor grasping for his wand. The only thing missing was an owl in a cage. It was also quite touching to stand on the bridge where Hagrid gives Harry his train ticket.

We had to be finished in time to be at the Odeon Leicester Square cinema by 4:00 P.M. We were finally going to see the movie we had been waiting for—*Harry Potter and the Prisoner of Azkaban.* The Odeon hosted the London premiere of the movie. Premium seats were reserved for the group.

After the viewing, we walked to the Radisson Edwardian Hampshire Hotel to discuss the movie. We were in awe as we stepped off the elevator to enter the meeting place. The penthouse suite's view was breathtaking. The general consensus on the movie—it's a hit! We also had the pleasure of meeting new fans who had arrived that morning for the weekend tour. Afterwards, some people headed back to the hotel while others stayed in central London to do some more sightseeing.

Quidditch, Wizard Games, and the Final Feast

This was our last day of the trip. We were both sad and excited at the same time. We knew that a special Harry-themed day was planned. We headed out to the Old Royal Naval College in Greenwich, six miles southeast of London. Located adjacent to the River Thames, it is one of the country's most famous riverside landmarks. Construction began in the fifteenth century and extensive remodeling has taken place throughout the years. The college originally functioned as a seaman's hospital and then was utilized as a training center for naval officers until 1998. It is currently used as a location for film and television productions and is open to the public for tours. Part of the college was reserved for our use.

Activities were available throughout the day, and we had the option of choosing which to attend. Although Hermione had difficulty with it, many of us tried our hand at "Divination." Our "Professor" covered the topics of palmistry (palm-reading) and tasseomancy (tea-leaf reading). We had a guidebook to aid us. However, even with that, some of us were unable to broaden our minds and decipher the true meaning of the soggy tea leaves at the bottom of our cups.

There was a fan-fiction workshop and a storytelling session. We had skittle bowling, which is English ninepins played with a wooden disk or ball. Our ninepins represented Death Eaters, which had to be put out of commission.

Outdoor activities included riding a mechanical dragon, playing wizard's chess, and searching a pond for "magical creatures." There was even a gyroscope ride, which did a wonderful job of simulating a ride on an out-of-control broom.

A Dementor's hand grasps the edge of the London theater showing the newly released *Harry Potter and the Prisoner of Azkaban* film.

Catherine Collins

Most popular by far was playing Muggle Quidditch. USA Team Handball, the National Governing Body for the Olympic Sport of Handball in the U.S., designed the game. They did an excellent job. Their representation was the closest we could get to playing Quidditch without flying on a broom. Games were held throughout the day, culminating with a final tournament. There were slight differences from the game Harry is used to playing. Our teams had nine players instead of seven. The additional two were designated Bludger Masters

Catherine Collins

A building on the premises of the Old Royal Naval College

whose job was to throw the Bludgers at the opposing team because obviously nobody knew the spell to enchant the Bludgers themselves! Chasers would throw the Quaffle to each other and the one closest to the hoops would attempt to score. The Keeper tried to block all shots. Beaters protected their teammates from stray Bludgers thrown by the Bludger Masters. No one knew when the Snitch would be released. Each team's Seeker would be poised and ready to dive for it. After countless games, the Fiery Phoenixes team emerged as our Quidditch champions.

After our fun-filled day, we had the Final Feast celebration. This was held in the stunning Painted Hall, recognized as probably the finest dining hall in the Western World. The walls and ceiling are decorated with James Thornhill's epic paintings. Commissioned from 1707–1726, they show *Peace* and *Liberty* triumphing over *Tyranny*, and depict Britain's role as a maritime power.

The Hall was set up to resemble Hogwarts' Great Hall; there was even a Head Table. We were served a traditional British feast. Many of the different foods we have read about in the Harry Potter books were included, and a few of us chose to dress for the occasion in wizard attire. Student uniforms were the most popular, but a few adults preferred to dress as professors. We all enjoyed Eric's video footage of the trip, which he projected onto a seven-foot screen. Prizes were given out to our Quidditch, Wizard Games, and Treasure Hunt winners. As a memento, each participant was given a beautiful limited edition, artist-signed glass pumpkin. Gini Garcia designed these special keepsakes in honor of our trip. We spent the rest of the evening reminiscing about the wonderful week. Finally, it was time to say good night. There were many long goodbyes and promises to keep in touch. Some of the participants stayed on for the Scottish Extension tour that would take them to more Harry Potter locations.

Early the next morning Eric and I said goodbye to Jeff and headed for Heathrow. As our plane took flight, we turned to each other and grinned in amazement at the adventure we had just experienced. Our love of a literary character and our trip into his world had expanded our own world in incredible ways, ones we could have never imagined.

About Catherine Collins: "My passion for Harry Potter began with the first movie. Never in my wildest dreams could I imagine where that would lead. It was short leap to reading the books, then working at online fan sites— TheQuidditchPitch.net (formerly TheDarkLord.net), HarryPotterFanZone.com, and MuggleNet.com. I've had the wonderful opportunity to interview the cast and crew of *The Prisoner of Azkaban* movie, and provide media coverage for the first ever HP Fan Trip and Spellbound! 2005. The best part is the wonderful friendships I have made. In the non-HP world, I am a registered nurse, devoted Trekkie, and Mom to two beautiful cats, Siri and Jadzia."

Harry Potter Conferences

There's a big difference between a conference and a convention: A conference (or symposium) is principally a gathering of academics who read from their submitted papers (the proceedings), which are then published after the event, usually in CD-ROM form (to save money) and sometimes in printed form.

In contrast, a convention is more informal, more fan-based, and although there are panels, the topics are usually not academic nor are there any readings of papers.

Usually titled from something in the Harry Potter universe, the U.S. conferences from the HP Educational Fanon have included Nimbus 2003 (Orlando, Florida), Nimbus 2005: The Witching Hour (Salem, Massachusetts), Lumos 2006 (Las Vegas, Nevada), and Prophecy 2007: From Hero to Legend (www.prophecy2007.org) in Toronto, Canada.

Also in the U.S., a competing conference, Phoenix Rising, will be held in New Orleans (May 17–21, 2007), a first-time Harry Potter–themed event put on by Narrate Conferences, a company that produces academic, literary, and educational conferences and events, according to its website (www.the phoenixrises.org).

In Europe, Accio 2005 marked the first Harry Potter conference (www.accio.org.uk). Like its American counterparts, the emphasis is on reading and subsequently publishing the proceedings.

In 2006 Harry Potter fans gathered at the University of Copenhagen in Denmark to attend Patronus 2006 (July 7–9).

Forthcoming conferences include: Sectus 2007 (www.sectus.org) in London, England, from July 19–22 and Accio 2007 (www.accio.org.uk), as well.

What to Expect

Because there's a strong component of academia at the Harry Potter conferences, the attendance is significantly less than a comparable convention. Lumos 2006, for instance, drew 1,200 attendees, but the World Science Fiction Convention (Anaheim, California) drew more than 5,000, and the San Diego Comicon routinely draws more than 100,000.

Despite the emphasis on delivering papers, the Harry Potter conferences are simply good fun for any Potter fan: a common room for informal get-togethers and hanging out with old and new friends,

Artist Gary Hall of Whirlwood Magick Wands with his display in the dealers' room at Lumos 2006.

an art gallery, a vendor's room, a life-size game of wizard's chess, a Quidditch match (land/water-based), viewing Harry Potter films, panels, and Hogwarts-style feasts at which the food is reflective of British fare.

For many, it's an ideal opportunity to meet with old friends and meet new ones, sharing a common bond: an interest in all things from the wizarding world.

Since many of these conferences co-mingle the academic with the traditional convention fare, I hope that future events include a costume contest, which is one of the highlights of any convention, as anyone who has attended a Worldcon will tell you: The time and effort put into a winning presentation are considerable, and the results certainly show it.

At Lumos 2006, the number of inventive costumes by attendees suggests that a costume contest would be a big hit.

Lumos 2006

I've met Draco Malfoy in the flesh . . . *and* his father.

I'm *not* kidding.

Draco's a young man with blonde hair and favors a black robe with a green liner, appropriate to his Hogwarts house, Slytherin. Should there be any doubters out there, I've got photographic proof of his Dark Mark and can provide his mailing address, as well.

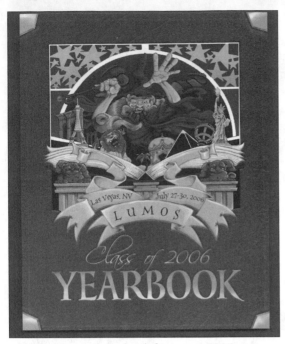

The program book for Lumos 2006

Or, to be a *little* more accurate, I've met a young British boy who changed his legal first name to Draco. The boy bears a permanent tattoo, a Dark Mark, and I saw him in the company of his father, Perseus, at Lumos, a Harry Potter conference held in Las Vegas, Nevada, in August 2006.

Perseus LePage, by the way, was also born in England, has long platinum hair, and bears a resemblance to Jason Isaacs, the actor who portrays Lucius Malfoy in the Harry Potter movies.

Lumos 2006 follows on the heels of two previous conferences, one held at Disney World in Orlando, Florida, and the other in Salem, Massachusetts. The Prophecy, the fourth conference, will be held in Toronto, Canada, in August 2007.

If you were to poll the 1,200 attendees who paid $180 to attend Lumos 2006, you'd likely find that the mostly female crowd—many of whom carried wands and dressed in school robes—made the trip to Sin City because it was the ideal opportunity to meet their online friends who preferred getting together at this smaller, more focused, and obviously more intimate gathering than a large media convention like Dragoncon or the San Diego Comicon, which annually draws tens of thousands of fans, mostly males.

Properly billed as a symposium instead of a convention, Lumos emphasizes its extensive, and impressive, list of papers that was delivered over a three-day period. The topics, ranging from the accessible to the strictly academic, provide enough of a variety so that there's something for everyone. In fact, there were so many topics—literary criticism, education, social sciences, legal, film, and fandom culture—that, at any given time, four different tracks of programming ran simultaneously.

Considering that all the events of Lumos 2006 had to be compressed in a three-day schedule, its organizers did a magnificent job, juggling a varied program that included not only the scheduled talks but other activities, as well: Water Quidditch, Magical Night Classes, Live Chess, opening and closing feasts, luncheons, movies (back-to-back Harry Potter films), and a trip to "Hogsmeade" (the Las Vegas Strip).

A vendor's room offered a wide selection of Harry Potter–related products, from wands to a complete wardrobe, and the nearby art gallery offered a selection of Potter-inspired art in multiple media.

Though a Common Room had been set aside for informal get-togethers, most attendees simply found a cozy corner or a table at one of the many eateries within the hotel itself. (The daytime temperature, averaging more than 100 degrees, guaranteed that most attendees stayed inside for the duration of the conference, unless they were watching, or participating in, Water Quidditch.)

After hours, most attendees used their time to hang out with friends or, if they felt more active, found themselves dancing to either Harry and the Potters or Draco and the Malfoys, two bands well known in the Harry Potter universe.

Since most of the attendees keep in touch by e-mail, message boards, and blogs, it's not surprising that the most popular event was a joint podcast with the two most prominent Harry Potter–related websites, The Leaky Cauldron and Mugglenet.com.

Dana is dressed to kill—as patriarch Lucius Malfoy—at Lumos 2006.

A far cry from the old days when fans who attended conventions relied on fanzines and snail mail to keep in touch, today's fans are hard-wired and use cell phones, instant messaging, MySpace, Facebook, Mac computers, iPods, PDAs, and (mostly) the web to keep in touch. Consequently, the principals at websites like The Leaky Cauldron and Mugglenet.com are well-known figures whose appearances at Harry Potter events like this inevitably draw a considerable crowd.

Kayla as Narcissa Malfoy strikes
a pose at Lumos 2006.

Wisely, the conference organizers deliberately avoid inviting film stars, who would simply steal the show. It's better, I think, to keep these events focused on the books and not the film celebrities known worldwide.

To this crowd, the names that matter are Steve Vander Ark (webmaster of The Harry Potter Lexicon), Dr. Edward Kern (author of *The Wisdom of Harry Potter*), Melissa Anelli (webmistress of The Leaky Cauldron), and Emerson Spartz (webmaster of Mugglenet.com).

In addition, there are in attendance numerous authors who have published books about J. K. Rowling and Harry Potter. From Muggles to magic, every topic imaginable is fair game at Lumos for the Muggle professors and the authors in attendance. They are eager to share their enthusiasm about Harry Potter with the attendees, who have an astonishing depth of knowledge about Rowling and her literary creation.

In fact, Rowling's own Potter fiction isn't enough to satiate the demand for stories. A surprising number of attendees have published online "shipping" stories in which characters from the books are incongruously paired (Harry and Draco, Hermione and Professor Snape) in a way that would make a Hungarian Horntail dragon blush. (Okay, so it's fan erotica that leaves little to the imagination.)

No matter. The attendees are a marked, and welcome, departure from the usual coat-and-tie types who meet at the Marriott for a business conference: There's not a suit in sight, but there are plenty of "students" and "faculty" in Hogwarts-inspired school house robes, Quidditch uniforms, and semiformal gowns.

Those interested in attending a Harry Potter conference have several choices on both sides of the pond:

1. Prophecy 2007: From Hero to Legend. August 2–5, 2007, in Toronto, Canada. The website is at hp2007.org.
2. Phoenix Rising. May 17–21, 2007, in New Orleans, Louisiana. The website is at www.thephoenix rises.org.
3. Sectus: An Unofficial Harry Potter Conference. July 19–22, 2007, in London, England. The website is at www.sectus.org.

Enlightening 2007

The organizers of this event have hit upon a novel idea: to have a Harry Potter get-together for the whole family. After all, Potter fans range in age from pre-teens to adults, so why not?

Billed as a "Harry Potter Camp for Families," Enlightening 2007 will be held on July 12–15, 2007, at the campus of the University of Pennsylvania; its gothic architecture is perfect for a Harry Potter–inspired event. The events planned have been broken down in terms of ages: 5–8 years old, the kid experience; 9–12, the tween experience; 13–17, the teen experience; and 18+, the adult experience.

As with all the other Harry Potter–related conferences and conventions, this is not officially sanctioned by Warner Bros.

Looking over the curriculum, it's obvious that a great deal of thought and imagination went into deriving age-appropriate activities so that everyone in the family

Some Topics Presented at Lumos

Presentations by scholars worldwide showed the diverse range of topics addressed at Lumos. Here's a sampling:

Bless Me, Dumbledore: A Latina Educator's Perspective on the Harry Potter Universe (Catherine L. Belcher)

Bloody Hell! Why Am I So Wild about Harry?, a roundtable discussion moderated by Cantor Amy O. Miller

Christmas at Hogwarts (Melissa McCrory)

Comrade Potter: A Marxist Reading of Harry Potter (Todd J. Ide)

The Fanon of Fantasy: How Harry Doesn't Quite Fit the Biscuit, a roundtable discussion moderated by Lee Hillman

Managing Your Harry Potter Fan Club (Lauren Shaw)

Making Magic with Watercolor, a workshop by "Glockgal"

Snape's Eyes (Dr. Edmund Kern)

A Study in Evil: Voldemort, the Malignant Narcissist

Where Magic Really Comes From: Knowledge, Choice, and Power in the Harry Potter Series (Stephanie Nettles)

Written in the Dark of Nox: Fanfiction and the Social Taboo (Megan Fowler)

would be fully occupied. Of course, all activities are drawn directly from the Harry Potter books, so loyal readers should feel right at home, so to speak, with the fantastic activities.

The admission price is variable, depending on when you register. Those who did so before September 30, 2006, got in the door for $275, but those who wait until the last minute will have to fork over $400.

From the course listing posted online, here's what the event organizers have planned, based on age group:

The Kid Experience

With an invitation delivered by Owl Post (i.e., U.S. mail), this is "designed to build their confidence and life science skills in workshops that focus on taking care of the world around us," including:

1. designing your own wand

2. designing your own pointed black hat

3. designing your own work robes for class wear

4. Herbology: a class involving pruning and repotting plants—perfect for aspiring potters

5. Care of Magical Creatures: create your own Monster Book of Monsters

6. Defense against the Dark Arts: use the martial arts to perfect balance and coordination skills

7. Potions: sharpen your skills in measuring ingredients and following recipes

8. Quidditch: learn its fundamentals, the rules of the game, and scorekeeping

9. attend an opening-night showing of *Harry Potter and the Order of the Phoenix*

10. attend a viewing of *Harry Potter and the Sorcerer's Stone*

11. participate in a scavenger hunt

12. Triwizard Tournament: compete against other houses

The Tween Experience

This group "will discover the science of magic and the magic of science as they work to solve the Great E7 Mystery."

1. Advanced Potions: practice potion-making

2. Astronomy: fill out your star chart and explore the facts and folklore behind the celestial bodies that share a name with Harry Potter characters

3. Beginners Fan Fiction Workshop: write and then act out scenes inspired by the Harry Potter novels

4. Divination: practice palm-reading, fingerprinting, and other crime scene investigation techniques

5. Quidditch: learn the basic skills for each position to determine the position you are best suited to play

6. Triwizard Tournament: negotiate obstacles and compete against other houses in this challenging contest

The Teen Experience

In contrast to the younger age groups, the teens are expected to actively contribute to the learning experience by creating new works in varying media, both traditional and electronic.

1. Advanced Fan Fiction: write a new scene using Harry Potter characters and give a dramatic reading to your classmates

2. Fan Art: produce a work of original art inspired by a character, setting, or scene from the Harry Potter novels

3. Comedy/Improv: write and perform a Harry Potter–themed comedy skit

4. A Cappella: compose a new tune, or compose a version based on an existing Wizarding Rock song

5. Podcast: for the film premiere night for *Harry Potter and the Order of the Phoenix,* produce a podcast of the scheduled festivities for (presumably) broadcast through the World Wide Web

6. Design: Conceptualize and design a castle intended to serve as a school of magic; design a brochure to promote the school to prospective students

7. Film: Using a scene from any of the Harry Potter novels, produce a short film

Other planned activities include: compete in a Quidditch tournament, participate in a speed debating book discussion, participate in after-hours social activities (dance to Wizard Rock music, engage in spirited discussions about the Potter books in groups, and play Harry Potter role-playing games).

The Adult Experience

Activities are designed for those who are knowledgeable about the books and those who are Harry Potter challenged.

For those who are not well versed in the Harry Potter canon, the casual fan, general tourist activities are available: explore the Penn campus, visit its Museum of Archaeology and Anthropology, shop 'til you drop in one of the boutique stores near the campus, play golf at the Hartefeld National Golf Course, visit nearby landmarks, or just plain relax. In other words, you're a die-hard Muggle and prefer not to experience the wizarding world.

But if you *do* have a taste for the fantastic, for the magical, then you can attend presentations on traditional topics focused on the Harry Potter canon (the kind of talks given at conferences like Lumos 2006), participate in an immersive workshop to enhance your skills at initiating a family dialogue using themes within the Potter books (e.g., class, race, loss, coming of age, etc.), and attend round-table discussions on a variety of HP topics.

Note: It's obviously easier to come up with activities for younger readers, but the events for the Harry Potter–savvy adult, while interesting, seem incomplete. Perhaps adults can act as "faculty" and "visiting professors" sharing their specific expertise in the classes for the youngsters. For instance, a real-world banker could explain the monetary system and how it works, and then talk about how it relates to Gringotts Bank.

Or adults could team up and act as supervisors in a clue-based, on-campus game with the youngsters, or . . . you get the idea.

Even those adults who have no knowledge of Harry Potter should attend an orientation class called "Magic for Muggles" in which the Harry Potter books are explained sufficiently so that when they attend an event with their children, they know what the kids are talking about.

But these are minor quibbles. I love the idea that this is a family-oriented event, with time allotted for both age-specific and whole-family events.

As is always the case, the first time around will be a learning experience for everyone, but there's certainly enough to keep everyone busy and, just as important, entertained.

For more information, go to their website at enlightening2007.org.

Collecting Autographs

A friend of mine, a professional autograph dealer, decided to collect the signatures of everyone connected to Stephen King, including the author himself, people with whom he has associated professionally, and television and movie directors, stars, and writers. He did it for his own enjoyment, collecting a scrapbook of signed photographs, playbills, movie tickets, posters, and so forth.

He had no intention of selling it, since this was done for his own amusement, but

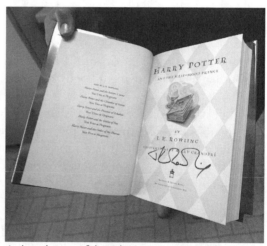

A signed copy of the 6th Harry Potter novel, given as a gift to supporters who bought orchestra seat tickets to Rowling's book reading in NYC (August 2006).

when the time came to sell, the scrapbook sold to the first buyer for more than $3,000—not a bad return for his well-spent time! (When the buyer resold the collection, it went for more than $5,000.)

I should point out that this prime collection took years to assemble, so please don't think you can get rich quick by collecting autographs.

For most fans, selling autographs is not a primary consideration; owning an original autograph from a favorite writer or film star is its own reward. A case in point is Bryony Evens, who approached Rowling for a signature at a 1998 book signing at the Cheltenham Literary Festival and got a warmly inscribed copy of *Harry Potter and the Goblet of Fire.* And no wonder: Evens, who worked at the Christopher Little Literary Agency, pulled the manuscript of *Harry Potter and the Philosopher's Stone* out of the slush pile and championed it. When Rowling, who had never met Evens, realized who had presented the book, she hugged Evens and on the title page signed her copy: "To Bryony—who really did discover Harry Potter."

It's unlikely Evens would part with her inscribed copy, nor should she. An important figure in Harry Potter publishing history, Evens was there *before* Pottermania struck.

First, a caveat: Beware of items purportedly signed and offered for sale by online auction houses. Without a documented history of ownership, authenticity is questionable. Obviously, there *are* legitimately signed collectibles for which no provenance will be offered, but do you want to take that risk?

Buying Tips

1. Buy from a reputable autograph dealer, who buys and sells from other reputable sources.

2. Don't expect to get a bargain. If the offer looks too good to be true, it is. You may end up buying a bogus signature.

3. Antiquarian book dealers offer signed copies of books that are most likely authentic. Because these people make their living buying Rowling collectibles, usually from trusted sources, the likelihood that a reputable dealer will sell you a bogus collectible is slim. Because their reputations are their livelihood, they are painstakingly scrupulous in what they buy and sell.

Rowling's Signature

Obviously, the most desirable signature is Rowling's, on the title page of one of her books.

Unfortunately, because of Rowling's popularity, book signings are out of the question. For *Harry Potter and the Order of the Phoenix,* there were no book signings scheduled, though she did in fact sign copies at a bookstore in her hometown of Edinburgh. As the witching hour approached, the all-kids audience was told to count down the last few seconds, and at the stroke of midnight, Rowling herself appeared, to the surprise and delight of all.

Reported the BBC, "J. K. had with her a huge wooden chest full of copies of *Harry Potter and the Order of the Phoenix,*" which were handed out as kids lined up to get copies signed.

Gushed one young fan, a nine-year-old girl named Sidra, "I shook her hand—I'm never going to wash it again."

That was the only book signing for *Order of the Phoenix,* which means that signed copies of that book are scarce indeed—rare as a dragon's egg.

At some point, Rowling may simply stop signing books, like best-selling author Stephen King, who recently announced an end to his own signings. Since 1974 King has signed tens of thousands books, posters, photographs, playbills, and other memorabilia. He even allowed fans to mail in copies of books for signatures, though only three copies per person. (To ensure fairness, King's secretaries set up a computerized database of names and addresses to track requests.) Recently, King said "no more," he's done enough and had enough, and so those seeking an autograph will have to buy one from a book dealer.

Getting J. K. Rowling's signature has become increasingly difficult and expensive. What, then, should you do?

Depending on your budget:

1. Buy a book signed by Rowling from an antiquarian book dealer. Go to www.abebooks.com and type Rowling's name and the book title in the search engine. (Be prepared for sticker shock!)

2. Buy a book from eBay, *if* the provenance is established; in other words, buy only if you have a reasonable assurance that the signature is the genuine article. (Her signature, large and loopy, is relatively easy to forge.)

3. Contact her directly through one of her publishers, who will forward the mail, but don't be surprised if you get no response. She gets more mail than any other author on the planet.

J. K. Rowling
c/o Scholastic
557 Broadway
New York, NY 10012
USA

J. K. Rowling
c/o Bloomsbury Publishing
38 Soho Square
London W1V 5DF
UK
Note: For best results, use this address.

Though Rowling has not, to my knowledge, spoken directly on the subject of fan mail, any professional writer will tell you that trying to respond personally with even a postcard is like trying to sweep the ocean back with a broom—it's an impossible task.

As for getting an autograph at one of her public events, it's logistically impossible. The crowds have become too large and, as I've said before, it's a case of pleasing a minority of fans at the cost of disappointing the majority. At that point, it's better for her not to sign books at all.

Note: For those of you who are willing to spend some time and take a chance, you may be able to catch Rowling after a press conference or on her way to or from a public speaking event.

At an August 2006 reading in NYC, several Rowling fans were able to get a little one-on-one time with her when she was, so to speak, offstage. It's not only a photo op, but Rowling is usually agreeable to signing a few autographs before moving on. If nothing else, it's an opportunity to get a few, unique snapshots with your digital camera.

Tips for Success

After a press conference, position yourself near one of the exits and wait until it lets out. Most press conferences run an hour or less.

Before a major speaking event, position yourself at one of the entrances at least two hours earlier. (In NYC, Rowling showed up one-and-a-half hours before the event.)

After the event, Rowling will want to make a quick exit. Again, position yourself near one of the exits.

If you're lucky, you'll get a one-of-a-kind photo.

And if you happened to drink a bit of *Felix Felicis* (a good-luck potion), you may be able to talk to her or get a book signed.

Film Celebrity Signatures

As for signatures from anyone other than Rowling, several options are available:

1. If the celebrity in question has an official website, signed memorabilia may be available for direct purchase. This is your best bet.

2. If the celebrity in question attends public functions to meet the public, you should show up early with pen and autograph book in hand and try to make your way to the front of the crowd.

3. Check conventions in your area—comic, science fiction, and film/media—since many film celebrities attend them to promote their latest projects. Though most celebrities will sign on the spur of the moment, planned signing events at these shows offer everyone the opportunity to get photos or memorabilia signed.

4. Send a personal letter to the celebrity directly, who typically has his or her mail handled by a professional agency. A heartfelt, handwritten letter will stand out, whereas a form letter will be ignored. In the autograph

trade, "graphers"—people who send 3 x 5-inch index cards for signatures—send out hundreds, if not thousands, of requests, using directories, mailing lists, and other reference sources. The reason they send out an index card is because it can then be matted and framed with a picture or other memorabilia for resale. In short, don't present yourself as a greedy "grapher." Instead, present yourself as a genuinely interested fan. Keep in mind that the average celebrity gets thousands of similar requests, so what makes *your* request/letter stand out from the pack?

Getting the Autograph by Mail

For most fans, the following procedure will be the easiest and most fruitful way to secure a genuine autograph:

1. Get the right address. Either subscribe to a celebrity address database service or send correspondence to a production company that can forward mail to the actors. In the case of Harry Potter films, one address suffices: Harry Potter Production in Leavesden Studios.

   Serious autograph collectors should consider subscribing to the Star Archive (www.stararchive.com), which has in its database 45,531 celebrities and their current addresses. A small subscription fee allows you to log on and search the site. It's more efficient than relying on printed directories, which may have outdated information.

2. Draft a personalized letter and read it over carefully several times to ensure that it says exactly what you want it to say. Ask for an autograph and be polite, not demanding. You are, after all, asking the celebrity for a freebie.

3. If you enclose anything for signing, keep in mind that the celebrity may take weeks, possibly months, to return it, *if* you get it back. In other words, there's *no guarantee* that what you send will be returned, so don't send anything you aren't willing to lose.

4. Provide a self-addressed, stamped envelope for the return of anything you submit (such as a photo or card), so the celebrity doesn't have to mail your freebie at his own expense.

5. Be prepared to wait as long as necessary, and realize that there's no guarantee you will get a response. But if you do, *keep the return envelope*, which is proof of delivery, with a postmark to help establish the provenance of the signed item.

6. After three to six months, if you hear nothing, send another request. If it's worth a first effort, it's worth a second one. After all, you have nothing to lose but a signed collectible!

J. K. Rowling on eBay

On September 12, 2005, J. K. Rowling, posting on her website (www.jkrowling.com), made it clear that insofar as her purported signatures are concerned, she has "advised eBay repeatedly . . . that many signatures for sale on their site appear to be fake, but have yet to see any reduction in the number of forgeries on offer. . . . The current situation has eBay profiting from the eBay users' relentless scamming of Harry Potter fans while, in effect, telling them that they have no one but themselves—or me—to blame."

Buyer beware! Before you buy anything purported to be signed by Rowling, remember that an authentic signature will be expensive and that reputable dealers can provide reasonable proof (provenance). Antiquarian booksellers who routinely deal with high-end collectibles are the best source, since their stock in trade is their reputation. Many fly-by-night operations couldn't care less, as long as they can fleece the customer, close up shop, and move on to the next victim.

7. Be suspicious of anyone who posts on an Internet message board, purporting to be a celebrity. *You can't be sure you're communicating with the celebrity.* More often, it's just a fan who likes to have some fun at your expense.

Most celebrities surf the Internet and post anonymously, though actor Rupert Grint, who plays Ron Weasley, does post to the BBC message board under the name of "permlessboy." He is, however, a notable exception.

Actor Names and Addresses

Although numerous Harry Potter fan websites provide mailing addresses, accuracy is suspect, especially since some simply repeat what has been posted elsewhere on the World Wide Web. Your best bet is to send your letter to the Leavesden Studios; in turn, the studio will forward your letter to the designated actor.

All of the actors and actresses in the Harry Potter films can be reached at:

[Insert here the name of the actor/actress]
c/o Harry Potter Production
Leavesden Studios
P.O. Box 3000
Leavesden, Hertfordshire
WD2 7LT
UK

Tim Kirk

Notable and Quotable:
The Real World of J. K. Rowling

Early in her career, Rowling gave hundreds of interviews, principally to newspapers, resulting in a bounty of quotes that provide snapshots on how she views the world.

Antichrist: "There's a lot about witchcraft and evil and spells and magic. I was taught at church that that was not good."

—a young Christian boy, Eric Poliner, quoted by Jodi Wilgoren in "Don't Give Us Little Wizards, the Anti-Potter Parents Cry," *New York Times* (November 1, 1999)

Being alone: "I can be very outgoing with the right people, but I have always liked to spend time alone. I have got the perfect temperament for a writer because I don't need to be surrounded by people all the time."

—Rowling in a Barnes & Noble interview (March 1999)

Best-sellerdom: "She is a money-making machine. The temptation to keep writing after the last of her seven planned Potter adventures must be irresistible. She could be the first billionaire author in history."

—Philip Beresford in "Harry Potter Sales Reach 250 Million," Reuters (November 17, 2002)

Booksigning at Borders gone bad: "'It was a total fiasco, really ugly,' said Matthew Demakos, another attendee. 'Irate parents were screaming; people who had bought books were demanding their money back. . . .' Young Allison Zimmer decided to express her disappointment in a letter she sent to the local newspapers. In part she wrote: 'A dark cloud fell over the parking lot. Lots of little kids were screaming and crying. If Borders could only see how many customers were upset they would be amazed.'"

—Shannon Maughan in "Keeping Up with Harry," *Publishers Weekly* (November 1, 1999)

Censorship: "For generations, we have had books based on fairies, witches, goblins, magic, all with differing views. We cannot remove something from this world because of fear and ignorance. These are children's books, and as long as they are not nasty, cruel, ridiculous in any way or show witches as evil, obscene creatures, then there is no cause for mudslinging or legal retaliation."

—Arch Priestess Tamara Forslun of the Church of Wicca (Australia) in "Look Out, Harry Potter!" *Education World* (April 10, 2000)

"If this subject offends people, that isn't what I want to do, but I don't believe in censorship for any age group, and this is what I wanted to write about. The book is really about the power of the imagination. What Harry is learning to do is to develop his full potential. Wizardry is just the analogy I use. If anyone expects it to be a book that seriously advocates learning magic, they will be disappointed. Not least because the author does not believe in magic in that way. What I'm saying is that children have power and can use it, which may in itself be more threatening to some people than the idea that they would actually learn spells from my book."

—Rowling in "Talking with J. K. Rowling," *Book Links* (July 1999)

Charity: "One day a week is spent doing 'charity stuff.' She has a charitable trust and is the patron of several groups, including one for single parents and the MS (Multiple Sclerosis) Society of Scotland (her mother died of the disease in 1990 at the age of 45). I say that I believe she gives quite a lot of money away anonymously and she stares at the carpet, lips pressed."

—Ann Treneman in "J. K. Rowling: The Interview," Timesonline.co.uk (June 20, 2003)

Childhood books: "If it's a good book, anyone will read it. I'm totally unashamed about still reading things I loved in my childhood."

—Rowling quoted by Elizabeth Gleick in "The Wizard of Hogwarts," *Time* (April 12, 1999)

Daydreamer: "I lived a lot in a fantasy world when I was younger and spent a lot of time daydreaming—to my parent's frustration."

—Rowling from a transcript of an online chat on BN.com (September 8, 1999)

Empowerment: "When I was younger, I think my greatest fantasy would have been to find out that I had powers that I'd never dreamt of, that I was special, that 'these people couldn't be my parents, I'm far more interesting than that.' I think a lot of children might secretly think that sometimes. So I just took that one stage further and I thought, 'What's the best way of breaking free of that?' Okay, you're magic."

—Rowling in response to a question from Skyler, an eight-year-old, who asked, "How did you get the idea of writing about magic?" during an interview by Margot Adler, *All Things Considered* (October 2000)

Fallout: "There's a lot of halo effect from Harry Potter that's positive and negative. Harry Potter is getting many people to read who wouldn't pick up a book. But what's happening is that it's eclipsing some of the literature. Kids don't want to read about animals, or they don't want to read fabulous things for their own age, or they're reading Harry too young. So we're spending a lot of time reminding parents that their kids are too young for 'Harry.'"

—Diane Garrett, owner of Diane's Books, quoted by Doreen Carvajal in "Booksellers Grab a Young Wizard's Cloaktails," *New York Times* (February 28, 2000)

Fantasy books: "More can be learned from them about the inner problems of human beings, and of the right solutions to their predicaments in any society than from any other type of story within a child's comprehension."

—Bruno Bettelheim, *The Uses of Enchantment* (1975)

Grief: "I know, of course, that these feelings are not unique to me, I know that guilt goes hand in hand with grief, as does its close relative, anger. I was very angry indeed: angry at myself, angry that my mother had died so young, angry at the illness that killed her, but also, and increasingly, angry at the care, or lack of it, that she had received."

—Rowling in "Multiple Sclerosis Killed My Mother," *Sunday Herald* (November 16, 2003)

Halloween: "Halloween, you'd not be surprised to know, is my favorite holiday."

—Rowling in *Time* magazine (October 30, 2000)

Heart's desire: "I was conscious that when I looked in the Mirror [of Erised], I would see exactly what Harry saw. But it was only when I'd written it that I fully realised where it had all come from. It is an enormous regret to me that my mother never knew about any of this, second only to the fact that she never met my daughter."

—Rowling quoted by Helena de Bertodano in "Harry Potter Charms a Nation," *Electronic Telegraph* (July 25, 1998)

Invisibility: "When asked what magical power she would like to possess and what she would do with it, Rowling replied, 'Invisibility. I would sneak off to a café and write all day.'"

—Rowling, quoted by Shannon Maughan, *PW Daily for Booksellers* (June 27, 2003), publishersweekly.com

Legal victory: "The court found 'clear and convincing evidence' that there was no infringement and that Stouffer had made false claims in presenting material to the court for characters that she neither created nor sold when she claimed she did. Stouffer, the judge wrote, 'engaged in a pattern of intentional bad faith conduct and failed to correct her fraudulent submissions,' and ordered her to pay $50,000 in attorney's fees and court costs."

—Jim Milliot and Steven Zeitchik in "Scholastic Rebuffs Potter Infringement Charges," *Publishers Weekly* (September 23, 2002)

Lightning bolt scar: "Shay Corrie almost died trying to save his friend, but was thrilled when he woke up in the hospital with a Harry Potteresque lightning bolt scar on his forehead."

—from the *Hogwarts Wire* online (October 30, 2003)

Literacy: "She is of outstanding distinction and has an international impact in her own field. She had an impact in reversing the worldwide trend in decreasing literacy. Her writing has attracted a huge number of children who previously had difficulties in beginning to read, and the society sees that her work has dispelled the myth that children lack the attention span to engage with longer books."

—Rowling lauded as an honorary fellow of the Royal Society of Edinburgh, as reported by Frank O'Donnell in "Rowling Joins Academic Elite," *Scotsman* (March 5, 2002)

Make-believe: "Come on, Jerry. It's just a story. The kids know it's make-believe; that's what novels are all about. Have you ever read one?"

—Jack Moseley in "Kids Have the Right to Read Harry Potter," *Arkansas News Bureau* (March 14, 2003)

Merchandising: "The magic is going. Soon there will be nothing special about Harry Potter. He'll be just another face on a cereal box. And a Coke can. And a toy. And candy."

—Matthew Flitton in "Harry Potter Merchandising Will Make the Magic Go Away," HardNewsCafe.usu.edu (November 28, 2001)

Merchandising, a kid's perspective: "J. K. Rowling created a feeling of magic when she wrote Harry Potter but all this merchandising and filmmaking is taking away that special feeling."

—Mark Luney, aged 14, quoted in "Harry Potter and Potty Ulster," childrens-express.org (January 1, 2002)

Merchandising nightmares: "I knew about the alarm clock. How do I feel about it? Honestly, I think it's pretty well known, if I could have stopped all merchandising I would have done so. And twice a year I sit down with Warner Bros. and we have conversations about merchandising and I can only say you should have seen some of the stuff that was stopped: Moaning Myrtle lavatory seat alarms and worse."

—Rowling in an interview conducted by Jeremy Paxman that aired on BBC Two (June 19, 2003), quoted in BBC News online

Money: "'But,' I ask, 'aren't you going to buy something, like a yacht perhaps?' This makes her bark with laughter."

—Ann Treneman in "J. K. Rowling: The Interview," *Times* (June 30, 2000)

Moviegoers: "In our world, not everyone is a reader first. There are people who go to movies and then realize there is a book."

—Barbara Marcus, President at Scholastic, quoted by David D. Kirkpatrick in "New Sign on Harry Potter's Forehead: For Sale," reprinted from the *New York Times* in the *Atlanta-Journal Constitution* (June 16, 2003)

Muggle: "Am I a Muggle? Yes, I am definitely a Muggle—a Muggle with an abnormal amount of knowledge about the wizarding world."

—Rowling interviewed in the *Connection* (October 12, 1999)

Parenting: "And I wouldn't mind being remembered as a good parent. But we won't know whether I've achieved that until my daughter writes *J. K. Dearest.*"

—Rowling quoted by J. F. O. McAllister in "The Shy Sorceress," a sidebar to "The Real Magic of Harry Potter," *Time* (June 23, 2003)

Parody: "'If Warner sues, we might as well roll up literary parody right now,' he said. Gerber said the book, which features an attempt to prevent a movie about the School of Hogwash from being made, is meant not only as entertainment, but as a serious comment on media conglomerates."

—on Michael Gerber's *Barry Trotter and the Unauthorized Parody,* from a story by Steve Zeitchik in *Publishers Weekly* (December 24, 2001)

Pet owls: "We are concerned by the surge in demand for owls because we don't think they make suitable pets. By their nature they are shy and reclusive birds, preferring to spend time in secluded places."

—Lucy Clark, spokesperson for the Royal Society for the Prevention of Cruelty to Animals, quoted in "Potter Sparks Pet Owl Demand," BBC online (December 18, 2001)

Poverty: "I remember reaching the supermarket checkout, counting out the money in coppers, finding out I was two pence short of a tin of baked beans and feeling I had to pretend I had mislaid a ten pound note for the benefit of the bored girl at the till. Similarly unappreciated acting skills were required for my forays into Mother care, where I would pretend to be examining clothes I could not afford for my daughter. All the time I would be edging ever closer to the baby-changing room where they offered a small supply of free nappies [diapers]."

—Rowling quoted by Clare Goldwin in "J. K. Rowling on her Days of Poverty," mirror.co.uk (May 20, 2002)

Privacy gone: "In fact, Rowling has tried to throw a cloak of invisibility around her family so they can live almost normal lives. But simple pleasures like strolling to the supermarket at home in Edinburgh or attending Jessica's Christmas pageant require constant vigilance against an army of tabloid reporters and the occasional stalker."

—J. F. O. McAllister in "The Shy Sorceress," a sidebar to "The Real Magic of Harry Potter," *Time* (June 23, 2003)

Proprietary fans: "In one sense, the boy wizard has slipped beyond her control; he is out there, everywhere, and legions of people feel a sense of ownership. But in the most important way, Harry still belongs to her. His future is in her head, as is that of the entire fictional universe she has set in motion."

—Paul Gray, "The Magic of Potter," *Time* (December 17, 2000)

Public relations nightmare: "It's really horrible. . . . So 10-year-old kids there have been told by a local paper that I'm getting out to sign. And then you have the police on the platform saying, 'Don't get out. It'll cause trouble.' So it's torturous as I'm just sitting there staring at crying children."

—Rowling commenting on a publicity tour nightmare, a train stop at which the local paper erroneously reported that she was there to sign books, quoted by Evan Solomon in "J. K. Rowling Interview," Canadian Broadcasting Company (July 2000)

Putin parodied: "The Russian radio station Ekho Moskvy reported that a group of Russian lawyers is preparing to take legal action against the film's producers. The lawyers apparently claim that the artists who created Dobby intentionally based him on Putin [president of Russia]. And that, naturally, shouldn't be allowed."

—Kathleen Knox in "Harry Potter and the Putin Imputation," atimes.com (January 29, 2003)

Quirky book: "I never expected to make money. I always saw Harry Potter as this quirky little book. I liked it and I worked hard at it, but never in my wildest dreams did I imagine large advances."

—Rowling quoted by Eddie Gibb in "Tales from a Single Mother," *Herald* (June 29, 1997)

Reclusiveness: "It makes me laugh, it really makes me laugh. It makes friends of mine laugh. I'm not reclusive. There are two reasons why I haven't done a lot of interviews recently. One, as I say, is I wanted to be working. An interview knocks out half a working day for me, and I was working ten-hour days on this book. I could not afford the time. To me, it was a waste of energy. I would rather be writing the book. And the other thing, which in my experience people tend to forget, is I'm still a single parent."

—Rowling quoted by Evan Solomon in "J. K. Rowling Interview," Canadian Broadcasting Company (July 2000)

Serendipity: "An interview with Rowling ran in the *Seattle Times* two days before she arrived in that city, and while the author was signing copies of *Harry Potter* in a bookstore in Seattle, a woman arrived, waving the newspaper clipping. When she asked if the store stocked the book, Rowling said, 'She had no idea I was there, and was quite pleased when the bookseller responded that not only did they have the book, but its author was sitting just behind her and would sign it for her. That was one of the most wonderful moments during my trip.'"

—Sally Lodge, from "Children's Authors and Illustrators Share Memorable Moments from Recent Book Tours," *Publishers Weekly* (January 4, 1999)

Nancy Stouffer: "It was as if some strange woman had come out of nowhere saying she was my children's mother . . . It was like a punch in the stomach. People think that if you have been successful, you are insulated from normal feelings of hurt, but you aren't."

—Rowling quoted by J. F. O. McAllister in "The Shy Sorceress," a sidebar to "The Real Magic of Harry Potter," *Time* (June 23, 2003)

Transition: "I don't know what I'll do now. I'm very nervous of just packing in my part-time teaching and becoming a full-time author, even though that is something I have always wanted to do."

—Rowling in "Book Written in Edinburgh Café Sells for $100,000," *Herald* (July 8, 1997)

Unauthorized books: "Rowling's legal team took exception to *The Irresistible Rise of Harry Potter* on the grounds that the colour scheme, typography and use of star symbols created the impression it was officially endorsed. . . . They objected to the purple colour scheme, the spiky typeface and the use of stars, and asked for a prominent disclaimer making it clear the book was not officially endorsed."

—Annabel House in "Potter Spin-off Spellbound by Legal Guardians," *Scotland on Sunday* (November 17, 2002)

Unfit literary fare: "These are not, however, books for adults. Unlike

Huckleberry Finn or *Alice in Wonderland,* the Potter series is not written on two levels, entertaining one generation while instructing another. Rather, it is in the category of Tom Swift and Dr. Dolittle; I was hooked on reading by them, but have laid aside my electric rifle and no longer talk to horses."

—William Safire, in an op-ed piece, *New York Times* (January 27, 2000)

Wands: "I drop in on two wand manufacturers. Allivan's is run by Dave Wedzik, whose prices range from $35 for a basic model up to $65 for a customised ebony version. 'We have had the occasional person ringing to say: My wand does not work,' says Wedzik. As for phoenix feathers: 'It has been difficult to find them lately. But we get calls about those, too.'"

—Roger Highfield at the Nimbus 2003 Harry Potter convention, reported in "All This Magic Makes My Brain Ache," Telegraph.co.uk (July 22, 2003)

Warner Bros. website: "The official Harry Potter website looks like it's had an awful lot of time and money invested in it. Given the amount of money JK's Harry has made everyone, though, they can probably afford it."

—From "Harry Potter Official Website," News.scotsman.com (June 5, 2003)

Welfare: "I had no intention, no desire, to remain on benefits. It's the most soul-destroying thing. I don't want to dramatise, but there were nights when, though Jessica ate, I didn't."

—Rowling quoted by Elisabeth Dunn in "From the Dole to Hollywood," *Electronic Herald* (August 2, 1997)

Witchcraft: "I have met thousands of children now, and not even one time has a child come up to me and said, 'Ms. Rowling, I'm so glad I've read these books because now I want to be a witch.' They see it for what it is. It is a fantasy world and they understand that completely. I don't believe in magic, either."

—Rowling in "Success of Harry Potter Bowls Author Over," CNN.com: Book News (October 21, 1999)

Part Two:
A Writer's Life

Tim Kirk

To understand and appreciate Rowling's life and work, it's essential not only to understand why she does what she does, but how she does it. Rowling's success has inspired countless people of all ages to pick up a pen and start writing. Some of those dreamers simply want to hold a finished book in their hands, but others have loftier goals—not only to publish, but also to become a best-selling author.

The Magic of Words: A Storyteller's World

I'm not writing for the money: It's for me and out of loyalty to fans.
—*Rowling, in an interview conducted by Ann Treneman for the* Times

Mike and Sully (*Monsters, Inc.*) play charades. The clue: Harry Potter.

To most the act of creative writing is a mystery—almost magic. To demystify the process, writer Harlan Ellison, best known for his essays, short fiction, and screenplays, has on numerous occasions set up his manual typewriter and typed out a short story from start to finish in one sitting, which is then photocopied, autographed, and given to customers who buy copies of his books from that store.

To counter the occasional charge from the nonbelievers that he's rigged the event—that he's a ringer—he'll ask someone to name specific story elements, which he'll then use to build a story. In other words, he's staking his reputation on the fact that he can write about anything, anywhere, and at any time. It's not magic, he says, it's hard work, imagination, creativity, and a lifetime of reading, writing, observing, and living life.

For nonwriters, the idea for a piece of writing can be likened to oyster grit. For nonwriters, who lack the imagination to create something from nothing, the grit will forever remain just a piece of dirt that irritates the oyster. But for writers, the grit may over time produce a pearl, a gem of a story.

In the world of creative fiction, the oyster bed of ideas realized by Rowling has yielded a rich bounty indeed. Journalists, who work on impossibly tight deadlines and want to catch the reader's attention, are quick to point out that she's richer than the Queen of England, that she owns three magnificent houses, that she's a rag-to-riches story. It's all part of Rowling's life story, but in the end, as Shakespeare reminds us, the play's the thing.

Rowling's early years before she finally hit it big sound similar to that of other successful writers. Like Stephen King, Rowling has always written for an audience of one (herself), never expected to make a fortune, taught school to support herself, and was finally freed to do what she felt was her life's work when a major subsidiary sale allowed her to quit teaching.

In Rowling's case, the odds certainly seemed stacked against her, because the captains of the book industry, especially children's book publishers, tend to look backward.

Unable to afford the cost of photocopying, Rowling typed out two copies of the first Harry Potter novel on a typewriter she bought for $80. Though there are conflicting reports in the media as to whom she sent the fledgling manuscript, the fact remains that the first publisher who saw the 80,000-word manuscript rejected it on the grounds that it was too long for a children's book. (Imagine trying to convince a child who compulsively read the first book in one unbroken reading session that it was too long; if anything, readers complain that her books are, like *The Lord of the Rings* books, too short.) Frankly, I'd hate to be the acquisitions editor or agent who rejected Rowling, since it's a mistake one can't afford to make twice. Writers like Rowling are so rare, you can count them on one hand, with four fingers hidden from view.

Fortunately for Rowling, she happened to send her manuscript to the Christopher Little Literary Agency in London, which remains her agency to this day—a rare enough circumstance in these times when writers are quick to leave at the first sign of a better offer. But no, Rowling is fiercely loyal to those who were there when she was a no-name author; and in turn, they are fiercely loyal to her.

To me the enduring genius of Rowling's Harry Potter novels is that, having invested seven years working on the first novel, and having meticulously mapped out the remaining six novels, using gridded paper that now occupies several boxes in her office, she was able to write an interlocking series instead of episodic novels. The result is that each book keeps the reader interested, always alert, picking up clues that will pay off in later books.

Currently, Rowling is working on book six, but we know nothing about it. As with book five, she's writing without the burden of facing a deadline, so when it's completed, she'll turn it in, and the publisher will crank up a publicity and marketing campaign to ensure that excitement reaches fever pitch.

Given that numerous fantasy novels revolve around the adventures (and misadventures) of boy wizards, what, one asks, makes Rowling's novels about Harry Potter so compelling and, judging from the dozens of editions published worldwide, so universally appealing?

Entire books have been written on that subject, for the world of academia has pounced on Rowling's fiction as virgin territory for theses; but the long and short of it is that Rowling is a world-builder whose fully imagined fictional universe harbors a sense of verisimilitude, a world we recognize and with which we are familiar, since it is anchored in the real world that coexists with the magical world.

It helps, too, that the characters are archetypal and immensely appealing—the orphaned wizard boy empowered beyond his imagining, and his loyal friends who stand by him through fair weather and foul, as the saying goes. It's an accessible story of good and evil, which is a theme that allows a writer to paint on a wide canvas. For Rowling, all the world's a stage and she's got the necessary space to create a fictional universe where, as in the real world, bad things can happen to good people—even death.

Often sudden and without warning, the fictional deaths are real to her. The characters are her literary creations to which she gave birth and, when they die, she can feel their acute pain. (Imagine how you'd feel if, in a perverse mood, Rowling killed off Harry Potter—you get the idea.)

When it was announced that an important character dies in book five, young readers wrote in to beg her to spare Ron Weasley because in their experience it's always the hero's best friend who gets killed.

There *is* a death in book five, but it's not someone you'd expect; and if you want to find out who it is, go read the book because I'm not telling.

But what I will tell you is that to Rowling the death was real, as she explained to BBC interviewer Jeremy Paxton in a June 19, 2003, broadcast. After writing the death scene, she was distraught and went into her kitchen to compose herself. As she recounted to Paxton:

> Well, I had rewritten the death, rewritten it, and that was it. It was definitive. And the person was definitely dead. And I walked into the kitchen crying and Neil said to me, "What on earth is wrong?" and I said, "Well, I've just killed the person." Neil doesn't know who the person is. But I said, "I've just killed the person." And he said, "Well, don't do it then." I thought, a doctor you know . . . and I said, "Well, it just doesn't work like that. You are writing children's books, you need to be a ruthless killer."

In other words, her husband, an anesthesiologist who sees life and death played out at the hospital and in the operating room, didn't intuit that his wife *had no choice.* The story is boss and the writer must be true to the book. Rowling did what *had* to be done, and just because it's fiction doesn't mean that the writer has a choice in the matter.

Vocationally, Rowling and her husband, Dr. Neil Murray, live in two different worlds: She's a dreamer, an imagineer, given to flights of fancy, with the power to make her imaginary stories real—so substantial that, as you're reading her novels, the world she's created seems real. Samuel Taylor Coleridge termed this the "willing suspension of disbelief" because as you fall through the pages of a book, the reality of the fictional universe—if it's consistent and true and resonates with verisimilitude—*seems* real to you. That's the power of Rowling's imagination at work, for *she* believes and therefore she can make *you* believe.

Vocationally, Rowling's husband lives in a Muggles world, whereas she lives in a wizarding world. When Dr. Murray witnesses a death in the course of his work, he's been trained to be clinically detached to keep him from being emotionally overwhelmed. Rowling, however, has to be a human receptor and live the lives of her characters to know them, to understand them, and to bring them to life, to make them ring true. So, understandably, when her characters die—and die they must, if she is true to the story—she feels their loss, she suffers their pain. To her and, by extension, her readers, fictional bereavement is *real.*

Rowling has expressed surprise that, because her books are so very British in setting and tone, the audience for them extends far beyond the borders of the United Kingdom. Indeed, part of the charm of the novels is precisely because of their setting. The British language, geography, and history are not only familiar but loved by readers who treasure the literature of the fantastic: Kenneth Grahame's *The Wind in the Willows,* J. M. Barrie's *Peter Pan,* A. A. Milne's *Winnie-the-Pooh,* Lewis Carroll's *Alice in Wonderland,* C. S. Lewis's *The Chronicles of Narnia,* Philip Pullman's *His Dark Materials* trilogy, and, of course, J. R. R. Tolkien's *The Hobbit* and *The Lord of the Rings.* It's a literary landscape with which we are already familiar, and one we love.

Give us a world we can lose ourselves in, we ask; give us a story well told; and most of all, give us characters we believe in and root for, as well as those we boo loudly. In short, give us a fully contained imaginary world where, for a brief period, we can leave our mundane world behind.

In C. S. Lewis's classic *The Lion, the Witch, and the Wardrobe,* Lucy goes into a closet and passes through a snow-filled world; so, too, we wish to get away from our world and leave our troubles behind.

Escapist fiction? Yes, for some, but in addition to that, it's fiction that illuminates. At its heart, the Potter novels are not about witchcraft and wizardry but about human values like honesty, loyalty, courage, sacrifice, and the enduring power of love.

Rowling's stories are so compelling that readers worldwide—young and old, of all races, creeds, colors, and nationalities—empathize with Harry Potter, the boy wizard who spent most of his early years thinking he was a Muggle, "just" Harry, as he put it, though those in the magical community know of him as "the boy who lived," the only one to survive a direct attack from Lord Voldemort.

At their core, the Harry Potter novels are about imagination, about self-empowerment, which is an appealing message no matter one's age or nationality. We want to believe in Harry Potter and, by doing so, harness the power of believing in ourselves. And we want to believe, if only for a few hours, in lions and tigers and bears. Oh my.

Though Rowling has yet to write an autobiography (I, for one, wish she would do so, or at least publish her memoirs, like Stephen King's *On Writing*) in the (mostly) speculative biographies on her and in numerous interviews, we've all heard the oft-repeated story of how she conceived of Harry Potter during a stalled train ride in England. Lacking paper, she was forced to remember everything and commit it to memory, starting with a fundamental question: Why doesn't Harry Potter know who he is? Because he's not what he seems—he's not an ordinary boy, he's a wizard. From that came the idea of Hogwarts, a school for young wizards, and from that the question of who else would be found at such a place—ghosts such as Nearly Headless Nick.

Of course, part of the fun is in trying to determine the linkages between her real life and imaginative fiction. And although such linkages obviously exist, as she's explained in interviews, the real magic is in how she's filtered these life experiences through her imagination and transmuted them into a fictional reality with substance and shape.

The bare bones, then: Ron Weasley is modeled after one of her best friends whom she met in high school, Séan Harris; Hermione Granger is a caricature of Rowling herself, a self-termed "swot" (a person who studies excessively); several professors at Hogwarts are drawn from those she knew when she was growing up; and Harry . . . well, he's the mystery. Harry Potter, as any writer might tell you, came from nowhere . . . and came from everywhere. To my mind, however, Harry Potter is very much a writer's construct, meaning he is at the heart of his novels and serves a purpose beyond that of the protagonist; he is in fact a metaphor for any writer who is initially unsure of herself and her talent, but then subsequently seeks to develop that talent to its fullest.

Let me explain: To a creative writer, most of the world *is* populated with Muggles (non-magic folk). A Muggle, as Rowling points out, is not necessarily a derogatory word; after all, Hermione Granger's parents are Muggles, yet wizards like Lucius Malfoy and his kind hold them in contempt. This is Rowling's way to write about bigotry, but without a preachy tone.

Regarding creative writing, you can either do it, or you can't. And if you can't, it means you can never understand what it's like to live in an imaginary world you've created and be constantly at war with a world that can't understand. As a writer, it's not that you *think* you're better but that you *know* you are different. Put simply, as a creative writer, you do think differently. Imagination, Nabokov once wrote, is an African dreaming up snow.

To put it in perspective, you may think up a story about a boy wizard, but that's just the bare shell of an idea; Rowling, on the other hand, dreamed up and fully imagined a boy wizard and his world that coexists (admittedly uncomfortably) with the real world, and then populated it with things like Quidditch, Diagon Alley, Hogwarts, the Ministry of Magic, and Aurors. It's the *execution* of the idea and not the idea itself that's valuable. Or to put it in terms of the currency to be found at Gringotts, the wizards' bank in the Harry Potter novels, the idea is worth a Sickle, but the proper execution of that idea is worth a Galleon.

Stephen King was not joking when he suggested, in an *Entertainment Weekly* book review of the fifth Potter novel, that Rowling should have her imagination insured by "Lloyd's of London (or perhaps the Incubus

Insurance Company) for the two or three billion dollars it will ultimately be worth over the span of her creative lifetime. . . ."

Rowling's books become, over the years, more imaginative, more substantial: The first novel (*Harry Potter and the Sorcerer's Stone*) is a straightforward narrative; the second novel (*Harry Potter and the Chamber of Secrets*) offers a compulsively readable narrative against the backdrop of the familiar school for wizards, Hogwarts, and adds a mystery; the third novel (*Harry Potter and the Prisoner of Azkaban*) offers the narrative, a mystery, and a wholly satisfying conclusion that lends depth to the story itself; the fourth novel (*Harry Potter and the Goblet of Fire*) is a braided, complex story with multiple storylines; and the fifth novel (*Harry Potter and the Order of the Phoenix*) delivers all of these previous elements, with the complexity of Harry Potter as he struggles with adolescence, as the story becomes increasingly darker in tone. In other words, the books are—unlike some of their paler imitations in the field—deeper, richer, more imaginative, and more fully developed with each successive installment.

Obviously, boy wizards grow in power as they master their craft . . . and so, too, has Rowling.

Harlan Ellison once pointed out that there are only a handful of fictional characters that are known around the world: Tarzan, Superman, and Sherlock Holmes, for example.

To that list we can safely add Harry Potter, but please don't take my word for it. Listen to Rowling's fans, who have bought millions of copies of her novels; listen to the critics who initially approached her work with a jaundiced eye and came away with appreciation; and listen to the millions who have discovered Harry, not through the books but through the films, which in turn brings them to the books, where they, too, become converts.

Come close and listen carefully as I whisper in your ear: *Harry Potter is one for the ages.*

Again, don't take *my* word for it, but you can safely take the word of master storyteller Stephen King, who reviewed *Harry Potter and the Order of the Phoenix* in *Entertainment Weekly* (July 11, 2003). After a thorough explication on why the novel is, as he put it, "a slam dunk," he poses the eternal question that every writer's work must face, the question of time's verdict on the work. On that note, King reassures us, we need not worry. As for whether or not Harry will be around a century from now—long after we have become dust—King concludes that Rowling's "is one series not just for the decade, but for the ages."

King, a former high school English teacher, then gives the novel a well-deserved top grade of A.

Coffee and Cafés Fuel Rowling's Creativity

Invisibility. I would like to sneak off to a café and write all day.
—*Rowling, when asked what magical power she'd most like to have,*
in response to a question posed to her at a public
appearance at London's Royal Albert Hall in July 2003

Imagine walking past your favorite bookstore and seeing a man in the display window banging away on a manual typewriter. You'd do a double-take, wondering if your eyes were deceiving you.

If it's Harlan Ellison, it's no joke: He is probably one of the few writers in the world who would ever *want* to write in such a setting and, more to the point, could pull it off. He's done this numerous times in the past, drawing large crowds, some of which pour into the bookstore to find out what's going on.

Stephen King is a frequent attendee at Red Sox baseball games in Boston; he carries a composition book and writes longhand between innings, oblivious to the curious who wouldn't mind sneaking a peek over his shoulder to see what he is writing.

Insofar as writing in public goes, Ellison and King are exceptions. Both of these demon-driven writers have shown a propensity for writing under any circumstances because they're hard-wired that way.

As for Rowling, I think she'd react with predictable horror at the mere prospect of writing in a bookstore's display window with passersby gawking at her. She does, however, love to write at cafés, if the coffee is hot, her cup is periodically refilled, and the other customers leave her alone, so words can pour out of her pen.

Unfortunately, the days when she'd park herself at a window table at Nicolson's in Edinburgh are history, as is the restaurant itself. Half-owned by her brother-in-law, the café made world-famous by her presence was sold to a restaurateur who transformed it into a Chinese buffet restaurant. (I think he missed a sure bet by not incorporating the word "dragon" into its title, for the obvious linkages to the Harry Potter universe, especially Rubeus Hagrid, who covets dragons.)

Even a change in venue to a café in a local museum in Edinburgh provided no refuge. Everything was fine, until a reader wrote a letter to the local paper to report with unbridled glee his Rowling sighting, after which she simply never returned. It wasn't enough for him to have seen her; he had to announce it to the world, as if to bask, for a few seconds, in the limelight that she so assiduously avoids. (If he had to live perpetually in that limelight as she does, he would have understood the rules; namely, we both know I'm here, but please respect my privacy. Don't bother me and don't go out and tell the world, because then you'll force me to leave, you selfish git!)

These days, Rowling is forced to write at home because the public has permanently driven her away from cafés.

In an essay for a book of autographs published by a small press, Stephen King noted that writers do their best work when they are observers and not the observed. The anonymity of the writer—the chronicler, the compulsive observer—is at the heart of all writers. But when a writer out in public is recognized, she can no longer do her job. Formerly invisible, she's now visible, exposed to naked scrutiny.

In Ernest Hemingway's *A Moveable Feast*, one sketch limns the problem Rowling and other writers who seek refuge in a café must face—the unwanted intrusion of others. As Hemingway wrote:

> The blue-backed notebooks, the two pencils and the pencil sharpener, . . . the marble-topped tables, the smell of early morning, sweeping out and mopping, and luck were all you needed. . . .
> Then you would hear someone say, "Hi, Hem. What are you trying to do? Write in a café?"

Your luck had run out and you shut the notebook. This was the worst thing that could happen. . . .

Now you could get out and hope it was an accidental visit and that the visitor had only come in by choice and there was not going to be an infestation. There were other good cafés to work in but they were a long walk away and this was my home café. It was bad to be driven out of the Closerie des Lilas. I had to make a stand or move.

Rowling would empathize with Hemingway, who was the first celebrity writer of modern times whose nonliterary exploits got as much press as his prose. The curious sought him out, just as they do Rowling. (In one instance, a fan traveled all the way from Japan with the hope that he'd meet Rowling in Edinburgh as she went about her appointed rounds. Disappointed that he never did, he reluctantly left for home.)

It would be nice, Rowling told an interviewer, if she could surrender some of her fortune to buy enough privacy to sit again at a café and blend in with the crowd. Unfortunately, Rowling is far too recognizable around the world, especially in Scotland and England, and even her wealth can't buy her that which she had when she was an unknown writer—the luxury of writing away from home, free of its distractions, with a bottomless cup of coffee on hand as she fills narrow-lined sheets of paper with magical words.

She now writes in the privacy of her home office, ensconced behind a nine-foot-high wall that encircles her property in Edinburgh, far from the crush of the common man and the madding crowd, where she dreams up her uncommon stories.

Harold Bloom, Stephen King, and Harry Potter: Strange Bedfellows Indeed

After Yale professor Harold Bloom attacked both Stephen King and J. K. Rowling—the former in the *Los Angeles Times,* the latter in the *Wall Street Journal*—a question arises: Is Harold a blooming idiot, as some might think, or does he know whereof he speaks?

Bloom has written or edited numerous well-regarded books: *Genius: A Mosaic of One Hundred Exemplary Creative Minds, The Western Canon: The Books and School of the Ages, Shakespeare: The Invention of the Human, How to Read and Why,* and—particularly pertinent to this discussion—*Stories and Poems for Extremely Intelligent Children of All Ages.*

Despite an impressive literary pedigree, Bloom's thesis—that King and Potter are, simply, popular literary trash—is suspect.

Upset that King was the 2003 recipient of the National Book Foundation's annual award, Bloom sneeringly wrote in the *Boston Globe* (Sept. 13, 2003), "By awarding it to King they recognize nothing but the commercial value of his books, which sell in the millions but do little more for humanity than keep the publishing world afloat." He suggested that if sales are the barometer of whether or not the award is justified, "perhaps next year the committee should give its award for distinguished contribution to Danielle Steel, and surely the Nobel Prize for literature should go to J. K. Rowling."

Bloom observed, "Our society and our literature and our culture are being dumbed down. . . ."

Citing other writers who he feels are deserving of the National Book Foundation's award—Thomas Pynchon, Cormac McCarthy, and Don DeLillo—Bloom concluded that honoring King is, in the end, "a terrible mistake."

In a separate op-ed piece for the *Wall Street Journal,* he took up arms against Rowling, while lambasting J. R. R. Tolkien as well. "The Harry Potter epiphenomenon will go on, doubtless for some time, as J. R. R. Tolkien did, and then wane."

Of Rowling's work Bloom had nothing good to say. One could almost hear him sighing loudly as he complained that readers of Harry Potter will not go on to read Lewis Carroll's adventures with Alice or Kenneth Grahame's *The Wind in the Willows*—an assertion that simply doesn't make sense, since devotees of children's literature do indeed cherish Carroll and Grahame, Baum (the Oz books), Tolkien, and a score of other writers who laid the groundwork for Ursula K. LeGuin, Philip Pullman, and Rowling.

Bloom concluded his op-ed piece by consigning Rowling to literary oblivion, dismissing the Potter books, based solely on a reading of the first book of the series and no more.

Bloom is way off his mark.

Unlike all other forms of mass entertainment—movies, plays, concerts, video games, and toys of every shape and description—reading is participatory and active; the others are passive.

At a time when parents are astonished that their kids will read anything at all, no wonder they are surprised when their children hungered to read the fifth Potter novel, a fact so unusual that numerous editorial cartoonists have drawn identical scenes: A stack of expensive, bulky electronic toys sit neglected, gathering dust, as a child is mesmerized by the latest Potter novel.

Citing Grahame's utterly delightful *The Wind in the Willows* as worthy reading, Bloom fails to recognize that what makes that book so memorable is *exactly* what makes the Potter books similarly enjoyable. It's the story of three friends—the boastful Toad who learns humility, the wise, fatherly Badger, and the steadfast Rat—celebrating their relationship and showing us very human values: hubris, loyalty, friendship, and sacrifice. Not coincidentally, these are the same values that are found (and celebrated) in the Potter novels. In other words, Grahame's book and the Harry Potter books have more in common than they do not, for Grahame and Rowling are of like minds.

Stephen King at the National Book Awards

For the highbrow literary community, it was a moment of unimaginable horror. Stephen King, whom they regard as little more than a hack, had beaten out scores of other writers to win a lifetime achievement award in American letters. The literary community immediately divided itself into two groups: those who, like Harold Bloom, felt the award was not deserved; and those who felt it was long overdue. That debate will rage on for years, but here's what King had to say:

> For far too long the so-called popular writers of this country and the so-called literary writers have stared at each other with animosity and a willful lack of understanding. This is the way it has always been. . . . But giving an award like this to a guy like me suggests that in the future, things don't have to be the way they've always been. Bridges can be built between the so-called popular fiction and the so-called literary fiction.
>
> Tokenism is not allowed. You can't sit back, give a self-satisfied sigh, and say, "Ah, that takes care of the troublesome pop lit question. In another 20 years or perhaps 30, we'll give this award to another writer who sells enough books to make the best-seller lists." It's not good enough. Nor do I have any patience with or use for those who make a point of pride in saying they've never read anything by John Grisham, Tom Clancy, Mary Higgins Clark, or any other popular writer. What do you think? You get social or academic Brownie points for deliberately staying out of touch with your own culture?

Grahame's novel delights us for the same reasons that the Potter books delight us. We read these novels not simply because we want diversion and escape—though the books provide those qualities in abundance—but because we want to know more about ourselves. The situations in which these fictional characters become embroiled and how they achieve ultimate resolution resonate in our lives.

Put differently, if Grahame's novel and the Harry Potter novels were nothing more than entertaining reads, neither Grahame nor Rowling would stand the test of time.

What Bloom has failed to recognize, much less acknowledge, is that what the books are about eclipses all other considerations. If the Potter novels were modest successes, hand-sold by independent booksellers, Bloom would still criticize them; but because the Potter novels sell so phenomenally well, they are suspect.

This is literary elitism of the worst sort. Though such elitism dismisses Rowling's novels for their supposed lack of cerebration, the fact remains that Rowling's novels are a matter of celebration. Bloom feels that children are better off reading other novels instead of Rowling's and King's. Mind you, this is the considered opinion of an educated man who has thought and written extensively on the subject of literary merit, so how can he be so obtuse?

Yes, one can fault Rowling for her excessive use of adjectives, a minor fault that Stephen King noticed and chided her for in his review of *Harry Potter and the Order of the Phoenix.* But taken on the whole, beyond the obvious storytelling engine that propels the reader from first to last page at a galloping pace, Rowling's books offer more, not less, as Bloom suggests. Far from being the literary equivalent of a McBook (A QUARTER MILLION SOLD!), Rowling's Potter novels speak to children in a vocabulary they understand, talking *to* them instead of down *at* them, and highlighting moral concerns—making the right choice as opposed to the easy choice—while affirming human values, especially loyalty and friendship and sacrifice. This raises the question: Does Bloom not see these attributes or does he choose to ignore them?

More the latter, I think. In Bloom's op-ed piece one can almost hear another sigh as he sees the ivory towers of academe crashing around him, a wasted literary landscape dotted not with the Grahames and Carrolls of the world but the Kings and Rowlings. He perceives a diminution of values and tastes, a dumbing-down of America, as he puts it.

I think the reading public is smarter than Bloom would admit, because there's plenty of room in bookstores for the Pynchons and DeLillos and McCarthys of the world, just as there's room for the Kings and Rowlings of the world.

Perhaps Bloom should worry less about whether Rowling's and King's books are the literary equivalent of McDonalds meals and think more about what worlds of imagination their books offer.

Harry Potter, Censorship, and Book Banning

You don't have to burn books to destroy a culture. Just get people to stop reading them.

—*Ray Bradbury, author of* Fahrenheit 451

Rowling finds herself in good literary company these days: Nobel prize–winning author Maya Angelou, America's best humorist and national treasure, Mark Twain, Nobel prize–winning author John Steinbeck, children's book author Judy Blume, and the celebrated recluse J. D. Salinger. They are all authors of some of the "100 Most Frequently Challenged Books of 1990–2000," according to the American Library Association. Rowling, of course, is high on the list.

At first glance, especially if one knows nothing about Rowling or her Harry Potter novels, it might seem appropriate until you crack open the covers of her books and realize that she's writing fantasy and not a how-to manual on ritual animal sacrifices. At second glance, one realizes that there's a world of difference between the fun, make-believe magic she writes about and the very real world of Satan worshippers. It's the critical difference between fantasy and reality, a distinction some choose not to make. Case in point: Reverend George Bender, the pastor of the Harvest Assembly of God Church in Penn Township, Butler County, in Pennsylvania.

Gathering at night in the parking lot behind his church, Rev. Bender expressed regret that attendance at his March 2001 book-burning was sparse. In a story by Carmen J. Lee of the *Post-Gazette*, she quotes him as saying: "I would have liked to have seen more visitors. But I think it worked out well. It made us pay attention to what we're doing. It makes us think about how to focus on the Lord as we should. I hope people understand our intentions, though I know some won't."

Most won't.

Like most censors quick to preach, quick to condemn, and too quick to burn anything that offends him, Rev. Bender never bothered to *read* the Harry Potter books he tossed in the bonfire, nor did he need to: He simply knew the books were the devil's work. "[He] was firm in describing the Potter books, specifically, and Disney productions, in general, as containing sorcery and witchcraft," wrote reporter Lee.

The problem, as pointed out in an article on the Education World website, is that because the Potter books have the trappings of witchcraft, that's more than enough for some people to damn them outright. Mark West, a college professor and author of *Trust Your Children: Voices against Censorship in Children's Literature,* observed, "They don't see it as fantasy. They see it as real. A small group of Americans can't accept fantasy that way. They really do care [about the book's impact], so they go against others' legal rights."

More than legal rights, such people are asserting their "superior" moral rights. They know what's best for them—and best for *you,* as well; they know what offends them—and want to make sure it won't offend anyone. They are smug in their ignorance, usually citing the Bible, that they are doing the Lord's work for the betterment of all by condemning, burning, and challenging the presence of Rowling's novels in public libraries and, especially, school libraries.

Christian author Berit Kjos, quoted in an article on the Education World website, explains the concerns of the Christian community:

> Christianity clashes with a love for witchcraft. . . . It is a religion that is very real and is spreading throughout the country. It makes me very uncomfortable when [children] are immersed in topics that make witchcraft very exciting. It can be very confusing for them.

It's not *children* who seem to be confused, for most children seem to understand the important distinction between fantasy and reality, between a world of make-believe and the real world.

Unfortunately, you can't argue with such paralogia, because it boils down to a matter of belief, of bedrock faith. The fossilized mindset of those who would want to censor Harry Potter cannot be changed. As Beverly Green, a Sunday school teacher from Eastman, Georgia, explained to Wired.com reporter Julia Scheeres, "*Harry Potter* is saying you can dabble in witchcraft as long as it's entertaining. If it's not good, it's evil. There ain't no in-between. When you start dabbling in demonic spirits, that's dangerous ground. You're opening up your home, yourself, to all kinds of attacks from the Devil."

The American Library Association

For anyone interested in knowing more about the ongoing and never-ending battle against censors, go to the ALA website (www.ala.org). It provides information and printed resources for readers and educators interested in free expression.

Well, maybe not necessarily from the Devil but from religious zealots who are supremely confident that they know best—and want *you* to know it, too, even if it means filing challenge after challenge, burning books, and putting their best efforts into banning books for *your own good!*

Echoing Green's comments, Reverend Jack D. Brock, citing Acts 19:19–20 of the Bible, encouraged members of his congregation to join him in a book-burning. The Harry Potter books, he explained, are "examples of our society's growing preoccupation with the occult. The Potter books present witchcraft as a generally positive practice, while the Bible expressly condemns all occult practices."

It's worth noting that, according to the online article from www.childrens books.about.com, Rev. Brock had never *read* the Potter novels but "had researched their contents."

Apparently, he didn't read closely enough, because if he had, he'd have found out that the books espouse qualities worth celebrating, as opposed to the "burn them all!" mindset of book-burners like Rev. Brock, who ardently believes that "stories like Harry Potter that glorify wizardry and sorcery will lead people to accept and believe in Satan."

Judy Blume, author of *Are You There, God? It's Me, Margaret, Superfudge,* and other children's books, is one of the most censored authors of our time. She wrote an op-ed piece for the *New York Times* (October 22, 1999) in which she observed that the backlash from religious fundamentalists against Rowling was only a matter of time: "I knew this was coming. The only surprise is that it took so long—as long as it took for the zealots who claim they're protecting children from evil . . . to discover that children actually liked these books. If children are excited about a book, it must be suspect."

Perhaps Blume's eight-year-old grandson said it best. After Blume tried to explain why some adults wanted to keep their children from reading

Harry Potter novels, he exclaimed, "But that doesn't make any sense!" No, it doesn't, but religious zealots will continue to condemn, criticize, and challenge Rowling's imaginative fiction because they prefer to curse the darkness and light bonfires, not candles.

So You Want to Be a Novelist? Advice for Budding Writers about Writing and Publishing

Though her critics complain she is churning out literary pap, Rowling is beloved by parents worldwide who are flabbergasted to see their children pick up a thick novel instead of a television remote. Similarly, she's celebrated by booksellers who haven't seen this much excitement over a book series in years, not to mention a jaded book industry that has seen all the conventional rules of publishing wisdom demolished by the Harry Potter phenomenon.

Sparking the imagination of a worldwide audience, Rowling's novels have been published in 55 languages in 200 countries in only a few short years.

What's happened is nothing short of magic. With the release of book five (*Harry Potter and the Order of the Phoenix*), Rowling's position as *the* best-selling author of all time is firmly established, and it's not likely anyone will soon challenge her dominance.

With such success, it's inevitable that a certain number of readers will be inspired to become writers. From children with stardust in their eyes to teenagers and the middle-aged (or older), readers are inspired by her example and some want to try their hand at what is arguably the oldest profession in the world, the art of telling stories.

Just as Woodward and Bernstein inspired generations of journalists who wanted to be investigative reporters to break stories like Watergate, Rowling has had a similar effect on aspiring writers. The recent bumper crop of first-time novelists—notably a British teen named Helen Oyeyemi who scored a record-breaking £400,000 advance from Bloomsbury for her novel *The Icarus Girl*—owe Rowling thanks for the public resurgence of interest in fantasy, which Tom Shippey (a Tolkien scholar) asserts is the dominant form of literature in our time, due in no small part to Tolkien and, more recently, Rowling.

Over the years, in media interviews, Rowling has commented on the process of writing, on editing, and on book publishing. I've culled her observations and added my notes (Lesson Learned) to put things in context.

Rowling's Time-Tested Words of Publishing Wisdom

"I don't think there's any subject matter that can't be explored in literature." (*Time,* October 30, 2000)

Lesson Learned: Don't be afraid to write about anything. Don't worry about what your friends, neighbors, parents, or critics think. Let your imagination run free.

"This is not vanity or arrogance, but if you look at the facts, very, very few people manage to write anything that might be a best-seller." (*Time,* September 20, 1999)

Lesson Learned: Because best-selling authors are all that we hear about in the media, and because most people have no idea that most professional writers are part-timers, the fantasy cherished by unpublished writers is that their work will be critical and financial successes. As Rowling points out, the odds are against making a fortune writing. It happens, but when it does, it's rare enough to make the news.

"Those five years really went into creating a whole world." Rowling speaking of the time spent in plotting the Harry Potter novels (*Time,* September 20, 1999)

Lesson Learned: Rowling is a master at plotting, but it takes time to get the details right, especially in a series in which key clues that will bear fruit later are planted early on. Writing such an airtight plot means that the imaginary world must be fully realized. If *you* believe, so, too, will the reader. Case in point, J. R. R. Tolkien's *The Lord of the Rings,* which took 13 years to write.

"If it's a good book, anyone will read it. I'm totally una-shamed about still reading things I loved in my childhood." (*Time*, April 12, 1999)

Lesson Learned: Read any-thing and everything and don't develop a snobbish idea as to what constitutes "literature" and what does not. Readers don't care. They want, simply, the best story you can tell. It's what they've paid for and it's what they deserve.

"I had been very realistic about the likelihood of making a living out of writing children's books . . . and that didn't worry me. I prayed that I would make just enough money to justify con-tinuing to write. . . ." (Salon.com, 1999)

Lesson Learned: In terms of what to expect of a writing career, keep your income expec-tations low. Editors at book pub-lishing houses tell first-time writers not to quit their day jobs. Even Stephen King didn't quit his day job until he sold his first novel, *Carrie*. He wisely waited until he had gotten a major sub-sidiary sale, which allowed him to quit teaching.

A Dozen Tips for Publishing Success

1. Read omnivorously.

2. Write, write, write!

3. Learn how to properly format a manuscript for submission.

4. Finish the work.

5. Get constructive criticism from several impartial sources.

6. Consult directories to research the best agent to represent you.

7. Write a one-page query letter and send it to several agents.

8. Be prepared to send in the fin-ished manuscript *only* if invited to do so.

9. If rejected by the agent, go on to the next one.

10. Repeat until you have represen-tation.

11. Start your next book immedi-ately.

12. Don't quit your day job.

"I always advise children who ask me for tips on being a writer to read as much as they possibly can." (Salon.com, 1999)

Lesson Learned: Writers are readers who read anything and everything they can get their hands on. They cannot *not* read. (A writer will read the text on a cereal box if nothing else is on hand.) If you don't enjoy reading, and reading a lot, you'll never be a writer.

"I didn't know anything about agents but I went to the library and looked up some addresses in the Artists' and Writers' Yearbook." (*Telegraph*, Spring 1997)

Lesson Learned: Do your research. Go to the standard references in the field and look up who may be interested in buying your book. Write a polite, short, to-the-point query letter; if interested, the agent will contact you to ask for a completed manuscript.

"I was about six and I haven't stopped scribbling since, but this is the first time I'd tried to get anything published." On submitting a book titled *Rabbit* to Penguin, which later reportedly turned down the first Harry Potter novel. (*Telegraph*, June 24, 1997)

Lesson Learned: At an early age, Rowling submitted work professionally. Though she submitted prematurely, it was an indication as to where her true interests and talents resided.

"I never expected to make any money." (*Sunday Times*, June 29, 1997)

Lesson Learned: A new writer isn't the next Charles Dickens and shouldn't have great expectations. If you're fortunate enough to get published, consider that its own reward. And if you make any money at it, consider that a bonus.

"I thought I am the luckiest person in the world. I am now being paid to do what I have been doing my whole life for nothing." (*Independent*, November 21, 1997)

Lesson Learned: Follow your bliss. It's the central thesis of Joseph Campbell's books. As Campbell explains, if you follow your bliss, you'll be happy, even if you don't make any money in the process.

But if you're lucky enough to write *and* make money, you should realize your good fortune.

"Yes, I've wanted to be an author as long as I can remember. English was always my favorite subject at school. . . ." (Amazon.com UK, 1999)

Lesson Learned: Writers discover early on that their great passion is writing. Understandably, their best subject in school is English. Pay attention to these early signs because they are indicators of where your true interests reside.

"I never really think in terms of ingredients, but I suppose if I had to name some I'd say humor, strong characters, and a watertight plot." (Amazon.com UK, 1999)

Lesson Learned: A work of fiction is not made by slavishly following a recipe. Think in terms of what makes a story a compelling read.

"Whenever someone younger asks me for advice in writing, I always say 'Read!', because that will teach you what good writing is like, and you will recognize bad writing too." (Barnes & Noble, March 1999)

Lesson Learned: Read, read, and then read some more. Reading will be an integral part of your life. If you read carefully and read enough, you may learn to recognize the good from the bad writing.

"I have got the perfect temperament for a writer, because I don't need to be surrounded by people all the time." (Barnes & Noble, March 1999)

Lesson Learned: Writing is a solitary act between you and a blank sheet of paper. Fill it with your best work. But if you are the kind of person who craves and needs an audience, consider an alternate career as a stand-up comedian or an actor.

"I just never really spoke about it, because I was embarrassed. And because my parents were the kind of parents who would have thought, 'Ah yes, that's very nice, dear. But where is the pension plan?'" (*School Library Journal*, September 1, 1999)

Lesson Learned: Budding word wizards and story sorceresses won't get much encouragement from their Muggle-thinking parents. In a list of jobs parents would prefer their children to consider—doctor, lawyer, teacher, or businessman—a career as a writer would definitely not be one of them.

"Here's the recipe for life: find what you do best and figure out a way to make it pay for you." (*Star-Ledger*, Newark, NJ, October 16, 1999)

Lesson Learned: This gets back to what Joseph Campbell affirmed. If you are good at something and it makes money, then you will have found your bliss. The hours of your life are short, so do you *really* want to spend the bulk of them doing work you hate with a passion?

"First you must read, then practice, and always plan." (*Boston Globe*, October 18, 1999)

Lesson Learned: This sounds simple, but it's not; it's a lifelong plan. Read extensively, in and out of the field you've chosen, to give your writing depth; write a lot, since you're going to have to get rid of the rubbish before you write narratives that shine like polished gems; and plan your work in depth because you don't need any rude surprises, and neither do your readers.

"And for their parents, don't tell them it's unrealistic. Never say that. Because even if they're not published, writing, well, writing is the passion of my life, so it's an important thing to do." (National Press Club, October 20, 1999)

Lesson Learned: Parents, don't discourage the dreamer. I wonder how many writers of talent never pursued their dreams because their parents kept telling them that it was stupid to even *dream* of being a writer. Life's full of disappointments, which your children will find out in due course, so why not let them believe in their dreams? Don't take that from them.

"I sat down to write something I knew I would enjoy reading. I do not try to analyse it and I don't write to a formula." (National Council for One Parent Families, September 29, 2001)

Lesson Learned: Write to please yourself. Don't write for any preconceived market.

"I doubt a writer who has got what it takes will need me to tell them this, but persevere!" (Scholastic, Fall 2000)

Lesson Learned: A truism: If you're an unpublished writer and *can* be discouraged, you *should* be discouraged, because real writers *never* give up!

"Persevere, but if everyone's turned you down, then it's time to try writing something else. And if that doesn't succeed, it *might* be time to think about a different career. But some great writers had lots of books rejected before they got published, so don't lose heart." (Yahooligans, October 20, 2000)

Lesson Learned: There comes a point when you have to accept your natural limitations and recognize that writing, despite your great passion for it, isn't one of your talents. It's one thing to persist, but another to waste the precious years of your life nurturing false hope, harboring an unrealizable dream.

"I enjoy the editing process, but I edit fairly extensively myself before my editors get to see the book. . . ." (Scholastic.com, 2000)

Lesson Learned: Good writing is rewriting. A first draft is the fun part; the second and subsequent drafts are where you polish the prose until the manuscript is letter-perfect. A good sentence, a good paragraph, a good chapter—all combine to make a good book.

Tim Kirk

If You Like J. K. Rowling, Try These Authors

By its very nature, good fantasy is timeless. And, from the current crop of best-sellers, good fantasy is also timely. There's no question that the public is hungering for good stories, no matter what universe they're set in. Today's readers (and viewers) have a cornucopia of irresistible choices because we are living in a golden age of children's books.

Most book industry professionals feel strongly that we'll never see another Harry Potter-like success in the short term, but wasn't that also the prevailing opinion in 1997 when the first Harry Potter novel was published?

No one—the author, editor, agent, publisher, booksellers, film moguls, or investors on Wall Street—could have imagined that The Boy Who Lived would become an international entertainment franchise. In 2003, according to Rowling's agent, the books had sold 250 million copies worldwide; today, the tally is at 300 million copies.

Though the numbers matter greatly to those in the book and film industry who have connections to the Harry Potter pie, readers are more concerned about a fundamental consideration: Is this a good story? Is it worth the investment of money and time? Is it a book I'd enthusiastically recommend to friends?

Forget the overblown hype from a publisher trying to convince you that his new author is "the next J. K. Rowling." The simple truth is that a book will find its own audience . . . or it won't. If it does, you'll see more books in the series; and if it doesn't, you'll see the book remaindered and then go quietly but permanently out of print.

If you find yourself wanting to roam outside the grounds of Hogwarts, check out these spellbinding storytellers.

Philip Pullman

To my mind, Pullman is the most imaginative and audacious writer in the fantasy field today. Pullman is a British writer. His Dark Materials, a trilogy of three books, is considered by many to be the best fantasy trilogy since Tolkien's *The Lord of the Rings,* which was published more than a half century ago.

October 2006 marked the tenth anniversary of the original publication of Pullman's first book in the series, *Northern Lights,* which was published in the U.S. under the title *The Golden Compass.* To celebrate its anniversary, Knopf issued a deluxe edition that features archival documents, scientific notes, and "found" letters by Lord Asriel.

The two books that followed were *The Subtle Knife* and *The Amber Spyglass,* both building on what had gone before. A short story, *Lyra's Oxford,* was published in 2003; this book includes a fold-out map of fictional Oxford and "souvenirs" from the past.

In the works: *The Book of Dust,* a collection of stories that tell the back stories for some of the main characters, including (according to www.bridgetothestars.net) how Lee and Iorek met, how Farder Coram and Serafina Pekkala fell in love, and the story of how Coulter and Lord Asriel met. (The book is currently being written, and I don't want to hazard a guess as to publication date.)

New Line Cinema's film adaptation of *The Golden Compass* is set for release on December 7, 2007. The official movie website is at goldencompassmovie.com.

The official website is at www.philip-pullman.com. Two great fan websites worth your attention are at www.bridgetothestars.net and www.hisdarkmaterials.org.

Cornelia Funke

A German writer, Funke had her writing career take off when Barry Cunningham "discovered" her after a German girl wondered why *The Thief Lord* wasn't available in English.

A professionally trained book designer and artist, Funke is winning new fans worldwide with each new book.

When *The Thief Lord* was published in the U.S. by Scholastic Books (Rowling's publisher), the book stole readers' hearts. More books followed: *Dragon Rider, Inkheart,* and *Inkspell.*

With forty books in print and more on the way, her brand of "magic realism" has made her an international favorite. In fact, British author/artist Clive Barker, in *Time 100,* wrote of her, "She is often called the German J. K. Rowling, but Cornelia Funke is a unique talent."

Her readers are breathlessly awaiting the publication of the third book in the Inkheart Trilogy, tentatively titled *Inkdawn.* Fortunately for her fans, she's already written more than 700 pages, although (as it's explained on her website), "Cornelia also says she still has lots to do, editing and re-writing parts of the text, before she will be ready to hand the story over to her publishers." She projects a Spring 2008 publication date.

Her website is at www.corneliafunkefans.com.

Naomi Novik

Born in 1973, Naomi Novik had her first novel, *His Majesty's Dragon,* published in March 2006. It was soon followed by *Throne of Jade* (April 2006) and *Black Powder War* (May 2006).

Her publisher, Del Rey Books, decided to debut her with a splash, issuing three books in close succession, to build up her audience as soon as possible.

The publishing strategy worked like magic. Issued as mass market paperbacks, the Temeraire series is open-ended; Novik is working on books four and five, which she hopes to see published, respectively, in 2007 and 2008.

Imaginatively crossing Patrick O'Brian's naval tales with Anne McCaffrey's dragon tales, Novik's Temeraire novels are a fresh departure from the tried-and-true (and clichéd) Tolkienesque fantasy setting; Novik uses the Napoleonic War between Great Britain and France as the backdrop, with a twist: Dragons serve as the equivalent of an air force.

If you need any further affirmation as to the potentially broad appeal of this series, filmmaker Peter Jackson optioned its film rights and told *The Hollywood Reporter:* "'Temeraire' is a terrific meld of two genres that I particularly love—fantasy and historical epic. I can't wait to see Napoleonic battles fought with a squadron of dragons. That's what I go to the movies for. . . . As I was reading these books, I could see them coming to life in my mind's eye. These are beautifully written novels, not only fresh, original and fast-paced, but full of wonderful characters with real heart."

Look to see more wonderful books from the pen of Naomi Novik, whose first three books I thoroughly enjoyed, as she finds a permanent place in the literary firmament as a rising star. She's got the real goods.

For more information, go to www.temeraire.org.

Christopher Paolini

If you have $12,050 burning a hole in your pocket and you just don't know what to do with it, you could always buy a copy of Christopher Paolini's first book, *Eragon*. Actually, let me make a small but important distinction: Paolini's *self-published* book was issued from Paolini International LLC, his family-owned small press that originally published 10,000 copies in trade paperback.

But luck (or fate) intervened in the form of Ryan Lindberg, who discovered it during a fishing trip at a bookstore in Montana and recommended it to his stepfather, writer Carl Hiassen, who had taken him on said trip. In turn, Hiassen brought it to the attention of Random House which, according to the *New York Times,* bought the rights to *Eragon* for "the middle six figures," publisher's code for approximately $500,000.

It was money well spent. The home-brewed edition was immediately put out of print as Random House began building the Paolini franchise with the republication of *Eragon,* followed by the publication of *Eldest,* to be followed by the third and final book in the series.

But long before Random House bought the book, it had garnered rave reviews on Amazon.com from enthusiastic, typically young, readers who found inspiration not only in the story itself but the real-life story *behind* the imaginary one: a teenage boy writes an epic fantasy and finds himself at the helm of an international book and movie franchise.

A cross-genre book inspired by Tolkien, Anne McCaffrey, and *Star Wars* (the Dragon Riders are the Jedi Knights of Paolini's Alagaësia), *Eragon* is a shining example of self-publishing at its best: The author gets intimately involved in every aspect of promoting the book, hand-selling the book at bookstores and going to schools to put on dramatic presentations to push book sales.

No doubt a lot of Paolini's motivation was the realization that the sale of his books was the family's livelihood—the sole source of income.

As Paolini told *USA Today,* "Let me put it this way. *Eragon* put food on the table. If *Eragon* had taken a month or two to become more popular, we would have had to move to the city and take jobs. It came that close."

It's not likely that the Paolini family is ever going to have to worry about moving or finding jobs, for *Eragon* (book 1) and *Eldest* (book 2) have each exceeded one million copies sold. The third book (as yet untitled) is also expected to hit more than a million.

Eragon, which was released as a major motion picture in December 2006, has grossed more than $60 million in the U.S. alone. Though receiving mixed reviews—detractors took glee in pointing out its heavy debt to Tolkien, McCaffrey, and George Lucas's *Star Wars*—its box-office success guarantees that this film franchise, now aloft, will schedule future flights for books 2 and 3.

The official movie website is at eragonmovie.com; the official Paolini website (Random House) is at alagaesia.com; and the best fan website is at shurtugal.com.

Tim Kirk

Notable and Quotable: On Writing and Publishing

Anticipation: "'I can't wait! I can't wait!' cries ten-year-old Alula Greenberg-White, hugging herself in expectation. It's 9 A.M. outside a large bookshop in north London and Alula is at the head of a queue of 100 excited children and parents. They peer through the windows at stacks of a 640-page novel, eyes searching for the small strawberry-blonde Pied Piper who has brought them here—and to bookshops round the globe—and who is somewhere inside nursing a coffee."

—Tim Boquet from "J. K. Rowling: The Wizard behind Harry Potter," *Reader's Digest* (December 2000)

Awards: "This business shouldn't be about awards but it's a vote of confidence and if there's the slimmest chance of winning I get terribly nervous."

—Rowling quoted by Anne Johnstone in "We Are Wild about Harry," *Herald* (January 26, 1999)

Being published: "The purest, most unalloyed joy was when I finally knew it was going to be a book, a real book you could see sitting on the shelf of a bookshop."

—Rowling quoted by Judith Woods in "Coffee in One Hand, Baby in Another—A Recipe for Success," *Scotsman* (November 20, 1997)

Books recommended: "Anything by Philip Pullman. Of modern writers there's a book called *Skellig* by an English author, David Almond, which I think is absolutely magnificent. Stuff I enjoyed when I was a child—I loved E. Nesbitt. I think she was a genius. Paul Gallico. He's out of print now. I really love his work, too."

—Rowling interviewed by Sean Bowler at a public talk at the National Press Club (October 20, 1999)

Booksigning: "The first time I ever had to do a reading which was to about four people, in fact so few people turned up at this bookshop that the staff felt really sorry for me and came and stood around and listened as well. I was shaking so badly I kept missing my line. I was terrified. But since then, I have found readings to be the most fantastic experience."

—Rowling quoted by Caroline Davies in "The Queen Meets Two of Britain's Best Loved Best-Sellers," *Daily Telegraph* (March 23, 2001)

Cafés: "I do still write longhand, and I do write away from the house whenever possible because it's very easy to get distracted when you're home. I use cafés as offices, really, with the added bonus that there's normally good music and someone to bring me coffee all the time, which is great."

—Rowling quoted by Jeff Baker in "Harry Potter: Need She Say More?" *Oregonian* (October 22, 2000)

Dreams: "I never, ever dreamt this would happen. My realistic side had allowed myself to think that I might get one good review in a national newspaper. That was my idea of a peak. So everything else really has been like stepping into Wonderland for me."

—Rowling quoted by Ann Treneman in "Joanne Rowling's Secret Is Out," *Independent* (November 21, 1997)

Editing: "Carving the books out of all her notes was a case of editing and condensing and sculpting it so the story moulded into shape. She had a mass of stuff on Harry that she had to edit down quite a bit. She figured Harry Potter would be a book for the obsessives. She figured it was a book for people who enjoyed every little detail that a story like Harry offers."

—from a BBC Special on Rowling (Christmas 2001)

Expectations: "I was totally realistic about what children's books involved. And that involves really no money at all. I mean, a lot of really great children's writers I know also do other work—they have to."

—Rowling quoted by Mark Phillips, CBSNews.com (July 9, 2000)

Fan fiction: "The author is 'flattered by genuine fan fiction,' said Neil Blair, an attorney for the Christopher Little Literary Agency, which represents Rowling. But she has been alarmed by 'pornographic or sexually explicit material [based on her characters] clearly not meant for kids.' Christopher Little began sending out letters last year because it feared 'the dangers of, say, seven-year-olds stumbling on the material as they searched for genuine [Harry Potter] material,' Blair said in an e-mail response to questions."

—Ariana Eunjung Cha in "Harry Potter and the Copyright Lawyer," *Washington Post* (June 18, 2003)

Fan mail: "'I could have been my own full-time secretary.' Now the American fan mail is diverted to and dealt with in America."

—Rowling quote, followed by statement by journalist Elizabeth Grice in "Harry's On Fire Again, Casting a Spell His Creator Can No Longer Ignore," *Daily Telegraph* (July 10, 2000)

Fantasy fiction: "I don't really like fantasy. It's not so much that I don't like it, I haven't really read a lot of it. I have read *The Lord of the Rings*, though. I read that when I was about 14. I didn't read *The Hobbit* until much later, when I was in my 20s. I'd started *Harry Potter* by then, and someone gave it to me, and I thought, yeah, I really should read this because people kept saying, 'You've read *The Hobbit*, obviously.' And I was saying, 'Um, no.' So I thought, well, I will, and I did, and it was wonderful."

—Rowling from an interview in *Newsweek* (July 10, 2000)

Favorite books: When asked if any one child stood out in her mind: "My favourite was the girl who came to the Edinburgh Book Festival to see me. When she reached the signing table she said, 'I didn't want so many people to be here—this is MY book.' That really resonated with me, because that's how I feel about my own favourite books."

—Rowling in an interview on Scholastic.com (October 16, 2000)

Finis: "I'm not going to say I'll never write anything to do with the world of Hogwarts ever again. Because I have often thought that (if I wrote) book eight, I think it would be right and proper that it should be a book whose royalties go to charity entirely. It could be the encyclopedia of the world (of Hogwarts) and then I could rid myself of every last lurking detail, but no: not a novel."

—Rowling in "Potter Author Knows How It Will All End," *Ananova* (December 2001)

Harry Potter: "He feels so real to me, I think it's going to break my heart to stop writing about him."

—Rowling quoted by Rosemary Goring in "Harry's Fame," *Scotland on Sunday* (January 17, 1999)

"The funny thing is that Harry came into my head almost completely formed. I saw him very, very clearly. I could see this skinny little boy with black hair, this weird scar on his forehead. I knew instantly that he was a wizard, but he didn't know that yet. Then I began to work out his background. That was the basic idea. He's a boy who is magic but doesn't yet know. So I'm thinking, well, how can he not know? So I worked backwards from that point. It was almost like the story was already there waiting for me to find it. It seemed to me [that] the most watertight explanation for him not knowing that he was a wizard was that his parents had been a witch and a wizard who had died and that he had been raised by Muggles, non-magic people."

—Rowling in an interview, *Connection* (October 12, 1999)

Job change: "Rowling also revealed that, when she decided to quit her teaching job and write full time, she announced her departure to her students, who were mainly from working-class backgrounds. She said one student asked her, 'Miss, are you going on the dole?' 'No,' she replied. 'I've got another career.' There was a pause, and then another student asked, 'Miss, are you going to be a stripper?' Rather than give the boy detention on her last day there, she thanked him for the compliment."

—Mark McGarrity from his profile on Rowling in "Harry Potter's Creator Meets Her Public," *Star-Ledger* (October 16, 1999)

Literature: "There are two books whose final lines make me cry without fail, irrespective of how many times I read them, and one is *Lolita*. There is so much I could say about this book. There just isn't enough time to discuss how a plot that could have been the most worthless pornography becomes, in Nabokov's hands, a great and tragic love story, and I could exhaust my reservoir of superlatives trying to describe the quality of the writing."

—Rowling quoted by Sarah-Kate Templeton in "How Lolita Inspired Harry Potter," *Sunday Herald* (May 21, 2000)

Magic rules: "There is legislation about what you can conjure and what you can't. Something that you can conjure out of thin air will not last. This is a rule I set down for myself early on. I love these logical questions!"

—Rowling quoted on swns.com

Jessica Mitford: "My most influential writer, without a doubt, is Jessica Mitford. When my great-aunt gave me *Hons and Rebels* when I was 14, Mitford instantly became my heroine. She ran away from home to fight in the Spanish Civil War, taking with her a camera that she had charged to her father's account. I wished I'd had the nerve to do something like that. . . . I think I've read everything she wrote. I even called my daughter after her."

—Rowling, quoted by Lindsey Fraser in "Harry and Me," *Scotsman* (November 9, 2002)

Muggle: "I think I derived 'Muggle' from the word 'mug,' which in Britain means a stupid person or a fellow who's easy to dupe."

—Rowling quoted by Roxanne Feldman in "The Truth about Harry," *School Library Journal* (September 1, 1999)

Names: "I used to collect names of plants that sounded witchy, and then I found this, *Culpeper's Complete Herbal,* and it was the answer to my every prayer: flaxweed, toadflax, fleewort, goutwort, grommel, knot grass, mugwort."

—Rowling quoted by Ed Bradley and Lesley Stahl in "Harry Potter Book Sales Skyrocket around the World," CBS' *60 Minutes* (September 12, 1999)

Nicolson's café: "It is an escapist book and by writing it I was escaping into it. I would go to Nicolson's café, because the staff were so nice and so patient there and allowed me to order one expresso and sit there for hours, writing until Jessica woke up. You can get a hell of a lot of writing done in two hours if you know that's the only chance you are going to get."

—Rowling quoted by Judith Woods in "Coffee in One Hand, Baby in Another—A Recipe for Success," *Scotsman* (November 20, 1997)

Practice: "I know this sounds like a teacher, but remember, I was a teacher before I began the Harry books. This is what works for me: First you must read, then practice, and always plan. Read as much as you can, because that teaches you what good writing is. Then, when you write, you will find your-self imitating your favorite writers, but that's OK, because it is part of the learning process. You will go on to find your own personal voice and style. Writing is like learning an instrument. When you are learning guitar, you expect to hit bum notes. And when you practice writing, you are going to write rubbish before you hit your stride. I know this sounds terribly boring, but it is much more productive to plan out exactly where you want to go when you sit down to write about something."

—Rowling quoted by Stephanie Loer in "All about Harry Potter, from Quidditch to the Future of the Sorting Hat," *Boston Globe* (October 18, 1999)

Romanticized: "Some articles written about me have come close to roman-ticising the time I spent on income support. The well-worn cliché of the writer starving in the garret is so much more picturesque than the bitter real-ity of living in poverty with a child."

—Rowling quoted in "Harry Potter Author: I Was Humiliated by Poverty," *Ananova* (May 20, 2002)

Sequels: "My terror when I first met the publisher after they'd taken the book was that they wouldn't ask for sequels. Because I had seven mapped, and I had boxloads of stuff on Harry."

—Rowling quoted by Rosemary Goring in "Harry's Fame," *Scotland on Sunday* (January 17, 1999)

Serendipity: "I don't know. It really is the weirdest thing. I was on a train journey in 1990 and the idea just came to me out of nowhere. It was really as though it just fell into my head. I have no idea where it came from."

—Rowling quoted in "Rowling Discusses the Adventures of Harry Potter," *CBS News: This Morning* (June 28, 1999)

Shameful secret: "It was a secret. People at the office used to ask me if I was coming down to the pub and I would say that I was going shopping. And then they would ask me what I had bought! I just felt embarrassed about saying, well, actually I'm writing a book. I've met so many people in bars who say they are writing a book and it means that they've written down a few ideas in a notebook. . . . I thought, I am the luckiest person in the world. I am now being paid to do what I have been doing my whole life for nothing. I can sit here and know that this book is actually going to be published. Then I suddenly realised: I am a writer. I'm being paid for it now. This is not my secret shameful habit that I don't tell anyone about any longer."

—Rowling quoted by Ann Treneman in "Joanne Rowling's Secret Is Out," *Independent* (November 21, 1997)

Slush pile: "These things can sit in a pile for ages. They're known as the slush pile. They're the unsolicited and, you know, it's the also-rans usually. And just by chance, two days afterwards, I picked up this pile and went to a lunch because somebody was turning up late. And inside, I started reading about Harry Potter and, you know, my toes curled."

—Christopher Little quoted in "The Magic behind Harry Potter," CBSNEWS.com (June 15, 2003)

Smarties prize: "It's a particularly wonderful award to win from my point of view, because the final judging is done by children, and they are obviously the people whose opinion matters to me most."

—Rowling quoted in "Children Pick Winner of $2,500 Literary Prize," *Herald* (November 19, 1997)

Stereotyping: "I was portrayed as a penniless, divorced, single mother, pushing a buggy round Edinburgh, on income support, and writing in play parks and cafés while the baby slept. Yes, of course I realise it was good copy—and yes, it was true; but I resented the reporter's implication that I should have gone out and got a proper job instead of sitting around writing. It wasn't a soft option. Not many people would have put up with those conditions. And then, just as I was able to feel secure for the very first time since my daughter was born, I was defined by what was in many ways the saddest part of my life. It was hard enough at the time, without having to relive it. It was dreadful—for a long time it stopped me writing. But don't get me started on that."

—Rowling quoted by Joanna Carey in "Who Hasn't Met Harry?" *Guardian Unlimited* (February 16, 1999)

Unauthorized biography by Sean Smith: "J. K. Rowling, the notoriously private author of the Harry Potter children's books, has reacted furiously to the publication of a new biography which rakes over her failed marriage, her miscarriage, and claims she fell out with her father when he remarried."

—From "Rowling Mad about Biography Published in September 2001," *Scotland on Sunday* (September 2001)

Writer?: "One of her pupils eventually discovered she was writing a book. The girl had turned up without pen or paper; Rowling gave her the obligatory telling off and sent her to get some from the notepad on her desk. 'She was ages at the desk, and I turned round and said, "Maggie, will you come back and sit down," and she went (putting on a Jean Brodie voice) "Miss, are you a writer?"' Rowling felt embarrassed, exposed. 'I think I said, "No, it's just a hobby."'"

—Rowling quoted by Simon Hattenstone in "Harry, Jessie, and Me," *Guardian* (July 8, 2000)

Writing: "My ideal writing space is a large café with a small corner table near a window overlooking an interesting street (for gazing out of in search of inspiration). It would serve very strong coffee and be non-smoking (because I've now given up for two years and don't want to be tempted) and nobody would notice me at all. But I can't write in cafés any more because I would get recognized a lot."

—Rowling quoted by Brian Ferguson in "J. K. Rowling's Fame Spoils Her Café Culture," *Edinburgh Evening News* (February 6, 2003)

Writing as career: "You've got to persevere, because it's a career with a lot of knock-backs, but the rewards are huge. It's the best thing in the world. Very rewarding. But it's not a career for people who are easily discouraged, that's for sure. And for their parents, don't tell them it's unrealistic. Never say that."

—Rowling interviewed by Sean Bowler at a public talk at the National Press Club (October 20, 1999)

Writing fame: "I am rarely recognized and I am very happy about that, because I like being an anonymous person! It usually happens when I'm writing in cafés, because the connection between me and cafés is strongly imprinted in Edinburgh people's minds. Occasionally I have handed over my credit card and people have recognised the name, which is a very comfortable level of recognisability. One shop assistant told me she had taken the second *Harry* book to read on her honeymoon! The most embarrassing occasion was when I took my daughter to see *A Bug's Life* with some friends, and a woman with a party of a dozen little girls asked me if she could take a picture of me with all her charges."

—Rowling quoted in "Harry Potter: An Interview with J. K. Rowling," Scholastic website (Fall 2000)

Writing for children: "If at the end of my life I had only ever published for children, I would in no way see that as second best. Not at all. I feel no need to write my Serious Adult Book."

—Rowling quoted by Emily Gordon in "The Magic of Harry Potter," *Newsday* (October 19, 1999)

Part Three:
Harry Potter–
Screen Magic

Tim Kirk

It is every writer's worst dream come true, a nightmarish situation: Hollywood beckons, siren-like, with buckets of money and honeyed words. Sell us your novel, they whisper, and we'll take you to the next level of success. Just sign on the dotted line and we'll make all your dreams comes true.

The reality, as far too many novelists have found out, is far different, and more sobering. A novel that took years to write must be compressed into a film script of 120 double-spaced pages. It takes a craftsman to distill the novel's essence and translate it into a screenplay, a dedicated director to translate it faithfully to the big screen, and an army of people behind the scenes to bring it all together.

For a few years Rowling resisted the blandishments of Hollywood. Rather than see her novels twisted out of shape, beyond all recognition, she tenaciously held onto the film and merchandising rights, until Warner Bros. finally won her hard-earned confidence.

Thus far four of the movies have appeared—careful translations of the wonderful texts, with casting perfection. Warner Bros. has pulled it off. They've delivered on their promise to Rowling to remain faithful to the books, and they've delivered on their promise to the fans, to give them the best movie-going experience money can buy and talent can assemble.

The Power of Imagination:
The Reality of Fantasy in Harry Potter

In the wake of the huge success of *The Lord of the Rings: The Return of the King,* the final installment of Peter Jackson's film trilogy based on J. R. R. Tolkien's novel, Hollywood and jaded critics alike have expressed surprise that fantasy is suddenly hot.

In truth, it isn't "suddenly" hot, it's *always* been hot. Of the 30 top-grossing movies of all time, only three are not fantasy, science fiction, comic-book related, or animated.

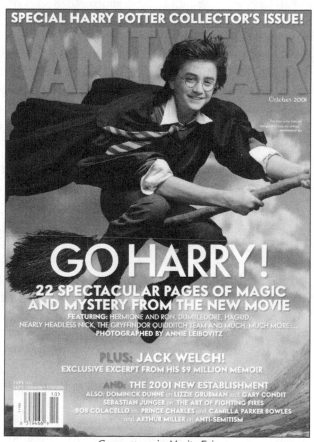

Cover story in *Vanity Fair*

As expected, the Harry Potter films are on the list. In terms of ranking,

Sorcerer's Stone is #4, *Goblet of Fire* is #8, *Chamber of Secrets* is #10, and *Azkaban* is #17. A sure thing: *Order of the Phoenix* will make the list as well.

In terms of a film franchise, Harry Potter will ultimately eclipse *The Lord of the Rings* for the simple reason that *Rings* is comprised of three films, whereas the Potter novels will, when completed, comprise seven films, each building on the success of its predecessors. Simply put, Rowling's Harry Potter novels will likely be the most successful film franchise in motion picture history, which is why executives at major film studios ardently wooed Rowling. Unlike most authors, she was initially cool to all overtures, including those from Warner Bros., the studio that eventually secured the Potter film franchise. At stake: not millions but *billions* of dollars.

Like other writers, Rowling had seen too many bad movies adapted from good books and was adamant that her novels not suffer the same fate. Better not to have a movie at all, she decided, than to have a bad one. The money was not an issue, but fidelity to the source material would be the key to unlocking the door to the Potter film franchise.

When Warner Bros. finally secured the rights, which included the lucrative merchandising rights estimated to be worth a billion dollars alone, the studio faced a situation in the marketplace similar to that faced by another studio, New Line Cinema, when it announced its film trilogy *The Lord of the Rings*.

The established base of readers, numbering in the millions, was protective of the author and the works, and if the early buzz on the Internet from the hard-core fans were unenthusiastic or, worse, condemnatory, it would prove to be a major obstacle. Again, as with *The Lord of the Rings*, the Harry Potter film franchise wasn't a gamble with merely one film but with several. The upside gain, however attractive, was soberly balanced by the downside risk. The studio could stand to make, or lose, a fortune.

As soon as the first Potter film was announced, fans chimed in on the Internet with the usual concerns. Who would be the director? Who would be cast? How close would the film hew to the book? Harry Potter fans were anxious to see a film adaptation, but only if it served the source material.

To make the first Harry Potter film a success, it would require a faithful screenplay, a committed director, state-of-the-art special effects, and, most important of all, a hand-picked cast that would forever be imprinted in the imaginations of Potter fans worldwide.

The common bond shared by all was a desire to meet, or exceed, the expectations of a hard-to-please worldwide fan base.

The screenwriter, Steve Kloves, worked hand-in-hand with Rowling to ensure that the book would be faithfully translated to the screen. It would be a real challenge, since the first Harry Potter book necessarily gets off to a slow start, establishing its back story and laying the groundwork for the six books to follow.

As with *The Lord of the Rings,* state-of-the-art special effects were necessary to give a realistic "look" to the first Potter film. With the $126 million budget for the film, however, that wouldn't be a problem. But even with a first-rate script and a big budget, the principal component to success would be the casting. Early on, when Steven Spielberg expressed an interest in helming the project, his choice for the pivotal role of Harry Potter was an American child actor, Haley Joel Osment, a fine actor but not whom Rowling had envisioned. To be true to the book, the film, she insisted, would not only have to be shot on location in England but have an all-British cast.

In hindsight, the casting was perfect. In fact, two of the crucial roles were filled by children with little or no prior acting experience: Emma Watson in the role of Hermione Granger and Rupert Grint in the role of Ron Weasley.

The key role of Harry Potter was, as one would expect, the most difficult to fill. The casting director screened 16,000 child actors, but none of them fit the bill. Then, two months before principal shooting was scheduled to begin, Steve Kloves (screenwriter) and David Heyman (producer) were in a movie theatre and saw Daniel Radcliffe in the audience. They knew they had found the right boy to play Harry Potter—a conviction reinforced when the screen test showed Radcliffe's considerable acting strengths.

The casting for the supporting roles of the faculty members at Hogwarts was relatively easy, since there was a large pool of adult talent from which to draw. Among them, the late Richard Harris as Dumbledore, Alan Rickman as Professor Snape, Maggie Smith as Professor McGonagall, and Robbie Coltrane as gameskeeper Rubeus Hagrid.

Throughout the entire process of filming, the common ingredient found among all—the actors, screenwriter, producers, and director—was a passion to get everything right, to translate Rowling's words faithfully to the big screen in a way that would satisfy not only the hard-core fans but the larger body of general filmgoers who would be new to Rowling's world.

When the trailer was finally released, the response was positive. Fans enthusiastically endorsed director Chris Columbus, who would go on to direct the second Harry Potter film, as well. (He declined to helm the third movie, citing the enormous strain and commitment required. It was time, he affirmed, for someone else to carry the torch.)

Any fears harbored by Warner Bros. over its substantial investment evaporated when the early reviews, mostly positive, came in. Early box-office receipts were also impressive, with a worldwide gross of $975 million dollars, second only to the box-office take of *Titanic.*

Supported by a well-orchestrated marketing and promotion campaign, and backed up with a selective merchandising line to complement the movie,

Barnes & Noble store display
of Harry Potter books

Harry Potter and the Sorcerer's Stone convincingly recreated Rowling's fictional universe with remarkable fidelity.

Rowling's magical world coexists with our own, populated with characters who, though able to draw on magic to help them get through life, deal with the usual problems of being human that magic cannot solve—the ache of losing one's parents, the sacrifices one makes for friends, the bonds of respect found in the student-teacher relationship, the difficulty in confronting one's fears, and the realization that in life hard choices must be made and their consequences accepted.

All of these are underscored by a scene in the movie when Harry, for the first time, sees his parents in the Mirror of Erised, which shows him that which he wants more than anything. Since his parents died when he was an infant, Harry has no memory of them.

As Rowling fans know, that scene came from the heart, for Rowling had lost her own mother, who never lived to see her daughter become the world's best-selling author, or to see her two grandchildren.

At the heart of Rowling's wonderful first novel is a heartfelt story of a boy who discovers his potential and is destined to take his rightful place in the wizarding world.

In book seven, Harry Potter will graduate from Hogwarts. It will be a moment of mixed emotions: a happy moment for readers who will have waited many years for that pivotal event, tempered by sadness because of the realization that there will be no more tales of the boy wizard. Though it's fun to contemplate the prospects of Harry Potter as an Auror, a professor or a headmaster at Hogwarts, or the Minister of Magic—imagine how that would infuriate Draco Malfoy!—the fact remains that Rowling is not likely to change her mind, to the infinite regret of her millions of readers worldwide.

Tim Kirk

Notable and Quotable: Film Quips

Films live and die on their casting.
—*Director Peter Jackson, who helmed the Tolkien film trilogy
(from the appendices of the extended DVD of* The Two Towers*)*

Acting is an interpretive art in which the best actors not only step into the roles and become the characters they portray, but also bring something of themselves to help bring the character to life.

The casting is key, as director Peter Jackson affirms: Pick the right person for the right role and the film will come alive.

All of the Potter films to date have benefited from superb casting choices.

To promote the films, the actors have collectively given hundreds of interviews, from which I've drawn the quotes that appear here, with my comments on the casting.

Sean Biggerstaff as Oliver Wood. The Quidditch team captain, Wood, an upperclassman, is confident and exudes a take-charge air as befitting his position. Sean Biggerstaff is a natural, giving a novice Harry Potter the benefit of his experience in Quidditch. A good performance with just the right touch of humor.

Biggerstaff got his first break when veteran actor Alan Rickman saw him in a production of *Macbeth* and recommended him to the casting director of the Harry Potter films.

Biggerstaff on his film character: "He's very sporty, slightly eccentric, and very passionate about Quidditch. Wanting to win the Quidditch House Cup is like the Holy Grail for him." (Quoted in *16 Magazine,* November 2001.)

David Bradley as Argus Filch. The caretaker of Hogwarts, Filch is a rather nasty man. He longs for the good old days when he could mete out positively medieval discipline—hanging students by their thumbs in the dungeon (or so he says). Less concerned with the student body, he seems more concerned about the welfare of his cat, Mrs. Norris. When someone puts a petrifying spell on her, it pushes him over the edge emotionally. He angrily names Harry Potter as the culprit and demands immediate justice. Ever so patiently, Dumbledore explains that the petrification is only temporary; Madam Pomfrey, the school nurse, will be able to administer the potion necessary to restore Mrs. Norris to her former state.

Bradley is a delightfully cantankerous caretaker, who brings his obnoxious characteristics to life.

Bradley on book five: "I heard that writer J. K. Rowling had killed off one of the characters in her last book and that she had cried afterwards, and I thought, 'Well, it can't be Filch—no one would cry over him.'" (Quoted by Marion McMullen in "Potter Villain Is Out for Blood," online at: http://icCoventry.co.uk, September 12, 2003.)

Kenneth Branagh portraying Professor Gilderoy Lockhart. Although Lockhart only briefly appears in book five, he steals the show in book two, *Harry Potter and the Chamber of Secrets.*

The first choice was Hugh Grant, who no doubt would have given a fine performance, but Branagh is now indelibly imprinted in our collective minds' eye, with his over-the-top performance. Flamboyantly dressed—he's quite the natty dresser—and full of himself, Branagh hams it up and hogs the limelight.

Branagh plays the role to the hilt and lends a much-needed humorous touch to an increasingly dark series of books.

Branagh on his film character: "Gilderoy Lockhart is a fantastically successful wizard and writer of many famous books which are now being used as textbooks at Hogwarts School. He is very much admired by the female students, which is very irritating to the boys. He is a narcissist, a gadfly, very full of himself, and faintly idiotic. But he can be rather touching at times. He amuses and intrigues us. Is he or isn't he a good guy? He is certainly a strange peacock of a man. (From "Interview with Kenneth Branagh" at countingdown.com, September 15, 2002.)

John Cleese as Nearly Headless Nick. Funnyman Cleese is perhaps best known for his work as part of the comedy troupe Monty Python, so it's no surprise that Cleese plays with brio the part of one of the ghosts that delightfully haunts Hogwarts. A haughty ghost whose head literally hangs by a thread, Cleese plays the role with the right touch of nobility, as befitting the ghost's lineage—Sir Nicholas de Mimsy Porpington.

Robbie Coltrane as groundskeeper and keykeeper Rubeus Hagrid. Standing eight feet, six inches tall in the novels (according to Rowling), Hagrid is a giant among men, physically and literally. In the film Coltrane must portray the gentle giant who can simultaneously show his strength and his compassion—two sides of a man of seeming contradictions. Coltrane brings a presence to this critical role, one that Rowling reportedly considered to be a crucial one in terms of casting. Larger than life, Coltrane plays the role of Hagrid to the hilt and convinces us that he's just an overgrown kid who dotes on Albus Dumbledore, whom he looks upon as a father figure.

Coltrane on his role: "I've seen the movie and, believe me, it looks fantastic and is so true and honest to the book." (Quoted by Louis B. Hobson in "Magic Monsters Set Loose" in the *Calgary Sun,* November 5, 2001.)

Christian Coulson as student Tom Riddle (Lord Voldemort). Coulson portrays the diabolical Lord Voldemort, whose given name was abandoned because of his Muggle heritage on his father's side. Coulson appears at the end of book two, when he announces that he is the true heir of Salazar Slytherin—not Harry Potter, which most students mistakenly believed.

Coulson provides a solid performance as an angry young man who has patiently bided his time to bedevil the wizarding world.

Coulson on his new fame: "It hasn't really changed me. People don't recognise me. Not long ago I walked past a group of people who had just seen the film, and were talking about Tom Riddle. They clocked me but had no idea who I was. That was kind of nice in a way. I can't imagine what life would be like if you couldn't take a bus or ride on the tube." (Quoted from a press conference for the first film in London prior to its release, from BBCi Films: Interviews on www.bbc.co.uk, undated.)

Warwick Davis as Professor Filius Flitwick and a goblin bank teller. Although the roles are quite different—a charming, diminutive professor who teaches charms at Hogwarts, and a goblin of serious mien at Gringotts, the wizard bank—Davis plays both well. A solid, creditable performance by an underappreciated actor, Davis's sympathetic portrayal of Professor Flitwick is delightful to see.

Davis on his role: "We were filming the Great Hall scene. I looked to my left, and I saw Maggie Smith, Alan Rickman, and Richard Harris; and then, on my right, I saw Robbie Coltrane. I thought to myself, 'It doesn't get any better than this.'" (Quoted from "Exclusive Interview with Professor Flitwick" on the website entertainment-rewired.com, November 15, 2001.)

Tom Felton as Draco Malfoy. The arch nemesis of Harry Potter, Draco Malfoy is not only a rich snob of the worst sort, but also prejudiced to the extreme. Proud of his heritage as a pureblood, Malfoy is a supercilious boy whose chief goal in life is to act as a foil to Harry Potter. After Harry becomes the Seeker for Gryffindor, it is no great surprise when Draco becomes the Seeker for Slytherin, so the two are pitted once again, not on the ground but in aerial combat.

Felton, as a actor, has a difficult challenge in portraying Malfoy because the character is essentially "flat." That is to say, the character is one-dimensional fictionally. He is always the bad egg, the one who insults Harry at every opportunity and sneers at Hermione Granger and anyone else he considers inferior. (It's worth noting that it is Granger, not Malfoy, who shines academically.)

Felton plays the role with a delicious evilness, a biting sneer, and a look of unrivaled contempt on his face at Potty and the Weasel, his nicknames for Harry Potter and Ron Weasley.

More a caricature than a fully developed character, Malfoy serves his purpose all too well, but one would wish for a more rounded character, so we could see Felton stretch himself as an actor in a role that, despite its one-note tone, is a fan favorite.

Felton on his role: "Inevitably, people have the impression that I'm as mean and nasty as Malfoy. The worst is the reaction of little kids. When five- or six-year-old fans see me, they often start to cry. They're terrified because they think I'm really Malfoy. They don't make the distinction between the actor and the character. One time, Chris Columbus's kids ran away when they saw me! [laughs] These reactions make me a little angry, but at least it proves I was con-vincing in my role. That's gratifying enough." (Quoted from an interview posted on an HP fan website, original source: *One Magazine,* November 2003.)

Ralph Fiennes as Lord Voldemort. Who can forget Fiennes's riveting role as Nazi concentration camp commandant Amoth Goeth in *Shindler's List?* Fiennes's interpretation of the clinically detached Goeth likely went a long way toward convincing the casting director for *Harry Potter and the Goblet of Fire* that he was the right actor to play the demanding, and pivotal, role of Lord Voldemort, who is at the dark heart of the Harry Potter novels.

Fiennes and his Death Eaters are among the scariest of all creations in fic-tion—scary enough to spook the King of Horror, Stephen King, who admitted as much to Rowling in the presence of 6,000 fans at Radio City Music Hall dur-ing a combined reading with John Irving—and Fiennes's performance in this film does not disappoint. He is truly awful, in the best sense of that word.

At movies.about.com, Ralph Fiennes tells Rebecca Murray that "I don't have a fan's investment in the books myself. I like the books. I admire the world of the books and the characters that she's created, but I'm not, as it were, an addict of 'Harry Potter.'"

On playing (again) an evil character, Fiennes told Murray, "Well, that was one of the blessings of a part like this where you're meant to be playing the distillation of evil, whatever that is, which can be anything. I think the one thing we were aiming for was a sort of question, a certain amount of unpredictability in him, so no one quite knows what he's going to do or say next, which I hope makes him slightly sort of dangerous."

Michael Gambon as Albus Dumbledore. The late Richard Harris had committed to the film series but passed on before the third began principal photography.

Gambon on his new, challenging role: "My friends' children come round and see me now, which they never did before. I'm getting letters from all over the world and kids knock on my front door, which is a bit of a nuisance, but you have to keep smiling and be nice. Being Dumbledore is a big responsibility." (Quoted by John Hiscock in "Dumbledore Makes Gambon Kids' Favourite" from News.Scotsman.com, as cited in *Showbiz Digest*, September 29, 2003.)

Brendan Gleeson as Professor Alastor "Mad-Eye" Moody. If there's one new character who steals the show, it's "Mad-Eye" Moody portrayed by Brendan Gleeson. In the film, actor Rupert Grint, as Ron Weasley, says, "Brilliant, isn't he? Completely demented, of course. Terrifying to be in the same room with him."

That's a pretty accurate assessment. In a brief film clip from www.ropes ofsilicon.com, Gleeson, on set and taking a break from the filming, explains his character's battered and world-weary physical appearance: "He's literally been through the wars and he's shaken."

Larger than life, forceful, and every bit a figure who has suffered numerous scars, both physical and psychic, Gleeson brings a manic intensity to the role, which is appropriate, considering the character's past: A legendary Auror, Moody lives up to his namesake, and then some. Fortunately, he's on the good side. . . .

Richard Griffiths as Vernon Dursley, Harry Potter's uncle. Griffiths is convincing in this role. The books portray Vernon as an unimaginative man who has never liked, and will never accept, Harry Potter in his life. Though he begrudgingly accepts Harry into his home, it's clear in book one that Uncle Vernon wants to keep Harry in his place. Harry's place, of course, is in the cupboard under the stairs, which is symbolic of Vernon's feelings: the cupboard is where you store things to keep them out of sight.

Griffiths portrays the blustery Vernon Dursley to perfection. We, as viewers, are absolutely convinced this is Vernon Dursley, the uncle from Hell.

Griffiths on the books: "The stories are becoming more dark and I think that's what makes them more attractive. Because the people that saw the first movie were 13- and 14-year-olds, they're growing along with the story. So it's natural of movies to also grow, and become more complex and mature. Of course there will always be new children of ten years, to see the first movie and repeat the cycle. They wouldn't be able to use the same people and repeat the stories changing just a little. It wouldn't be fun." (Quoted on a HP fan website, zanzaro.com, from Omelete.com during a launch party for the second film, undated.)

Rupert Grint as Ron Weasley. Among the cast of characters, three are critical: Harry Potter, Ron Weasley, and Hermione Granger. Of the three, only Rupert Grint has no prior film experience, which makes his standout status all the more remarkable. In the books, Ron is Harry's best friend. The youngest boy in a wizard family long on love but short on money, Ron gets the family hand-me-downs and is used to a life of genteel poverty. Actor Rupert Grint plays Ron Weasley to perfection. By turns self-effacing, incredulous, fearful, or angry as the occasion requires, Grint's nuanced performance brings Ron Weasley from page to film screen with astonishing fidelity. Unaffected, unabashedly normal in every way, with the right touch of regret at having been born in a poor wizarding family, Grint as Weasley is picture-perfect. He is my favorite among all the child actors in the Potter films. In short, bloody brilliant!

Grint on his role: "It all started when I was watching this English children's television programme called *Newsround*. The show told you how to audition for a part in Harry Potter and so I sent in a letter because I really wanted to play the part of Ron. But, for weeks I heard nothing. So, I was looking on the *Newsround* website one day and saw how another kid had sent a video of himself. So, my mum helped me to make an audition tape with me doing a rap of how much I wanted to be in the film, reading some lines as Ron which I wrote myself and also dressing up as my drama teacher. That was the most embarrassing part as she's a woman! I sent it in and the next thing I knew I was being called by the casting director. And then I was doing screen tests! And then I got the part!" (From a fan website, rupertgrint.net, undated.)

Richard Harris as Albus Dumbledore. The late Richard Harris defined the character on screen. The book takes great pains to establish the character as one of worldly wisdom and restraint. We know, for instance, that he's held in wide regard among the wizarding community and considered the only one who could face, and best, Lord Voldemort in a wizards' duel. (Who, one wonders, would be Dumbledore's second? I'd vote for Alastor Moody.)

Harris fits his role like a hand in a racing glove. It's hard to imagine anyone filling his considerable shoes, but Michael Gambon is likely up to the challenge. Even still, everyone will fondly remember Harris as Dumbledore from the first two Potter films as the wise wizard and father figure for Harry Potter, a role he brought to life.

Harris on the child actors in the film series: "They're very good, actually. They were terrific. What amazed me about them was that they were so confident. They weren't intimidated by anything, like Maggie Smith or myself, or Robbie Coltrane, or anybody. I was kind of enamoured by it." (Quoted in a profile by Claire Bickley in the *Toronto Sun,* November 13, 2001.)

Harris's commitment to the film series: "That huge commitment caused him to turn the role down at first, but the production had a secret agent close to him to change his mind. The books were the favourites of Harris' then 11-year-old granddaughter Ella.

"She called me up and she said to me, 'If you don't do it, I'll never speak to you again.' So I said, 'Okay, I'll do it.'

"Ella spent two days on the film's set and has a background role as a student in a Hogwarts dining hall scene." (Profile by Claire Bickley in the *Toronto Sun,* November 13, 2001.)

Ian Hart as Professor Quirrell. People are sometimes not w-w-w-what they s-s-s-seem. Case in point: The stuttering Professor Quirrell, the new Defense against the Dark Arts teacher in the first year Harry Potter attends Hogwarts. Quirrell first meets Harry at the Leaky Cauldron, where the young boy wizard is surprised that everyone there not only knows his name but respects him—a hitherto unknown experience, since he's used to being ignored or mistreated. Hart delivers a noteworthy performance as a disarming admirer of Harry Potter and one who, when faced with the prospect of a troll on the loose in Hogwarts, faints in fear.

At the end of the first film, he shows himself as he actually is: Far from being a stuttering, squeamish professor, he's actually someone far more powerful, allied to the dark side.

Hart on his audition: "Even before my audition, there were several pages missing from my script because those bits were so unbelievably secret not even I was allowed to see them. I'm not usually attracted to big-budget American films. . . . I only decided to do this one because it's a different kind of role. There are a lot of special effects in the film so, from a technical point of view, it was a challenge." (From "Wild at Heart" in *Nova* magazine, June 2001.)

Shirley Henderson as Moaning Myrtle (a student-turned-ghost). Although ghosts haunt Hogwarts, most roam throughout the entire building—all except one: Moaning Myrtle, who hangs out in the girl's bathroom, where she died under suspicious circumstances. Myrtle's nickname is apt, since she bemoans her fate and laments her early, and unforeseen, passage into the spirit world. (She is, in fact, the only student-turned-ghost.)

Actress Shirley Henderson steps perfectly into the role of Moaning Myrtle, with the right tone of indignation and sorrow, balanced by righteous anger at her lamentable circumstances. She didn't choose death—it chose her.

Sweet on Harry but harsh on Ron, Moaning Myrtle, stuck in limbo, has made her troubled peace with her life as a ghost.

Henderson (aged 37) on her role: "I loved Harry Potter, but I thought it was crazy me getting a part in it. I didn't think I'd get it because she's a schoolgirl. It was great fun: When you're a ghost, you're flying through the air in a harness and it's quite physical. I'd never done any special effects before." (Quoted from the newspaper website scotsman.com, August 19, 2003.)

Joshua Herdman as Gregory Goyle. A crony of Draco Malfoy, Goyle is an appendage of Draco.

John Hurt as Mr. Ollivander. The proprietor of Ollivander's Wand Shop, which is a store frozen in time, has a remarkable memory. Remembering every wand he's ever sold, he tells Harry Potter that he distinctly remembers selling wands to his parents, and wondered when the son would show up to get his wand.

Hurt plays the part as if he's been in the business of selling wands for a long time. Picking among the many boxes of wands in his store, he finally finds the *only* wand for Harry—a wand he was destined to own.

Though only on the screen briefly, Hurt more than fits the bill: He is tailor-made as a storekeeper in Diagon Alley.

Hurt on acting: "Well, yes, pretending to be other people is my game and that to me is the essence of the whole business of acting." (Quoted by Geoff Andrew in the *Guardian*, April 27, 2000.)

Stanislav Ianevski as the Bulgarian Seeker, Viktor Krum, a final year student from Durmstrang Institute. In his screen debut, Ianevski perfectly fits the role of Viktor Krum, who makes a dramatic appearance in *Harry Potter and the Goblet of Fire*. In the lead position, he flies into the stadium hosting the Quidditch World Cup competition, flanked by his fellow Quidditch teammates. Ianevski does a dramatic front-to-back flip on his broom as he soars around the stadium, to the delight and amazement of all, especially an awestruck Ronald Weasley who breathlessly proclaims, "There's no one like Krum. He's like a bird the way he rides the wind. He's more than an athlete—he's an artist!"

From *Sugar Magazine*, Ianeveski on Krum: "He's a mixture of good and bad. I think he's more of a good guy, but some spells are cast on him to make him look bad. But he falls in love with Hermione, so he must have a soft side. . . ."

Jason Isaacs as Lucius Malfoy. A confident wizard with supercilious manners, Lucius is the father of Draco Malfoy—not surprisingly, like father, like son. The father is contemptuous of any witch or wizard not born in a wizarding family; purebloods like himself, he believes, are the only ones worthy of being taught magic. Non-magic witches and wizards shouldn't even be allowed to enroll at Hogwarts—"mudbloods," he derisively calls them.

Jason Isaacs is memorable as Lucius Malfoy. Fearsome when angry, placating when necessary, politically suave as the situation dictates, he exhibits a range of emotion that we don't see in his son, Draco, who walks around Hogwarts with a perpetual sneer and an insulting manner whenever he sees Harry Potter or his friends.

Knowing what will happen in book five, all one can say about Jason Isaacs is that we expect a great performance from him, and he will surely deliver.

Isaacs on his role: "I probably shouldn't mention this in public, but [Rowling] has actually sent me an early draft of the next book, which is called *Harry Potter and the Chronicles of Lucius,* which is all about Lucius's early romantic adventures. She's warned me it might change before publication, so I'll wait and see." (Quoted by Alec Cawthorne in "Harry Potter and the Chamber of Secrets" from BBCi Films Interviews, November 2002.)

Toby Jones as the voice of Dobby the house-elf. A wonderfully realized character, Dobby appears on the scene as a hand-wringing, deeply concerned elf who will stop at nothing to prevent Harry Potter from returning to school for his second year—an attempt that is doomed to failure, but not before Dobby uses all the powers at his command to dissuade, then physically bar, Harry, even at the risk of injury.

Though CGI technology can create a computerized person, it cannot create that person's voice. In this regard, Toby Jones's voice blends seamlessly with Dobby, a downtrodden house-elf who is overly emotional when Harry Potter simply recognizes his existence and is minimally polite—a stark contrast to Dobby's usual condition of servitude, in which he's used, abused, and misused by the Malfoy family.

Toby Jones's voice ranges from contrite to adamant as the occasion dictates. I'm looking forward to seeing more of Dobby and hearing more of Jones.

Matthew Lewis as Neville Longbottom. Pertually put-upon, Longbottom, in the second movie, laments, "Why is it always me?" Unsure of himself and bedeviled by Slytherins, especially their head, Professor Snape, Longbottom's role is more than aptly filled by Matthew Lewis, who plays the part so convincingly that one wonders if the young actor had similar experiences in school. I suspect, though, that he's simply a good actor, and one whose role in the upcoming films will become increasingly visible and more important as he assumes his rightful place in the wizarding world.

Lewis on the scene in which Hermione Granger temporarily immobilizes him with a petrification spell: "I kept doing it and doing it—I even practised at home with my brother—but eventually they had to get a stunt man in because my legs kept flying up at the ends." (Quoted by Clare Youell in "Potter Boys Reveal COS Acting Secrets" from BBC Newsround, November 15, 2002.)

Miriam Margolyes as Professor Sprout. The professor of Herbology, Sprout is jovial and down to earth. Margolyes fittingly plays the part and makes us wish she had been given a bigger supporting role in the book and, therefore, the films. A delightful visual interpretation, Margolyes has certainly got at the root of the character.

Margolyes on her role: "It's a very friendly set. Chris Columbus, the director, has a sweet personality—he only looks about 12, actually. And the kids are delightful: they like each other very much. . . . I enjoyed myself a lot. . . . I was delighted with it: I was terribly good, and I think the film is terribly good." (From "Harry Potter Exclusive: Interview with Professor Sprout," a RealAudio interview conducted by Dominic King from www.bbc.co.uk, Radio Kent film, January 16, 2000.)

Harry Melling as Dudley Dursley. In real life Harry Melling is undoubtedly a prince of a fellow, a fine young lad, which is a stark contrast to the character he plays—a bullying git named Dudley Dursley, who enjoys bedeviling Harry Potter and making his life as miserable as possible. Dudley is a whining, obnoxious, self-centered brat of a boy, which Melling portrays to perfection. Given a choice of roles, Melling might prefer a more winsome role, but somebody's got to play the bad guy, and in this case Melling is very good as the very bad Dudley.

On his role: "It was fun playing the baddie, though—more challenging." (Quoted on an online site, www.thisisheartfordshire.co.uk, September 18, 2001.)

Gary Oldman as Sirius Black. I am twitching, I tell you, twitching with anticipation to see Oldman as Sirius Black. Though we only have a brief teaser to give us a taste of what is to come in June 2004, the snippets of footage with Oldman are delightful. I especially love the "WANTED" poster with Oldman laughing maniacally—the perfect touch—and the shot of him in Azkaban, as he turns his gaze toward the viewer.

In the third Potter film, Sirius Black is on center stage and in the spotlight, and I'm telling you now, even without the benefit of Professor Trelawney's crystal ball, I feel confident in saying that Oldman is going to steal the show. Something wicked—though not in an evil sense: think British slang—this way comes!

Robert Pattinson as Cedric Diggory. The Hogwarts champion who will compete in the Triwizard tournament, Diggory is described by Rowling as "an absurdly handsome 17-year-old," which is tough to live up to. Pattinson, however, effortlessly fits the description. He comes across in the film just as Rowling portrayed him: a confident, older student in Hufflepuff who is well regarded among his peers and proves his mettle in the Triwizard tournament, as well. On his role, Pattison told the BBC that "I think he's a pretty cool character. He's not really a complete cliché of the good kid in school. He's just quiet. He is actually just a genuinely good person, but he doesn't make a big deal about it or anything. He's just like, whatever. I can kind of relate to that. He's not an unattractive character at all and his storyline is a nice [one] to play."

James and Oliver Phelps as Fred and George Weasley. Twin brothers (obviously), they are perfectly cast as the Weasley twins, magical pranksters whose career goals are nontraditional. They want to make a living as full-time inventors and vendors of magical novelties.

Think of what a discussion around the Weasley dinner table must be like around O.W.L. time—Molly stressing the need to do well on the exams, Arthur automatically endorsing his wife's view, and Fred and George exchanging knowing glances, since they have no intention of following in their father's footsteps by joining the rank-and-file at the Ministry of Magic.

James and Oliver Phelps are a pure delight and, knowing what comes in book five, I'm very much looking forward to seeing them in that film, from the first practical joke on poor Dudley Dursley to their grand joke on Professor/High Inquisitor/Headmaster Dolores Umbridge.

On their roles. James: "It was a once in a lifetime experience, to see how it's created." Oliver: "Working alongside such big name actors was fantastic; it hasn't really sunk in yet." (From an interview on www.oliver-phelps.com, undated.)

Clémence Poésy as Fleur Delacour. Best known for her roles in several French movies, Poésy plays the impossibly beautiful and unobtainable Fleur Delacour, the kind of beautiful and irresistible girl at whom men throw themselves . . . in vain. In *Harry Potter and the Goblet of Fire*, Poésy comes across as beautiful and distant, but in the end proves to be warm and accessible.

On her role, Poésy told *Empire Online*: "She's a bit cold. She's the kind of girl I used to hate when I was in high school! She always has tons of people behind her, doing everything perfectly, which is impossible. I talked about it with Mike [the film's director] and said, 'Do you want it to be snobby?' and he was like, 'Oh, you know . . .' and I said, 'She's French, right?' and he said, 'Yeah, exactly!' Mike has got a great sense of humour and that's what's in the book; she's a bit of an image people might have about French girls!"

Daniel Radcliffe as Harry Potter. All the king's horses and all the king's men couldn't put this film franchise together again if the casting for Harry Potter weren't dead-on. A casting challenge on the scale of Everest, Harry Potter is so well defined in one's imagination, due in large part to the visual interpretations by Mary GrandPré, that it seemed nearly impossible to find a child actor who could fit the bill.

In fact, even after interviewing thousands of young boys, with principal shooting scheduled to begin in a few weeks, the key role remain unfulfilled, a casting director's nightmare.

By luck, Daniel Radcliffe showed up on the radar, though not in a way anyone had envisioned. He was sitting in the audience at a movie theater and providentially spotted.

Radcliffe is superb as Harry Potter. Perfectly cast, Radcliffe—no matter what else he does in the film community—will be forever remembered for his role as Harry Potter.

To watch Harry Potter in the books grow up is a reader's delight; and to watch Radcliffe's interpretation of the character in the film versions is a corresponding delight.

Daniel Radcliffe is an extraordinarily talented young actor who has carried the awesome (a word I use sparingly) responsibility of carrying the film series to date. These are films that gross nearly a billion dollars each!

If, as Rowling writes, the wand chooses the wizard, then it's not too far-fetched—especially under the circumstances under which the actor was discovered—to assume that the film picks the actor. In this case, it was an inspired choice and a wonderful performance by an indisputably gifted young man.

Rowling may have given us Harry Potter, but Radcliffe has *shown* us Harry, and done so brilliantly.

Radcliffe on Emma and Rupert: "We get along really well because we're all quite like our characters and Rupert's very funny, Emma's very intelligent, and I'm in between because that's how Harry is, I think." (Quoted from "Daniel Radcliffe: Full Interview," conducted by Lizo Mzimba, from BBC Newsround on: http://News.bbc.co.uk, October 24, 2002.)

Chris Rankin as Percy Weasley. The character of Percy Weasley is a good example of how Rowling has very carefully thought out how fictional characters should grow. The straight-laced, by-the-book Percy Weasley is professionally interpreted by Chris Rankin, who delivers a solid performance. Walking a thin line between being fussy and too stiff, Rankin has the right touch. For instance, in a scene from the first film, Percy encounters Draco Malfoy, who spies what he thinks are his cronies Crabbe and Goyle, who are in fact not. Percy walks up and puts Malfoy in his right place—a small but memorable moment.

A young man whose life is defined by rules, Percy is wonderfully brought to life by Chris Rankin.

Rankin on his role: "I feel very happy that people appreciate the work I do and who I am. I still think that I'm the same guy I was before Potter came along. I'm no celebrity, and I don't want to be. I like doing the work I do, it's just a job at the end of the day, and if people get enjoyment out of it—I've done the job well. Percy's a great character, so I'm not suprised there's websites about him!" (Quoted from "My Interview with Chris Rankin" by an uncredited staffer of a fan website, www.percyweasley.com, January 25, 2003.)

Miranda Richardson as tabloid reporter Rita Skeeter. As fans know, J. K. Rowling has had her fill (and then some) with adult reporters, who long ago began intruding in her life—banging on her door to demand interviews and ambushing her in public—to the point where she has had to literally take refuge behind the towering nine-foot wall that surrounds her Edinburgh home, protected by electronic security.

Rita Skeeter is, to Harry Potter, an annoying character buzzing around him in *Harry Potter and the Goblet of Fire,* always seeking a new angle that she can write about with a touch of exaggeration.

Dressed in a tight-fitting green outfit, sporting curly platinum blonde hair and ruby red lipstick, Richardson is without question a scene stealer, using a Quick Quotes Quill to dictate her imaginative stories.

On her role, she told www.timesonline.co.uk, "It's sort of irresistible to be part of this great leviathan that is Harry Potter. The sense is it's part of history, and for that reason it's great. As it would have been to be part of *The Lord of the Rings.* And I like the fact that kids everywhere are clutching a hardback book to their chests and huddling off into corners, getting absorbed in a new world."

In 2003, Richardson had a small "preview" of Hogwarts, spoofing Hermione Granger in a skit for Comic Relief. Her one regret is that one of her lines was dropped. In one scene, in which she's wearing a small replica of a key piece of Quidditch gear, she asks innocently, "Are you looking at my Snitch?"

According to Steve Vander Ark's website, the Harry Potter Lexicon, the Snitch is "a walnut-sized golden ball with silver wings, the most important of the four balls used in Quidditch. A Snitch is bewitched to avoid capture for as long as possible within the boundaries of the pitch. The capture of the Snitch ends the game and gives the team whose Seeker caught it 150 points, which usually determines which team wins the game."

Alan Rickman as Professor Severus Snape. Rickman is best known for his film roles as a bad guy—the Sheriff of Nottingham in *Robin Hood* and the terrorist mastermind in *Die Hard,* to name two that come immediately to mind.

Professor Snape is portrayed by Rowling as a very skilled potions master at Hogwarts, but his career aim is to teach Defense against the Dark Arts, which tells us much about the character and his nature.

Rickman plays this role in a controlled, understated manner. The word *precision* comes to mind when I think of how he portrays Snape. He is in total control of his lines and delivers them exactly.

In the first book, Snape tells his first-year class about the beauty of potion-making, a subtle scene in which we begin to understand why he harbors such love for this difficult, exacting craft. In the film (scene 14 on the DVD), Rickman bursts in on his class and carefully, deliberately, performs this scene with understated control. He is clearly in command and as an actor delivers his lines with confidence, with the students hanging on his every word.

Rickman brings his considerable acting talents to bear in his interpretation of Snape—one that's a standout in a film series filled with memorable characters played by good and great actors.

Rickman on the first Harry Potter film: "It looked tremendous to me. I think the thing is that whenever . . . I was on the set and children were coming in and visiting, the endless refrain was, 'Wow! It's just like the book!' And I think that was certainly Chris Columbus's and the producers' aim: to be faithful to J. K. Rowling's imagination. And I think, given the fact that at the end of the screening last night the entire cinema stood up and cheered, I guess they've done it!" (Quoted by Tim Sebastian on BBC Hardtalk, November 7, 2001.)

Fiona Shaw as Petunia Dursley. The perfect wife for Vernon Dursley—she is similarly unimaginative and excessively concerned with appearances, though blinded to the shortcomings of their obnoxious son. Aunt Petunia is pure caricature: the class-conscious housewife who dotes excessively on her son and whose job is to support her husband blindly.

Fiona Shaw steps into this role and becomes Petunia Dursley, convincing us that, like her husband, all is not right in the world unless she finds continual fault with nephew Harry Potter, whom she resents.

A first-class, professional performance by Shaw complements the performances by actors Richard Griffiths and Harry Melling.

Shaw on her role: "Bad? Me? No, but I am very honoured to be Aunt Petunia. It is great to be part of a cultural touchstone, the film's very exciting and beautifully directed by Christopher Columbus." (Quoted from "Harry Potter's Wicked Aunt" in www.empireonline.co.uk, November 28, 2000.)

Maggie Smith as Professor Minerva McGonagall. As Rowling has pointed out in interviews, McGonagall is a powerful witch. The head of Gryffindor house, she is a key figure at Hogwarts.

The role is demanding—in fact, crucial, according to Rowling, who was concerned about its casting—but Maggie Smith is more than capable of filling the role. One of England's most celebrated actresses, Dame Maggie Smith is a consummate professional, a pro's pro. She delivers a carefully nuanced role, which she seems to fill without exertion.

In one film scene, she confronts Harry and Ron, who have just barely escaped a direct attack by the aptly named Whomping Willow. A miserable Ron sighs, resigned to his fate, and says he'll get his things now and leave Hogwarts, because he's been expelled. Maggie Smith, in her role as the head of Gryffindor, delivers the line, "Not today, Mr. Weasley." How she delivers that line with dry wit and precision makes her a joy to watch. In the vernacular of Harry Potter-aged kids, Smith RULES.

Smith on why she committed to the film series: "It's very simple really. Harry Potter is my pension." (Quoted by Chloe Fox in "Spellbinding" on www.telegraph.co.uk, January 14, 2004.)

David Tennant as Bartemius Crouch, Jr. The son of Bartemius Crouch, Sr., the Minister of Magic, the son falls far from the tree: In the opening scene, we see him in the company of Peter "Wormtail" Pettigrew, Nagini, and the Dark Lord himself, Lord Voldemort. We know, then, that he's no good and up to no good, as well. As the storyline in *Harry Potter and the Goblet of Fire* unfolds, it's clear that the son is not merely a bad apple but rotten to the core, as well.

David Tennant gives an outstanding performance; regrettably, he gets few scenes but still manages to steal the show. As actor Daniel Radcliffe told *SFX Magazine*, "I'll tell you what—I wish there was more of David Tennant in *Goblet of Fire*. He plays Barty Crouch, Jr. He only got a few scenes and he's brilliant in all of them. He's so absolutely, fantastically watchable. . . . I would love to work with him again. He's also the nicest person."

Verne Troyer as Griphook the Goblin. Best known for his role as "Mini Me" in the Austin Powers films, Troyer has only a brief appearance in one scene, when Harry Potter and Rubeus Hagrid go to Gringotts to make withdrawals. Harry needs cash for school supplies and Hagrid needs to pick up a special package on the instruction of Albus Dumbledore.

Troyer's walk-through is all too brief (more, please, about the Gringotts' goblins). Though Troyer is diminutive in real life, he's a giant of an actor.

Julie Walters as Molly Weasley. The mother that Harry Potter never had, Molly Weasley is the wife of Arthur Weasley and the mother of six boys and one daughter, all of whom have gone to or are currently enrolled in Hogwarts. As longtime readers know, there's more to her than meets the eye—particularly obvious in book five—and her role becomes increasingly more visible in each book.

Screenshot of Alivans.com, a webstore that sells wands

Julie Walters plays well the part of Molly Weasley. She steps into the role and becomes the character. An endearing interpretation, Walters portrays Molly exactly as Rowling has written her—she runs the Weasley household, lays down the law with her own children, dotes on Harry Potter, and can still be like a giddy schoolgirl when in the presence of someone famous and flamboyant like Gilderoy Lockhart. (Ron is right: She fancies Lockhart, but of course downplays that notion.)

Hers is a solid performance that in the films to come will require rising to the occasion and reaching new heights of character interpretation.

Walters on her role: "Since playing Mrs. Weasley in *Harry Potter*, I've had a lot of children asking me for autographs. But usually it is women who say, 'I did an Open University course after seeing *Educating Rita.*' . . . Anyway, we live a very ordinary life so we don't come into contact with the starry thing. We live in a small community where everyone knows us and I'm just the local actress who opens the fetes. . . ." (Quoted from "The Actress Next Door" by an uncredited staff writer on www.theage.com.au, October 11, 2003.)

Emma Watson as Hermione Granger. The only character that Rowling has admitted is drawn from a real person, Hermione is a "swot," a brainy girl who uses her intelligence to mask her insecurities. It's a portrait of Rowling herself, who in high school was a prefect, as is Hermione in book five.

The danger for any young actress attempting this role is striking the right balance, achieving the right tone. If played too tightly, Granger would appear as unsympathetic and such a know-it-all that we as viewers would find her off-putting, like Ron Weasley does in his initial meetings with her. But in time a grudging friendship between them develops into a bona fide friendship, and she, Ron, and Harry become inseparable.

Emma Watson is brilliant as Hermione Granger. The initial scene with her on the train as she first meets Harry and Ron tells us everything we need to know about her interpretation of the character. We are in good hands. Watson *is* an endearing know-it-all, who is initially an aggravation, subsequently an annoyance that borders on grating, and finally one who realizes when to obey the rules and when to break them (Percy Weasley, take note!).

Watson is an accomplished young actress who has to display a wide range of acting skills to pull off this challenging role. Fortunately for the film series, she is not only up to the challenge but throws herself into her role with unbridled enthusiasm.

Watson on what she doesn't like about her character: "She's a bit too [concerned with] rules. She overdoes it when Harry gets the Firebolt and she seeks out Professor McGonagall. She was obviously worried, but I probably would've had a talk with my friend before I sought out a teacher." (Quoted from "Emma Watson: Hermione" in *Nickolodeon Magazine,* October 30, 2001.)

Mark Williams as Arthur Weasley. The husband of Molly Weasley, Arthur is an employee at the Ministry of Magic, which gives us glimpses into its inner workings. Williams plays the role to perfection, whether it's showing delight and surprise when discovering that his sons have brought Harry Potter to his home as they all gather around the kitchen table for a hearty breakfast, or his childlike curiosity when he discovers that Ron, George, and Fred took his enchanted Ford Anglia for an unauthorized flight; he excitedly asks them how it went, and then assumes a mock-angry tone after being chided by his wife, who really runs the house and rules the roost.

Williams on his role: "It's a great film to work on. It's like all your favorite actors. Julie Walters is my wife, which is fantastic!" (Quoted from the *Johnny Vaughan Show* on BBC 1, September 23, 2002.)

Bonnie Wright as Ginny Weasley. The only daughter of Arthur and Molly Weasley, Ginny is initially awestruck when first encountering Harry up close, when she sees him at the family breakfast table. It turns out that she had been talking about Harry all summer to her bemused brother Ron, who says a little talk about Harry is okay, but she had become tedious, going on endlessly about poor Harry.

As with other secondary characters in the series, Ginny grows up. The speechless schoolgirl in the first film becomes a key figure in the second film, as she becomes more confident in herself—a difficult thing to do when you've been raised in a family of boys with no older sister to confide in.

Bonnie Wright strikes no wrong tones in her interpretation of Ginny Weasley. A loyal Gryffindor to the core, as are her brothers and Harry Potter, Ginny is a character to watch—as is the talented Bonnie Wright.

Wright on stardom: "I have had a few people recognise me in public. But I wouldn't like everybody to recognise me. I can still walk across the street and not be noticed. If I was Daniel Radcliffe I think I would find it much harder to deal with." (Quoted from "BBCi Films: Bonnie Wright. *Harry Potter and the Chamber of Secrets,*" an interview conducted by Jamie Russell, undated.)

Harry Potter and the Sorcerer's Stone

I really wanted to get back to a darker, sort of edgier action-adventure kids' film, and this just fit into what I was getting obsessed with. At the same time, I knew I wanted to work with kids. . . . Emma and Rupert had never ever done a film before. So it was great to work with these kids who were fresh.

—Director Chris Columbus
interviewed by www.scifi.com

For an industry wholly dependent on imagination, it's amazing to me that studios pass on projects that, even beforehand, seem to be no-brainers. Case in point: Peter Jackson's *The Lord of the Rings*.

Disney, after looking at the numbers for its previous fantasy films, took a pass; so did all the other studios, except one. New Line Studios took the risk—not with one but three films—and reaped the rewards. Now the suits (the businessmen in the boardroom) are optioning everything that even smacks of fantasy, and have sent errand boys to bookstores to scour the shelves clean for any book with a dragon, wand, or wizard on its cover.

A Harry Potter bookend

In Rowling's case, film interest was always high, but she fended off all offers—including one from Warner Bros., who would eventually buy into the franchise big-time—because of concerns that Hollywood would twist, tear, and reshape her beloved stories into an unrecognizable, bland product.

Unlike their brethren in the book trade, writers in Hollywood are on the bottom of the totem pole. Once a writer sells his property to a studio, the fervent wish among the suits is that the pesky writer will somehow vanish and leave them alone to make the movie their way.

It's a culture clash that, more often than not, has resulted in bitter feelings between writers (the creative talent) and the suits (the noncreative business types), with the result that what finally appears on the screen bears only a passing resemblance to the original storyline.

You see, in Hollywood, it's all about money. It's about stars' salaries, production and promotion costs, and the "talent" (the actors). The author is merely the inconvenient but indispensable speed bump on the path to getting the film to fruition.

In the case of Harry Potter, the stakes were higher because there would be not one property at stake but a franchise: seven interrelated films that, if successful, would be a hugely profitable film property.

Rowling, more concerned about control than cash, wisely held off until she had reassurances in writing that guaranteed her carefully constructed imaginative universe would not be populated by characters acting in strange or unseeming ways. Either tell the stories my way, she said firmly, or don't tell them at all.

Given the potentially lucrative income from ticket sales, DVD sales, and licensing, the lure of Harry Potter meant that the suits would, regretfully but necessarily, make concessions.

In a move that surprised the film industry, Rowling insisted that all the cast members be British. Just as she didn't want American characters making appearances in her very British book, she also didn't want American actors with fake British accents tromping around in her backyard, so to speak.

I'm sure the British actors were thrilled to hear that news, since the American and British film industries are worlds apart in terms of compensation: in the U.S., actors get residuals, but in the U.K., British productions pay flat rates only, with no further income.

This explains why an actor like Dame Maggie Smith, one of the most esteemed in her profession, was happy to be a continuing character, Professor Minerva McGonagall, for the film series. As she pointed out in several interviews, the film franchise would be her retirement account.

Rowling's insistence on an all-British cast proved to be the right one, and the casting across the board proved to be felicitous choices. For the first

Harry Potter film, some of the biggest names in British films would sign up: Richard Harris (as Professor Albus Dumbledore), Robbie Coltrane (as Rubeus Hagrid), John Hurt (as Mr. Ollivander), John Cleese (as Nearly Headless Nick), and Alan Rickman (as Professor Severus Snape), to name a few.

Though the adults were superbly cast, the choices for the child actors—the linchpin to the film's success—proved to be positively inspired. Of the three principal characters, two had never before appeared in any film (Rupert Grint playing Ron Weasley, and Emma Watson as Hermione Granger), but the difficulties in finding the perfect boy to play Harry Potter proved to be a casting director's nightmare. Until fairly late in the game, the crucial role of Harry Potter remained unfilled, despite casting calls throughout England that drew thousands of hopeful Harrys.

As was clearly obvious to all, the child actor who portrayed Harry Potter would be carrying not only this film but the franchise itself: The right choice would go a long way toward establishing the franchise on firm ground, whereas the wrong choice would cripple, if not kill, it.

In the end, it wasn't the tried-and-true casting calls that produced the actor in question but a chance encounter when the producers, stymied in their search for Harry, went to see a movie for diversion and, a few rows up, they spied the perfect Harry Potter: actor Daniel Radcliffe, who two years earlier had played a young David Copperfield in a television adaptation of Dickens's novel of the same name.

But the big question was: Could this child actor step into this demanding role and fit the bill? Or would the producers have to postpone production to go back and find another actor?

Radcliffe's young shoulders proved more than capable of carrying the burden of the film. A completely believable Harry Potter, Daniel Radcliffe absolutely owned the role.

With crew and cast assembled, a watchful world holding its collective breath, and Potter fans worldwide speculating endlessly on the World Wide Web as to every casting choice and airing every concern, Chris Columbus's enchanting adaptation gave shape and substance to the wizarding world that Rowling had explored for five years before committing the first book to print.

Unlike so many other Hollywood stories, this one had a fairy-tale ending because everyone really did live happily ever after: the actors were part of a franchise that would guarantee income for their retirements; Warner Bros. realized a return on its investment of time, money, and effort; and the fans generally found more to like than not in what would be the first film in an ongoing series.

But now that the first film had proven to be successful, would history repeat itself with Harry Potter film #2, or was it just a fluke? As Hollywood knows all too well, a promising first, and even second, film doesn't a franchise make, as shown by *The Terminator* series.

That was the $100 million question (the budget for the film), and one that weighed heavily on the minds of the suits at Warner Bros.

Warner Bros., 2001. Running time: 153 minutes. November 16, 2001. (DVD issue: May 28, 2002.) Budget: $130 million. Worldwide gross: $975 million.

Awards: Best Live Action in the category of Family Film from the Broadcast Film Critics Association.

Credits

Source: novel by Joanne Rowling
Screenwriter: Steve Kloves
Director: Chris Columbus
Producers: David Heyman, Mark Radcliffe (no relation to actor Daniel Radcliffe)
Cinematographer: John Seale
Composer: John Williams
Costume Designer: Judianna Makovsky
Editor: Richard Francis-Bruce
Executive Producers: Chris Columbus, Michael Barnathan, Duncan Henderson, Mark Radcliffe
Production Designer: Stuart Craig
Visual Effects Supervisor: Rob Legato

Cast (Actor: Fictional Character)
Bayler, Terence: The Bloody Baron, Slytherin ghost
Biggerstaff, Sean: Oliver Wood, Gryffindor Quidditch captain
Bradley, David: Mr. Argus Filch, caretaker
Cleese, John: Nearly Headless Nick, Gryffindor ghost
Coltrane, Robbie: Rubeus Hagrid, groundskeeper
Dale, Emily: Katie Bell
Davis, Warwick: Professor Flitwick and Goblin bank teller
Fearon, Ray: Firenze, centaur
Felton, Tom: Draco Malfoy
Fisher-Becker, Simon: The Fat Friar, ghost
Griffiths, Richard: Uncle Vernon Dursley
Grint, Rupert: Ronald "Ron" Weasley
Harris, Richard: Headmaster Albus Dumbledore
Hart, Ian: Professor Quirrell
Herdman, Joshua: Gregory Goyle

Holmes, David: Adrian Pucey
Hurt, John: Mr. Ollivander
Lewis, Matthew: Neville Longbottom
Melling, Harry: Dudley Dursley
Murray, Devon: Seamus Finnigan
Phelps, James: Fred Weasley
Phelps, Oliver: George Weasley
Radcliffe, Daniel: Harry Potter
Rankin, Chris: Percy Weasley
Rickman, Alan: Professor Severus Snape
Shaw, Fiona: Aunt Petunia Dursley
Smith, Maggie: Professor Minerva McGonagall
Spriggs, Elizabeth: The Fat Lady, Gryffindor
Sutherland, Leilah: Alicia Spinnet
Taylor, Danielle: Angelina Johnson
Troyer, Verne: Griphook the Goblin
Walters, Julie: Molly Weasley
Wanamaker, Zoe: Madam Hooch
Watson, Emma: Hermione Granger
Waylett, Jamie: Vincent Crabbe
Wright, Bonnie: Ginny Weasley
Youngblood, Luke: Lee Jordan

Selected Reviews

Daily Mail (U.K.): "I am happy to report that it truly is a wizard show. I suspect that fans of all ages will want to see it again and again. . . . Shooting the movie in British locations with a mostly British crew and all-British cast helped ensure that the film has been mostly free of the saccharine gloss that has choked the life out of many a Hollywood film.

"And the controlling hands of author J. K. Rowling and producer David Heyman have kept the picture true to the novel."

Daily Telegraph (U.K.): "When Steven Spielberg turned down the director's job to make *A.I.*, the choice of *Home Alone* filmmaker Columbus over the other candidates such as Ivan Reitman, Brad Siberling, and Terry Gilliam initially came in for criticism from Harry Potter fans. Many felt Columbus's tendency toward sentimentality—as demonstrated in *Stepmom* and *Bicentennial Man*—would be highly unsuitable for the weird and wonderful world of Harry Potter. But he has managed to keep the saccharine to a minimum, and instead allows Rowling's story to unfold almost exactly as she wrote it. . . . Screenwriter Steven Kloves has managed to retain all the essential elements of the book, while, by necessity, paring down and omitting a few of the minor characters. . . . [But] the stars of the film are its three children, on whose shoulders its credibility rests.

"Daniel Radcliffe . . . is in almost every frame and is a wonderful Harry, often bemused but always determined to do the right thing. . . ."

Jack Gardner for the Rochester *Democrat and Chronicle:* "There's magic galore in *Harry Potter and the Sorcerer's Stone*—even a Muggle like me can see it. The most eagerly anticipated movie adaptation of a novel since *Gone with the Wind* is a rousing success. . . . All told, the film propels the filmmaker into rarefied Spielberg and Lucas territory. *The Sorcerer's Stone* is the first of what will almost certainly be the most popular series of fantasy films since *Star Wars.*"

E-Wired: "The cast could not have been more perfectly assembled. Rupert Grint was 'bloody brilliant.' Emma Watson shined as the almost-goody-goody Hermione, and Daniel Radcliffe, well, he *is* Harry Potter—the boy we have been awaiting so very long to see. . . . I thank the cast all kindly for bringing these characters to life, characters that have meant so much to myself, and millions of others."

Hollywood Reporter: "Fortunately, all hands involved in the production have faithfully observed the mantra 'It's the book, stupid.' Taking only a few shortcuts and hewing as close to the spirit of a literary work as any movie can, *Harry Potter* vividly imagines the world of wizards, magic school, and mystical creatures found in Rowling's series of children's adventure books. Clearly, the sky's the limit, not only for worldwide box office but video, DVD, television, and merchandising."

Jonathan Foreman for the *New York Post:* "Adapting books for the screen is not easy to do well. It's even harder if fidelity to the original material is a major priority—and with *Harry Potter and the Sorcerer's Stone* it was more of a priority than in any of Hollywood's biblical epics."

James Berardinelli for *ReelViews:* "Viewed exclusively as a piece of cinema—something extraordinarily difficult to do with this property—*Harry Potter and the Sorcerer's Stone* stands out as a solid piece of entertainment. The film's spell may not be as potent as that of the book, but there's still some magic in what Columbus and his crew have wrought."

Joe Baltake for the *Sacramento Bee:* "If every movie that's greedily earmarked as a cinematic franchise could be as immaculately conceived as Chris Columbus's *Harry Potter and the Sorcerer's Stone*, there would be no reason to complain about the crass commercialization of films."

Jeff Strickler for the *Star Tribune:* "This is not a great movie, but it is a very good one. That's quite an accomplishment in light of the parameters forced upon him: He had to make a movie that works on its own terms for viewers who aren't familiar with the book, while appeasing the legion of Harry devotees who consider the source material the Holy Grail of kid lit."

Richard Corliss for *Time:* "How to make a film out of such a cinematic experience that 100 million readers have seen in their minds' eyes? Either by transferring it, like a lavishly illustrated volume of Dickens, or transforming it with a new vision. Columbus, along with screenwriter Steve Kloves and the Potter production team, chose Column A and made a handsomely faithful version, with actors smartly cast to type."

TV Guide: "Based on the first of Rowling's mind-bogglingly popular novels, Chris Columbus's lavishly appointed film aims for fidelity to the source in all things. And if it's a little airless, in the manner of certain *Masterpiece Theater* adaptations of literary masterworks, no matter. Fans will be so relieved to find the world they love transplanted to the screen intact that they won't mind a bit."

HARRY POTTER AND THE CHAMBER OF SECRETS

"Hermione Granger" (Erin Golden) of Barnes & Noble prepares to transfigure a plush doll back into the real Mrs. Norris.

In his second film adaptation, Chris Columbus wasted no time in getting to the story at hand, since exposition explaining the backstory of Harry Potter, the world of Muggles, the wizarding world, and Hogwarts was not necessary. Consequently, we are introduced to Dobby, an endearing magical creature whose servitude to a wizarding family puts him at odds with himself: On one hand, the diminutive creature's eyes shine with awe because he considers Harry Potter to be a great wizard; and on the other, Dobby goes to extraordinary lengths to keep Harry from going back to Hogwarts—for the young wizard's own good.

Dobby, however, fails in his attempt to convince Harry to give his word not to return, so Dobby forces the issue: His mayhem is engineered to force Harry to remain in the Muggle world at the Dursley residence, with his bedroom windows barred to prevent escape.

But Harry does manage to escape and make his way to Hogwarts, no matter how many obstacles Dobby erects to bar him.

At Hogwarts, the real fun (or mischief) begins, when Harry must decipher an age-old puzzle: What ancient creature is housed in the school's fabled Chamber of Secrets, and what is its connection to Rubeus Hagrid and Moaning Myrtle?

At the center of the mystery is a riddle—Tom Riddle, actually—that Harry must solve. Suffice it to say, Tom Riddle's boyish looks are disarming, for beneath his carefully cultivated exterior he conceals much and shows little . . . until it's time to reveal his hand.

The real surprise (and delight) this time around is the performance of Kenneth Branagh, who as Hogwarts's new Defense against the Dark Arts professor, Gilderoy Lockhart, plays the role with brio. Branagh rises to the occasion with an over-the-top performance that brings levity to an otherwise increasingly dark story.

A thoroughly convincing secondary universe, the wizarding world as envisioned by Rowling has been ably brought to life by Columbus who has discovered what Potter fans already knew: What we see of Hogwarts whets our appetite for more, as Columbus serves up a satisfying portion that will hold fans over until the release of the next film, *Harry Potter and the Prisoner of Azkaban*.

Warner Bros., 2002. Running time: 161 minutes. November 2002. (DVD issue: April 11, 2003.) Budget: $100 million. Worldwide gross: $869 million.

Credits

Source: novel by Joanne Rowling
Screenwriter: Steve Kloves, Joanne Rowling
Director: Chris Columbus
Producers: David Heyman, Chris Columbus
Cinematographer: Roger Pratt
Composers: John Williams, William Ross
Executive Producers: Michael Barnathan, David Barron, Chris Columbus, Mark Radcliffe
Production Designer: Stuart Craig
Special Effects Supervisor: John Richardson

Cast (Actor: Fictional Character)

Biggerstaff, Sean: Oliver Wood, Captain of the Quidditch team for Gryffindor

Bradley, David: Mr. Argus Filch, caretaker of Hogwarts

Branagh, Kenneth: Professor Gilderoy Lockhart, Hogwarts teacher of Defense against the Dark Arts

Burke, Alfred: Armando Dippet

Cleese, John: Nearly Headless Nick

Coltrane, Robbie: Rubeus Hagrid, groundskeeper

Columbus, Eleanor (Chris Columbus's daughter): Susan Bones

Coulson, Christian: Tom Riddle

Dale, Emily: Katie Bell

Davis, Warwick: Professor Filius Flitwick

Enoch, Alfred: Dean Thomas

Felton, Tom: Draco Malfoy

Glover, Julian: voice of Aragog the Spider

Griffiths, Richard: Harry Potter's uncle, Vernon Dursley

Grint, Rupert: Harry Potter's best friend, Ronald "Ron" Weasley

Hardy, Robert: Minister of Magic, Cornelius Fudge

Harris, Richard: Albus Dumbledore, headmaster at Hogwarts

Henderson, Shirley: ghost student, Moaning Myrtle

Herdman, Joshua: Gregory Goyle

Isaacs, Jason: Lucius Malfoy, father of Draco Malfoy

Jones, Toby: voice of Dobby the house-elf (for the Malfoys)

Lewis, Matt: Neville Longbottom

Margolyes, Miriam: Professor Sprout, Hogwarts teacher of Herbology

Mitchell, Hugh: Colin Creevey

Murray, Devon: Seamus Finnigan

Padley, Gemma: Penelope Clearwater

Phelps, James: Fred Weasley

Phelps, Oliver: George Weasley

Radcliffe, Daniel: Harry Potter

Randell, Edward: Justin Finch-Fletchley

Rankin, Chris: Percy Weasley

Rickman, Alan: Professor Severus Snape, Hogwarts teacher of Potions

Shaw, Fiona: Harry Potter's aunt, Petunia Dursley

Smith, Maggie: Professor Minerva McGonagall

Sutherland, Leilah: Alicia Spinnet

Walters, Julie: Molly Weasley

Watson, Emma: Hermione Granger

Waylett, Jamie: Vincent Crabbe

Williams, Mark: Arthur Weasley

Wright, Bonnie: Ginny Weasley
Yeates, Jamie: Marcus Flint
Youngblood, Luke: Lee Jordan

Selected Reviews

Roger Ebert for the *Chicago Sun-Times:* "What's developing here, it's clear, is one of the most important franchises in movie history, a series of films that consolidate all of the advances in computer-aided animation, linked to the extraordinary creative work of Rowling, who has created a mythological world as grand as *Star Wars,* but filled with more wit and humanity. Although the young wizard Harry Potter is nominally the hero, the film remembers the golden age of moviemaking, when vivid supporting characters crowded the canvas. The story is about personalities, personal histories, and eccentricity, not about a superstar superman crushing the narrative with his egotistical weight."

Kirk Honeycutt for TheHollywoodReporter.com: "More than ever, the film must rely on its technical crew. Nick Dudman's imaginative creature and makeup effects, Roger Pratt's painterly cinematography, Lindy Hemming's flamboyant costumes, and Stuart Craig's labyrinthine sets that melt into many visual and special effects all convincingly usher us into the realm of the fantastic."

Kenneth Turan for latimes.com: "Perhaps as an acting choice, perhaps because of the effects of the illness that eventually took his life, Harris plays Dumbledore with a quavering but resolute frailty that gives the character an effective gravity. His speech about the life span of his beloved phoenix, Fawkes, one of those creatures that 'burst into flames when it is time for them to die,' provides an unintentional valedictory to an impressive career."

Lou Lumenick for nypost.com: "*Harry Potter and the Chamber of Secrets* proves that sometimes you can have too much of a good thing. Crammed full of labyrinthine plot twists, this second installment will delight Potter-crazy kids even as their parents grow restless at the 2-hour-and-41-minute running time."

A. O. Scott for nytimes.com: "Mr. Columbus, once again working with the screenwriter Steve Kloves and a cast of talented children (especially Emma Watson, who plays the brainy and intrepid Hermione) and grown-up British luminaries, has acquitted himself honorably. . . . My fellow critics and I may occasionally fault a movie for departing, in detail or in spirit, from its literary source, but the grousing of a few adult pedants is nothing compared to the wrath of several million bookish ten-year-olds."

William Arnold for seattlepi.com: "Best of all, the second Potter movie reunites its adult cast: Richard Harris, Maggie Smith, Robbie Coltrane, John Cleese, Alan Rickman, Julie Walters, and others—a veritable Who's Who of British actors that single-handedly elevates the proceedings out of the kid's movie genre into something special."

HARRY POTTER AND THE
PRISONER OF AZKABAN

T he moment I read the book, I was hooked. It's a myth for our times. You read about Fudge and the Ministry of Magic—that's Tony Blair! And Guantánamo is not that different from Azkaban. There are Dementors over there, too.

—*Director Alfonso Cuarón*

Before talking about Cuarón, let's talk about Chris Columbus. He, as the director, went into the breach with not only the first Harry Potter film but the second as well.

Long before the first film illuminated the movie screens, fans on the World Wide Web debated the pros (but mostly the cons) of Columbus as director. The more strident fans wailed, "But he directed the saccharine *Home Alone* and its sequel!"

The fans needn't have worried. Columbus knew that the fans' expectations had been ratcheted up to stratospheric heights, compounded by the pressure of delivering a big-budget film, and the first in what was almost certain to be an enduring and highly profitable franchise.

The long and short of it: Columbus delivered the goods. Working hand-in-hand with the screenwriter and with Rowling herself, Columbus brought to the screen a magical and enchanting movie that put the collective fears of Potter fandom to rest.

Some Potter fans, muttering under their butterbeer, were quick to point out that the films weren't dark enough in tone. Rowling didn't write the proverbial pink-and-blue bunny rabbit children's story but instead necessarily wrote a dark fantasy story that, along the way, would become increasingly somber, as the power of Lord Voldemort grew in strength, with death in his wake.

Enter Alfonso Cuarón.

A highly regarded director whose credits included *A Little Princess* and *Y Tu Mamá También,* Cuarón came to *Harry Potter and the Prisoner of Azkaban* with the considerable cachet. No one, it seemed, doubted his ability to bring to the screen the increasingly darkened landscapes of the wizarding world. Rowling herself, who loved his adaptation of *A Little Princess,* spoke for the multitude of Potter fans who felt that teenage angst was the essential heart of the third book; Harry, Ron, and Hermione weren't children anymore but, in fact, young adults grappling with adolescence.

Like Columbus, Cuarón remained true to the source material by taking to heart Rowling's suggestions on how to approach the project. In an online interview (filmforce.ign.com), Cuarón observed: "The first thing she told me was don't be literal with this book; be faithful to the spirit of the book, . . . And I have to say, she is a person that has such a big respect to the filmmaking process. She is not a person who is going to say, I like or dislike. She would say, 'That makes sense in that universe, but it doesn't make sense in *this* universe.'"

Cover story in *U.S. News & World Report* about Pottermania

With Rowling's input firmly in mind, Cuarón delivered a powerful film, a sustained dark medley that hit all the right notes with viewers. What Cuarón probably didn't know is that in readers' polls, this book is among the favorite books in the series.

Not surprisingly, this film is the fan favorite as well, owing much to the mystery that surrounds the prisoner of Azkaban, and the struggles—internal and external—that Harry, Ron, and Hermione must endure as they continue to grow up in an increasingly dangerous world where somewhere in the background, and in darkness, Lord Voldemort and his followers, the Death Eaters, are gathering their strength to mount a final assault against all that is good in the wizarding world.

The financial and critical success of the third film practically guaranteed that Cuarón would be asked to return once again to helm *Harry Potter and the Goblet of Fire,* but he declined. As Cuarón pointed out in numerous interviews, he'd love to do it again, but not so soon. So, perhaps, we may see him for the seventh (and last) Potter novel, which will be a perfect fit of director and film project: The final confrontation between Harry Potter (played by Daniel Radcliffe, we hope) and Lord Voldemort (played by Ralph Fiennes, who makes his first appearance in *Harry Potter and the Goblet of Fire*) will be as dramatic as Gandalf's confrontation with his arch nemesis, Sauron, in J. R. R. Tolkien's *The Return of the King.*

In the meantime, Muggles everywhere wait anxiously for the release of *Harry Potter and the Goblet of Fire,* to be directed by Mike Newell.

Warner Bros., 2004. Running time: 141 minutes. May 2004. (DVD issue: November 2004). Budget: $130 million. Worldwide gross: $249 million.

Credits

Source: novel by Joanne Rowling
Screenwriter: Steven Kloves
Director: Alfonso Cuarón
Producers: Chris Columbus, David Heyman, Mark Radcliffe
Associate Producers: Chris Carreras, Paula DuPré Pesman
Cinematographer: Michael Seresin
Composer: John Williams
Executive Producers: Michael Barnathan, Callum McDougall, Tanya
    Seghatchian
Production Designer: Stuart Craig
Special Effects Supervisors: Mark Bullimore, et al.

Cast (Actor: Fictional Character)
Bradley, David: Argus Filch
Christie, Julie: Madame Rosmerta
Coltrane, Robbie: Rubeus Hagrid
Felton, Tom: Draco Malfoy
Ferris, Pam: Aunt Marge
French, Dawn: The Fat Lady (painting)
Gambon, Michael: Albus Dumbledore
Gardner, Jimmy: Ernie the Bus Driver
Griffiths, Richard: Uncle Vernon Dursley

Grint, Rupert: Ron Weasley
Hardy, Robert: Cornelius Fudge
Herdman, Joshua: Gregory Goyle
Ingleby, Lee: Stan Shunpike
Lewis, Matthew: Neville Longbottom
Melling, Harry: Dudley Dursley
Murray, Devon: Seamus Finnegan
Oldman, Gary: Sirius Black
Phelps, James: Fred Weasley
Phelps, Oliver: George Weasley
Radcliffe, Daniel: Harry Potter
Rankin, Chris: Percy Weasley
Rawlins, Adrian: James Potter
Rickman, Alan: Professor Severus Snape
Shaw, Fiona: Aunt Petunia Dursley
Smith, Maggie: Professor Minerva McGonagall
Somerville, Geraldine: Lily Potter
Spall, Timothy: Peter Pettigrew
Tavaré, Jim: Tom the Innkeeper
Thewlis, David: Professor Remus Lupin
Thompson, Emma: Professor Sybill Trelawney
Walters, Julie: Mrs. Molly Weasley
Watson, Emma: Hermione Granger
Waylett, Jamie: Vincent Crabbe
Williams, Mark: Arthur Weasley
Wright, Bonnie: Ginny Weasley

Selected Reviews

Michael Rechtshaffen for *The Hollywood Reporter:* "The third time's definitely the charm. . . . Thanks to the revitalizing imprint of . . . director Alfonso Cuarón, *Harry Potter and the Prisoner of Azkaban* is a deeper, darker, visually arresting, and more emotionally satisfying adaptation of the J. K. Rowling literary phenomenon, achieving the neat trick of remaining faithful to the spirit of the book while at the same time being true to its cinematic self."

David Sterritt for *The Christian Science Monitor:* "How do you keep a movie franchise from growing stale? One way is to put a different director on the case, bringing a fresh eye—and, ideally, a set of fresh ideas—to what might otherwise seem like yet another vacation to the same place you visited last year. . . . Stretching the PG rating to its breaking point, Mr. Cuarón has directed the creepiest and scariest Potter picture yet—and to my mind, the best."

Stephanie Zacharek for www.salon.com: "The first true Harry Potter movie—the first to capture not only the books' sense of longing, but their understanding of the way magic underlies the mundane, instead of just prancing fancifully at a far remove from it."

Harry Potter and the Goblet of Fire

In this film, Harry Potter faces his greatest challenge and worst fears as he keeps a date with destiny: fire-breathing dragons! malevolent shrubbery! underwater merpeople! Lord Voldemort and his Death Eaters! "Mad-Eye" Moody! But they are nothing compared to what Harry Potter must now confront. Now an adolescent, he must face his deepest, darkest fear: having to ask a girl out for a first date to a dance . . . the winsome Cho Chang.

In Harry's case, it's the Yule Ball, and the prospect of asking a girl out petrifies him. As he tells his friend Ron Weasley, "I think I'll take the dragon right now."

Harry's dilemma is at the heart of this long story—Rowling's longest novel to date—that ran 157 minutes on the silver screen. The movie runs along two parallel tracks: Harry as an unexpected competitor at the Triwizard Tournament and Harry as a tormented adolescent who has noticed, and been noticed by, girls for the first time in his young life.

As Rowling has pointed out, as the Harry Potter series progresses, the books get longer and darker; this is certainly the case with *Goblet of Fire*, which meant that director Mike Newell had to cut to the chase. What wound up on the cutting room floor, so to speak, was an elongated storyline about Hermione Granger's efforts to liberate the Hogwarts house-elves, despite their disinterest, by starting an organization called S.P.E.W. Explained producer David Heyman to *SCIFI Wire*, "Anything that doesn't really relate to Harry and Harry's journey is less relevant. . . . [S.P.E.W.] is Hermione's issue. Not to say Hermione's [not important]. Hermione's a vitally important character. But you have to make some choices."

It was a wise choice.

The film starts off with a bang (a riveting scene involving Lord Voldemort) and immediately shifts to Harry and the Weasley and Diggory family members as they make their way to a Portkey that transports them to the Quidditch World Cup.

Then, not surprisingly, things take an ominous turn: The Dark Mark appears above the camping grounds where the Quidditch World Cup is held and the Death Eaters make their dramatic appearance.

The film rockets on to an unforgettable climax (no, I'm not going to tell you), and it's up to Harry to make sense of everything that's happened, especially the decidedly odd behavior of "Mad-Eye" Moody, who is clearly *too* helpful to Harry in preparing for the Triwizard Tournament.

Rowling has stated several times in interviews that what happens in this book sets the stage for what is to follow, and she's got a good point. The midpoint in the series, *Harry Potter and the Goblet of Fire* is a far cry from the more innocuous first book, which is clearly more for children. Make no mistake: This book (and the film adaptation) is a deeper, richer experience. Harry and his pals have learned much, but they have more to learn.

Rowling does not disappoint with her fourth novel—and nor does Mike Newell, who has shown that he can capably helm a clearly challenging book to film adaptation.

The general consensus, echoed by Devin Faraci (www.Chud.com), is that "it's the first franchise where each movie is better than the last one. . . ."

Warner Bros., November 2005. Running time: 157 minutes. (DVD issue, March 2006.) Budget: $150 million. Worldwide gross: $892 million.

Credits

Source: novel by Joanne Rowling
Screenwriter: Steven Kloves
Director: Mike Newell
Producer: David Heyman
Cinematographer: Roger Pratt
Composer: Patrick Doyle
Co-producer: Peter MacDonald
Executive Producers: David Barron, Tanya Seghatchian
Production Designer: Stuart Craig

Cast (Actor: Fictional Character)
Bjelac, Predrag: Igor Karkaroff
Bradley, David: Argus Filch

Coltrane, Robbie: Rubeus Hagrid
Davis, Warwick: Professor Flitwick
Fiennes, Ralph: Lord Voldemort
Gambon, Michael: Albus Dumbledore
Gleeson, Brendan: Professor Alastor "Mad-Eye" Moody
Grint, Rupert: Ron Weasley
Hardy, Robert: Cornelius Fudge
Ianevski, Stanislav: Viktor Krum
Isaacs, Jason: Lucius Malfoy
Leung, Katie: Cho Chang
Lewis, Matthew: Neville Longbottom
Lloyd-Pack, Roger: Barty Crouch
Mandy, Angelica: Gabrielle Delacour
Oldman, Gary: Sirius Black
Pattinson, Robert: Cedric Diggory
Phelps, James: Fred Weasley
Phelps, Oliver: George Weasley
Poésy, Clémence: Fleur Delacour
Radcliffe, Daniel: Harry Potter
Richardson, Miranda: Rita Skeeter
Rickman, Alan: Professor Severus Snape
Smith, Maggie: Professor Minerva McGonagall
Spall, Timothy: Peter Pettigrew
Tennant, David: Barty Crouch, Jr.
Tour, Frances de la: Madame Maxime
Watson, Emma: Hermione Granger
Williams, Mark: Arthur Weasley
Wright, Bonnie: Ginny Weasley

Selected Reviews

Devin Faraci for www.Chud.com. "*Goblet of Fire* is a real achievement as a film in a lot of ways. The book was the toughest adaptation yet, but you don't feel anything missing in the final film. Mike Newell was new to this genre and to the sheer amount of [special] effects, but the movie is effortless and lovely, with both a charming eye for detail and a vision of grand spectacle. But the best achievement may be in just how much of a damn good film it is. It's a real competitor for a spot in the list of great 'coming of age' movies."

Michelle Alexandria for *Eclipse Magazine*. It's "one of those rare films that does it all, and never loses itself along the way. It successfully blends together action, adventure, comedy, and mystery to form an almost perfect film."

Jami Bernard for the *Daily News*. "This new Harry Potter movie makes things right, even if—as Harry and pals nervously acknowledge at the end—everything will be different from now on."

William Arnold for the *Seattle Post-Intelligencer*. "Still, in the end, the movie's chief joy is less its fantasy visuals or eccentric characters than the privilege it offers of allowing us to watch our old friends, the three principals—now awkward teenagers—struggle with hormonal surges and the rites of puberty. . . . Amazingly, director Mike Newell makes it work, giving the lengthy sequence some of the high anxiety and social humor of his *Four Weddings and a Funeral*. In his scheme of things, fighting a dragon is nothing compared to the terrors of a first date."

Premiere Magazine. "The fourth novel in J. K. Rowling's magical saga of the boy wizard is a sprawling, sumptuous, richly textured book, nearly unfilmable in all its excesses, tangents, and brilliantly tortured plot twists. Mike Newell's adaptation judiciously trims down the story to its barest and most crucial elements: 14-year-old Harry's long-awaited confrontation with Voldemort, the unspeakably evil wizard who murdered his parents. In so doing, Newell puts his own stamp on the franchise and delivers the best *Potter* movie yet filmed."

Notable and Quotable: Film Clips

Book to script: "The challenge always for me is keeping it from being four hours. What I honestly think is magical about what Jo does is the details. And so my first drafts are always chock-full of details."

  —Steve Kloves, screenwriter, quoted on Disc 2 of *Harry Potter and the Chamber of Secrets* DVD

Casting Harry: "Dan is great. It was a very difficult process. Finding Harry was very hard. It was like trying to find Scarlett O'Hara, this one. And I think everyone was getting slightly desperate. And I was walking down the streets of Edinburgh and London and looking at boys who passed me in a very suspicious-looking way. You know, I was thinking, could it be him? And then the producer and director walked into a theater one night and found Dan, an actor, who is just perfect. I saw his [screen] tests and I really had everything crossed that Dan would be the one, and he is."

  —Rowling on Dan Radcliffe, from "J. K. Rowling Discusses Surprising Success of *Harry Potter*," an interview on *Larry King Live* (October 20, 2000)

Chris Columbus: "At last it can be told: despite the $900 million it made at the global box office, despite its ranking as the highest-grossing film of 2001, director Chris Columbus was not entirely happy with *Harry Potter and*

the Sorcerer's Stone. 'I always thought we could have gotten the visual effects better,' he says. The pacing of the film, he admits, was a bit sluggish. 'The first 40 minutes of the first Harry Potter film were introductions.'"

—Jess Cagle from "When Harry Meets SCARY," *Time* (November 11, 2002)

"Not all the news is good. Harry Potter will soon be appearing at a multiplex near you. The initial project is being helmed by Chris Columbus, a filmmaker of no demonstrable ingenuity; one doubts if the director of *The Goonies,* one of the loudest, dumbest, and most shriekingly annoying children's movies ever made, is up to bringing Rowling's scatty wit and vibrant imagination to the screen. (I hope, on behalf of the millions of children who love Harry, Hermione, and Ron Weasley, that Columbus will prove me wrong.)"

—Stephen King in the *New York Times* (July 23, 2000)

Disappointed viewer: "I must regretfully admit I am disappointed in both of the film versions of Harry so far. They have first-rate casts and a number of really nice scenes here and there, but they somehow always fail to come together."

—Cartoonist/writer Gahan Wilson in "Harry Potter and the Amazing Success Story," *Realms of Fantasy* (August 2003)

Emotional connection to characters: "It is what the characters say, not how they look, that enables us to make an emotional connection with them. Though some of the excellent cast manage to act their way beyond the special effects (notably Alan Rickman's Snape, Robbie Coltrane's Hagrid, and Emma Watson's Hermione), many characters get lost in the dazzle of light and sound that filmmakers feel compelled to throw at us. If characters, and not scenery, had the starring role, viewers could become as involved with the film as they were with the novel."

—Author Philip Nel in "Bewitched, Bothered, and Bored: Harry Potter, the Movie," *Journal of Adolescent and Adult Literacy* (October 2002)

Fidelity to the novels: "As I recently said to my biographer, when I first started to get offers from film companies, I initially said 'no' to all of them. I am not against cinema—I actually love good movies. However, the vital thing for me was that the studio which eventually got the production contract, Warners, promised to be true to the book, and I have great faith in their commitment to that."

—Rowling quoted in "Exclusive: Writer Rowling Answers Her Readers' Questions," *Toronto Star* (April 22, 2003)

Film rights: "I did not feel I was far enough into the series, I didn't want 'non-author-written sequels' where a film company could have taken my characters and sent them off to Las Vegas on holiday, or something equally mad. I finally said 'yes' when I knew I was far enough into the books to make it very difficult for the filmmakers to take Harry and company off in directions I didn't want them to go."

—Rowling quoted in "Rowling Despaired of Ever Finishing *Harry*," nzoom.com (May 19, 2003)

Harry Potter #1: "As any reasonable person would have expected, it's a big and often sloppy Hollywood production with some bad computer graphics, a syrupy score from John Williams, and a focus on storybook adventure rather than Rowling's oddball characters."

—Andrew O'Herir in a review of *Harry Potter and the Sorcerer's Stone,* Salon.com (November 16, 2001)

Steve Kloves: "When I first met the screenwriter Steve Kloves, the fact that he was American did indeed make me wary, as I felt that he could very well be careless and insensitive with my creative baby. But as soon as he said his favorite character was Hermione, he completely won me over because she is the character who is closest to me. Steve also won my confidence by saying how protective both he and the production team were about my book, and that they were determined to avoid that usual Hollywood gaucheness."

—Rowling quoted in "Exclusive: Writer J. K. Rowling Answers Her Readers' Questions," *Toronto Star* (April 22, 2003)

Merchandising: "So where, cynical parents sated by *Phantom Menace* merchandise this summer must be wondering, is the movie? Where are the toys? How can this be just a book? Warner Bros. has the film and merchandise rights to the first book, but there will be a lull before American children see their personal image of Harry replaced by a face on a movie screen or have a chance to buy a certified Nimbus 2000 broomstick."

—Eden Ross Lipson in "Book's Quirky Hero and Fantasy Win the Young," *New York Times,* Books (July 12, 1999)

"Warner Bros.' huge marketing juggernaut has been cranking merchandise into the marketplace for more than a year, so you can already 'get' Harry via coffee mug, sweatshirt, lightning-bolt scar stickers, or mantelpiece figurine rather than getting him by reading. Thankfully, the stuff in most cases is so ugly that it helps even the youngest readers separate the wonderfully illustrated books from the movie hype."

—Tracy Mayor in "Kiss Harry Potter Goodbye," Salon.com (November 6, 2001)

Movie as marketing vehicle: "By now we're all used to heavy marketing campaigns for movies. But movies that actually feel like two-hour-plus marketing campaigns are a relatively new phenomenon. Perfunctory, competent, well-oiled, and yet still stultifyingly dull, *Harry Potter and the Chamber of*

Secrets sells itself dutifully minute-by-minute—it's the hardest-working movie in show business."

—Stephanie Zacharek in "The Trouble with Harry," Salon.com (November 15, 2002)

Movie deal: "Ms. Rowling has a deal giving her 1% of box office profits and it is thought she will net five pence for every £1 of Potter merchandise sold. Disney has already paid £49 million for the U.S. TV rights to the film."

—Susan Woods in "Rowling Conjures Up House for Close Friend," *Scotsman* (April 8, 2002)

Movie realism: "Instead of trying to overtake the readers' imagination, we've just given them the best possible version of the book, which means steeping it in reality . . . I wanted kids to feel that if they actually took that train, Hogwarts would be waiting for them."

—Chris Columbus quoted by Jeff Cagle in "The First Look at Harry," *Time* (November 5, 2001)

Protectiveness: "But I sold it to people I trusted, and so far my trust has not been misplaced. We're looking at an all-British cast. At first that looked like an impossibility. There was many a director who couldn't see that working at all. I would say things are going really well at the moment. People have to understand that no one could feel as protective as I do about these characters."

—Rowling quoted by Malcolm Jones in "The Return of Harry Potter," *Newsweek* (July 1, 2000)

Dan Radcliffe: "Having seen Dan Radcliffe's screen test, I don't think Chris Columbus could have found a better Harry."

—Rowling quoted by Laura Miller in "Harry Potter Kids Cast," Salon.com (August 22, 2000)

"It's really funny, but there were a couple of people at school and they had never talked to me before, but as soon as I got the part they started e-mailing me and pretending we were best friends. My close friends have been totally cool about it. At least, I hope they have. And anyway, Mum and Dad keep me leading a normal life. I have some close friends and they are the same now as before I did this. They want to know about it—of course they do—and some of them have come on set to have a look. But nothing's changed."

—Daniel Radcliffe quoted by Tracey Lawson in "Spellbound," News.scotsman.com (June 14, 2003)

Scriptwriter spotlighted: "I've never been involved with a picture that anyone was remotely interested in before I'd handed in the script. Certainly not

a picture that people are interested in doing articles on before I'm even finished with the polish on the first draft."

—Screenwriter Steve Kloves quoted by Michael Sragow in "A Wizard of
Hollywood," Salon.com (February 24, 2000)

Steven Spielberg: "The Edinburgh-based writer made the aside at the
Scottish charity premiere of *Harry Potter and the Philosopher's Stone* at the Ster
Century Cinema in Leith. Rowling praised Columbus for remaining true to
her book, then added: 'Thank God it wasn't Spielberg.' She then jokingly
added: 'Do you think we could be sued for that?'"

—From "Rowling Has a Dig at Spielberg," *Edinburgh Evening News*
(November 7, 2001)

Unhappy film fan: "In the Harry Potter Usenet group alt.fan.harry_potter,
one potterphiliac entitled her posting 'Nooooooo' and suggested that the
film ought to be called *Harry Potter and the Mainstream Inflate-a-Budget Crap."*

—Laura Miller from "Fans Hate Director Picked for Harry Potter Film,"
Salon.com (March 30, 2000)

Right: Perseus LePage and his son Draco (yes, that's his real name—he legally changed it) strike a pose in front of a Harry Potter display in the dealer's room at Lumos 2006.

Below: Perseus LePage and his son Draco display their Dark Marks, which are permanently tattooed on their forearms.

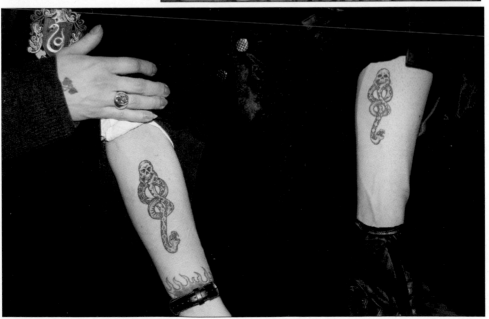

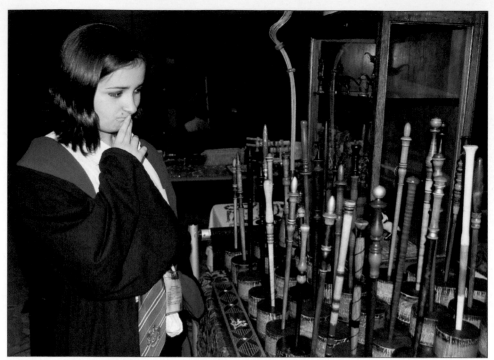

Paula Cella Geanau of Slytherin House looks at the amazing display of Whirlwood Magick Wands at Lumos 2006.

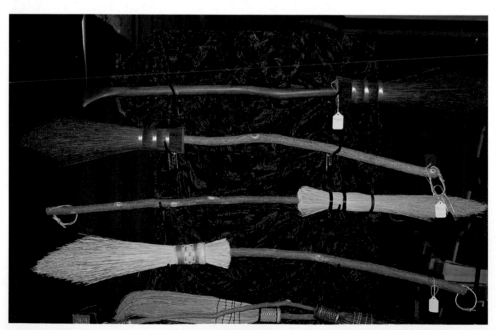

Master wandmaker Alivan's displays a selection of brooms at Lumos 2006.

Lucius Malfoy (Dana) strikes a pose.

The Malfoy family: Draco (Sam), Narcissa (Kayla), and Lucius (Dana) at Lumos 2006

Draco Malfoy (Sam) strikes a pose.

Witches and wizards gather to practice casting spells on one another at Lumos 2006, with the result that a stunning spell claims a victim!

Artist Tim Kirk points to a fantasy portrait he
drew of a Lumos 2006 attendee as she looks on.

Tim Kirk, in the dealers' room, begins another fantasy portrait at Lumos 2006.

In the dealers' room, a reader checks out the selection of Harry Potter books for sale.

A young Harry Potter fan in costume at Lumos 2006

Miryam Copper-Smith in full regalia at Lumos 2006

Clockwise from top left: Ron Weasley™ in casual gear, Hermione Granger™ in weekend togs, and Harry Potter™ out of the classroom (courtesy Tonner Doll Company, Inc.)

The Triwizard™ cup from Harry Potter and the
Order of the Phoenix (courtesy Tonner Doll Company, Inc.)

The Quidditch™ set: the trunk, a Quaffle™, two Bludgers™, the Golden
Snitch™, and a Beater™ bat (courtesy Tonner Doll Company, Inc.)

Draco Malfoy™ in school robes
(courtesy Tonner Doll Company, Inc.)

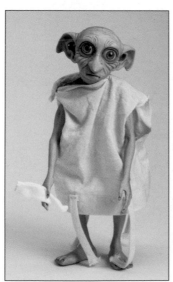

Dobby, the House-Elf™ (courtesy Tonner Doll Company, Inc.)

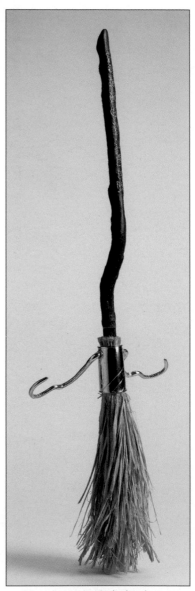

Harry Potter's Firebolt™ broom
(courtesy Tonner Doll Company, Inc.)

Ron Weasley™ at Hogwarts™
(courtesy Tonner Doll Company, Inc.)

Hermione Granger™
at Hogwarts™
(courtesy Tonner Doll Company, Inc.)

Harry Potter™ as
Gryffindor™ Seeker™
(courtesy Tonner Doll Company, Inc.)

Harry Potter™ at Hogwarts™
(courtesy Tonner Doll Company, Inc.)

The storefront to Whimsic Alley in Santa Monica, California

A statue of Dobby™ stands guard
at the entrance of Whimsic Alley.

Artist Britton McDaniel puts her hand between the bricks at Platform Nine and Three-Quarters at Whimsic Alley.

Whimsic Alley's fine selection of books, journals, owls cages, and other accessories on display

The entrance to Whimsic Alley

Head wizard Stan Goldin in his store, Whimsic Alley

J. K. Rowling preparing to read from *Harry Potter and the Half-Blood Prince* in NYC's Radio City Music Hall (August 2, 2006)

John Irving answers questions after his reading at NYC's Radio City Music Hall (August 2, 2006).

Stephen King reads from "The Revenge of Lard Ass Hogan" in NYC's Radio City Music Hall (August 2, 2006).

The irrepressible, inimitable Whoopi Goldberg whoops it up in her introduction of King, Irving, and Rowling at NYC's Radio City Music Hall (August 2, 2006).

Stephen King, J. K. Rowling, and John Irving take questions from the audience at NYC's Radio City Music Hall (August 2, 2006).

Part Four:
A Look at the Books

Tim Kirk

ewcomers to Harry Potter's world will likely feel a bit over-whelmed, which is understandable: six books, four movies (and more on the way), and a wealth of dedicated websites exploring every nook and cranny of the Harry Potter universe—it all confuses rather than clarifies.

This section is devoted to a book-by-book look at the six Harry Potter novels in print. By focusing on the principal texts, the newcomer will find negotiating the overwhelming amount of information about Rowling and the Harry Potter novels much more manageable.

My general recommendations for reading the Potter canon:

1. Read the books in order. Not only are the novels chronological, but Rowling plotted them in exquisite detail, which means that each book builds on what has gone before. Little details that seem insignificant will, in later books, resonate with meaning and importance.

2. Keep your eyes open for the clues. Rowling employs the literary technique of foreshadowing to build anticipation and whet readers' appetites. There is nothing superfluous in the novels. Everything has been inserted for a reason, even if it's not readily apparent at first glance.

3. Enjoy the movies but realize that they are interpretive, not literal, and thus the reader is advised to go to the primary source, the novels, to get the story straight.

In this section I'll discuss the story behind the story (the facts surrounding the book's publication), the publishing history of the book, reviews, awards, and a summation of where the book fits in with the rest of the series.

I will not provide a detailed plot summary, since the first-time reader will want to discover it in the reading.

HARRY POTTER AND THE
PHILOSOPHER'S/SORCERER'S STONE

I never dreamt this would happen. My realistic side had allowed myself to think that I might get one good review. That was my idea of a peak. So everything else really has been like stepping into Wonderland for me.

—Rowling quoted by
Ann Treneman in
"The J. K. Rowling Interview,"
Times (June 20, 2003)

The first Potter novel was published in the United States as *Harry Potter and the Sorcerer's Stone* because Scholastic didn't feel American readers would understand the allusion in the British title, *Harry Potter and the Philosopher's Stone*.

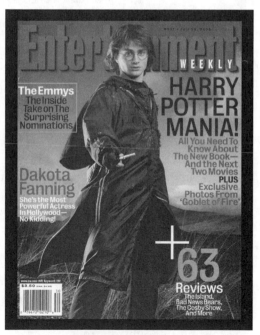

Actor Dan Radcliffe as Harry Potter rates the front page of *Entertainment Weekly*.

At Whimsic Alley, a bricked wall—platform 9 3/4

Dedication

"For Jessica, who loves stories,/For Anne, who loved them too;/And for Di, who heard this one first."

The dedication is for her daughter, Jessica; her late mother, Anne; and her sister, Dianne.

Background

Once upon a time there was a single mother on welfare who became rich and famous by writing her way out of poverty by writing the best-selling series of all time—in other words, an enchanting Cinderella story, in which the handsome prince (the publisher) discovers the beautiful but hitherto ignored blonde heroine.

That's the story journalists writing about Rowling like to tell, since it romanticizes the world of the aspiring writer and offers hope to the millions of others who think that they, too, can go from obscurity to fame with their fiction. (If only it were that easy!)

Rowling undoubtedly rolls her eyes whenever she reads another story that plays up that oft-repeated narrative hook, since it oversimplifies the plain truth. A lifelong writer, she spent most of her adult life working. In fact, she had gotten an £8,000 grant from the Scottish Arts Council to work on the Potter novels *after* she had sold the first book to Bloomsbury. In other words, the journalists showed us a snapshot of a specific moment in her life, but it wasn't representative of the whole.

Like most first-time authors, Rowling faced an uphill battle in getting her first novel published, since she had to confront all the preconceived notions the publishing industry harbors of first-time authors, especially those who want to write children's books.

Though Rowling has a powerful imagination, neither she nor anyone else could have imagined the salutary effect she'd have on the genre. She would go on to transform it permanently, bringing it into the mainstream, like Stephen King did for horror/suspense fiction.

When she submitted her novel to the Christopher Little Literary Agency, two early readers—Bryony Evens and Fleur Howle—championed it in-house and recommended it to their boss, Christopher Little.

After Rowling signed the standard artist-agent contract, Little began submitting the over-80,000-word novel to British publishers, who raised what then seemed quite sensible objections: It is too long for a children's book and, besides, boys won't read a children's book written by a woman.

In hindsight, both objections seem laughable, but at the time they seemed perfectly reasonable; in fact, the latter objection prompted the agency to recommend that Rowling not write under her name but under an abbreviated, gender-free name: J. K. Rowling instead of Joanne Rowling.

Again, in hindsight, the British publishers who passed on what turned out to be the most lucrative literary franchise of our time seem foolish, but this is commonplace in the book industry. Publishing houses rise, and fall, on the wisdom of book acquisitions.

Bloomsbury Publishing wisely decided to take a chance on this unknown but obviously talented writer who, incidentally, was skilled as an illustrator, as well. The offer from Bloomsbury was modest, but Rowling didn't care. She would realize her dream of seeing a book with her name on it in a bookstore.

On June 26, 1997, the book went to press with a modest first printing, most of which sold to libraries and independent booksellers.

Early reviews from newspapers in England were positive, heralding a new voice, but with such modest sales, Rowling could not hope for anything but supplementary income from her writing.

The turning point arrived when the book came to the attention of a publisher in the United States, which would prove to be the world's largest market for Harry Potter books. Janet Hogarth, formerly on the staff at Bloomsbury's children's book division, had recently begun working at Scholastic and championed the book to the firm's editorial director, Arthur A. Levine, who was en route to an international book fair in Germany.

Levine read the book and loved it, determined to bid whatever was necessary to secure U.S. rights. Soon thereafter, a spirited auction resulted, with Levine bidding furiously, fending off the competition. The result: Levine kept bidding until he had won the U.S. rights for a figure some in the industry felt excessive, especially for a children's book by a first-time novelist.

In sharp contrast to the modest first U.K. printing, Scholastic planned an unprecedented print run of 50,000 copies. The combination of a record advance and a large first printing made news worldwide, and so began the legend of J. K. Rowling. Newspapers ran stories about her as a single parent on the dole who became rich by writing her way to success—a great story, but rather fanciful.

By this time Rowling had finished and turned in the second book in the series, *Harry Potter and the Chamber of Secrets,* and the big question on everyone's mind was whether or not publishing history would repeat itself. Would her second book repeat the success of the first, or was she a one-book wonder?

About the Book

For readers worldwide, this book is pure magic. Though novels about student wizards are (pardon the expression) old hat, Rowling has reinvigorated not only the fantasy field but children's literature, as well.

What makes this book all the more surprising—and make no mistake, the book is *full* of delightful surprises—is that it came not from an established writer with a long publication history but from an unknown writer who didn't even have a short story to her credit.

In short, the odds didn't favor the young author or her fledgling novel, which makes it all the more remarkable that within six years Rowling would sell a record quarter-billion copies of her Harry Potter novels one through five. Greatly exceeding her modest expectations, her books would go on to make book-publishing history.

"A wonderful first novel," wrote a reviewer for the *New York Times,* which certainly sums up the book succinctly. The story of an orphaned boy who lives with his depressingly ordinary relatives—the monstrous Dursley family—Harry Potter is not what he seems. In fact, Harry himself doesn't know who he is, since the Dursleys go to extraordinary lengths to shield his true identity from him and everyone else. As far as Vernon and Petunia Dursley are concerned, and as far as Harry knows, he is just another non-magical boy—a Muggle. But when owl-delivered letters from Hogwarts inexplicably arrive at the Dursley residence for Harry, his uncle intercepts them and, with characteristic glee, burns them in the fireplace.

To his uncle's dismay and mounting frustration, the trickle of letters increases, so he takes the family off to a remote shack by the sea, never realizing that what he's dealing with is beyond his imagination. Indeed, when the letters fail to be delivered, the final letter is hand-delivered, not by an ordinary postman but by a half-giant named Rubeus Hagrid, who is on a mission to deliver an acceptance letter to Harry Potter, inviting him as a first-year student to a magical educational institution, Hogwarts School of Witchcraft and Wizardry.

Kept in the dark about his past and, indeed, his family, Harry Potter had no idea that he was already a legend in the magical community. "You're a wizard, Harry," says Hagrid, to the great surprise of the young boy, who may have had an inkling because strange things happened when he willed them, but he didn't realize why.

Hagrid rescues Harry Potter from his Muggle world and takes him to Diagon Alley, which is his first encounter with the wizarding community. From there, it's on to Hogwarts, along with the other first-year students, on the Hogwarts Express, a train that picks students up at Platform Nine and Three-Quarters in London and transports them to a geographical point far to the north.

At Hogwarts, Harry Potter realizes his place in the universe is in the wizard-ing world, where great things are expected of him. The son of James and Lily Potter—a wizard and Muggle-born witch—Harry Potter has a singular distinc-tion. He is famous because, as an infant, he survived a direct attack by a power-ful dark wizard named Lord Voldemort who failed in killing Harry, despite the employment of the deadliest of all curses, the feared Killing Curse.

Far from being just another fledgling wizard in the magical world, Harry Potter is the only one who has ever survived a Killing Curse and is therefore unique. He is "the boy who lived" when countless others died, including Harry's parents. The attack also sealed his destiny, inextricably linking it to Lord Voldemort's, with the promise that a hellacious showdown is inevitable in the last book in the series.

Will Lord Voldemort finally finish what he failed to do many years ago and kill Harry Potter, or will the boy wizard take his place in the wizarding world by defeating the most feared dark wizard of all time?

In the first chapter of the book, Professor McGonagall makes a prophetic observation about the boy wizard. "He'll be famous—a legend—I wouldn't be surprised if today was known as Harry Potter day in the future—there will be books written about Harry—every child in the world will know his name!"

Professor McGonagall spoke the truth.

Selected Reviews

Booklist: "Rowling's first novel is a brilliantly imagined and beautifully written fantasy that incorporates elements of traditional British school sto-ries without once violating the magical underpinnings of the plot. In fact,

Rowling's wonderful ability to put a fantastic spin on sports, student rivalry, and eccentric faculty contributes to the humor, charm, and, well, delight of her utterly captivating story."

New York Times Book Review: "A wonderful first novel. Much like Roald Dahl, J. K. Rowling has a gift for keeping the emotions, fears, and triumphs of her characters on a human scale, even while the supernatural is popping out all over. The book is full of wonderful, sly humor [and] the characters are impressively three-dimensional (occasionally, four-dimensional!) and move along seamlessly through the narrative. *Harry Potter and the Sorcerer's Stone* is as funny, moving, and impressive as the story behind its writing. Like Harry Potter, [Rowling] has wizardry inside, and has soared beyond her modest Muggle surroundings to achieve something quite special."

Publishers Weekly: "Readers are in for a delightful romp with this award-winning debut from a British author who dances in the footsteps of P. L. Travers and Roald Dahl. . . . There is enchantment, suspense, and danger galore (as well as enough creepy creatures to satisfy the most bogeymen-loving readers, and even a magical game of soccer-like Quidditch to entertain sports fans) as Harry and his friends Ron and Hermione plumb the secrets of the forbidden third floor at Hogwarts to battle evil and unravel the mystery behind Harry's scar. Rowling leaves the door wide open for a sequel; bedazzled readers will surely clamor for one."

School Library Journal: "After reading this entrancing fantasy, readers will be convinced that they, too, could take the train to Hogwarts School, if only they could find Platform Nine and Three-Quarters at the King's Cross station."

Awards (U.K. and U.S.)

American Library Association Notable Book
Booklist Editor's Choice
Booksellers Association/Bookseller Author of the Year (1998)
British Book Awards: Children's Book of the Year (1998)
FCBG Children's Book Award: overall winner, and Longer Novel category
   (1998)
Nestle Smarties Book Prize (1998, Gold Medal)
New York Public Library Best Book of the Year 1998
North East Book Award (1999)
North East Scotland Book Award (1998)
Parenting Book of the Year Award 1998
Publishers Weekly Best Book of 1998
Scottish Arts Council Children's Book Award (1999)
Whitaker's Platinum Book Award 2001

Summation

To categorize *Harry Potter and the Sorcerer's Stone* as a children's novel—that is to say, a novel that only a child would enjoy—is to ignore the enormous appeal that the novel holds for adults, a fact that surprised everyone, especially Bloomsbury, who found adults in England shielding their copies behind newspapers, since they didn't want to be seen in public reading a children's book. As a result, Bloomsbury then issued the novels with two different covers—one for children, and one for adults.

While it's certainly possible for a children's book to sell well on its own, this novel clearly appealed to two sensibilities. Children loved its sense of fantasy and humor, its enormously appealing rite of passage story. They identified with a powerless child who realizes his potential to assume his rightful place in the world.

Adults, who also love a well-told story, appreciated it for the same reasons children did, but realize that the novel offers more. As Rowling pointed out, the book serves as a metaphor to explore the world of imagination. You are either a Muggle or, so to speak, a magician; you either believe in the status quo and a world of rules and order . . . or a world of imagined possibilities, where human potential can be realized.

For children and adults alike, the novel speaks volumes. We empathize with Harry Potter because we can all see a little bit of Potter in ourselves.

HARRY POTTER AND THE CHAMBER OF SECRETS

"Harry Potter" (Taylor Kincaid, an employee at Barnes & Noble) takes a break from the hectic Potter Party.

Dedication

"For Séan P. F. Harris,/Getaway driver and foul-weather friend."

This refers to her college pal, who is one of her best friends.

Background

Rowling submitted the manuscript for this book to her British publisher in early July 1997, two weeks after the U.K. publication of *Harry Potter and the Philosopher's Stone.*

This second book in the series was published in the U.K. in July 1998, but wouldn't see publication in the U.S. until June 1999. The problem, as Scholastic soon discovered, was that some eager fans wouldn't wait for the U.S. edition; instead, they ordered the British edition from the U.K. division of Amazon.com, which undercut the sales of the U.S. edition.

To make matters worse, the third book in the series, *Harry Potter and the Prisoner of*

Azkaban, would be scheduled for publication in the U.K. on July 8, so the problem was compounded. U.S. fans began ordering significant quantities of the U.K. edition, since the U.S. edition wasn't scheduled for publication until September.

To Bloomsbury's and Scholastic's dismay, Web-savvy U.S. readers upset the delicate order of balance. The appetite for Harry Potter books was so great that Scholastic's marketing and sales plan were seriously undercut by the built-in delay in publication between the U.K. and U.S. editions—a problem they would finally correct with the fourth book, *Harry Potter and the Goblet of Fire.*

About Book Two

Contrary to popular belief, lightning *can* strike twice, but it's rare, and especially so in the book field where the promise of a first novel sometimes turns out to be an empty one. The writer, having said all he wanted to say in his first novel, cannot resist the siren call for a second book, which the publisher hopes will be just as, if not more, successful. Far too often, however, the second novel doesn't reach sales, or readers', expectations.

Part of Rowling's great genius in constructing the series was in biding her time. Until she had thoroughly explored her fictional world and knew exactly, book by book, what would happen and when, she refrained from publishing. Consequently, the first book got off to a necessarily slow start, with 113 of its 309 pages just to get Harry to Hogwarts, at which point the real fun begins and the book builds up its momentum, like a train streaking down the tracks at top speed.

In the second book in the series, two facts become obvious. Nothing in the first book is accidental. In other words, there are clues, seemingly innocuous, to what will become important in the books to follow. Also, Rowling dispensed with the back story—telling us who Harry Potter is and why he's so famous in the wizarding community—to get on with the main story. As a reviewer for *Booklist* put it, "The magical foundation so necessary in good fantasy [is] as expertly crafted here as in the first book."

By page 12 of the second novel, we know Harry Potter's got a problem on his hands because Dobby, a house-elf, visits him in his room at the Dursley residence to warn him not to come back to Hogwarts, and does everything in his considerable power to drive the point home.

Having established the main character, the supporting cast (Rubeus Hagrid, Ron Weasley, and Hermione Granger), and the faculty at Hogwarts, Rowling can concentrate on the story at hand. At Hogwarts, the Chamber of Secrets is the stuff of legend. It reportedly resides deep within the bowels of the school, undiscovered despite numerous searches over its more than thousand year history. Though the present faculty is quick to point out that talk of the Chamber of Secrets should be discounted, if not dismissed outright, the talk among the students is animated, especially when things take a somber tone with Hogwarts students turning to stone.

Does the Chamber of Secrets actually exist? And, if so, has someone opened it—presumably, the destined heir of Slytherin—to allow the fabled monster to escape and run amuck at Hogwarts? No one—living or dead—is spared. Animals, students, and even ghosts are all at risk, as pesky poltergeist Peeves warns everyone.

Readers love a good mystery wrapped within a well-told tale, and with her second book, Rowling doesn't disappoint. She, in fact, has written an engaging book series that promises to deliver more with each installment, as Harry Potter learns more about himself and his eventual place in the wizarding world.

In the second novel we also learn much more about the delightful wizarding world. We are taken to the enchanted home of the Weasleys, where clocks tell more than time, where dishes wash themselves, and the family garden is populated with talking gnomes, who must periodically be weeded out.

This book adds to the cast of memorable characters Gilderoy Lockhart, a flamboyant and excessively vain braggart who shows up with a flourish at a bookstore to sign copies of his many books, required texts for Hogwarts students, since he's the newest addition to its faculty. (His books are more fiction than fact, however!) We also learn more about Nearly Headless Nick, a ghost at Hogwarts who is certainly the most interesting of the lot. Add to that mix and an engaging assortment of new magical creatures, good and bad, and spiced with a delightful sense of humor throughout, and the end result is, as the British would say, a simply smashing read.

Of course, at the heart of the book is the mystery about the Chamber of Secrets, which must be solved by Harry Potter, who is still very much a fledgling student wizard, unsure of himself and his place in the magical world.

By the second book in the series, we know we are in good hands. Rowling has delivered the literary goods once again and whetted our appetite for the third novel, just as any good writer should.

Selected Reviews

Booklist: "Harry Potter's exploits during his second year at Hogwarts completely live up to the bewitching measure of *Harry Potter and the Sorcerer's Stone.* The magical foundation so necessary in good fantasy [is] as expertly crafted here as in the first book."

Los Angeles Times: "*Harry Potter and the Chamber of Secrets* is a wonderful sequel, as suspenseful, charming, and ultimately satisfying as its predecessor."

A *Publishers Weekly* starred review: "Fans who have been anxiously awaiting the return of young British wizard Harry Potter (and whose clamor caused the Stateside publication date to be moved up three months) will be amazed afresh. And newcomers will likely join Harry's delighted legion of followers, for this tale is perhaps even more inventive than its predecessor, *Harry Potter and the Sorcerer's Stone.* Picking up shortly after his first year at Hogwarts School of Witchcraft and Wizardry, orphan Harry is spending the summer with his detestable Muggle (non-witch) aunt's family. Rowling briskly sets the action rolling with a mysterious warning from an elf named Dobby. The pace accelerates as Harry, now 12, is rescued from his bedroom imprisonment by his best friend Ron Weasley and his irrepressible older twin brothers in a flying car. Their school year gets off to a bad start when Harry and Ron crash-land the car at Hogwarts. More trouble soon follows, first from Harry's old nemesis, supercilious Draco Malfoy, then from a mysterious something that is petrifying Muggle-born students, culminating with Harry and Ron's friend Hermione. And once more, it's up to Harry to save the day. Rowling might be a Hogwarts graduate herself, for her ability to create such an engaging, imaginative, funny, and, above all, heart-poundingly suspenseful yarn is nothing short of magical."

School Library Journal: "Fans of the phenomenally popular *Harry Potter and the Sorcerer's Stone* won't be disappointed when they rejoin Harry, now on break after finishing his first year at Hogwarts. The novel is marked throughout by the same sly and sophisticated humor found in the first book, along with inventive, new, matter-of-fact uses of magic that will once again have readers longing to emulate Harry and his wizard friends."

USA Today: "Those needing a bit of magic, morality, and mystical worlds can do no better than opening *Harry Potter and the Chamber of Secrets.* As she did in *Harry Potter and the Sorcerer's Stone,* Rowling delivers plenty of ghoulish giggles. And in young Potter she has created a hero as resourceful, brave, and loyal as Luke Skywalker himself."

Wall Street Journal: "Harry's enchanted world is a refreshing break from the all-too-familiar settings of many of today's novels."

Awards (U.S. and U.K.)

American Library Association (ALA) Best Book for Young Adults (1999)
American Library Association (ALA) Notable Book
Booklist 1999 Editor's Choice
Booksellers Association/Bookseller Author of the Year 1998
British Book Awards (1998): Children's Book of the Year
FCBC Children's Book Award (1998): Overall winner, and Longer Novel
    Category
Gold Medal Smarties Prize (1999)
National Book Award, U.K. (1999)

North East Book Award (1999)
North East Scotland Book Award (1998)
School Library Journal (1999), Best Book of the Year
Scottish Arts Council Children's Book Award (1999)
Whitaker's Platinum Book Award (2001)

HARRY POTTER AND THE
PRISONER OF AZKABAN

Dedication

"To Jill Prewett and Aine Kiely, the Godmothers of Swing."

The dedication refers to her two fellow teachers with whom she taught at Encounter English School in Porto, Portugal. She also shared an apartment with them while there.

Background

This book is tightly written with a plot that keeps the reader turning pages at a furious rate. Not surprisingly, the book is a critical favorite as well. A reviewer for *USA Today* observed: "It's three for three for British author J. K. Rowling, who scores another home run with *Harry Potter and the Prisoner of Azkaban.*"

At Lumos 2006, Petra proudly wears a Sirius Black prison shirt.

This third book in the series would be the last one to see initial publication in the U.K. because Rowling's publishers realized that only a simultaneous release worldwide would satisfy the fans. For *Azkaban*, U.S. readers simply ordered from Amazon.co.uk, rather than wait three more months for the domestic edition from Scholastic.

The thousands of orders siphoned off from Scholastic prompted Rowling's publishers to put in place a new policy: Effective with the fourth book, Harry Potter would be released in the U.K. and the U.S. on the same day, with foreign translations to follow as soon thereafter as possible.

The book's success was a sign of the times, marking a turning point for Rowling, now an international phenomenon. Mobbed at a book signing in New York City, Rowling realized that what had been planned as an ordinary book signing turned into an extraordinary event: an exercise in logistics on a larger scale than her publishers had anticipated. The long line of readers that stretched around the city block underscored her growing popularity. Clearly, Rowling's popularity was off the charts and a routine book signing was no longer feasible. Rowling regretfully resigned herself to the undeniable fact that there could be no more book signings, no matter how much the fans wanted it, and no matter how much she wanted that one-on-one contact with her readers. There were, after all, millions of fans . . . but only one writer to satisfy the demand.

About the Book

The tone of this book is considerably darker than the preceding books. At its heart: Sirius Black—an escapee from Azkaban prison—is reportedly looking for Harry Potter. As the Minister of Magic marshals his forces, enlisting Aurors and Dementors alike in a search for Black, Harry Potter has his own problems to deal with on the home front: In the Muggle world, Harry is under siege from his Aunt Marge, who has come to visit. After repeatedly insulting Harry and his parents, the final insult triggers Harry into unintentionally using magic: Marge is inflated and floats out of the house, to the shock of everyone present. Angry beyond words, Harry packs up and leaves, wanting to escape not only Uncle Vernon's barrage of demands but whoever may be on the way from the Ministry of Magic. His use of magic outside Hogwarts is a serious school infraction, especially since this is the second time it has happened. (The first time, a house-elf named Dobby was the culprit, but the Ministry fingered Harry.)

On the lam, Harry unwittingly summons the Knight Bus, which provides emergency transportation for stranded witches and wizards, and it takes him to the Leaky Cauldron, where Cornelius Fudge, the Minister of Magic, awaits him. The good news is that Harry is still alive and unharmed;

the bad news is that Sirius Black—one of the most dangerous criminals ever to be incarcerated in Azkaban—is not on a witch but a wizard hunt, looking for Harry . . . but to what end?

The wizarding world has issued an all points bulletin, so to speak, alerting everyone that it's a serious matter indeed: Sirius Black is loose and no one—in the Muggle world or wizarding world—is safe. Dementors, under order from the Ministry of Magic, are at Hogwarts on guard duty; Ron and Hermione's friendship becomes increasingly frayed; and all indications are that this third year will be Harry's most troubling yet.

Questions abound: Why does Sirius Black want to kill Harry? What's the secret behind the Shrieking Shack? And, most important, will Harry survive his inevitable encounter with Sirius Black?

Rowling delivers the goods with a riveting tale, with twists, turns, and surprises galore.

Selected Reviews

Publishers Weekly: "Rowling proves that she has plenty of tricks left up her sleeve in this third Harry Potter adventure, set once again at the Hogwarts School of Witchcraft and Wizardry. Right before the start of term, a supremely dangerous criminal breaks out of a supposedly impregnable wizards' prison; it will come as no surprise to Potter fans that the villain, a henchman of Harry's old enemy Lord Voldemort, appears to have targeted Harry. In many ways this installment seems to serve a transitional role in the seven-volume series: While many of the adventures are breathlessly relayed, they appear to be laying groundwork for even more exciting adventures to come.

"The beauty here lies in the genius of Rowling's plotting. Seemingly minor details established in books one and two unfold to take on unforeseen significance, and the finale, while not airtight in its internal logic, is utterly thrilling. Rowling's wit never flags, whether constructing the workings of the wizard world (just how would a magician be made to stay behind bars?) or tossing off quick jokes (a grandmother wears a hat decorated with a stuffed vulture; the divination classroom looks like a tawdry tea shop). The Potter spell is holding strong."

Booklist: "What results once again is a good story, well told, one that is not only a cut above most fantasies for the age group but is also attractive to readers from beyond both ends of the spectrum. . . . We wait impatiently for the next episode."

New York Review of Books: "The Harry Potter stories belong to an ongoing tradition of Anglo-American fantasy that takes off from Tolkien and C. S. Lewis. . . . What sets Rowling's books apart from their predecessors is partly a lighthearted fertility of invention that recalls L. Frank Baum's Oz books. Even more important is the fact that hers is a fully imagined world, to which she has a deep, ongoing commitment."

School Library Journal: "Isn't it reassuring that some things just get better and better? Harry is back and in fine form in the third installment of his adventures at Hogwarts School of Witchcraft and Wizardry. . . . The pace is nonstop, with thrilling games of Quidditch, terrifying Omens of Death, some skillful time travel, and lots of slimy Slytherins sneaking about causing trouble. This is a fabulously entertaining read that will have Harry Potter fans cheering for more."

Awards (U.S. and U.K.)

American Library Association Notable Book
Booklist 1999 Editor's Choice
Booksellers Association/Bookseller Author of the Year
British Book Awards Author of the Year
FCBC Children's Book Award 1999/Longer Novel category
Gold Medal Smarties Prize (1999)
Los Angeles Times Best Book of 1999
New York Public Library Title for Reading and Sharing
Whitaker's Platinum Book Award (2001)
Whitbread Award for Children's Literature

HARRY POTTER AND THE GOBLET OF FIRE

Dedication

"To Peter Rowling,/In Memory of Mr. Ridley/And to Susan Sladden,/Who Helped Harry Out of his Cupboard."

The dedication refers to her father, Peter Rowling; to Mr. Ronald Ridley, who was in part the fictional basis for the character of Ronald Weasley; and to Susan Sladden, whom I haven't been able to identify.

Background

Mindful of U.S. readers who wouldn't wait for the U.S. edition of the Harry Potter book to be published—preferring instead to order from Amazon.com UK—Bloomsbury and Scholastic wisely decided to

"Ron Weasley" (Kenneth Douglas) mans the cash register at a Barnes & Noble bookstore during a Potter Party.

release book four simultaneously, thus ensuring that British book sales didn't undercut the U.S. book sales.

By now Rowling was a publishing phenomenon with books that sold in the millions of copies. Good for her publishers, but not necessarily good for the fans, since it meant large crowds turned up for her every public appearance, especially bookstores, at which the demand for signed copies far exceeded supply.

The long and short of it: The publicity tour for this book proved to Rowling and her publishers that such tours were no longer logistically possible in the U.K. or the U.S. At a widely publicized public appearance at King's Cross station, children crowded anxiously to get a glimpse of Rowling, but were disappointed when the press corps forced their way to the front lines, taking photos and shouting for her. Elsewhere on the tour, in the U.S., a small bookstore was overwhelmed with capacity crowds, for which police were called in as frustrated parents nearly exchanged blows.

For Rowling, the book tour—backed by a multimillion-dollar publicity and marketing campaign—made it abundantly clear that, rather than help sell books, her fame and popularity were actually hindrances. A literary superstar, she could not possibly satisfy even a fraction of the demand for her time from the media, from bookstores requesting personal appearances, and from other organizations asking for her presence at their events.

Clearly, decisions would have to be made regarding future promotions, since things—as this book tour amply proved—had gotten way out of hand.

About the Book

Harry Potter and the Goblet of Fire is the midbook in the series, with a count of 734 pages. In this book, Harry Potter grapples not only with the unexpected developments concerning Sirius Black from the previous book, but also with a new challenge. He is, inexplicably, a fourth contender for a Triwizard Tournament for which traditionally only three contenders are selected by the Goblet of Fire. But choose him it does, and so he competes against a fellow Hogwarts student and also top students from the two other wizarding schools in Europe, Durmstrang and Beauxbatons.

The novel opens with a hilarious entry by Arthur Weasley and his sons, Fred and George, who use Floo Powder to arrive at the Dursley residence to pick up Harry Potter, for whom they have a ticket to an international Quidditch tournament. What happens at that tournament, however, foreshadows what is to come. The Triwizard Tournament is more than simply a test of will and skill among four contestants; its true purpose is far more sinister.

A deeper, richer novel than the three previously published novels, carefully textured and painted on a wide canvas, *Harry Potter and the Goblet of Fire* is the kind of book Potter fans willingly lose themselves in, as they explore heretofore unseen aspects of the magical world in which Harry Potter is, for obvious reasons, a focal point.

Rowling points out that far from being children's novels per se, the books will necessarily get darker in tone and more horrific as the series progresses. Indeed, in this latest installment, a significant character dies. It will be, as Rowling has warned us in several interviews, one of many to come.

Far from being a children's fantasy in which everyone lives happily ever after, the Potter novels are imbued with a naturalistic element that gives them a dark touch; a reminder to everyone, even Harry Potter, that we all have to grow up—a painful process in which hard choices must be made, choices that will shape our lives for the years to come.

Selected Reviews

Publishers Weekly: "Even without the unprecedented media attention and popularity her magical series has attracted, it would seem too much to hope that Rowling could sustain the brilliance and wit of her first three novels. Astonishingly, Rowling seems to have the spell-casting powers she assigns her characters: this fourth volume might be her most thrilling yet. The novel opens as a confused Muggle overhears Lord Voldemort and his henchman, Wormtail (the escapee from book three, *Azkaban*), discussing a murder and plotting more deaths (and invoking Harry Potter's name); clues suggest that Voldemort and Wormtail's location will prove highly significant. From here it takes a while (perhaps slightly too long a while) for Harry and his friends to get back to the Hogwarts school, where Rowling is on surest footing. Headmaster Dumbledore appalls everyone by declaring that Quidditch competition has been canceled for the year, then he makes the exciting announcement that the Triwizard Tournament is to be held after a cessation of many hundreds of years (it was discontinued, he explains, because the death toll mounted so high). One representative from each of the three largest wizardry schools of Europe (sinister Durmstrang, luxurious Beauxbatons, and Hogwarts) is to be chosen by the Goblet of Fire; because of the mortal dangers, Dumbledore casts a spell that allows only students who are at least 17 to drop their names into the Goblet. Thus no one foresees that the Goblet will announce a fourth candidate: Harry. Who has put his name into the Goblet, and how is his participation in the tournament linked, as it surely must be, to Voldemort's newest plot? The details are as ingenious and original as ever, and somehow (for catching readers off-guard must certainly get more difficult with each successive volume) Rowling plants the red herrings, the artful clues, and tricky surprises that disarm the most attentive audience. A climax even more spectacular than that of *Azkaban* will leave readers breathless; the muscle-building heft of this volume notwithstanding, the clamor for book five will begin as soon as readers finish installment four."

Booklist: "Harry's fourth challenging experience will more than live up to his myriad fans' expectations. . . . The carefully created world of magic becomes more embellished and layered, while the amazing plotting ties up loose ends, even as it sets in motion more entanglements."

Kirkus Reviews: "Another grand tale of magic and mystery, of wheels within wheels oiled in equal measure by terror and comedy, featuring an engaging young hero-in-training who's not above the occasional snit, and clicking along so smoothly that it seems shorter than it is."

Stephen King in the *New York Times Book Review:* "I'm relieved to report that Potter four is every bit as good as Potters one through three. . . . The fantasy writer's job is to conduct the willing reading from mundanity to magic. This is a feat of which only a superior imagination is capable, and Rowling possesses such equipment."

Janet Maslin in the *New York Times:* "As the midpoint in a projected seven-book series, *Goblet of Fire* is exactly the big, clever, vibrant, tremendously assured installment that gives shape and direction to the whole undertaking and still somehow preserves the material's enchanting innocence. . . . This time Rowling offers her clearest proof yet of what should have been wonderfully obvious: What makes the Potter books so popular is the radically simple fact that they're so good."

Awards (U.S. and U.K.)

American Library Association Notable Book
Booklist Editors' Choice (2000)
Children's Book Award in 9–11 category (2001)
New York Public Library Book for the Teen Age
Publishers Weekly Best Children's Book (2000)
Scottish Arts Council Book Award (2001)
Whitaker's Platinum Book Award (2001)
Winner of the Hugo Award, Best Novel category (World Science Fiction Convention)

HARRY POTTER AND THE
ORDER OF THE PHOENIX

Dedication

"To Neil, Jessica, and David, who make my world magical."

The dedication refers to her second husband, Neil Murray, her daughter from her first marriage, and her son from her second marriage.

Background

The book industry has a tried-and-true game plan to guarantee as many copies of a book as possible will be sold by its publication date. The plan involves sending out hundreds of galleys well before the book's publication to guarantee early reviews, sending out hundreds of review copies to newspapers and magazines, and, most importantly, scheduling media appearances on television—all

At Whimsic Alley, a room filled with odd curios, swords, walking sticks, and accessories of every kind for the well-equipped wizard

designed to snare the attention of a jaded public and get them to buy books.

All of this is predicated, of course, on the completion of the book itself, which in this case became a matter of growing concern to all. The book industry wanted Rowling's latest to help draw attention to books as best-sellers; booksellers wanted it to help their bottom line; and most of all, readers clamored for it because they simply wanted to read it.

This fifth book, however, was plagued with unanticipated delays that dogged it, postponing publication time and again. As a result, the media started running stories about Rowling's presumed writing block. In the absence of truth, speculation ran rampant, but the simple truth was that a confluence of several events delayed the book: She needed to get off the restrictive publishing treadmill that demanded books on demand to suit the publisher's schedule; she wanted to write two short books for Comic Relief, a charity; she was distracted by a meritless lawsuit in which she was later vindicated; but most of all, she needed relief from the overwhelming presence of the media, with reporters showing up at her home in Edinburgh, banging on her door, and demanding interviews.

The biggest problem was the deadline, so Rowling wrote to her publisher and offered to pay back the advance, since she no longer wanted the burden of having to produce on demand. Understandably, Rowling's publisher declined her offer and told her to keep the advance. Write the book on your own schedule, they told her, and when it's done, we'll be happy to publish it. Everyone— the publisher, the booksellers, the media, and the fans—would just have to wait.

As it turned out, the wait would be three years, during which the publisher did not stand idle. Pumping $4 million into promoting the book it didn't even have on hand, Scholastic embarked on a "stealth" book campaign:

1. No early review copies.

2. No book signings.

3. No media coverage except a BBC interview (in the U.K.) and a profile with Katie Couric (from NBC-TV).

4. A countdown clock on her U.K. publisher's website—a device quickly adopted worldwide by Potter fan websites.

5. Midnight parties scheduled worldwide. Books would go on sale on June 21, 2003, only one minute into the new day.

All, it seemed, was going according to plan, but as poet Robert Burns reminds us, in the affairs of mice and men, things can often go awry. In Rowling's case, an unscrupulous employee smuggled unbound copies out of the printing plant, with the hope of selling chapters to a local newspaper. (His plan failed. The paper cooperated with the police and set up a sting operation.)

On a more serious note, an entire truckload of copies in England was stolen weeks before publication date, which understandably caused grave concern at Bloomsbury. Where would these copies show up? Would they be sold on the black market as under-the-counter sales? Would copies be shipped immediately to the Pacific Rim, where printing pirates would be quick to manufacture facsimile editions for sale? Would copies show up for sale on the Internet? Nobody knew, but everyone feared the worst.

In the end, the worst that happened was that, in the U.S., a handful of stores mistakenly put copies out a few days early, but when Rowling's publisher explained that if they couldn't observe the embargo this time around, they might not get *any* books the next time around, merchants everywhere got the message: It's one thing to get a Howler, but quite another to be sent to Azkaban. For merchants, not getting books six or seven would be the equivalent of a prison sentence—a form of economic death.

Things settled down as the witching hour approached, when booksellers quietly began opening up specially marked boxes overprinted with text ("Harry Potter and the Order of the Phoenix/J. K. Rowling/DO NOT OPEN BEFORE JUNE 21, 2003"). Meanwhile, the master countdown clock on the website of Bloomsbury Publishing ticked down to its final seconds until its message changed to the declaration everyone had been waiting for: IT'S HERE!

Finally, *Harry Potter and the Order of the Phoenix* saw light—moonlight, as it turned out. At an hour when most families were fast asleep, scores of parents with sleepy-headed kids were at bookstores nationwide, picking up their reserved copies of the biggest Potter novel to date—870 pages.

In my small corner of the world, southeast coastal Virginia, local bookstores stocked up on copies and held midnight parties. The local chain stores, with heavy discounting, got the bulk of the customers. At a Barnes & Noble superstore in nearby Virginia Beach, more than a thousand Potter fans (many of them children, and in costume) showed up, as store staffers handed out plastic round-framed eyeglasses, which were eagerly snapped up and donned. It was a curious sight: nearly a thousand children all wearing thick plastic glasses with round frames.

For those who waited until the next day, virtually no copies of the novel were to be had. I checked out two stores and found them sold out. At a local Books-a-Million in Williamsburg, Virginia, I saw dozens of customers, with kids in tow, leaving the store empty-handed; the college bookstore at William and Mary, run by Barnes & Noble, had also sold out but promised copies as soon as possible; and a Barnes & Noble superstore in Newport News, Virginia, which had sold out its allotment, set up a special table near the entrance as staffers queried customers coming in, "Are you here to pick up your reserved copy of *Harry Potter?*"

For those who hadn't reserved copies at local stores or hadn't ordered through Amazon.com, the *only* hope locally was Costco, a warehouse chain with two pallets of books on hand, which is where I bought my own copy.

By the time night fell on publication day, two things were clear: Nobody predicted that the demand for first-day copies would exceed supply, nor did anyone predict that on top of a 6.8 million first printing, a Hagrid-sized second printing of 1.7 million copies would be needed to fill the immediate demand.

The quarter million words that comprised book five proved to be no obstacle for Potter fans who, like Tolkien fans, hungered for more.

As for Rowling, the presumption was that she'd either be far away from Edinburgh, which was the focus of international attention on publication day, or she'd be holed up and inaccessible to all. The least likely scenario—a local appearance—turned out to be Rowling's game plan.

Expecting store clerks to hand out copies of Rowling's latest, customers were astonished when Rowling herself appeared at a Waterstone's to hand them out. One of the customers, an awestruck young girl who excitedly shook Rowling's hand, told a BBC reporter that she'd never wash that hand again.

In short order, millions of Potter fans cracked open their copies to immerse themselves once again in his imaginative universe. The first page began, "The hottest day of the summer so far was drawing to a close and a drowsy silence lay over the large, square houses of Privet Drive." There would be, happily, 869 more pages to go.

The end result, all agreed, was a satisfying novel that delivered on the promise Rowling made to her readers with her first Potter novel: Harry Potter would grow and change with each passing book, and his life experiences would prepare him for the inevitable—a final showdown with the "Lord Voldy-thing," as Vernon Dudley called him.

Scores of reviews began appearing in newspapers, in magazines, and on websites worldwide, but I think Stephen King, writing in *Entertainment Weekly*, said it best: "I think Harry will take his place with Alice, Huck, Frodo, and Dorothy, and this is one series not just for the decade, but for the ages."

When all was said and done, the fifth Harry Potter novel had sold an astonishing 12 million copies worldwide, which will not be eclipsed by any book—until the next Potter novel is published.

The old one-two punch of a best-selling novel, fueled by successful film adaptations, catapulted the camera-shy (read: glum-looking) writer into the limelight. In fact, in an annual assessment of entertainers with clout, Rowling ranks fifth in a list of the top 101 entertainers.

To give you a sense of where she fits on the 2003 year's list, compiled by *Entertainment Weekly,* look at the high-powered names of some of those who preceded her (Steven Spielberg and Tom Hanks) and those who followed her (Oprah Winfrey, Tom Cruise, and Peter Jackson).

As anyone with any experience in Hollywood will tell you, it's a telling ranking. Writers are traditionally considered bottom-feeders in the food chain in that industry. That Rowling would not only make the list but be in the top ten attests to her power position. Rowling—make no mistake—has clout.

About the Book

If Potter fans thought *Harry Potter and the Goblet of Fire,* at 734 pages, was a long read, what would they make of the fifth book in the series? At 870 pages, *Harry Potter and the Order of the Phoenix* is the longest Potter novel to date.

As promised by Rowling, Harry Potter is growing up; in fact, his growing pains, as he wrestles with the demons of adolescence, might be off-putting to younger readers, but anyone who is currently going through the pain of adolescence or remembers having gone through it will recognize themselves in Harry Potter.

An admittedly darker novel than its predecessors, it begins with the traditional framing device. We see Harry at the Dursley residence before he leaves for Hogwarts; but unlike the previous books, elements of the magical world come to haunt the Muggles world, and it's up to Harry to defend not only himself but Dudley Dursley, who, like Harry, is no longer a child. Dudley, in fact, has a natural talent for boxing—honed, no doubt, by years of bullying others—but shows his true colors when he's confronted by the unprecedented arrival of the Dementors.

Soon thereafter, events move into high gear as Harry is met by an Advance Guard that come to the Dursley home to escort him to the headquarters of the Order of the Phoenix.

The magical world is divided on whether or not Lord Voldemort has in fact returned. The Ministry of Magic's Cornelius Fudge toes the party line and seeks to placate the wizarding community by reassuring them that You-Know-Who has certainly *not* returned, but Albus Dumbledore, Harry Potter, and others know better. They know the truth, that Lord Voldemort *has* returned, which divides the community into those who believe and those who don't.

Cornelius Fudge clamps down on Hogwarts by installing one of his lieutenants, a froglike-looking woman named Dolores Jane Umbridge, whose sickly sweet demeanor belies her true nature—she's not honey but, in fact, poison. Umbridge, who joins the faculty as the newest Defense against the Dark Arts teacher (one new one per school year, thus far), soon becomes the instrument of draconian enforcement by the Ministry of Magic—a High Inquisitor. The position gives her enormous power over the faculty and student body, as well. That power becomes absolute when she is appointed the Headmaster of Hogwarts, replacing Albus Dumbledore. Morale at Hogwarts reaches a new low, but uneasy is the head that wears the crown, so to speak. As a major battle shapes up, those at Hogwarts must choose; so, too, must choices be made in the wizarding community when the believers and the nonbelievers must put aside their differences and hang together—or hang separately.

The Order of the Phoenix, the members of which are devoted to Albus Dumbledore, bookends the novel. The Order is prominently featured in the beginning and at the end of the book, though I would have liked to read more about its history and about the members' important role in the battle against Lord Voldemort's followers, the Death Eaters, and Voldemort himself.

By the end of the novel, an endlessly patient and imperturbable Albus Dumbledore explains to an enraged Harry Potter that it's time for frankness. His destiny, Dumbledore tells him, is inextricably linked to Lord Voldemort in ways that cannot be ignored.

It's important for Harry to know because he is destined to meet Lord Voldemort for what will undoubtedly be the battle of his life—a one-on-one fight to the death with Lord Voldemort.

Most frightening of all: Rowling doesn't guarantee that Harry Potter will survive the encounter. She is asked that, of course, by readers and the media at virtually every opportunity, but mum's the word. Don't expect the lock-lipped author to divulge the details because she won't, unless you have some Veritaserum handy—the truth serum that forces someone to talk.

For parents who are concerned about the darkness of this novel, be forewarned. Rowling has made it abundantly clear that the last two novels will be even darker. There will be more preordained deaths because the logic of the story, worked out years ago, requires them. Clearly, books six and seven are not likely to be appropriate reading material for young children. But older teens and adults are likely to find them to be irresistible reads.

Selected Reviews

Publishers Weekly: "Year five at Hogwarts is no fun for Harry. Rowling may be relying upon readers to have solidified their liking for her hero in the first four books, because the 15-year-old Harry Potter they meet here is quite dour after a summer at the Dursleys' house on Privet Drive, with no word from his pals Hermione or Ron. When he reunites with them at last, he learns that the *Daily Prophet* has launched a smear campaign to discredit Harry's and Dumbledore's report of Voldemort's reappearance at the end of book four, *Harry Potter and the Goblet of Fire.*

"Aside from an early skirmish with a pair of Dementors, in which Harry finds himself in the position of defending not only himself but his dreaded cousin, Dudley, there is little action until the end of these nearly 900 pages. A hateful woman from the Ministry of Magic, Dolores Umbridge (who, along with minister Cornelius Fudge, nearly succeeds in expelling Harry from Hogwarts before the start of the school year), overtakes Hogwarts—

Fan Travels Halfway around the World for PHOENIX

The *Scotsman* reported that Akira Sadakato, a college student, flew from Japan to Edinburgh, Scotland, to buy a copy of the fifth Potter novel. The paper reported that the young man walked into an Internet café in town and, according to owner Richard Hind, "said it was his dream to meet J. K. Rowling and get his books, which he had in his rucksack, signed. . . . He came in on Thursday and said he was going back to stay in Edinburgh to buy the book when it came out at midnight on Friday."

GrandPré's toadlike portrait of her is priceless—and makes life even more miserable for him. She bans him from the Quidditch team (resulting in minimal action on the pitch) and keeps a tight watch on him. And Harry's romance when his crush from the last book, Cho Chang, turns out to be a major waterworks (she cries when she's happy, she cries when she's sad). Readers get to discover the purpose behind the Order of the Phoenix and more is revealed of the connection between Harry and You-Know-Who. But the showdown between Harry and Voldemort feels curiously anticlimactic after the stunning clash at the close of book four.

"Rowling favors psychological development over plot development here, skillfully exploring the effects of Harry's fall from popularity and the often isolating feelings of adolescence. Harry suffers a loss and learns some unpleasant truths about his father, which result in his compassion for some unlikely characters. (The author also draws some insightful parallels between the Ministry's exercise of power and the current political climate.) As hope blooms at story's end, those who have followed Harry thus far will be every bit as eager to discover what happens to him in his sixth and seventh years."

Leslie Rounds for *Children's Literature:* "This is a thrilling read. Those

Almost £308 a Word: Rowling's Outline for Book Five

Raising money for charity, Sotheby's generated £28,260 with the sale of a brief outline Rowling wrote that detailed book five. Reportedly purchased by an American who wanted to have a unique gift for his children who love Harry Potter . . . the details of the outline were not revealed by the buyer . . . though a few words were made public, whetting fans' appetites: "Thirty-eight chapters . . . might change . . . longest volume . . . Ron . . . broom . . . sacked . . . house-elf . . . new teacher . . . dies . . . sorry."

who enjoyed the previous books are not likely to be disappointed, and Rowling will probably add even more Potter fans with the publication of this volume."

Laura (from Shepshed, Leiceistershire, England), aged 14, who speed-read the book in two hours and 19 minutes after it was officially published: "I'd give it nine out of ten. It was really good. Now I'm going home and read it slowly."

Michael Cart for the *Los Angeles Times*: "In fleshing out her plot, Rowling devotes considerable attention to . . . coming-of-age aspects of Harry's personality, making him a richer and more psychologically complex character than ever before. There's no doubt that Harry is growing up, and the process isn't always pretty, although he remains wonderfully appealing and, when necessary, heroic."

Bethany Schneider, who attended a midnight book release party at her local bookstore, for News day.com: "What I participated in very early Saturday morning was an international phenomenon, complete with adults in capes and children with scars scrawled across their foreheads. But Rowling is not surfing on her success, nor is she sliding on the childish charm of her characters. She is hauling them and herself forward through troubled and changing waters."

Eva Mitnick, Los Angeles Public Library, for *School Library Journal*: "Children will enjoy the magic and the Hogwarts mystique, and young adult readers will find a rich and compelling coming-of-age story as well."

Lev Grossman for *Time* magazine: "Just when we might have expected author J. K. Rowling's considerable imagination to flag . . . she has hit peak form and is gaining speed."

Deirdre Donahue for *USA Today:* "The book richly deserves the hype. All the qualities that marred the fourth book . . . have evaporated. Indeed, the faux gothic horror of the fourth has been replaced by a return to the wonderful, textured writing of the three earlier novels. . . . *Order of the Phoenix* allows the reader to savor Rowling's remarkably fertile imagination."

Robin Videmos for the *Denver Post*: "The [Potter] legend has grown with each succeeding volume, not because she's written to a formula but because she continues to deliver the same combination of enticing elements without allowing them to become predictable."

Emma Pollack-Pelzner for the *Yale Review of Books:* "Although the *Harry Potter* series' intricately worked-out moral content, fun character relationships, and vividly imagined world make them rewarding reading for anyone, don't let these books elbow aside ones that you loved as a child; just add them to your list."

SCHOLASTIC AND SIMON & SCHUSTER/CBS CORPORATION

PRESENT

AN EVENING WITH

HARRY
CARRIE
& GARP

J. K. ROWLING · STEPHEN KING · JOHN IRVING
READ TO BENEFIT DOCTORS WITHOUT BORDERS & THE HAVEN FOUNDATION

AUGUST 1 & 2 · 7:30PM

SCHOLASTIC   SIMON & SCHUSTER   CBS CORPORATION

Tickets available at www.ticketmaster.com

RADIO CITY MUSIC HALL

MSG ENTERTAINMENT

The brochure used to promote "An Evening with Harry, Carrie, & Garp"

Harry Potter and the Half-Blood Prince

Dedication

"To MacKenzie, my beautiful daughter, I dedicate her ink-and-paper twin."

Background

Unlike *Harry Potter and the Order of the Phoenix*, which was plagued by sundry delays, *Harry Potter and the Half-Blood Prince* met with relatively few. Cloistering herself in her Edinburgh home, Rowling fended off repeated questions from fans and journalists until she was ready to announce its completion—an announcement made on her official website on December 22, 2004, followed later with the news that its publication date had been set for July 16, 2005.

With book publication only half a year away, Scholastic would have to marshal all of its resources to orchestrate a timely release. In the interim, the book world scrambled to make preparations for the release of what would predictably be the book of the year in terms of visibility and sales.

Quick to respond to the news, online bookselling giant Amazon.com announced that it was taking orders at 40 percent off—a deep discount that sacrificed profits for market share. It was a move that other retailers imitated. Almost overnight, preorders for the new book catapulted it to the #1 position on Amazon's list of bestsellers.

Following the successful marketing strategy of *Harry Potter and the Order of the Phoenix*, one that not only whetted the public's appetite but created a buying frenzy, Scholastic implemented a time-tested plan: countdown clocks posted

At one minute past midnight, cartons of *Harry Potter and the Half-Blood Prince* are finally opened.

online and positioned in retail stores, no advance review copies whatsoever, no pre-publication interviews months in advance, and as little information as possible about the book, even at the annual BookExpo—the industry trade show—in May.

Predictably, Harry Potter fan sites went into high gear as Rowling's publishers fast-tracked its production. With only six months from completion of the book to its publication, Rowling's publishers had no time to waste. The book had to be edited, copyedited, typeset, designed, illustrated, printed, bound, and shipped to booksellers worldwide, who would receive their orders in white book cartons with prominent green lettering clearly marked: "DO NOT OPEN before July 16, 2005."

As the orders poured in, eclipsing advance orders for the previous book, Scholastic announced a record-breaking first printing: 10.8 million copies for its $29.99 book. Unlike the last time, Scholastic wanted booksellers to be well stocked, so that on Saturday, when most of the shoppers would go out in search of the book, copies would be available, thus avoiding the nightmarish scenario that had played out countless times across the country with *Order of the Phoenix*, when parents went into bookstores and left empty-handed with disappointed kids in tow.

Although Scholastic had rushed back to press, additional copies took weeks to print, bind, and ship, with the result that brick-and-mortar retailers lost out to online sellers, warehouse chains (Costco and Sam's Club), and other vendors that supplied copies to those same customers.

Scholastic was also aware of the fact that this would be one of only two remaining opportunities to debut a new Harry Potter novel. The franchise, Rowling has stated firmly, will end with the seventh novel.

Given the facts at hand, Scholastic built its marketing campaign around the question: "Who is the Half-Blood Prince?" Wanting to keep the public guessing, the contents of the book were not only shrouded in secrecy but legally protected with "John Doe" lawsuits that would be invoked if anyone revealed the details of the book early and spoiled the surprise for fans who wanted to find out what happens on their own.

To enhance security of the shipped books, major chain booksellers cordoned off secure areas in their warehouses to prevent the possibility of someone pilfering a copy from existing stock before the release date. No question, every copy—as far as Rowling was concerned—had to be accounted for before the book release.

Considering the millions of copies being printed worldwide, there were bound to be a few slip-ups, but with few exceptions, the secrecy strategy worked well; everyone—from book distributors to journalists—understood that this was all part of the game plan. As the book's publication date neared, arrangements were made at Edinburgh Castle to hold a party of special magnificence: Rowling would play host to cub reporters, who would hold a press conference after being given a signed copy of the book to read beforehand. These young teenagers realized they were lucky indeed to be hand-

The Harry Potter "countdown clock" sent by Scholastic to all its accounts

picked for the "job" of interviewing Rowling, but few of them likely knew that Rowling, disgusted with the aggressiveness of the press, had shut the door on virtually all reporters, save a handful. The intrusiveness of the press—badgering her family, banging on her front door, and writing stories speculating about her wealth but not the books that earned it—combined to create a situation in which the media, by and large, was simply not welcome. Though Rowling clearly understood the role of media and its importance in affecting book sales, the media circus that had manifested in recent years forced her to take matters into her own hands; the press no longer had uncontrolled access to her personal or professional life.

The bottom line: The 70 "reporters" who covered the release of the book at Edinburgh Castle were, in every instance, the youngest ever to see print in their respective publications. Rowling wouldn't have it any other way.

For most of the book-reading world wanting to celebrate the release of the book, it meant attending one of the thousands of midnight parties hosted by booksellers, who had their staff dress up in Hogwarts robes and act as hosts to the kids who would have to stay up way past their bedtimes to get their hands on the new book.

At exactly one minute past midnight on Saturday, July 16, 2005, the green-labeled cartons of books were opened worldwide and the penultimate Harry Potter novel found its way into eager hands: young and old, male and female, cutting across international boundaries; finally, the sixth Harry Potter novel was made available to a worldwide Potter-hungry audience.

It was Christmas in July, judging from the rapt expressions of each child who finally held the book in his or her hands. The children had two things in common: a look of pure joy and a desire to get home as soon as possible to begin reading.

The truly impatient, the die-hard fans, burned the midnight oil and stayed up all night and read the 652 page novel, enchantingly illustrated by Mary GrandPré, whose artwork has become inextricably linked to Harry Potter. Likewise, journalists rushed to get their reviews in print, since the embargo guaranteed that no one could review the book before publication date: The race was on to be the first.

Four Potter fans wearing plastic round glasses at Barnes & Noble get their photo taken behind and around a Harry Potter standee.

On Saturday, when millions of readers worldwide opened the book to read the first line ("It was nearing midnight and the Prime Minister was sitting alone in his office, . . ."), it was as if a silence had descended on the world: iBooks, iPods, cell phones, PlayStations, DVDs, and other electronic gadgets were turned off and put aside as eager Muggles found themselves back in the wizarding world where

Harry Potter would doubtless find himself tested but hopefully not bested by dark forces.

The enchanting magic of Rowling's well-told tale would hold those readers spellbound; the new novel, in fact, would be judged online by those polled by the BBC to be the readers' favorite, eclipsing the much-loved *Harry Potter and the Prisoner of Azkaban*.

From the beginning, Rowling has made it clear that the Harry Potter novels aren't, in fact, traditional children's books. Usually, children's books share much in common—traits that have, in terms of literary reputations, put them as second-class works unworthy to stand in the first rank of books. Unfortunately, too many children's book authors have been hidebound by these perceptions, with the result that their works have been excessively diluted.

Where are the children's books in which the characters actually grow from book to book, as opposed to episodic adventures experienced in a world where time stands still for them?

Where are the children's books that deal with life's unpleasantries and ugly truths, and grow darker in tone as the series wends its way to its conclusion?

Where are the children's books that aspire to more than being didactic? Children, according to those who like to write such books, need instruction, and detailed instruction, at that!

Rowling gives children a lot more credit than, often, their own parents do. Children, after all, see the magical goings on in the wizarding world as a literary device; some of their parents, however, see far more and feel the books are merely thinly disguised propaganda for indoctrinating children into the occult.

The great genius of Rowling is that her books are rigorously plotted, so each book builds on that which has gone before; moreover, the books become increasingly, and necessarily, darker in tone because of what is inevitable: a life-and-death battle between Harry Potter and the Dark Lord, He-Who-Must-Not-Be-Named. It's a battle that's foreseen in the stars, as a stargazing centaur notes: The planet Mars is in ascendancy.

Harry Potter is an infant when we meet him in the first book, but will come of age as the series concludes. Harry Potter makes the transition from child to adult as the series unfolds, which is pivotal to the books' success: The young readers, too, see that Harry's adventures (and misadventures) mirror his life; they, too, witness firsthand the passage of years. They are, in a very real way, growing up with Harry Potter, just as they've watched child actor Daniel Radcliffe (as Harry Potter in the film adaptations) grow up to become a young adult.

About the Book

In this sixth book, Harry is close to coming of age, for in the wizarding world, witches and wizards come of age at 17, whereas in the Muggle world, people come of age at 18. The tone of the book is increasingly darker, since Harry must now deal with the inescapable fact that he is—like it or not—the "Chosen One," a label applied to him by the *Daily Prophet*, the official newspaper of the wizarding world.

Unlike his classmates who only have to worry about graduating from Hogwarts, Harry has a much greater calling: He is seen as the only one who can defeat the Dark Lord himself. He is the wizarding world's last hope. Otherwise, that world (and ours) will be plunged into chaos, as the Dark Lord and his minions, the Death Eaters, run amuck in both the wizarding and Muggle worlds.

In this book, Harry necessarily spends a lot of time with Headmaster Albus Dumbledore, who takes him more fully under his wing. Together, they delve into the Dark Lord's past and glean clues that they hope will prove useful to Harry in his final battle with Lord Voldemort, the most anticipated fictional confrontation since Sherlock Holmes and his arch nemesis, Professor Moriarty, duked it out at Reichenbach Falls.

As any student of military history knows, "know thyself" is the first rule of combat, and "know thy enemy" is the second. In this sixth book, Harry discovers much more about himself and his place in the wizarding world, and learns a lot about his enemy, the Dark Lord, who emerges as a character with a haunted, and dark, past.

As for the book's principal mystery, the identity of the "Half-Blood Prince" is revealed and, without giving anything away, it's not someone you would expect. This figure, however, proves pivotal in the book and is essential for setting up the premise of the seventh, and final, book in the series.

So, you ask, is the book good? Is it worth your investment of time and money?

Absolutely.

If you've read the first five books in the series, you will definitely want to read this sixth book because it ties up a lot of loose ends and offers an emotional ending that will likely stun you—a quick jab to the heart.

Although one can quibble about Rowling's occasional overuse of adjectives, the plotting, the storytelling, and the sheer power of her imagination make the book required reading.

The only note of disappointment—already noted by numerous fans—is that the seventh book will be Rowling's final ride on the Hogwarts Express . . . and ours, as well.

Given the increasingly darker tone of the books, the pivotal question is whether or not Harry Potter will survive his inevitable encounter with the Dark Lord. Though fans are hopeful that Harry will live, and perhaps go on to become an Auror, there are no guarantees in the wizarding world; anything can, and will, happen and all bets are off. Harry may survive . . . or he may not.

Only Rowling knows for sure, and she's not telling. The final chapter in book seven is already written, safely stored, presumably in a bank vault, after curious children visiting her home searched the cupboards for the notebook containing the handwritten conclusion. The afterword, notes Rowling, relates the fates of all the characters, or at least those who live.

Though the Harry Potter experts at Mugglenet.com are adamant that Book #7 will not be out in July, citing a conflict with the movie release date of film #5, I disagree. Look for the final book to be published on July 21, 2007.

Selected Reviews

Deidre Donahue for *USA TODAY:* "There is really only one flaw in the sixth installment of J. K. Rowling's series, *Harry Potter and the Half-Blood Prince:* It is not a kid's book."

Robert Crum for *The Observer* (U.K.): "As usual, Rowling's prose runs the gamut from torpid to pedestrian, but her plot—driven by the quest for the identity of the Half-Blood Prince—always clips along inventively. . . ."

Marta Salij for the *Detroit Free Press*: "Rowling manages, this time, to put together the story with none of the flab that marred the nearly 900-page Book 5. *The Half-Blood Prince* is 652 lean pages, in which the essential plot . . . has just the right [number] of side stories."

Deepti Hajela for the Associated Press: "And, yes, there is another major death. Seriously major. Break out the tissues. No matter how well you think you know these books, don't assume you really know who anyone is, or what they are and aren't capable of. . . . This is a powerful, unforgettable setup for the finale. The hardest thing about *Half-Blood Prince* is where it leaves us—in mourning for who has been lost, anxious to learn how Rowling will wrap up a saga that millions wish would go on and on."

Emily Green for the *Los Angeles Times:* "The good news is that Harry is courageous and true. The bad news is that Voldemort's agents have more Peruvian Vanishing Powder on their side. This is a book for children of mettle. It will reward them richly, but they must not whine, they must be sunny and true and, above all, brave. The ending is almost too much to bear. I haven't cried so hard since Charlotte the Spider died."

Christopher Paolini (author of *Eragon* and *Eldest*) for *Entertainment Weekly:* "And though I finished *The Half-Blood Prince* only a few hours ago, I have to ask her the question that every author who's just published a novel dreads hearing: So, when's the next book coming out?"

Magic at Midnight: HARRY POTTER AND THE HALF-BLOOD PRINCE Is Released in the U.S.

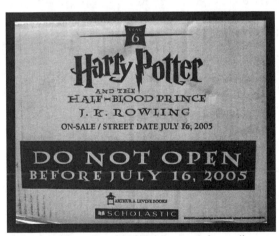

The warning printed in bright green ink on all cartons containing *Harry Potter and the Half-Blood Prince*

The popularity of Harry Potter in the U.S. meant that when it came time to choose which Potter party to attend, even in my small corner of the world (southeast Virginia), the venues included a Books-a-Million, a Barnes & Noble affiliated with the College of William and Mary, a Barnes & Noble superstore in nearby Newport News, or—depending on whether I'd be willing to spend an hour on the road—a multiplicity of possibilities in Richmond, Virginia.

My first choice was Newport News, since I know several of the employees personally, including a personable Harry Potter look-alike named Kurtis Wiley who, not surprisingly, is often pressed into service when a new Harry Potter is released.

Since Kurtis made it clear to me that he had another pressing engagement that night, his absence meant that I'd stay in town to attend the Barnes & Noble event at the college bookstore in Williamsburg. Besides, the B&N

at Newport News was expecting a record crowd, based on the attendance realized when the previously published Potter book hit the stores. And did I really want to push my way through hundreds of overly excited children?

The B&N in Williamsburg is set on Duke of Gloucester Street, which is owned by Colonial Williamsburg. In the winter, when an occasional snowstorm blankets the area, that part of town recalls a Dickensian Christmas, with its cobblestone streets, old-fashioned lampposts, and period houses. In other words, it's not Muggle London, but close enough, especially if you have a modicum of imagination.

When we arrived at 11:00 P.M., the bookstore's parking lot had already filled up. At both entrances, store employees dressed up as characters from the Harry Potter universe were positioned to pass out the freebies: a green wristband with the book's release date and a full-color

Copies of the sixth Harry Potter novel with name bands for customers who reserved them

poster with the new book prominently featured, surrounded by cover art from the previous titles.

To facilitate purchases, numbered wristbands were passed out to every person who had reserved a book. The thinking behind those wristbands was that it would insure an orderly checkout of books when numbers were called.

With more than an hour to go and the second floor blocked off, the first floor was packed, as children stood in line to get lightning-shaped designs drawn on their foreheads and to get their photos taken behind a standee (a life-size cardboard cutout or frame) with a hole in the middle.

To help pass the time, televisions with DVDs were set up to play the film adaptations.

To lend the right touch, store employees dressed in costume. "Hermione Granger" carried a plush cat toy and a wand, "Ron Weasley" had carrot-red hair and towered above everyone else, and "Harry Potter" wore round glasses and sported a curious lightning-shaped scar on his forehead. There was even a hobbit-sized man, whose name tag read "Professor Flitwick."

At exactly one minute after midnight, book trolleys were rolled into position, each book marked with a name band, and sealed boxes were opened and books extracted for the customers who had shown up without having reserved a copy.

The employees manned the cash registers and a mad rush ensued as customers jockeyed for position. Though the initial plan was to call customers using the numbered wristbands, the plan was quickly abandoned as the lines grew and the store's manager decided that the easiest strategy was simply to get everyone's order rung up as quickly as possible.

Most of the attendees were adults who obviously would have preferred to wait until the next morning to get a copy, but their children likely wanted their copies first thing in the morning, instead of waiting until the stores opened at 10:00 A.M.

No matter what those children usually do on a Saturday, *this* Saturday would be different. They would not be going to Little League baseball games, not shopping, not visiting friends, not playing video games, and not talking on cell phones. They would, instead, be quiet and still—an unnatural state for them as a rule—and immerse themselves in the wizarding world, following the latest adventures of Harry Potter, known to his fellow wizards and witches as "The Boy Who Lived."

For parents who agonized over how to get their recalcitrant children to read, the hassles of staying up until midnight to get the Potter novel were forgotten when they saw how their children read with rapt attention, transfixed for 652 pages.

The book's release was indeed magic at midnight—the party I attended was one of 6,000 in the U.S. alone—but the real magic was on Saturday when readers everywhere, from grandchildren to grandparents, enjoyed a worldwide communal experience: the timeless pleasure of reading a well-told tale. That is the *true* magic to be found in the enchanting tales of Harry Potter.

Quidditch Through the Ages, Fantastic Beasts and Where to Find Them, and Conversations with J. K. Rowling

Quidditch Through the Ages, by Kennilworthy Whisp. Whizz Hard Books, 56 pages (September 2001).

Fantastic Beasts and Where to Find Them, by Newt Scamander. Obscurus Books, 42 pages (September 2001).

During the prolonged—and for some, unendurable—wait for *Harry Potter and the Order of the Phoenix*, Rowling published two books under two different pen names: Kennilworthy Whisp and Newt Scamander. Though fans preferred the feast of words promised in the eagerly anticipated *Order of the Phoenix*, these two literary appetizers more than fit the bill.

Sold as a boxed set for $12.95, these two books belong on the shelf of any Harry Potter fan. Written as fundraisers for Comic Relief, a charity based in England, these books provide information on two topics of great interest to Potter fans: the sport that all wizards love (Quidditch), and the beasts that populate Rowling's imaginative fictional universe.

Quidditch Through the Ages is packaged as a book from the Hogwarts library. On the first page, a dire warning from Hogwarts librarian Irma Pince virtually guarantees that borrowers will return the book in good condition. Albus Dumbledore, in his introduction to the book, knows all too well the hidden hazards thereof. Even after removing the protective spells on the book, he cautions readers that Madam Pince is known to add jinxes to them as well, as the Professor found out when he "doodled absentmindedly" in a library book and,

Comic Relief

Poverty, as Rowling found out, is no laughing matter. Unfortunately, far too many people around the world find themselves in dire circumstances and must rely on the charity of strangers to survive.

To support Comic Relief, Rowling wrote two books, both published under pen names, that were published in the U.K., the U.S., Canada, Australia, New Zealand, and Germany. These books (*Quidditch Through the Ages* and *Fantastic Beasts and Where to Find Them*) have raised £15.7 million, with money going all over the world.

In Rowling's native England, the money raised by Comic Relief goes to help a broad spectrum of people—disabled people, young people living in the streets, troubled teens, older people, people living in deprived communities, and immigrants experiencing discrimination.

Regarding Comic Relief, Rowling points out in an interview published online at the scholastic.com website that all those involved in printing, selling, and distributing her two charity books have donated their time and services, just as she has. The result is that the lion's share of the cover price (80 percent) goes to the charity, and not for overhead. In other words, at this charity, your money will go further than with some others, and both Comic Relief and Rowling are grateful for all the support.

Harry Potter fans have shown, time and again, that when it's time to give back to the community, they do so without hesitation. Why not, then, extend the effort internationally and reach beyond your backyard?

"There is something wonderful about the idea that laughter should be used to combat real tragedy and poverty and suffering and it is just the most wonderful thing," Rowling observed in the online interview published on the Scholastic website, which promotes the two charity books.

"You will be doing real magic by buying these books," she told a young boy who interviewed her for Scholastic, and she's right: Buy the books and know that the money is going to a great cause. Like Hedwig, give a hoot! Go to www.comicrelief.com and make a donation online today. As Rowling has said, every dollar (or pound) will help.

---

to his surprise, found himself under attack. The book, he said, beat him "fiercely about the head."

Not surprisingly, *Quidditch Through the Ages* is free of the usual doodlings, markings, and defacements that often mark student texts.

As for the text itself, its "reviews," printed in the front of the book, run from the straightforward ("The definitive work on the origins and history of Quidditch," says Brutus Scrimgeour, author of *The Beaters' Bible*) to the whimsical ("I've read worse," from reporter Rita Skeeter in the *Daily Prophet*). We also find out that the book's author, Kennilworthy Whisp, has penned other books, including (as you'd expect) more books on Quidditch.

In ten short but informative chapters, Quidditch is thoroughly covered, with art illuminating the text. Required reading for all Hogwarts students, magically minded Muggles everywhere will find much of interest in Whisp's explication of the wizarding sport that Rowling says most closely resembles basketball in our world.

Fantastic Beasts and Where to Find Them, unlike *Quidditch Through the Ages*, is a student text, and so is defaced, torn, illustrated, and annotated by Harry Potter, Ron Weasley, and Hermione Granger. In fact, this facsimile is Potter's own copy, as evidenced by the sticker on the front cover.

As with *Quidditch Through the Ages*, Professor Albus Dumbledore contributes an introduction, in which he writes: "Newt's masterpiece has been an approved textbook at Hogwarts School of Witchcraft and Wizardry ever since its publication and must take a substantial amount of credit for our students' consistently high results in Care of Magical Creatures examinations—yet it is not a book to be confined to the classroom."

Found in every magical household, *Fantastic Beasts* is a delightful text, filled with fabulous beasts of all kinds; the first entry tells the specifics about the dreaded Acromantula, which earns the highest Ministry of Magic classification of five Xs, to which Potter (or Weasley) has added nine more Xs, for good reason. The book, arranged from A to Z, ends with Y for "Yeti" (also known as Bigfoot, the Abominable Snowman).

The two books are conveniently packaged in a sturdy slipcase bearing the legend, "J. K. Rowling: Classic Books from the Library of Hogwarts School of Witchcraft and Wizardry."

Conversations with J. K. Rowling, by Lindsay Fraser. Trade paperback, 96 pages, $4.99, Scholastic, October 2001. Cover art by Mary GrandPré.

This is billed on the cover as "The *Only* Authorized Biography of J. K. Rowling," but the billing is somewhat misleading. It's not a biography. It is more accurate to say this is a short interview supplemented by an overview of Rowling's books, a distinction made clear when it was originally published in England by Mammoth, an imprint of Egmont Children's Books, as *Telling Tales: An Interview with J. K. Rowling*.

The book is set in large type with wide margins. The first half is an interview with Rowling, a traditional one-on-one sit-down chat; the second half is comprised of an overview of the books, supplemented with previously published interview material from *Entertainment Weekly, O, The Oprah Magazine, Larry King Live,* and *Newsweek*.

The cover art by Mary GrandPré, who is the artist (cover and interior) for the U.S. editions of the Potter novels, is a portrait of Rowling.

Bottom line: Recommended, with reservations—this short interview of 46 pages is padded with filler material to bulk out the book to its 96 pages.

Readers wanting a full-fledged biography are better served by Sean Smith's book, *J. K. Rowling: A Biography*. Albeit unauthorized, it does cover her life more thoroughly than any other biography currently on the market, though it does make me wish she'd write a memoir or work with another writer to give us an authorized biography.

The Wizard Rockumentary:
A Movie about Rocking and Rowling

If you attended Lumos 2006, you undoubtedly saw Mallory and Megan Schuyler making the rounds. Twin sisters, they teamed up to create *The Wizard Rockumentary*, a documentary of Wizard Rock; specifically, rock bands inspired by the works of J. K. Rowling's magical world.

Megan (house: Ravenclaw) is a producer/video editor at a production company in Washington state; Mallory (Gryffindor) is a writer and graphic art enthusiast who works at an art gallery/bookstore. Together, these 21-year-old diehard Harry Potter fans have pooled their cash to create GryffinClaw Productions LLC, "fueled by our humble savings and pure stubbornness. This project and the bands that it documents personify creativity, nerve, and perseverance. If nothing else, we hope that this documentary will inspire people to follow their dreams and do what they love. You CAN start a band. You CAN write a book. You CAN make a movie."

The Schuylers' film has taken them all over the map, interviewing and filming bands with Harry Potter–inspired names: The Switchblade Kittens, "Weird Sisters," The Hermione Crookshanks Experience, The Whomping Willows, The Hungarian Horntails, The Cedric Diggorys, Fred and George, The Parselmouths, Harry and the Potters, Draco and the Malfoys, The Remus Lupins, Ron and the Weasleys, Snidget, The Moaning Myrtles, and Roonil Wazlib.

Most are, of course, indies that use the Internet to promote their music with free samples, compact disc recordings, and downloadable music. Though small, these bands are spirited, and they have two things in common: they love the Harry Potter books and they **ROCK!**

Because the documentary (excuse me, the *rock*umentary) is still in the works, you'd best go to the official website to get updates. The principal photography is done and the project is now in its editing phase. In the meantime, go to their website and check out some of their recommended links to wizard bands and set your phasers on stun . . . er, fun.

Now, let me get out of the way so Megan and Mallory—two of the most delightful Harry Potter fans you could ever hope to meet—explain what they're all about.

Like so many others, we are dedicated Harry Potter fans and have long been wishing for a way to contribute to the wizarding community. The opportunity presented itself when we realized that Wizard Rock, which has brought us so much enjoyment, is still relatively unknown to the vast majority of HP fans. So, in celebration of the HP music scene, we decided to create The Wizard Rockumentary: a feature-length documentary on Wizard Rockers and the HP following (think "Trekkies" but way cooler because it's Harry Potter!). We hope that this documentary will expose the wizarding community to the joy that is Wizard Rock!

Barry Trotter: The World's Most Famous Wizard

Barry was born in the bean-patch of a squalid Sussex commune. After his hippie parents died, Barry lived with his Muddle relatives (the Dimsleys), tormenting and being tormented, until he was forcibly enrolled at Hogwash. Valumart is constantly trying to kill him, but Barry always survives, so nobody takes Barry seriously. As a result of one of these assassination attempts, Barry has a scar shaped like an interrobang on his forehead. He drinks too much, eats like a pig, sleeps until noon, and owes everybody money. All in all, he's pretty happy.

—from the characters and glossary list on the official Barry Trotter web-site (www.barrytrotter.com)

Do you know what an "Acromandela" is? It's "a gigantic black spider with a passion for civil rights. Native to South Africa, one lives in the Forsaken Forest."

What about the curse, "Aveda Neutrogena"? It's "one of the forbidden spells; it causes death-by-moisturization."

How about the spell "Openadoora"? It's "a spell that opens doors (duh)."

Welcome to the crazy world of Barry Trotter, the subject (so far) of three books by humorist Michael Berber, who (according to the bio provided on the Barry Trotter website) originally self-published the first book in the series after mainstream publishers passed on it because of legal concerns. (Note: parody is considered fair-use under copyright law, which is why Berber need not worry.)

Unlike the Tolkien parody, *Bored of the Rings,* which was a half-hearted attempt to compress 500,000 words into one tenth its length, resulting in a slim volume that lost steam as the writers worked their way through the book, Berber is more ambitious. To date he's published three good-sized books in the series, selling (by his estimate) 700,000 copies worldwide.

The three books in print include *Barry Trotter and the Shameless Parody* (originally published as *Barry Trotter and the Unauthorized Parody*), *Barry Trotter and the Unnecessary Sequel,* and *Barry Trotter and the Dead Horse.*

Gerber has held up a funhouse mirror that irreverently translates the Hogwarts School of Witchcraft and Wizardry into the Hogwash School of Wizardry and Witchcrap, and Muggles into Muddles. In other words, if you have a *very* broad sense of humor and a bit of tolerance, you'll likely find these three books will tickle your funnybone.

Obviously, as is always the case with humor writing, it's best to try before you buy, so Gerber has conveniently provided the first chapters of each book in Adobe PDF form on the Barry Trotter website.

After reading the characters and glossary list, I downloaded the first chapter to *Barry Trotter and the Shameless Parody* and found myself laughing out loud. What better compliment can I give this book?

Obviously, I wasn't alone in thinking so, since there are various editions for Australia, Germany, Japan, Spain, Sweden, Portugal, Russia, China, Taiwan, Brazil, Estonia, and England, with Korea, France, and Finland on the way, according to Gerber.

And, just as obviously, Gerber will likely trot out more books in this series for those of you who have acquired a taste for his brand of humor.

And now, as comedian Steve Martin would say, if you'll excu-u-u-s-e me, I've got to get back to the characters and glossary list to learn more about the world of Barry Trotter, in which there's "a rare and quite mysterious medical condition in which the sufferer grows progressively younger. Treated with geezerwort and kidsbane," the disease is called . . . Youthanasia.

Notable and Quotable:
The World of Book Publishing

Artist on writer: "I don't talk to J. K. We're not buddies or anything. I met her about four years ago in Chicago, and she's a great lady, but I don't speak with her, really. The publisher often doesn't want the author and illustrator [of children's books] to speak."

—Mary GrandPré quoted by Dan Nailen in "Harry Potter Artist Speaks at Library," *Salt Lake Tribune* (November 16, 2003)

Audiobooks: "So, in *Order of the Phoenix* there are 134 characters, but more than 60 of them are brand new. The challenge was trying to find new voices and accents. I thought I'd explored them all when I invented five, let alone 100. I have to go instinctively now; the first voice I think of, I go with that. Nobody's complained yet, including J. K. Rowling. She's the one we try to please."

—Audiobook reader Jim Dale, quoted by Shannon Maughan in "The Voices of Harry Potter's World," *Publishers Weekly* (July 14, 2003)

Book contracts: "[Christopher] Little may even consider offers from other publishers for the next three books. Although reports have long suggested that

Bloomsbury and Scholastic have a contract for the whole series, Little says this is not the case: 'I negotiate on a book-by-book basis,' he says."

—Sheryle Bagwell, *Australian Financial Review* (July 19, 2000)

Book sales: "Over decades or centuries, Shakespeare and Dickens, Keats and Wordsworth, or Agatha Christie and P. G. Wodehouse may have sold more books, but no one within living memory can match the phenomenal number sold by J. K. Rowling over the past six years."

—Brian MacArthur, "Sales of Harry Potter Books Speak Volumes," Timesonline.co.uk (June 20, 2003)

Boys reading: "The most phenomenal thing is that boys who didn't read are devouring this book. And the book seems to have awakened in children a realization that reading is entertainment."

—Margot Sage-El of Watchung Booksellers, quoted by Bernard Weintraub in "New Harry Potter Book Becoming a Publishing Phenomenon," *New York Times* (July 3, 2000)

British to American English: "But although there are many legitimate reasons for praising the series—the exciting plots, the new young readers being drawn to books, the quality of the writing—I am disappointed about one thing: the decision by Scholastic, publisher of the American edition, to translate the books from 'English' into 'American.' . . . By insisting that everything be Americanized, we dumb down our own society rather than enrich it."

—Peter H. Gleick in an op-ed piece, "Harry Potter, Minus a Certain Flavour," *New York Times* (July 10, 2000)

Censorship: "I don't think there's any subject matter that can't be explored in literature. Any subject matter at all. I really hate censorship. People have the right to decide what they want their children to read, but in my opinion they do not have the right to tell other people's children what they should read."

—Rowling quoted in *Time* (October 2000)

"With Harry Potter, the perceived danger is fantasy. . . . According to certain adults, these stories teach witchcraft, sorcery, and satanism. But hey, if it's not one 'ism,' it's another."

—Judy Bloom, *New York Times* (October 22, 1999)

Child's view of licensing: "None of the kids are crazy about it. Some people say how stupid it is that they are coming out with Harry Potter toothbrushes and things like that. I think they should just stop with the books and movies, otherwise it just goes sort of overboard into a more Disney thing."

—Nine-year-old Emma Bradford quoted by David D. Kirkpatrick in "New Sign on Harry Potter's Forehead: For Sale," *New York Times* (June 16, 2003)

Children's books as cool: "There's not a particle of me that's troubled by the idea that adults might be reading children's books. They jolly well should be. Thank you, J. K. Rowling, for making it cool to read children's books."

—Brenda Bowen, executive vice president and publisher of Simon and Schuster Children's Publishing, quoted in "The Trouble with Harry," *Book* magazine (May/June 2003)

Christian fundamentalists: "When fundamentalists look at Harry Potter, they see a seething Hieronymous Bosch painting, a grotesque and frightening world rife with sin and temptation and devilry. . . . It's odd, though, that when one looks at a child reading a Harry Potter book, lost in a private world, one senses something entirely different. Just a child, secure in a place that is impenetrable to adults and their interpretations. Children read for the same reasons adults do: to escape. Why is it that some adults want to drag them back to their own world of fears and discord? Perhaps because if a book is selling like Harry Potter sells, you can't very well leave it to children."

—Philip Kenicott in "A Scholar Who Gives 'Harry' the Evil Eye," *Washington Post* (November 23, 2003)

Collectibles: "Meanwhile, a hard-backed version of a Harry Potter book bought by a woman from Swindon for £10.99 five years ago was sold at auction yesterday for £13,000. Dominic Winter Book Auction in Swindon, which sold the book, said it was one of just 300 printed. Only a few are privately owned. It was bought by a book dealer from Bristol."

—David Lister in "Bidder Pays £28,000 for Harry Potter Secrets," www.independent.co.uk (December 13, 2002)

Exasperating adult: "In the last tour, in the U.K., I finally lost my temper. And I have a fairly long fuse for my readers, but halfway down a queue of about a thousand people, I had to make a train. This was a train to see my daughter, so this was not a thing I wanted to miss. Halfway down the line, I've got this guy with every bit of Harry Potter paraphernalia he could get his paws on and he wanted them all personalized. And I said to him, 'If I do this for you, that means 12 children at the end of this queue won't get their books signed.' And he argued, and I lost my temper. But eBay . . . explains a lot of it."

—Rowling quoted by Frank Garcia in "Harry Pottermania in Vancouver," *Dateline* (November 16, 2000)

Glasses: "Potter was drawn with spectacles because, Ms. Rowling said, she had worn thick glasses as a child and was frustrated that 'speccies were swots but never heroes.'"

—Rhys Williams in "The Spotty Schoolboy and Single Mother Taking the Mantle from Roald Dahl," *Independent* (January 29, 1999)

Harry Potter illustrations: "I love the look of the American books, especially the chapter illustrations."

—Rowling quoted on scholastic.com (October 16, 2000)

Hogwarts headaches: "A pediatrician says he had three otherwise healthy children complain of headaches for two or three days last summer. It turns out all had been reading the 870-page *Harry Potter and the Order of the Phoenix* in marathon sessions."

—Stephanie Nano, Salon.com (October 29, 2003)

HP1: "A four-year-old American girl is in critical condition in the hospital after apparently trying to fly on a broomstick, like the characters in *Harry Potter and the Philosopher's Stone,* it was reported today. . . . Police in Shelby, North Carolina, told TV reporters the girl crawled onto a kitchen counter, straddled a broom, and then jumped off shortly after watching the film."

—From "Girl, 4, Critical after Harry Potter Broomstick Stunt," *Edinburgh Evening News* (July 22, 2002)

"Of all the questions that children asked me, the most memorable was from a boy in San Francisco, who asked me why Harry's aunt and uncle don't send him to an orphanage if they hate him so much. This is a very important question and it has an answer, but I can't give it without ruining the plot of the fifth Harry Potter book. I have been waiting a long time for someone to ask me that question and I was stunned that I had to travel across the Atlantic to hear someone put his finger on it."

—Rowling quoted by Sally Lodge in "Children's Authors and Illustrators Share Memorable Moments from Recent Book Tours," *Publishers Weekly* (January 4, 1999)

"On the whole *Harry Potter and the Sorcerer's Stone* is as funny, moving, and impressive as the story behind its writing. . . . But like Harry Potter, she has wizardry inside and has soared beyond her modest Muggle surroundings to achieve something special."

—Michael Winerip in a review of the book, *New York Times* (February 14, 1999)

"So much of *Harry Potter and the Sorcerer's Stone* was written and planned before I found myself a single mother that I don't think my experiences at that time directly influenced the plots or characters. I think the only event in my own life that changed the direction of 'Harry Potter' was the death of my mother. I only fully realized upon rereading the book how many of my own feelings about losing my mother I had given Harry."

—Rowling quoted by Margaret Weir in "Of Magic and Single Motherhood," Salon.com (March 31, 1999)

"This book [*Philosopher's Stone*] saved my sanity. Apart from my sister I knew nobody. I've never been more broke and the little I had saved went on baby gear. In the wake of my marriage, having worked all my life, I was suddenly an unemployed single parent in a grotty little flat. The manuscript was the only thing I had going for me."

—Rowling quoted by Anne Johnstone in "Happy Ending, and That's for Beginners," *Herald* (June 24, 1997)

"When I got that first phone call, we had no idea this little kid was going to be on everyone's shelves and be a phenomenon. When that first call came, the publisher was saying, 'It might be part of a series, but we'll probably do just one.'"

—Harry Potter artist Mary GrandPré quoted by Dan Nailen in "Harry Potter Artist Speaks at Library," *Salt Lake Tribune* (November 16, 2003)

HP3: "Rowling took time to say a cheery 'hello' to each of the 100 children who waited in line to have Rowling sign her latest book, *Harry Potter and the Prisoner of Azkaban.* She told one child who said proudly that she, too, was a writer: 'You keep writing, and one day when you're famous, we'll meet again.'"

—Karen McPherson in "'Harry Potter' Goes to Hollywood," *Post-Gazette National Bureau* (October 21, 1999)

"We can't know where J. K. Rowling will take our Harry. But if her series goes on the way it's started, Harry will be 17 by the last installment. . . . Maybe by then J. K. Rowling will have achieved what people who love the best children's books have long labored after: breaking the spell of adult condescension that brands as merely cute, insignificant, second-rate the heartiest and best of children's literature."

—Fantasy author Gregory Maguire in a review of the novel *Lord of the Golden Snitch, New York Times,* Books (September 5, 1999)

HP4: "416. That is how many times I respond in a reasonable tone [to my daughter], explaining patiently that we will have to wait until July 8, the worldwide publication date for all English language versions [of *Harry Potter and the Goblet of Fire*]."

—Michelle Slatalla in "Waiting for Harry Potter in Long Lines on the Net," *New York Times* (April 27, 2000)

"A few seconds past the wizarding hour of midnight Saturday, the most annoying and unnecessary marketing campaign in publishing history finally delivered the goods. J. K. Rowling's *Harry Potter and the Goblet of Fire* would have sold millions of copies had its U.S. and British publishers simply dumped them in bookstores, unannounced, and then got out of the way as word of mouth spread among stampeding Pottermaniacs."

—Paul Gray in "The Wait Was Worth It," *Time* (July 8, 2000)

"For all its frenzy of publicity, this book has arrived like a midsummer night's dream. Enter it and you find a place where the enemies are obsessed with racial purity and the heroes are the ones who have to learn tolerance, community, and reaching across boundaries of fear. If children learn and adults re-learn that lesson in this season of reading, they will find the book very rewarding indeed."

—Steven R. Weisman in "A Novel That Is a Midsummer Night's Dream," *New York Times,* Editorial (July 11, 2000)

"It is worth remembering right about here, that *Harry Potter and the Goblet of Fire* is not a Hollywood summer blockbuster, although its weekend grosses will probably be announced in a breathless press release. It is a book, a really long book, with no moving images, soundtrack, or joysticks. Reading it or listening to someone else read it aloud requires a modicum of silence, the exact antithesis of all the bells and whistles and clarions that heralded its arrival."

—Paul Gray in "Harry Is Back Again," *Time* (July 17, 2000)

"It was the knowledge, unprecedented in a life devoted to the solitary practice of reading, that last night and throughout this weekend, I and millions of other people, young and old, will all be reading the very same book."

—Laura Miller in "Pottermania at Midnight," Salon.com (July 8, 2000)

"It's the end of an era in the context of the whole series of books. For Harry his innocence is gone."

—Rowling quoted by Alan Cowell in "All Aboard the Potter Express," *New York Times* (July 10, 2000)

"The first Harry Potter book was the best. It went into such vivid detail. I really wanted to go to King's Cross and find Platform Nine and Three-Quarters. The first book was the base, the second built the characters, and the third gave the background. So I was excited about the fourth book. Unfortunately, there were too many subplots—like Harry falling in love and the House-elves—that took away from the main Voldemort plot. I enjoyed reading *Harry Potter and the Goblet of Fire,* but *Harry Potter and the Philosopher's Stone* is still my favourite."

—Lucy Barton, aged 14, quoted by Fiona Barton and Lesley Yarranton in "Fear Stalks the Hogwarts Express," *Mail on Sunday* (July 9, 2000)

"The working title had got out—*Harry Potter and the Doomspell Tournament.* Then I changed *Doomspell* to *Triwizard Tournament.* Then I was teetering between *Goblet of Fire* and *Triwizard Tournament.* In the end, I preferred *Goblet of Fire* because it's got that kind of 'cup of destiny' feel about it, which is the theme of the book."

—Rowling quoted by Jeff Jensen in "Rowling Thunder," *Entertainment Weekly* (August 4, 2000)

"There has never been anything like this in the history of book-selling. I think this could be the most profitable book we ever sold. If we can get kids hooked on a seven-book series, hopefully we could get them hooked on reading for life."

—Vice Chairman of Barnes & Noble, Steve Riggio, quoted by David D. Kirkpatrick in "Harry Potter Magic Halts Bedtime for Youngsters," *New York Times* (July 9, 2000)

HP4 book tour and the media: "I'd really love to talk to some children, if I ever manage to finish with you lot."

—Rowling quoted by T. R. Reid in "All Aboard the Publicity Train," *Washington Post* (July 9, 2000)

HP5: "Ms. Rowling has imagined this universe in such minute and clever detail that we feel that we've been admitted to a looking-glass world as palpable as Tolkien's Middle-earth or L. Frank Baum's Oz. The wizards, witches, and Muggles who live there share complicated, generations-old relationships with one another and inhabit a place with traditions, beliefs, and a history all its own—a Grimm place where the fantastic and fabulous are routine, but also a place subject to all the limitations and losses of our own mortal world."

—Michiko Kakutani in *"Harry Potter and the Order of the Phoenix,"* New York Times (June 21, 2003)

"But what really makes the Harry Potter series great is its dual nature. It's a fantasy wrapped around a nightmare, an unreal, escapist fiction with an icy core of emotional pain that is very real."

—Lev Grossman in "That Old Black Magic," *Time* (June 30, 2003)

"I'd spend £1,000 on it if I had to."

—Sinead Miller, aged 13, on what she'd pay for the fifth Harry Potter novel, quoted by Chris Heard in "Potter Mania Sweeps Nation," BBC News: UK Edition (June 21, 2003)

"If you were simply craving a megadose of the old Hogwarts magic, along with the promised twists and surprises (a romance, the death of a key character), then the new book is worth every Potter-deprived minute. J. K. Rowling's great gift—her ability to conjure a rich, teeming, utterly believable alternative world—hasn't failed her."

—Elizabeth Ward in "Harry Potter, Still Quite the Charmer," *Washington Post*'s Book World "For Young Readers" column (June 24, 2003)

"In the U.S., the president of the New York Public Library donned white gloves to accept a signed first edition delivered by armoured car. 'We put the white gloves on only for the most special books,' the library head, Paul LeCler, told the Associated Press news agency."

—From "World Greets New Harry Potter," BBC News (June 21, 2003)

"It is written for people whose imaginative lives are confined to TV cartoons, and the exaggerated (more exciting, not threatening) mirror-worlds of soap, reality TV, and celebrity gossip."

—Author A. S. Byatt in "Harry Potter and the Childish Adult," *New York Times* (July 7, 2003)

"The nation's children are up in arms. Where is their annual fix of the young magician? At this rate they will have to compensate—shock, horror—by reading other—do they know there are any?—books for children by the likes of Philip Pullman, Jacqueline Wilson, Anne Fine, Lemony Snicket, Joan Lingard, and Teresa Breslin."

—Giles Gordon in "Publish or Be Damned," *Scotsman* (September 20, 2002)

"The publisher already has distributed 3 million bumper stickers, 400,000 buttons, 50,000 window displays, and 24,000 stand-up posters with countdown clocks. . . . Scholastic has also sent out more than 15,000 'event kits' to bookstores and other retail outlets, where parties are planned all over the country."

—From "Publisher Preps for Potter," MSN Entertainment News (June 5, 2003)

"Thus a multiethnic multiculture of warlocks, mermaids, mugawumps, trolls, vampires, fairies, dwarfs, ghouls, mummies, pixies, gnomes, banshees, wood nymphs, dementors, boggarts, veelas, animagi, and parselmouths."

—John Leonard in *"Harry Potter and the Order of the Phoenix:* Nobody Expects the Inquisition," *New York Times Book Review* (July 13, 2003)

"We knew it was big—the massive first printing, the media hype, the midnight release parties, the assured instant-best-seller status. But perhaps nobody knew *Harry Potter and the Order of the Phoenix* would be this big, this fast. According to reports from Scholastic, an estimated five million copies of the book were sold on Saturday, its first day of release."

—PW staff in *"Harry* Makes History—Again," *Publishers Weekly* (June 23, 2003)

Licensing: "I would do anything to prevent Harry from turning up in fast-food boxes everywhere. I would do my utmost. That would be my worst nightmare."

—Rowling quoted by David D. Kirkpatrick in "New Sign on Harry Potter's Forehead: For Sale," *New York Times* (June 16, 2003)

"In 1998, Rowling sold worldwide licensing rights to Warner for about $500,000 (a price now considered insanely low), although she does receive unspecified royalties based on licensing revenues. For example, she gets an estimated $1 to $1.50 for each Harry video game that is sold. About 75 products have been licensed so far. Hard as it is to believe, that's not so many for a brand of this visibility, part of a strategy by Warner to sell a modest number of licenses for a massive number of dollars."

—Gordon T. Anderson in "Harry Potter and the Big Wad of Cash," CNNMoney.com (June 20, 2003)

"I've had some very weird offers. A margarine company wanted to put Harry on its margarine, if you can believe it."

—Rowling quoted by Katy Abel in "Harry Potter Author Works Her Magic," *Family Education* (summer 1999)

"Ms. Rowling created the characters, and she has the right to kill them off . . . or turn them into Happy Meal action figures, if that's where her heart lies. But the sentimentalists among us are going to mourn the days when Harry existed only in books, which were smaller than breadboxes."

—Gail Collins in an op-ed piece, "Moby Dick on a Broom," *New York Times* (July 7, 2000)

"We're getting over 100 inquiries a day, whether it's the Sony Corporation or Microsoft or Boeing, to people that make cups and saucers."

—Christopher Little quoted by Ed Bradley on *60 Minutes* (September 12, 1999)

Literary power of Potter: "Parents report reading levels jumping four grades in two years. They cannot quite believe this gift, that for an entire generation of children, the most powerful entertainment experience of their lives comes not on a screen or a monitor or a disc but on a page."

—Nancy Gibbs in "The Real Magic of Harry Potter," *Time* (June 23, 2003)

Magical book: "One little girl said her books were 'magic.' Rowling told her that that was the nicest compliment she had ever received. Eventually more than 1,000 fans filed through."

—Linton Weeks in "Charmed, I'm Sure," *Washington Post* (October 20, 1999)

Magical reality: "What makes the Harry Potter books fly, so to speak, is not so much their otherworldliness as their fidelity to the way things really are (or were, at least, when quills and parchment were still more common than computers): Wizards, Harry Potter's world suggests, are only regular Muggles who've been to the right school."

—Pico Iyer in "The Playing Fields of Hogwarts," *New York Times,* Books (October 10, 1999)

Master plan: "I want to finish these seven books and look back and think that whatever happened to me—however much this hurricane whirled around me—I stayed true to what I wanted to write. This is my Holy Grail: that when I finish writing book seven, I can say—hand on heart—I didn't change a thing. I wrote the story I meant to write. If I lost readers along the way, so be it, but I still told my story. The one I wanted. Without permitting it to sound too corny, that's what I owe to my characters. That we won't be deflected, either by adoration or by criticism."

—Rowling quoted by Linda Richards in "January Profile: J. K. Rowling," januarymagazine.com (October 2000)

Model for Hermione Granger: "She is a caricature of me: I was neither as bright nor as annoying as Hermione. At least, I hope I wasn't, because I would have deserved drowning at birth. But she, like me, lightens up. As I went through my teens, things actually got better. I began to realize that there was more to me than just someone who got everything right."

—Rowling quoted by Helena de Bertodano in "Harry Potter Charms a Nation," *Electronic Telegraph* (July 25, 1998)

Muggle technology: "But one of the interesting things about Hogwarts in the Potter books is that it contains no technology at all. Light is provided by torches and heat by massive fireplaces. Who needs electricity when you have plenty of wizards and magic wands? . . . Technology is for Muggles, who rely on contraptions because they cannot imagine the conveniences of magic. Who wouldn't choose a wizard's life?"

—Paul Gray in "Wild about Harry," *Time* (September 20, 1999)

Occult: "The books are written in a very amusing way, but those underlying tones of death, murder, and the occult is what scares us. Especially here in the States with all the violence we've had in our schools. A lot of that has been linked to kids getting involved in the occult. . . . It's too violent. There were parts that really scared us, and we didn't want [our son] to lose his innocence."

—David Williamson, a parent protesting the Harry Potter novels, quoted by Celia Farber in "Harry Potter's Toughest Foe," *Sunday Herald* (October 17, 1999)

Panned: "The cultural critics will, soon enough, introduce Harry Potter into their college curriculum, and the *New York Times* will go on celebrating another confirmation of the dumbing-down it leads and exemplifies."

—Harold Bloom in an op-ed piece, "Can 35 Million Book Buyers Be Wrong? Yes," *Wall Street Journal* (July 11, 2000)

"The writing was dreadful; the book was terrible. . . . Rowling's mind is so governed by clichés and dead metaphors that she has no other style of writing. . . . Later I read a lavish, loving review of Harry Potter by the same Stephen King. He wrote something to the effect of, 'If these kids are reading Harry Potter at 11 or 12, then when they get older they will go on to read Stephen King.' And he was quite right. He was not being ironic.

When you read 'Harry Potter' you are, in fact, trained to read Stephen King."

—Harold Bloom, from "Dumbing Down American Readers," *Boston Globe* (September 24, 2003)

Parent-child relationship: "This book has opened up a whole new relationship between my ten-year-old son (who definitely had no passion for reading) and myself (a person who has such a love for reading). We have the best time talking about the characters and the stories! I do believe this has made my son love reading, which is a gift any parent will appreciate! But I think the best part is the quality time we spend reading and talking about the adventures."

—Beth A., in a letter (*Time*, July 11, 2000) responding to "Extra! Extra! Page One of the New 'Harry Potter,'" *Time* (July 7, 2000)

Phenomenon: "Does the word 'miracle' mean anything to you? What we're talking about here is a foreign import with no television show, no movie, and no celebrity. It's a noisy world, and it's hard to get attention for a children's book."

—Nancy Pines, children's book publisher at Simon and Schuster/Pocket Books, quoted by Doreen Carvajal in "Children's Book Casts a Spell over Adults," *New York Times* (April 1, 1999)

Plotting: "It is a lot of work to create an entire world. It was about five years to finish the first book and to plot the remaining six books, because they were already plotted before the first book was published; and book two was started before book one was finished. Yeah, so I spent an awful lot of time thinking about the details of the world and working it out in depth."

—Rowling quoted in "Interview with J. K. Rowling," *Connection* (October 12, 1999)

Popularity: "We've never had a [children's book] author who has risen as quickly as J. K. I think she might well be regarded as highly as Roald Dahl."

—British book reviewer Julia Eccleshare quoted by William Plummer and Joanna Blonska in "They're Wild about Harry," *Entertainment Weekly* (July 9, 1999)

Private world: "I always find it very hard to talk about the book in these terms because I find it very, very difficult to be objective . . . To me, they remain my private little world—I was writing about Harry for five years before anyone else read a word of him—and it is still an amazing feeling to me to be in a room, as we are today, with people whose heads are also populated with these characters because, as I say, for five years, they were my private secret. From the moment I had the idea for the book, I could just see a lot of comic potential in the idea that wizards walk among us and that we are foolishly blind to the fact that the reason that we keep losing our car keys is that wizards are bewitching them for fun."

—Rowling quoted in "James Naughtie Talks to J. K. Rowling about One of Her Novels," Radio 4's Book Club Programme (August 1, 1999)

Quidditch: "I invented Quidditch while spending the night in a very small room in the Bournville Hotel in Didsbury, Manchester. I wanted a sport for wizards, and I'd always wanted to see a game where there was more than one ball in play at the same time. The idea just amused me. The Muggle sport it most resembles is basketball, which is probably the sport I enjoy watching most. I had a lot of fun making up the rules and I've still got the notebook I did it in, complete with diagrams, and all the names for the balls I tried before I settled on Snitch, Bludgers, and Quaffle."

—Rowling quoted in an interview on Amazon.co.uk (1999)

Rowling's imagination: "The fantasy writer's job is to conduct the willing reader from mundanity to magic. This is a feat of which only a superior imagination is capable, and Rowling possesses such equipment."

—Stephen King in a book review of HP4 for the *New York Times*

Science in Harry Potter's universe: "Irrespective of the specific title of the course, the 'magic' in the fiction is being analyzed by applying concepts of physics, chemistry, biology, and engineering. This honors course creatively packages scientific principles in a contemporary way that will interest today's students."

—Catherine R. Gira, Frostburg State president, on George R. Plitnik's physics course, "The Science of Harry Potter," quoted by David Dishneau in "Harry Potter Gets Some Class at College," Associated Press (September 21, 2003)

Selecting Hogwarts students: "The Ministry of Magic doesn't find out which children are magic. In Hogwarts there's a magical quill which detects the birth of a magical child and writes his or her name down in a large parchment book. Every year Professor McGonagall checks the book and sends owls to the people who are turning 11."

—Rowling quoted in "The 24 Most Intriguing People of 1999," *People* (December 31, 1999)

Showing up unannounced at a hometown bookstore: "When *Goblet of Fire* was published, I was desperate to go into a bookshop at midnight and see children's reactions, so this time I'm really pleased I could. Much of the pleasure of being published for me is meeting the children who are reading the books."

—Rowling quoted in "JK in City for Spell at Harry Launch," News.scotsman.com (June 21, 2003)

Tim Kirk

The Final Exam: A Trivia Quiz for Muggles

Anyone can claim to be a Harry Potter expert, but do you really know your stuff? Here are questions that will tax your knowledge of J. K. Rowling and the Harry Potter Universe.

The Real World of J. K. Rowling

1. In which country was J. K. Rowling born?
    a. Scotland
    b. Ireland
    c. England
    d. Narnia

2. Where did J. K. Rowling's parents meet for the first time?
    a. On a train traveling from London to Scotland
    b. At Waterstone's, a bookstore in London
    c. At Merton College in Oxford, England
    d. In Munchkin City in the Land of Oz

3. Which of the following authors does J. K. Rowling count among her favorites?
    a. Stephen King
    b. Philip Pullman
    c. Jane Austen
    d. Bilbo Baggins

4. Known to the world as J. K. Rowling, what do the first two initials in her name stand for?
    a. Julie Kathleen
    b. Joanne Kathleen
    c. Jill Kathleen
    d. Jenny Kathleen

5. At Wyedean Comprehensive, Rowling was appointed:
    a. Head Girl
    b. Student librarian
    c. Student assistant
    d. Captain of the soccer team

6. Before Rowling wrote Harry Potter, she had written two works that remain unpublished. These works are:
    a. books of nonfiction
    b. books of essays
    c. adult novels
    d. juvenile fantasy

7. Though Rowling applied to Oxford, she was not accepted, and she subsequently attended which university?
    a. University of Exeter
    b. Harvard University
    c. The School of Hard Knocks
    d. Merton College

8. The idea of Harry Potter was conceived while she was traveling:
    a. on foot
    b. on a plane
    c. on a double-decker red bus in London
    d. on a train

9. After college graduation, she taught English in which country?
    a. the Republic of China
    b. Portugal
    c. Vietnam
    d. France

10. Rowling's first marriage ended in failure, after which she moved to:
    a. Edinburgh, Scotland
    b. Cambridge, England
    c. Paris, France
    d. Los Angeles, California

11. Drinking coffee and writing longhand, Rowling penned fiction at a public place:
    a. Starbucks
    b. The Cock and Bull restaurant
    c. Nicholson's restaurant
    d. McDonald's restaurant

12. Writing the first Harry Potter novel and plotting out the remaining novels in the series took Rowling:
    a. one easy year
    b. two moderately difficult years
    c. three torturous years
    d. five long years

13. Realizing that she would need a literary agent to represent her to book publishers, Rowling's work caught the eyes of those at which literary agency?
    a. Christopher Little Literary Agency
    b. Chris Columbus Literary Voyages
    c. Bryony Evens Agency
    d. Creative Artists Agency

14. Though several U.K. publishers passed on Harry Potter, one firm took the chance on Rowling, a first-time novelist. Who was that publisher?
    a. Fly By Night Publishers
    b. HarperCollins
    c. Bloomsbury
    d. Reader's Digest Condensed Books

15. Rowling's first book advance—money loaned to an author that is hopefully repaid by book sales—was:
    a. 500 British pounds
    b. 1,500 British pounds
    c. 15,000 British pounds
    d. 150,000 British pounds

16. At the Bologna Book Fair in Germany, Arthur Levine, the editorial director at Scholastic Books, saw and fell in love with the first Harry

Potter book. By the time the bidding war ended, he had committed to spending:
a. $1
b. $10,000
c. $100,000
d. $1,000,000

17. The book advance from Scholastic allowed Rowling to buy:
    a. a cup of Starbucks coffee—barely
    b. a two bedroom flat in Edinburgh, Scotland
    c. a loft apartment in downtown London
    d. an Apple computer with laser printer and a 30-inch cinema display

18. In a highly publicized (and subsequently dismissed) lawsuit, J. K. Rowling was accused of plagiarism from an American author whose book was titled:
    a. *The Legend of Rah and the Muggles*
    b. *Muggles and More Muggles*
    c. *Rah, Rah, Rah for the Muggles*
    d. *The Muggles from Mudworth*

19. From the beginning, Rowling has adamantly insisted that the Harry Potter saga would encompass:
    a. six novels
    b. seven novels
    c. eight novels
    d. as many novels as the public is willing to buy

20. After the final book in the Harry Potter series is published, Rowling has said in interviews that she plans to publish an accessory book as a charity project. According to interviews with her, this book will cover:
    a. An encyclopedia of Hogwarts and the wizarding world
    b. A concordance to every word in the Harry Potter canon
    c. A keepsake book
    d. A book of spells

21. Rowling, who has been blessed with good and great fortune, generously donates to charities that resonate personally with her. Because of the difficult time she endured when she returned from Portugal, she's become an ambassador and a generous contributor to:
    a. the National Council for One Parent Families
    b. the Humane Society
    c. the Society for the Prevention of Cruelty to Authors (SPCA)
    d. the TCBS (the Tea Club and Barovian Society)

22. What is the address of J. K. Rowling's official website?
    a. www.jkrowling.com
    b. www.rowlingindough.com
    c. www.iwroteharrypotter.com
    d. www.flightsofimagination.com

23. When in London, J. K. Rowling stays in a Georgian-style house in which London suburb?
    a. Kensington
    b. Oxford
    c. Buckingham Palace
    d. Hyde Park

24. J. K. Rowling has penned two charity books. What are her two pen names?
    a. Newt Scamander
    b. Kennilworthy Whisp
    c. Frog Salamander
    d. Kennelworthy Whisk

25. Rowling was approached by numerous film studios that were interested in the Harry Potter books. She initially turned them all down, but one company persisted and finally won her over. Which studio won the franchise?
    a. Warner Bros.
    b. MGM Studios
    c. Twentieth Century Fox
    d. Disney's Mouseworks

26. Which nocturnal hunting animal has become popular among kids as a result of the Harry Potter novels?
    a. cats
    b. dogs
    c. toads
    d. owls

27. Commissioned especially for book cover art and for licensing properties, artwork of Harry Potter has been rendered by many talented artists. Who illustrates the U.S. editions of the Harry Potter books?
    a. Mary GrandPré
    b. Kinuko Craft
    c. Irina Ivanova
    d. Britton McDaniel

28. What is the most famous Harry Potter fan website?
    a. www.hpana.com
    b. www.mugglenet.com
    c. www.harryisnumberone.com
    d. www.whenharrymethermione.com

29. The Harry Potter novels are available in virtually every popular format except:
    a. electronic books (ebooks)
    b. signed, limited editions
    c. print-on-demand books (POD)
    d. Ipod recordings

30. J. K. Rowling appeared as herself in a famous television animated series in a cameo:
    a. *Beavis and Butthead*
    b. *The Simpsons*
    c. *The Saturday Morning Funnies*
    d. *Spongebob Squarepants*

31. J. K. Rowling's homes can be found in all the following locations *except*:
    a. Edinburgh, Scotland
    b. Kensington, London
    c. Pertshire, Scotland, on the banks of the River Tay
    d. Dublin, Ireland

32. Though J. K. Rowling graduated from the University of Exeter in England, she received an honorary degree from which university in Scotland?
    a. The University of St. Andrews
    b. The Robert Gordon University
    c. The University of Edinburgh
    d. Napier University

33. What U.S. magazine erroneously reported that J. K. Rowling is a billionaire?
    a. *Forbes*
    b. *Time*
    c. *Newsweek*
    d. *U.S. News & World Report*

34. What major U.S. news magazine featured Rowling on its cover, with art by Mary GrandPré?
    a. *Time*
    b. *Newsweek*
    c. *U.S. News and World Report*
    d. *Muggles Monthly*

35. At a public talk given at the Royal Albert Hall in London, Rowling expressed her grave displeasure at a certain person whom she'd love to see boiled in oil. What is the profession of that person?
    a. member of Parliament
    b. tax collector
    c. solicitor
    d. journalist

36. Rowling has written novels that will likely never see publication. How many are there?
    a. one
    b. two
    c. three
    d. dozens

The Film World of Harry Potter

37. Who is the child actor who plays the key role of Harry Potter?
    a. Haley Joel Osment
    b. Liam Aiken
    c. Jacob Smith
    d. Daniel Radcliffe

38. Who is the child actress who plays the key role of Hermione Granger?
    a. Emma Watson
    b. Gemma Padley
    c. Emily Dale
    d. Bonnie Wright

39. Who is the child actor who plays the key role of Ronald Weasley?
    a. Alfred Enoch
    b. Tom Felton
    c. Rupert Grint
    d. Matt Lewis

40. Who directed the first two Harry Potter movies?
    a. Chris Columbus
    b. Amerigo Vespucci
    c. Ferdinand Magellan
    d. Steven Spielberg

41. Who directed the third Harry Potter movie?
    a. Chris Columbus
    b. Alfonso Cuarón

    c. Steven Spielberg

    d. Gary Wood

42. The cast of all the Harry Potter movies is unique in film-making because:
    a. The cast is overwhelmingly British
    b. The cast is evenly divided between Muggles and wizards
    c. The cast are all members of SAG (Screen Actors Guild)
    d. The cast is international in membership

43. For the most part, the Harry Potter films have been shot in:
    a. Ireland
    b. England
    c. Scotland
    d. Isle of Man

44. What famous U.S. director expressed an interest in, but subsequently passed on, helming the first Harry Potter film?
    a. Ron Howard
    b. Jonathan Demme
    c. Steven Spielberg
    d. Terry Gilliam

45. What Harry Potter novel perpetuated the rumor that, because of its length, it would be made in two films?
    a. *Harry Potter and the Goblet of Fire*
    b. *Harry Potter and the Order of the Phoenix*
    c. *Harry Potter and the Half-Blood Prince*
    d. *Harry Potter and the Dark Lord Duke It Out*

46. Who is the screenwriter of the first three Harry Potter film adaptations?
    a. Steve Kloves
    b. Steve Anise
    c. Steve Chives
    d. Steve Cardamom

47. For *Harry Potter and the Prisoner of Azkaban*, a new director was needed because the man who helmed the first two films felt:
    a. He wasn't getting enough money.
    b. He was getting enough money, but he felt he needed a well-deserved and long overdue break.
    c. He was getting a bloody fortune and wanted to enjoy it at a south sea island, far from the madding crowd.
    d. He played rock/paper/scissors with another director—and lost. (Game strategy: always pick paper because most people pick rock.)

48. Who conducted the scores for the first three Harry Potter films?
    a. John Williams
    b. Howard Shore
    c. John Tesh
    d. Vangelis

49. Which British actor who played Headmaster Albus Dumbledore died between the second and third films?
    a. Richard Griffiths
    b. Richard Harris
    c. Richard Bremmer
    d. Richard Ricardo

50. The super-hard question in this category: Who provided the voice-over of Harry Potter in the first movie? (Hint: He also provided the voice of Harry Potter in a video game. I know, that doesn't *really* help, does it?)
    a. Joe Sorebutts
    b. Joe Sowerbutts
    c. Joe Blow
    d. Joe Butts

Miscellany

51. Whose voice is heard on the Harry Potter audio books sold in the U.S.? (Hint: He holds the world record for the greatest number of voices in a single audio recording.)
    a. Run DMC
    b. Jim Dale
    c. Steve Martin
    d. Martin Short

52. What famous member of the British comedy team, Monty Python, made his ghostly appearance in the first Potter film?
    a. John Cleese
    b. Eric Idle
    c. Graham Chapman
    d. Michael Palin

53. What famous castle in England was used for the exterior shots of Hogwarts?
    a. Alnwick Castle
    b. Dunboy Castle
    c. Pendennis Castle
    d. Buckingham Palace

54. What prominent London landmark is seen in the second Harry Potter film?
    a. Big Ben
    b. The London Eye
    c. The Tower of London
    d. The Victoria & Albert Museum

55. According to Rowling's literary agent, her Potter novels have reached a new high in terms of copies in print. Sold in more than 200 countries and translated into 60 languages, what benchmark was reached?
    a. A billion
    b. A quarter billion
    c. A half billion
    d. Like McDonald's hamburgers, "billions and billions" sold

56. Like clockwork, all of the Harry Potter novels appeared when the publisher has promised, except one. Which Harry Potter novel ran late?
    a. the third novel
    b. the fourth novel
    c. the fifth novel
    d. the sixth novel

57. What famous writer raved enthusiastically about the Harry Potter novels in the August pages of *The New York Times*?
    a. J. D. Salinger
    b. Stephen King
    c. Stephen Spignesi
    d. David Lowell

58. A famous author dismissed the Harry Potter novels by saying they are "written for people whose imaginative lives are confined to TV cartoons, and the exaggerated (more exciting, not threatening) mirror-worlds of soaps, reality TV, and celebrity gossip." Who is that author?
    a. A. S. Byatt
    b. Terry Pratchett
    c. A. S. Bile
    d. Harold Bloom

59. At a Sotheby's auction of a Rowling-inscribed set of Harry Potter novels, one of them, *Harry Potter and the Goblet of Fire*, fetched an astounding sum, owing to it being an associational copy (that is, inscribed to family or a friend). How much did that copy sell for?
    a. $10,000
    b. $30,000

    c. $48,000

    d. $75,000

60. Referring to the previous question, to whom was that copy inscribed? Rowling's:

    a. literary agent

    b. first husband

    c. father

    d. sister

ANSWERS

The Real World of J. K. Rowling

1. c
2. a
3. c
4. b
5. a
6. c
7. a
8. d
9. b
10. a
11. c
12. d
13. a
14. c
15. b
16. c
17. b
18. a
19. b
20. a
21. a
22. a
23. a
24. a & b

25. a
26. d
27. a
28. b
29. a
30. b
31. d
32. c
33. a
34. a
35. d
36. b

The Film World of Harry Potter

37. d
38. a
39. c
40. a
41. b
42. a
43. b
44. c
45. a
46. a
47. b

48. a

49. b

50. b

Miscellany

51. b

52. a

53. a

54. a

55. b

56. c

57. b

58. a

59. c

60. c

Tim Kirk

Books about Rowling and Harry Potter

The number of books about J. K. Rowling and Harry Potter continue to pour forth from writers who find eager publishers rushing to press with them. This list, then, is incomplete; check Amazon.com with a search on both subjects for what has been recently published or is forthcoming.

59³/4 Fabulous Sites for Harry Potter Fans, by Barbara J. Feldman. Surfnetkids.com, 2003. Adobe PDF book. Lists approximately 60 websites of interest to Potter fans, including the official sites, games, screensavers, postcards, discussion boards, fan fiction, etc. My first thought is, *"only* 60 sites?" My second thought: Do your own Google search and come up with your own list, which will be more updated.

All about J. K. Rowling, by Shaun McCarthy. Raintree, 2003. 32 pages. A brief biography.

Beacham's Sourcebook for Teaching Young Adult Fiction: Exploring Harry Potter, by Elizabeth D. Schafer and Elizabeth D. Sullivan. Beacham, 2000. 528 pages. A resource guide especially useful to students and teachers, this book's 20 chapters provide background information and a chapter-by-chapter and book-by-book look at the Potter novels with projects and activities appropriate for students. Most useful for its excellent bibliography.

Beatrix Potter to Harry Potter: Portraits of Children's Writers, by Julia Eccleshare. National Portrait Gallery Publications (U.K.), 2002. 136 pages. This covers the exhibition of the same name that took place in May–August 2002 in the Porter Gallery. The exhibit, which drew more than 100,000 visitors, included paintings, drawings, sculptures, and original manuscripts.

Boys and Girls Forever: Children's Classics from Cinderella to Harry Potter. Penguin, 2002. 240 pages. Fourteen essays culled from the *New York Review of Books,* written by a well-known critic whose "essays are consistently entertaining, enlightening, and erudite." Recommended.

A Champion's Prediction Journal for Harry Potter Fans, by Leslie Durhman and Susie Worden. Superior Siblings LLC, 2002. 50 pages. A journal for recording your responses to 100 questions posed by the authors regarding the contents of *Harry Potter and the Order of the Phoenix.*

Character Education: The Legacy of the Harry Potter Novels, by Stefan Neilson. Aeon Hierophant Pub: Vintage, 2001. 128 pages. A psychologist examines Harry Potter's experiences as life lessons for parents and educators seeking guidance and instruction.

A Charmed Life: The Spirituality of Potterworld, by Francis Bridger. Image Books, 2002. 176 pages. A theologian and principal of Trinity College (Bristol, England) examines the Potter novels in the context of J. R. R. Tolkien's and C. S. Lewis's novels, steeped in Christian faith.

A Closer Look at Harry Potter: Bending and Shaping the Minds of Our Children, by John Houghton. Kingsway Communications, 2001. 96 pages.

Conversations with J. K. Rowling, by Lindsey Fraser. Arthur A. Levine Books, 2001. 96 pages. This book is divided into three parts: an interview conducted especially for this book, an overview of the first four Harry Potter novels, and quotes from the media on Rowling and Harry Potter, culled from print publications. Short but illuminating.

The Definitive Harry Potter Guide Book Series: The Prisoner of Azkaban, by Marie Lesoway. Suggit Group Ltd., 2001.

A Detective's Analysis of Harry Potter and the Mysteries Within, by Mary C. Baumann. Authorhouse, 2004. 228 pages. A print-on-demand book.

Fact, Fiction, and Folklore in Harry Potter's World: An Unofficial Guide, by George Beahm, illustrated by Tim Kirk and Britton McDaniel. Hampton Roads Publishing, 2005. 256 pages. Thematically arranged (creatures, wizards, artifacts, and places), this book has 300 separate entries that delve into the myths, legends, folklore, and facts that are an integral part of the Harry Potter universe. (Yes, Sirius Black will be in the next edition.)

Faith Journey through Fantasy Lands: A Christian Dialogue with Harry Potter, Star Wars, and The Lord of the Rings, by Russell W. Dalton. Augsburg Fortress Publishers, 2003. 160 pages. In this Christian's look at these pop culture powerhouses, Dalton suggests they are popular because of their religious elements. He recommends the books be used as pathways for open discussion with fellow Christians, for faith-sharing, especially with younger people.

Fantasy and Your Family: Exploring The Lord of the Rings, *Harry Potter, and Modern Magick,* by Richard Abanes. Horizon Books, 2002. 300 pages. A thought-provoking discussion organized in four sections: an overview of fantasy literature, Tolkien's *The Lord of the Rings,* Harry Potter, and pro/con arguments about Harry Potter.

Females and Harry Potter: Not All That Empowering, by Ruthann Mayes-Elma. Rowman & Littlefield Publishers, 2006. 160 pages.

Friends and Foes of Harry Potter: Names Decoded, by Nikita and Chitra Agarwal. Outskirts Press, 2005. 160 pages. Originally a creative writing project, this book is written by two sisters, a fifth grader and a sophomore high school student. Organized by house and by friend or foe, the young authors analyze each character's name to derive its significance. For instance, Professor Pomona Sprout (who teaches herbology) is aptly named, for Pomona is the Roman goddess of fruit trees and horticulture. A fun book for fans who would enjoy digging beneath the surface of the names to learn more about their historical and mythical origins.

From Alice to Harry Potter: Children's Fantasy in England, by Colin Manlove. Cybereditions, 2003. An e-book available online from Amazon.com in Adobe Reader format. An overview of children's literature spanning 150 years and 400 English classics, where the genre flourishes. An in-depth and informed discussion that puts this wide body of literature in broad context.

From Homer to Harry Potter: A Handbook on Myth and Fantasy, by Matthew T. Dickerson and David O'Hara. Brazos Press, 2006. 272 pages. An ALA review notes that this is "an informative, highly entertaining examination of the literature of faerie throughout the centuries. . . ." Recommended.

From Shakespeare to Harry Potter: An Introduction to Literature for All Ages, by Connie Ann Kirk. Xlibris Corp., 2004. 129 pages. A print-on-demand book. An accessible guide to the world of literature from the classics to pop cult favorites. Recommended.

God, the Devil, and Harry Potter: A Christian Minister's Defense of the Beloved Novels, by John Killinger. New York: St. Martin's/Griffin, 2004. 208 pages. A defense of the Harry Potter novels written by an ordained clergyman who has doctorates in theology and literature. (For a similar discussion, see *A Charmed Life.*)

The Gospel According to Harry Potter: Spirituality in the Stories of the World's Most Famous Seeker, by Connie Neal. Westminister John Knox Press, 2002. 166 pages. An explication of the Potter texts in light of Christian beliefs. Read this instead of books by other Christian writers who see her texts as platforms espousing occultism.

Guide to the Harry Potter Novels, by Julia Eccleshare. Continuum International Publishing Group, 2002. 112 pages.

Harry Potter and the Bible: The Menace behind the Magick, by Richard Abanes. Horizon Books, 2001. 275 pages. A former minister, Abanes specializes in writing about the occult. This book is divided into two parts: The first part summarizes the first four Potter novels and discusses the elements of occultism to be found; the second part is an overview of occult in the U.S., putting it in the context of fantasy literature as a genre, with a discussion of the controversy of Potter books used as texts in public schools.

Harry Potter Collectibles. CheckerBee Publishing, 2000. 128 pages. As the author of two editions of *Stephen King Collectibles,* in which I list every known book edition with price valuations and other materials that the King fan would likely want to know about, I would assume (based on the title alone) that *Harry Potter Collectibles* would be similar, but it's not. It is not only many years out of date but covers companion-style material that has no place in a book like this. This book of marginal interest cannot be recommended, at least until it's updated, tightly focused on true collectibles, and can serve as an authoritative price guide.

The Harry Potter Companion, by "Ascascias Riphouse." Virtualbookworm.com Publishing, 2004. 540 pages. A print-on-demand book. A general-interest book about Harry Potter and the wizarding world, unfortunately marred (as is often the case with POD books) with numerous typographical errors.

Harry Potter and International Relations, by David H. Nexon and Iver B. Neumann. Rowan & Littlefield Publishers, Inc., 2006. 224 pages. An anthology themed to understanding world politics through the imagined world of Harry Potter.

Harry Potter, Narnia, and The Lord of the Rings: What You Need to Know about Fantasy Books and Movies, by Richard Abanes. Harvest House Publishers, 2005. 297 pages. A Christian-based book comparing and contrasting the three most popular fantasy book/movie franchises in our time.

Harry Potter Online Directory, by JLJ Marketing. Online Trading Academy, 2003. 300 pages. On CD-ROM only. Active links on the web broken down by category: directories, education, discussions, fan sites, games, fun, kids, news, official, the books, the movies, videos and MP3, reviews, images, and interactive. Unfortunately, this is a PC-enabled product only—an important fact not pointed out by its publisher or online booksellers.

Harry Potter and Philosophy: If Aristotle Ran Hogwarts, eds. David Baggett, Shawn Klein, William Irwin. Open Court, 2004. 250 pages. An anthology of 17 pieces from a philosophical perspective.

Harry Potter and the Sorcerer's Stone: A Unit Plan, by Marion B. Hoffman on CD-ROM and printable PDF. Teacher's Pet Publications, Inc., 2001. 202

pages. Intended for teachers looking to use the book as a point of departure for discussions with children, the manual has "study questions, quizzes, writing assignments, discussion questions, unit tests, vocabulary worksheets, daily lesson plans, group and individual assignments and activities worksheets, games, puzzles, bulletin board ideas, and written objectives for the guide and each lesson."

Harry Potter! The Best Websites & Web Journal, compiled by Anthony M. Swinsinski. Lightning Rod Publishers, 2005. 42 pages. From what I can tell online, single entries comprise one paragraph in length; the remainder of the pages have blank lines for you to fill in your own comments.

Harry Potter, You're the Best: A Tribute from Fans the World Over, ed. Sharon Moore. Griffin, 2001. 128 pages. A follow-up book to *We Love Harry Potter!,* this book is a tribute, with letters from young readers and fun stuff for them as well; she includes crossword puzzles, word jumbles, and a resource list of books recommended for Potter fans.

Harry Potter's World: Multidisciplinary Critical Perspectives (Pedagogy and Popular Culture), ed. Elizabeth E. Heilman. Routledge, 2003. 304 pages. A welcome addition to the growing body of books on Harry Potter from the academic community. Edited by a college professor, this collection of essays is organized in four sections: Cultural Studies Perspectives; Reader Response and Interpretive Perspectives; Literary Perspectives: The Hero, Myth and Genre; and Sociological Perspective. This is an illuminating book that sheds considerable light on the Harry Potter phenomenon in all its varied dimensions.

Henry Potty and the Pet Rock: An Unauthorized Harry Potter Parody, by Valerie Estelle Frankel. WingSpan Press, 2006. 112 pages.

The Hidden Key to Harry Potter: Understanding the Meaning, Genius, and Popularity of Joanne Rowling's Harry Potter Novels, by John Granger. Zossima Press, 2002. 384 pages. Its thesis is that, like C. S. Lewis and J. R. R. Tolkien, Rowling is at heart a Christian writer—the hidden key, as it were, to unlocking her fiction. Whether or not you agree, the fact remains that Christians are divided as to whether or not her books should be banned or bought. There are advocates within the Christian community for both positions. For everyone else without an axe to grind, this speculative book is fascinating reading, as it is neither a spirited defense nor a polemic against the perceived "evils" of Harry Potter novels.

The Hidden Myths in Harry Potter: Spellbinding Map/Book of Secrets, by David Colbert, illustrated by Virginia Allyn. St. Martin's Griffin, 2005. 32 pages. Colbert, who has made a name for himself as the author of *The Magical Worlds of Harry Potter,* goes back to the well to repackage the information in a format especially useful to children: a fold-out, full-color map and reader-friendly text with short entries and charming illustrations. A delightful book, this would make a great birthday gift or stocking stuffer for a child who is young enough to believe in dragons and witches but not old enough to read Colbert's *The Magical Worlds of Harry Potter.*

If Harry Potter Ran General Electric: Leadership Wisdom from the World of Wizards, by Tom Morris. Currency, 2006. 272 pages. A former philosophy professor, Morris draws lessons of leadership from Harry Potter and his adventures in the wizarding world. This book is a sequel to Morris's *If Aristotle Ran General Motors.* This book is intended for managers in the business world.

Imagining Faith with Kids: Unearthing Seeds of the Gospel in Children's Stories from Peter Rabbit to Harry Potter, by Mary Margaret Keaton. Pauline Books & Media, 2005. 312 pages.

An Interview with J. K. Rowling. Egmont Children's Books, 2002. 74 pages. The title is somewhat misleading, since the interviews herein are conducted with four authors, only one of whom is Rowling. (The others are Anne Fine, Michael Morpurgo, and Jacqueline Wilson.)

The Irresistible Rise of Harry Potter, by Andrew Blake. Verso, 2002. 118 pages. A sociological discussion explaining the success of the Harry Potter novels in light of English culture and education.

The Ivory Tower and Harry Potter: Perspectives on a Literary Phenomenon, ed. Lana A. Whited. University of Missouri Press, 2004. 418 pages. A critical anthology.

J. K. Rowling, by P. M. Boekhoff and Stuart A. Kallen. Gale Group, 2002. 48 pages. A short biography written for older children, ages 9–12.

J. K. Rowling, by William Compson. Rosen Publishing Group, 2003. 112 pages. Part of a series (Library of Author Biographies), this is a general biography that discusses her life and works.

J. K. Rowling, by Ann Gaines. Mitchell Lane Publishers, 2001. 32 pages. A short biography for children, which needs updating.

J. K. Rowling, by Mary Hill. Children's Press, 2003. 24 pages. A magazine-length article in book form written especially for young children, ages 4–8.

J. K. Rowling, by Stuart Kallen. KidHaven Press, 2002. 48 pages. A book in

a series about inventors and creators.

J. K. Rowling, by Carl Meister. Checkerboard Library, 2002. 24 pages. A very short biography written especially for young children.

J. K. Rowling, by Joan Price. World Almanac Library, 2004. 48 pages. For young readers.

J. K. Rowling, by Colleen Sexton. Lerner Publications, 2006. 112 pages. An A&E biography. The best of the bios for children. Recommended.

J. K. Rowling, by SparkNotes Editors. SparkNotes, 2003. 176 pages. From its "Library of Great Authors" series.

J. K. Rowling, by Bradley Steffens. Lucent Books, 2002. 104 pages. This one provides an overview of the Harry Potter phenomenon, a short biography, discussions about the Potter books, the Potter movies, and speculations on what Rowling may do after she's finished with the series. Recommended.

J. K. Rowling, by Bradley Steffens. Lucent Books, 2006. 112 pages. Biography. Recommended.

J. K. Rowling, ed. Gary Wiener. Greenhaven Press, 2003. 142 pages. A book in a series of literary companions to contemporary authors. An anthology of articles about Rowling and Harry Potter.

J. K. Rowling: Author, by Joanne Mattern. Ferguson Publishing Co., 2005. 122 pages. Part of the Ferguson Career Biographies series, intended for young adults.

J. K. Rowling: Author of Harry Potter, by Karen Leigh Harmin. Enslow Publishers, 2006. 128 pages. Part of a series called "People to Know Today." A biography.

J. K. Rowling: A Biography, by Connie Ann Kirk. Greenwood Publishing, 2003. 155 pages. The middle ground between the short and skimpy biographies and Sean Smith's (so far) definitive biography. Kirk has done her homework and conducted extensive research, which shows. Recommended, especially for students.

J. K. Rowling: A Biography, by Sean Smith. Michael O'Mara Books (distributed in the U.S. by Andrews McMeel Publishing), 2003. 240 pages. An eight-page color photo insert; the book is indexed. This is an expanded edition of this book, originally published in England in 2001. Sean Smith is the author of *Kylie Confidential*, a biography of pop star Kylie Minogue, published by Michael O'Mara Books (U.K.). His previous writing credits include writing a column for a national newspaper in England.

A straightforward accounting of her life, this biography draws principally on the author's firsthand trips and on selected interviews with people who knew her (notably Bryony Evens). Smith did not have the benefit of having the participation of Rowling, her family members, or her close friends.

Not surprisingly, Rowling has distanced herself from this unauthorized book, reportedly because of its emphasis on her personal life, which she now aggressively shields from the media; but overall there's more to like about this book than not.

The book covers her life in sufficient detail to give the reader a sense of Rowling's love for her fictional creation, Harry Potter. Unfortunately, it also suffers from padding, as seen in a tedious recounting of her accepting an honorary degree from her alma mater.

For this U.S. edition, prices have been converted from pounds to dollars, but there are many instances in which words or phrases of British origin have not been Americanized, which will be confusing to readers.

Though unauthorized, this is a book worth adding to your collection. More useful for its scope than for its revelations, it's recommended, though with reservations.

J. K. Rowling: Her Life and Works, by Charles Lovett. Sparknotes, 2003. 173 pages. Covers first three novels in detail. Indexed.

J. K. Rowling: The Wizard behind Harry Potter, by Marc Shapiro. New York: St. Martin's/Griffin, 2001. 164 pages. Billed as "new and revised," this book badly needs updating. It lacks information about the most recent novel *(Harry Potter and the Order of the Phoenix)*. It also has no mention about Rowling's new husband or son—two serious omissions. A "freelance entertainment journalist," Shapiro has published a dozen celebrity biographies, most (if not all) unauthorized. Lacking an index, this biography, aimed mostly toward young readers, draws entirely

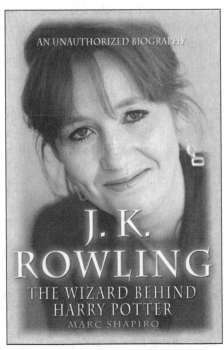

from secondary sources, like magazines, newspapers, and electronic media profiles and interviews. A basic introduction to Rowling and her fictional universe, this book lacks the depth that makes Sean Smith's book the better choice. Recommended for those who want a general, not detailed, biography.

J. K. Rowling's Harry Potter Novels: A Reader's Guide, by Philip Nel. Continuum Publishing Group, 2001. 96 pages. A general overview, with a brief biography, an examination and review of the novels, and recommendations for further reading and discussion.

Kids' Letters to Harry Potter from Around the World, ed. Bill Adler. Carroll and Graf, 2002. 195 pages. Compiler Bill Adler has solicited assistance from booksellers who have forwarded letters to him written by children worldwide. It's a cute idea, but the letters tend to sameness. Compounding the problem, follow-up interviews merely echo what has gone before.

Looking for God in Harry Potter, by John Granger. Saltriver, 2006. 256 pages. Written by a Christian father of seven home-schooled kids, this book won a hard-earned rave review from *Publishers Weekly:* "This is obviously a painstakingly researched book. It is easily the best examination to date of the spiritual legacy of 'the boy who lived.'" A devout Christian, Granger's thesis is: "I am convinced that the fundamental reason for the astonishing popularity of the Harry Potter novels is their ability to meet a spiritual longing for some experience of the truths of life, love and death taught by

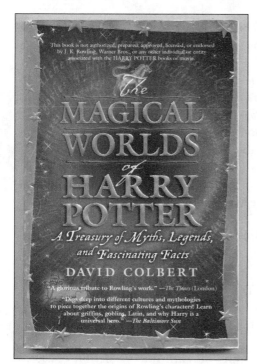

Christianity but denied by a secular culture. Human beings are designed for Christ, whether they know it or not. That the Harry Potter stories 'sing along' with the Great Story of Christ is a significant key to understanding their compelling richness." Recommended.

The Magical Worlds of Harry Potter: A Treasury of Myths, Legends, and Fascinating Facts, by David Colbert. Berkley Publishing Group, 2002. 209 pages. Fifty-three alphabetized essays ranging in length up to six pages, posing questions about the myths and legends alluded to in the Potter novels, as in "Did alchemists really search for a magic stone?" and "Have witches always flown on broomsticks?" Since Rowling does not answer these questions, it's up to others to explain the linkages between her fiction and myth and history texts. Recommended.

Mapping the World of Harry Potter, ed. Mercedes Lackey. Benbella Books, 2006. 240 pages. Fourteen essays about Harry Potter, ranging from the academic to the general: "Hermione Granger and the Charge of Sexism" by Sarah Zettel to "Why [a character] Had to Die" by Lawrence Watts-Evans.

Meet J. K. Rowling, by S. Ward. Powerkids Press, 2003. 24 pages. A very short biography written for children.

Mugglenet.com's What Will Happen in Harry Potter [Book] Seven: Who Lives, Who Dies, Who Falls in Love, and How the Adventure Finally Ends, by Ben Schoen and Emerson Spartz. Ulysses Press, 2006. 180 pages. Those who are frequent visitors to mugglenet.com will recognize the names of the authors, who have taken a page from the speculative books by Galadriel Waters (a Tolkien-inspired pen name). Questions under discussion include: Will Hogwarts be open for Harry's final year? If so, will Harry be in attendance? Will Harry's quest for the remaining Horcruxes be rewarded? Severus Snape—good or bad guy? And will Harry survive the final battle with Lord Voldemort?

Although these questions will become moot when the seventh Harry Potter novel is published, the general reader will likely want to discover the answers to them on his own instead of reading speculations prior to its publication.

My Year with Harry Potter: How I Discovered My Own Magical World, by Ben Buchanan. Lantern Books, 2001. 112 pages. The magic of Harry Potter's novels can be found in their transformational effect on readers. An inspiring memoir written by an 11-year-old boy who was inspired by the Potter universe to create a board game, which he entered in his school's Invention Convention.

Mythmaker: The Story of J. K. Rowling, by Charles J. Shields. Chelsea House Publishers, 2002. 112 pages. Another short biography on Rowling that is too similar to its competition and, therefore, doesn't stand out. Reviewers have pointed out that there are errors that mar the book.

New Clues to Harry Potter, Book 5, by Galadriel Waters, illustrated by Professor Astre Mithrandir. Wizarding World Press, 2003. 88 pages. A supplementary book to her previous book *(Ultimate Unofficial Guide to the Mysteries of Harry Potter)*, this book discusses clues found in *Harry Potter and the Order of the Phoenix.*

Nimbus 2003 Compendium, eds. Edmund Kern and Rose Highfield. Xlibris Corporation, 2005. 530 pages. The proceedings from the conference, the scope and breadth of the subjects covered make this a worthy addition to a library collection or for those with an interest in Harry Potter academia. Recommended.

A Parent's Guide to Harry Potter, by Gina Burkart. InterVarsity Press, 2005.

112 pages. (Also audio book and CD. Hovel Audio, 2006.) In an explanatory "review" on eBay, the author says that she explains "how Harry Potter fits into the fairy tale genre and how fairy tales often help children release their fears. . . . I show parents that these books aren't about magic at all, rather they show that magic does not solve problems. It is love that saves and protects Harry."

The Plot Thickens . . . Harry Potter Investigated by Fans for Fans, edited by Galadriel Waters. Wizarding World Press, 2004. 277 pages. The anonymous Galadriel Waters—clearly named after Galadriel, Lady of Lórien, from J. R. R. Tolkien's *The Lord of the Rings*—once again conjures up another volume specifically intended for hard-core fans, who, in fact, are the contributors to this anthology. Ranging from speculations to discussions of everything imaginable, the editor explains: "What is this book about? Of course, it's about sleuthing Harry Potter. The discussions in this anthology delve deep into the riddles surrounding our favorite boy wizard, as the mysteries of J. K. Rowling's series become increasingly intricate. We are in the heart of the septology, and our heads are brewing with questions about the characters, the plot, and even the wizarding world. . . . This book is your recipe for a cauldron-ful of thought-provoking discussions. However, it's not just a slew of clues. You are about to be entertained with some of the most intriguing character profiles, brain teasers, and plot analyses you have ever read." Fun reading for fans who can't get enough.

Pokemon & Harry Potter: A Fatal Attraction, by Phil Arms. Hearthstone Publishing Ltd., 2000. 152 pages. Pastor Phil Arms's thesis is that games like Pokemon and books like Harry Potter are in fact a supernatural battle for the minds of children everywhere and, therefore, must be fought. Phil's call to arms, unfortunately, may rally some Christian soldiers marching off to war, but most will find this inflammatory book full of sound and fury signifying nothing.

Predictions in Stone for Harry Potter Fans, by Leslie Durhman and Susie Worden. Superior Siblings LLC, 2002. 50 pages. The authors predict plot points to *The Chamber of Secrets* and, in this journal, suggest you write your own predictions, then read the novel.

Predictions through Time, by Leslie Durhman and Susie Worden. Superior Siblings LLC, 2002. 50 pages. The authors predict plot points to *Goblet of Fire* and suggest you do the same, then write them down in this journal.

The Psychology of Harry Potter: The Boy Who Lived, by Dr. Neil Mulholland. Benbella Books, 2007. 240 pages. According to its publisher, this is an anthology of articles written by psychologists that use characters from the Harry Potter books to discuss psychological disorders: Is Harry a cranky adolescent or suffering from real post-traumatic stress disorder? Is Voldemort evil incarnate or a misguided boy now twisted beyond recognition? Is Snape treacherous or struggling for redemption?

Reading Harry Potter: Critical Essays, by Giselle Liza Anatol. Praeger Publishers, 2003. 248 pages. An assistant professor of English at Kansas State University, Anatol has edited an excellent collection of essays that students, scholars, and teachers will find useful.

Readings on J. K. Rowling, by Peggy J. Parks. Greenhaven Press, 2003. 192 pages. Part of the "Literary Companion Series." From the publisher's website, "Authors in this anthology examine Rowling's life and work and tackle the controversies, both artistic and moral, surrounding the Harry Potter books."

Re-Reading Harry Potter, by Suman Gupta. Palgrave Macmillan, 2003. 224 pages. Suman Gupta teaches at the Open University (U.K.). From the publisher's website:

> This book is the first extended analysis of the social and political implications of the Harry Potter phenomenon. Arguments are primarily based on close readings of the first four Harry Potter books and the first two films, and a "text-to-world" method is followed. This study does not assume that the phenomenon concerns children alone, or should be lightly dismissed as a matter of pure entertainment as the amount of money, media coverage, and ideological unease involved indicates otherwise. The first part of the study provides a survey of responses (both of general readers and critics) to the Harry Potter books. The second part examines the presentation of certain themes, including gender, race, and desire, with a view to understanding how these may impinge on social and political concerns of our world.

Return of the Heroes: The Lord of the Rings, Star Wars, Harry Potter, and Social Conflict, by Hal G. P. Colebatch. Cybereditions, 2003. An e-book available online from Amazon.com in Adobe Reader format. We live, as Colebatch asserts, in a cynical age; why, then, are works of heroic fantasy like *The Lord of the Rings, Star Wars,* and the Harry Potter novels so phenomenally successful? Far from being reflective of our age, this book celebrates a different age, when traditional values held sway, and speaks of the health, not the demise, of our culture.

Scholarly Studies in Harry Potter: Applying Academic Methods to a Popular Text, ed. Cynthia Whitney Hallett. Edwin Mellen Press, 2005. 275 pages.

A Scholastic Literature Guide to Harry Potter and the Goblet of Fire. Scholastic Professional Books, 2000. 24 pages. Written for teachers to stimulate classroom discussion for 8–11 year-old students.

A Scholastic Literature Guide to Harry Potter and the Sorcerer's Stone. Scholastic Professional Books, 2000. 18 pages. Written for teachers to stimulate classroom discussion for 8–11 year-old students, this slender book offers summaries, discussions, and cross-curricular activities. A poster, a timeline of Harry Potter, is also included.

The Science of Harry Potter: How Magic Really Works, by Roger Highfield. Penguin, 2003. 368 pages. A British science writer uses elements of Harry Potter's world as the basis of discussion for Muggle-related technologies. Unlike *The Science of Star Trek,* where there's a direct correlation between fact and fiction, this particular book is a bit of a stretch. For instance, Rowling is adamant that Quidditch was not inspired by any specific sporting game, but the author attempts to link it to a sixteenth-century Mesoamerican game called Nahualtlachti. Interesting and though-provoking, but in the end, magic is magic and science is science.

Selected Papers from Nimbus–2003 Compendium: We Solemnly Swear These Papers Were Worth the Wait, compiled by Penny Linsenmayer, Ebony Thomas, Lee Hillman, and Heidi Howard Tandy. Published by HP Education Fanon, Inc. (printed by Xlibris Corporation, a print-on-demand publisher), 2005. Hardback, $36.99; trade paperback, $26.99. 530 pages. Endnotes. Available from Amazon.com.

As with *Star Trek, Star Wars,* and *The Lord of the Rings,* Harry Potter fandom—firmly entrenched in popular culture—has already hosted conventions in the U.S. and England, with more scheduled worldwide.

What makes the Nimbus conventions unique is that the HP Education Fanon assembles under its umbrella an international collection of fans, critics, and scholars who, despite their various backgrounds, come together to celebrate all things Harry Potter.

The first published proceedings from the first-ever Harry Potter convention, this telephone directory–sized book collects the papers read at the conference, as a sampling of topics suggests: "Harry Potter: Are They Children's Books?" "Justice in the Wizarding World," "Harry Potter and the Prisoner of Azkaban: A Case against the Death Penalty," and "It's Not Easy Being Hermione: Harry Potter and the Paradox of Girl Power."

Firmly entrenched in popular culture, the Harry Potter phenomenon is winning advocates in academic circles in which Potter is taken seriously, and with no apologies. Clearly, the Harry Potter phenomenon is still going strong, building momentum as the seventh, and last, book sees print in the summer of 2007. Until then, Potter fans should acquaint themselves with this informative compendium that celebrates the fictional life and times of this famous boy wizard.

So You Think You Know Harry Potter, by Clive Gifford. Hodder Children's Books, 2002. A trivia quiz book with more than 1,000 questions.

The Sorcerer's Companion: A Guide to the Magical World of Harry Potter, by Allan Zola Kronzek and Elizabeth Kronzek. Broadway Books, 2001. 304 pages. Allan Kronzek is a professional magician (see *A Book of Magic for Young Magicians: The Secrets of Alkazar*) and Elizabeth Kronzek (his daughter) is a writer. For readers who want to know more about magic as practiced in the real world, this book is indispensable. Drawing on diverse sources, the Kronzeks bring a wealth of knowledge about magic to bear. The Potter fan who isn't aware of all the historical references to the magical elements of Rowling's fiction will find this book compulsively readable and entertaining.

SparkNotes: Harry Potter and the Sorcerer's Stone. SparkNotes, 2002. 72 pages. A study guide with a plot overview; character lists; a discussion of the book's themes, motifs, and symbols; a summary and analysis of each chapter; key facts; study questions; essay topics; and recommended resources.

Sticks and Stones: The Troublesome Success of Children's Literature from Slovenly Peter to Harry Potter, by Jack Zipes. Routledge, 2002. 240 pages. A collection of essays in which the author poses, and answers, provocative questions about the success of children's literature and its value in an increasingly commercialized world.

Storybook Travels: From Eloise's New York to Harry Potter's London, Visits to 30 of the Best-Loved Landmarks in Children's Literature, by Colleen Dunn Bates and Susan La Tempa. Three Rivers Press, 2002. 288 pages. Thirty itineraries for parents who wish to visit worldwide destinations themed to children's literature. (Note: A similar book, specific to England, is Mealanie Wentz's *Once Upon a Time in Great Britain: A Travel Guide to the Sights and Settings of Your Favorite Children's Stories,* from St. Martin's: Griffin imprint, 2002.)

Teaching Fantasy Novels: From The Hobbit to Harry Potter and the Goblet of Fire. Teacher Ideas Press, 2003. 192 pages. Recommended by *VOYA* (*Voice of Youth Advocates,* a library magazine). Twenty books are thoroughly discussed and keyed to "meaningful and enjoyable activities. . . . This book is a great way to ensure that the fantasy texts young people love get considered as the excellent literary choices so many of them are. There is substantial material from which to build entire units, or the questions and activities could be used as supporting materials." Recommended.

There's Something about Harry: A Catholic Analysis of the Harry Potter Phenomenon (audiobook, two cassette tapes). Surprised By Truth Seminars, 2002. Patrick Madrid (publisher of *Envoy* magazine), Tony Collins, and Michael O'Brien weigh in on "the real issues at stake" behind the phenomenon itself.

Triumph of the Imagination: The Story of Writer J. K. Rowling, by Lisa Chippendale. Chelsea House Publishers, 2001. 112 pages. This is a book in a series that celebrates "Overcoming Adversities." It's a biography for young adults, with a discussion of Harry Potter books one to four.

Ultimate Unofficial Guide to the Mysteries of Harry Potter, by Galadriel Waters and Astre Mithrandir. Wizarding World Press, 2003. 442 pages. The name of the publishing house, as well as the pen names drawn from Tolkien (Galadriel = Lady Galadriel, Mithrandir = Gandalf), suggest that it's a fun-filled look at the Potter books, taking its cue from Rowling's in-depth, celebrated plotting. Arranged by Potter book, with short summaries and a discussion of all the clues, this book is for the die-hard fan who recognizes that the game's afoot and, like Sherlock Holmes, enjoys tracking down clues.

The Ultimate Unofficial Harry Potter Trivia Book: Secrets, Mysteries, and Fun Facts, including HALF-BLOOD PRINCE, Book 6, by Daniel Lawrence. iUniverse, 2005. 119 pages. Indexed. A print-on-demand book, this book is composed of two parts.

The first part includes general Harry Potter questions, history, books 1–5, movies 1–3, characters, Hogwarts, charms, spells, creatures, beasts, and locations.

The second part includes general questions about J. K. Rowling, books 6 and 7, and movies 4 and 5.

Since this is essentially a self-published book, the author might have arranged the material in a more chronological fashion: Rowling, Harry Potter, books 1–7, and a section on movies 1–5.

Sources for the questions are listed in the back of the book, along with detailed answers to the questions.

Unauthorized Harry Potter Book Seven News: "Half-Blood Prince" Analysis and Speculation, by W. Frederick Zimmerman. Nimble Books, 2005. 132 pages. A print-on-demand book, 92 pages focus on a chapter-by-chapter analysis of book six; the remaining pages cover speculations that are under discussion at Harry Potter fan websites. When it comes to hard information on book seven, Rowling is keeping her cards close to her chest, so books like this are largely educated guesses and suppositions. This kind of book is intended for die-hard fans who want every scrap of information about Harry Potter, as opposed to the more general reader. (Note: there are several variant editions with varying titles, available in e-book form.)

An Unofficial Muggle's Guide to the Wizarding World: Exploring the Harry Potter Universe, by Fionna Boyle. ECW Press, 2004. 466 pages. Indexed. (Note: This book is currently out of stock or possibly out of print. It is currently not available from online booksellers.) Boyle's book covers the first five Harry Potter novels and does so in an intriguing fashion by focusing on the Muggle and wizarding worlds. The introduction sets the tone by explaining who Harry Potter is, and then takes an in-depth look at the characters in the series, Hogwarts, other wizarding schools, the Triwizard Tournament, Quidditch, the wizarding world, and the Muggle reader's world, with a translation guide from British to American words, key differences between the books and films, a wizarding tour of Britain, and how to host your own Harry Potter party. The book concludes with a list of resources on the web. Sources, endnotes, and an index follow.

Much of this same information will be published, and in much greater detail, in Rowling's proposed encyclopedia to Hogwarts and the wizarding world, which she has discussed in several interviews. Rowling's nonfiction book will obviously be the final word on the subject, so fans will want to add it to their collection. (Don't look for Rowling's encyclopedia to be published until at least 2008, since book seven won't likely be published until July 7, 2007.)

We Love Harry Potter!, ed. Sharon Moore. New York: St. Martin's Press, 1999. 120 pages. A collection of letters from children praising the Potter novels. The term "déjà vu" comes to mind.

What's a Christian to Do with Harry Potter?, by Connie Neal. Waterbrook Press, 2001. 224 pages. A balanced book that looks on both sides of the fence: those who feel the Potter books are the work of the devil, and those who don't.

Who Killed [Rowling character]?, edited by John Granger. Zossima Press, 2006. 236 pages. More than just speculation on the character (whose name is in the title) killed in *Half-Blood Prince*, this thought-provoking book brings together six Harry Potter "detectives" (as they call themselves) as they examine the puzzles, riddles, and murders found in Book 6. Add this one to your bookshelf!

The Wisdom of Harry Potter: What Our Favorite Hero Teaches Us about Moral Choices, by Edmund M. Kern. Prometheus Books, 2003. 296 pages. An associate professor of history at Lawrence University, Kern is a popular speaker at Harry Potter conferences. Writes Kern in the book's preface, "Rowling's development of a moral system . . . has deep historical roots in Stoic philosophy. Fate shapes Harry's life, but his responses to it are not unlike what ancient philosophers such as Zeno, Marcus Aurelius, or Seneca would suggest. His choices and actions are all his own. He meets circumstances beyond his control with resolve and accepts that he must maintain his inner goodness and direct it outward in order to act on behalf of others." Recommended.

Wizard! Harry Potter's Brand Magic, by Stephen Brown. Cyan Communications, 2005. 192 pages. For the business community, this book discusses how the Harry Potter books are a marketing phenomenon.

Wizards: The Quest for the Wizard from Merlin to Harry Potter, by John Matthews. Barron's Educational Series, 2003. 144 pages. A fascinating overview of wizards through the ages.

Part Five:
Spellbinding Storytellers—
J. K. Rowling,
Stephen King,
and John Irving
in New York City,
August 2006

Tim Kirk

The Press Conference: J. K. Rowling, Stephen King, and John Irving Read from Their Books at Radio City Music Hall (August 1-2, 2006)

I feel like I've just been told the Beatles and the Stones are warming up for me.

—J. K. Rowling at the press conference, after both Stephen King and John Irving observed that they were the "warm-up dance" for her

In comparison to other entertainment industries, book publishing is the smallest of worlds; so small, in fact, that when disaster struck one of its most prominent practitioners, the reverberations were felt halfway around the world. This is exactly what happened on June 19, 1999, when the media reported that Maine writer Stephen King had been rushed to the hospital after being struck by a van near his summer home in Center Lovell, Maine.

As King recounted in an essay titled "On Living," in *On Writing: A Memoir of the Craft,* he was "actually lying in death's doorway" as a helicopter whisked him away to Central Maine Medical Center in Lewiston.

During the long and painful period that followed—known as physical therapy to those who haven't experienced it, and pain and torture to those who have, according to King—he couldn't write but he could read.

If memory serves, one of the long books that took him away from his pain and misery was one of J. K. Rowling's Harry Potter novels, which she had sent him, probably *Harry Potter and Prisoner of Azkaban.*

King later sang her praises and wrote informed reviews of *Goblet of Fire* and *Order of the Phoenix,* returning the favor.

In October 2005, Stephen King and John Irving wrote to J. K. Rowling, inviting her to come to the U.S. and, to benefit charity, read from a Harry Potter novel at Radio City Music Hall. Rowling quickly agreed. There would be two nights of readings; the first night would benefit King's own Haven Foundation, and the second night would benefit a favorite of Rowling's, Doctors Without Borders (Médecins Sans Frontières), which had first come to her attention when she worked for Amnesty International.

Stephen King commented: "This is like a dream come true for me. It's a chance for me to read with two great writers while supporting two very deserving organizations at the same time. I think this is going to be quite an event and, worthy causes aside, it is a chance for fans to see some amazing imaginations at work, live and in person, on one of America's greatest stages."

John Irving commented: "I first met Stephen King at a reading—another charitable event. The writer André Dubus had been hit by a car while assisting a fallen motorcyclist. Dubus lost use of both legs; he had no medical insurance. I organized a series of readings at the Charles Hotel in Cambridge, Massaachusetts, to raise money to pay for his hospitalization and rehabilitation. One winter night, in 1981, I read with Stephen. We've been friends ever since. He recently gave a charitable reading for an elementary school my wife and I co-founded in Manchester, Vermont. I said I would read for his charity of choice in return, and together we wrote to J. K. Rowling and asked her to join us. I not only look forward to the reading; I am looking forward to meeting Ms. Rowling, whom I credit with introducing an entire generation of readers to long, complicated, plotted novels."

Rowling commented: "For me, this was a unique opportunity to raise money for two great, important causes; read to American fans for the first time in six years; and get to meet and read alongside Stephen King and John Irving. Stephen pretended to be in suspense about my answer, but frankly, this was easily one of the most enticing propositions ever put to me in an envelope."

On May 10, 2006, the *New York Times* ran a brief story headlined, "J. K. Rowling Is Coming to New York for Charity Reading." In the body of the piece, it added that she would join "Stephen King and John Irving at a charity reading at Radio City Music Hall."

As Scholastic (Rowling's publisher) and Simon & Schuster (King's and Irving's publisher) got the word out through the usual publicity channels, the collective fan base of all three authors effectively used the Internet to really get the word out. On their respective websites, the authors put the word out, as well.

Major Harry Potter fan websites devoted to J. K. Rowling picked up the story and, predictably, were deluged with requests for more information. The Leaky Cauldron, devoted to Rowling, had gotten frantic emails from fans wanting to know the date of the engagement and when tickets would be available. Sue Upton of The Leaky Cauldron wrote, "We CANNOT get you tickets and do not yet know HOW to get tickets—there isn't even a set date yet, so please stop e-mailing. As soon as we know, you'll know!" Moreover, the site reported, "We do NOT know what book Jo will be reading from, and are working to find out more."

Ticket prices, Sue wrote, would "range from $12.50 to $100 apiece, with $1,000 family packages including four orchestra seats and a signed book from each of the authors."

At ten o'clock on May 12, 2006, Ticketmaster began selling tickets for both nights of readings set for August 1 and 2. By that time, more information had been made available, but not enough to satiate Potter fans: there would be surprise guests for both nights to introduce each writer; a press conference would be held at 10:00 A.M. on the 1st, for which media credentials were checked out (professional media only); no photography would be allowed during the reading itself; and, finally, those who paid for $1,000 tickets (500 seats per night) in the prime orchestra section would be allowed to e-mail a question to Scholastic, who would then cull a dozen to be answered by the authors at the event itself.

Not surprisingly, fans e-mailed Harry Potter websites with requests for more information. Would there be an official book signing? Would there be a webcast? Could a member from a prominent fan website get something signed by Rowling? Does anyone know where Rowling would be staying? Can someone at the website get a backstage pass? Would there be a red carpet and an opportunity to perhaps get a closer glimpse of Rowling and perhaps a signature? And can we bring cameras?

The short answer to all of those questions: no.

You buy a ticket and get the best seat you can afford; anything else would be a bonus. If you were lucky, well, you might just get an autograph—if you knew where to hang out.

In addition to the press conference and the two nights of readings, LeakyMug (the Leaky Cauldron website) and Mugglenet.com arranged with Barnes & Noble at Union Square to hold a podcast with its principals, which would follow on the heels of a similar podcast held on July 29 in Las Vegas at the J.W. Marriott Resort & Spa, where 1,200 fans would show up to attend Lumos 2006, a Harry Potter symposium.

The two leading Harry Potter fan websites gather for an August 2, 2006, podcast at Barnes & Noble's Union Square store, drawing more than one thousand fans. From left to right: Mugglenet.com's Andrew Sims, Jamie Lawrence, Emerson Spartz (founder/webmaster), and Ben Schoen; The Leaky Cauldron's Sue Upton, John Noe, and Melissa Anelli.

Also ongoing at the time: Scholastic had sent key members of two Harry Potter fan websites—The Leaky Cauldron and Mugglenet.com—on the road, along with one of their editors, Cheryl Klein, to promote the release of the sixth Harry Potter novel, which had just been published in trade paperback.

This was promising to be two days and nights to remember.

For Rowling fans, her arrival in the Big Apple was big news, but for Muggles in the city, the record heat wave—with temperatures nearing 100 and the power grid taxed to the max—got the headlines. Meanwhile, members of the world's media set up in a hallway at Radio City Music Hall, where Rowling and her fellow authors would field questions at a press conference that Scholastic estimated would run an hour.

To insure the press conference would run smoothly, Scholastic issued coordinating instructions before the event by e-mail to the invited media, who were told to arrive no earlier than 8:30 A.M. but no later than 9:30 A.M., when the doors would close.

Anxious to get a good seat or a good camera position, anxious to get out of the heat and into the air-conditioned coolness of Radio City Music Hall, and anxious to avail themselves of what was an enticing spread of breakfast food and drink (coffee, orange juice, fruits, donuts, bagels, and assorted pastries), news/food hungry media hounds were in place and ready at 10:00 A.M., when the press conference was scheduled to start.

According to the folders handed out to the media, three people would speak before the floor would be opened up for general questions: Billy DiMichele of Scholastic (the event organizer), Jack Romanos (president and CEO of Simon and Schuster, the book publisher for King and Irving), and Dick Robinson (president and CEO of Scholastic, the book publisher for

John Irving, J. K. Rowling, and Stephen King at a press conference on August 1, 2006

Rowling). At the tail end of the press conference, time would be allotted to photographers for the staged photo opportunity.

Billy DiMichele set the stage, so to speak, by talking about the event in terms of Stephen King's involvement, noting, "I really doubt there's another author who could have conceived of a fundraiser of this scale and delivered on that vision. It's precisely that combination of vision and ambition that placed Stephen King on the nation's best-seller lists, and he's been there since 1973, which led him to publish more than 40 memorable books and made him the recipient of the National Book Foundation medal for Distinguished Contribution of American Letters.

"That said, it's my privilege and an honor to introduce a man who himself has the magic of Harry, the heart of Carrie, and like Garp is a real Yankee—Stephen King."

A round of polite applause.

"One of America's most innovative and talented novelists with a string of best-sellers, John Irving tackles topics ranging from feminism and religion to wrestling, tattooing, and New England life. *The World According to Garp* launched him into the stratosphere of authors; he continues to share his humor and intelligence with such works as *The Cider House Rules, A Prayer for Owen Meany, The Fourth Hand,* and most

Stephen King applauds after being introduced by Dick Robsinson (of Scholastic books).

287

J. K. Rowling looks at Stephen King as he answers a question at the press conference.

recently, *Until I Find You: A Novel.* He has been honored by a list of prestigious awards, but the one that may surprise you is that he is an inductee in the National Wrestling Hall of Fame. Ladies and gentlemen, John Irving."

Again, polite applause, after which Dick Robinson spoke, introducing his most famous and bankable author, J. K. Rowling.

"I'm Dick Robinson of Scholastic, the lucky U.S. publisher of Harry Potter, the best known, best-loved character on planet Earth, and of J. K. Rowling, Harry's brilliant creator.

"From the moment I met Jo, then unknown, eight years ago, I was touched by her graceful confidence, born of her sure foreknowledge that Harry Potter would be one of literature's great characters. I was also struck by her artist's supreme gift of matchless concentration, the mind completely and at all times absorbed in the consistency of the whole seven-book story that she had imagined from the beginning.

"And not only was her commitment to the developing story absolute, but it was accompanied by a parallel of readers. Her story and its readers have been linked in her mind from the beginning, even as the readers grow older, and the story artfully unfolds through the years.

"Our company is thought of by teachers, parents, and children as a place to find great stories and great books to help you read and learn. Nothing we have done in 86 years, however, matches the impact of Harry Potter opening millions of minds to a great story and making reading the best way to learn about yourself. For all of this, thank you, Jo Rowling."

Polite applause, then questions were fielded from the assembled press corps. (Note: I've reworded the questions posed, since some of them were unintelligible.)

A question for Rowling: What can you tell us about the progress of the seventh, and last, Harry Potter novel?

Rowling: I'm well into the writing of it now. There's so much I could say. To an extent, the pressure's off because it's the last book, so I feel quite liberated. I can just resolve the story now, and it's fun—fun in a way that it hasn't been before because finally I'm doing my resolution. I think some people will loathe it and some will love it, but that's the way it should be.[1]

A question for King: How much money do you expect to raise for your respective charities?

King: I think we're going to be able to raise at least $250,000 for each charity, which for three people who write books is a lot of money. When we set out to do this, we decided that we would do two nights; one to benefit the charity of my choice, Haven Foundation, to raise money for freelance artists who find themselves after catastrophic accidents and diseases with no resources for themselves, and one designated by Jo, Doctors Without Borders, and she can talk very cogently about that.[2]

As I say, all of this came out of the fact that last year I read for John's charity, which was Maple Street School in Vermont, and he said he would read for me. And so while I read for a small school, I dragged him to Radio City Music Hall, and he came along!

A general question for all three authors: What advice do you have for young people wanting to become writers?

Rowling: The first thing you should do is read. By reading you'll not only increase your vocabulary, but you'll learn what kind of writing you like and learn how to analyze it. And the other thing is to accept that you'll waste a lot of trees.[3]

Irving: I certainly support reading. If you're lucky enough to be a writer, as you get older, you find that you'd rather write than read. So you better have read a lot when you're young because the more you write, you develop the capacity to spend more hours of the days doing that. For the last ten or 15 years, I found ways to be writing almost all of the time, and I'm not really as good a reader as I used to be.[4]

I'm grateful that, as Jo said, I read some writers—Charles Dickens, especially—who became the model of the form for me.

King: You have to read, and you have to hold out hope, too, because as a young writer you have to remember that we will all die.[5]

A question for Rowling: What will you miss most about the Harry Potter series?

Rowling: Everything. I've loved writing it. I will miss it hugely, but I always planned seven books and this particular ending, so if I get through it and do what I meant to do when I first committed to this story, then I'll be proud.

Then I'll probably go through a mourning period and then have to give something else a try.[6]

A question for King: Fiction is often reflective of a particular community area. Is that true for you?

King: I think we all have a tendency to write about places that we know best. It's where we feel most comfortable and grounded.[7]

Writing feels to me like being on a tightrope, anyway.

A question for all three authors: What are your thoughts on killing off your characters?

Rowling: John's killed off more than I have, so I think he should go first.

Irving: Because I never begin writing a novel until I know the major emotional things that happen in it, especially what happens at the end, I have a kind of casualty list of which characters make it and which characters don't before I write the first word. So that process of deliberation that sometimes precedes the writing of a novel by as much as a year or 18 months means that by the time I get to write those death scenes, I've lived through the lives and deaths of those characters for many months, sometimes several years. Therefore, I'm not truly emotionally affected when it comes to writing those scenes. It's as if they've already happened and I'm just remembering things. But I think that's a direct result of my needing to know the ending of the story before I ever imagine where it might begin.

Rowling: I understand why an author would kill a character from a point of view of not allowing others to continue writing after the original author. I don't always enjoy killing my characters. I didn't enjoy killing the character who died at the end of book six. I'm being discreet just in case anyone hasn't finished the book. I really didn't enjoy doing that, but I had been planning that for years. As John says, it wasn't quite as poignant as you might imagine. I'd already done my grieving when it actually came to writing it.[8]

King: I don't enjoy it either, and I don't always know. I don't plan the books out very clearly. There are writers who plan and I think there are people who fire missiles the way that the United States fires missiles. I fire them the way Hezbollah fires missiles: I have a certain idea of where they're going to land, but if they get within 12 miles one way or another, I'm happy. I wrote a book called *Cujo* and it's about a mother and a son trapped in a car by a rabid dog. I thought I had a pretty good idea of what was going to happen at the end. I thought that the little boy would be okay, but the little boy *wasn't* okay, and that really shook me.

I had a book called *Pet Sematary* that disturbed me so much that I put it in a drawer. I ended up publishing it only because of a contractual issue . . . well, things happen. I felt like I had to publish the book, and I did, and I did it with a lot of distress because I felt the audience would think, "Oh, this is the most dreadful thing," but they loved it. John, I think that you said your son is reading it now, and he seems to be liking it a lot and I'm thinking, "My goodness!"

But the thing is, I've written other books where the strangest things happen. I wrote a book called *The Dead Zone* which begins with a character named Greg Stillson. In the prologue, he kicks a dog to death in the dooryard, and I wanted to establish this character as a real awful person in the beginning who covers it with this cheerful, smiling, happy "Hey, I'm just a good ol' fella" kind of Willie Stark kind of thing going on, and I got more letters, "How can you do that to that dog?"

You write people back and you want to be nice to them and you say, "I'm sorry you don't like that," and I'm thinking to myself: Number one, it was a dog, not a person, and number two, the dog wasn't even real—I made that dog up. That was a fake dog, a fictional dog. But people get very involved, and I get involved too, and I've written books and I know what Jo has been through. And I can tell you too that when I read *The World According to Garp,* there's a scene in that book that is so distressing to me that it's one of the few times I did not sleep that night. And I'm case-hardened. I've read a lot of books, but I spent that night awake. Thanks very much, John.

For King or Irving: Do either of you have advice for Rowling as she comes to the end of her series?

Rowling: [looking at King] Kill him!

King: Do I have any advice? I just want the story to be fair—that's what I always want. I want to read the book. I love that series. I want to read the book and I have total confidence because I read the other books. Man, I'm just up for it, that's all.[9]

Irving: My fingers are crossed for Harry, that's all. I'm just hoping.

To Rowling: Why did you choose Doctors Without Borders as your charity choice, and why have you not been in the U.S. for six years?[10]

Rowling: The reason I wanted to nominate Doctors Without Borders (which is Médecins Sans Frontières in Britain) is that I used to work for Amnesty International, and that's when I first came across the organization. I noticed that every time there was a situation, like the war in Lebanon, Doctors Without Borders were some of the first people on the ground. They were a very effective organization, and also as the name clearly states, it doesn't matter what your religious affiliation is, it doesn't matter what your ethnic group is, it doesn't matter what your circumstance is. If you are physically in need they will help you or do everything they can to help you. So they've been an organization I've always supported financially, since having money and having made money, and I thought that if we were doing one great charity that deals with a specific group, I thought it would be great if we did a charity that deals literally with the world.

[As for my long absence,] you didn't say anything wrong. I absolutely love coming here, and I particularly love coming to New York—it's one of my favorite cities. But during that six years I've been pregnant twice, I've had small children, and that's really why we weren't doing the long flights and the tours. They're old enough to travel now. So it's great to be back.

To Rowling, posed by a child reporter from Time *magazine:* In book six, why did [a main character] have to die?

Rowling: I did an interview last year in which I was asked this question. In the genre in which I'm writing, you usually find that the hero has to go on alone. There comes a point when his support falls away and to be truly heroic he has to act alone. Harry is not completely alone; he still has his two faithful sidekicks. So that's why. In these sort of epic sagas, the hero eventually has to fight alone.[11]

To Rowling: Is the final book going to be different from its predecessors?

Rowling: It is different to an extent. The essential plot is what I've always planned when working toward the end. But a couple of characters I expected to survive have died and one character got a reprieve, so there have been some fairly major changes, I suppose.

To all three authors: Are you comfortable reading your own work onstage?

King: I don't mind reading my own work. I know it best. That's fine. The challenge is to find something that can hold a broad audience.

Irving: My only discomfort with what I'm reading tonight is it's from something relatively old, something I've not read or been in touch with for a number of years, but Steve and I have talked about what we were going to read and we recognize that we see ourselves as the warm-up dance for Jo. We imagine that there's going to be mostly *her* audience there, and I don't think that Stephen King and John Irving generally write material that's terribly suitable for younger people. So Steve and I had to go looking for those occasionally more innocent moments in our earlier work, so to speak. So I would say in the case of this reading I love the idea of reading with Steve and Jo in this wonderful space, but I'm a little intimidated by the age of the audience—it's not my usual audience.[12]

Rowling: I feel like I've just been told the Beatles and the Stones are warming up for me.

To tell you the truth I'm not that comfortable reading my own work, and that's why I'm going to be doing a shorter reading tonight and taking some questions. I do think that the people who are coming to hear me read would probably rather ask questions than hear me do a long reading. I would like to think so anyway because I'm not very comfortable doing it. I don't think I'm particularly good at reading.[13]

A question for Rowling: **How do you feel when your readers accuse you of being a sadist, and how do you feel about wrapping up the series?**

Rowling: When fans accuse me of sadism, which doesn't happen that often, I feel I'm toughening them up to go on and read John and Stephen's books. They've got to be toughened up somehow. It's a cruel literary world out there, so I'm doing them a favor.

How do I feel about the series ending? On the one hand, I am going to feel sad. Harry's been an enormous part of my life and it's been quite a turbulent phase of my life as well; he was always a constant. So there will be a sense of bereavement, but there will also be a sense of liberation because there are pressures involved in writing something this popular; and wonderful though it's been, I think that there will also be a certain freedom in escaping that particular part of writing Harry Potter.

The final question, posed to Rowling: **What's next in terms of your writing?**

Rowling: I have a shorter book for children that's half written, so I think I'll probably go to that next.[14]

It was 40 minutes past the hour and, with the Q&A finished, the authors stood up to pose for the cameras. Photographers surged forward with digital cameras and began firing a blinding barrage of light, catching all three authors by surprise. As photographers shouted, giving stage direction ("Hey, Jo!" and "Look *this* way, Jo!"), and as the writers looked like deer in the headlights, it became obvious that with each passing minute, what was supposed to be a sedate photo opportunity had turned into a melee.

The three authors were gobsmacked by the relentless barrage of flashguns firing, and after a few minutes, they were mercifully ushered off stage through a side door to their right, and the press conference officially ended.

Notes

1. It's every author's bane: When is the next book coming out? The pressure, writer Harlan Ellison once wrote, is enough to drive an author crazy. In Rowling's case, the answer is that, based on her progress on previous books and the rapidity with which Scholastic has been able to get a new book to press, my guesstimate is this: July 7, 2007.

2. All three authors have donated generously of their time, money, and effort to charitable causes, including sizable anonymous donations. The two-day webcast brought in additional money, but not from Apple's Mac users whose browsers were incompatible with the streaming video from MSN—a problem MSN hopes to correct in the future, according to an event spokesperson. In such instances, a DVD recording would raise millions, but no plans had been made for commercial release in a fixed format.

3. For aspiring writers, the best advice on writing I've ever read is Stephen King's memoir/tutorial, *On Writing*. He echoes what Rowling said: read a lot and write a lot. There's no other way.

4. For pro writers, the pressing urge to write, to tell the stories, becomes increasingly important as the years go by. By the time a writer has built a career and is in his fifties or sixties, time is of the essence: Barring a major medical malady or, in King's case, an accident not of his making, time is better spent writing than reading, though King points out in *On Writing* that there's always time to take "sips" of reading by always carrying a book with you when you're out in the public: a strategy that not only turns waiting time into reading time, but keeps people at bay, as well. (Who wants to be so rude as to interrupt a reader deep in a book?)

5. This is a stock King answer. In numerous interviews over the years, he's said that when he was younger, he wondered if he'd ever have a book on the best-seller lists, where all the slots were taken by the same people time and again. But, King said, he had hope because, sooner or later, they'd have to pass on, thus making room for a newer generation of readers. (Leave it to a morbid writer like King to think of it in such grim terms!)

6. Rowling's great genius is that she spent five years plotting out the Harry Potter novels, which is why the books are so airtight in every possible way: She has left nothing to chance. But, as she's said, and others at the top of their game have said, all good things must finally come to an end, and it's best to leave when you're in fine form. For writers, particularly, this is a concern because commercial considerations—in this case, hundreds of millions of dollars—are big inducements. After all, who wouldn't like to read more about Hogwarts and the wizarding world? Who wouldn't like to read about Harry (if he survives—and that's a big if) as a fledgling Auror as he grows from young adult to adult? There are many more stories to be set in Rowling's fantasy world of Harry Potter, but alas, she holds the key to that door and she's locking it forever to further access.

7. It's natural for a writer to want to set his stories in a milieu in which he's comfortable. For that reason, King tends to set his stories in Maine (most often, rural settings); Rowling tends to write about England; and Irving tends to write about New England. A writer has enough to worry about in the storytelling process without having to think about the landscape in which the tales are set.

8. From a writer's point of view, killing off characters is not done lightly; in fact, it's

only done when the story demands it. Characters, as writers have found, take on a life of their own and essentially must live their own lives. In Rowling's case, she's been adamant that her grand plot necessitates the death of characters, major and minor, which is one reason why she's cautioned parents that the Harry Potter novels are not necessarily children's novels, in the sense that good will necessarily triumph and everyone will live happily ever after. Her books, she's cautioned us, are not fairy tales; and as the characters grow and mature, they learn about themselves and the world they must live in, and that death (whether natural or sudden and unexpected) is a natural component of life. The big question is: Will Harry die? To Rowling's great credit, after ten years of Harry Potter in print (six books), no one will know for sure until the seventh, and last, novel is published. Now that's storytelling!

9. King's comments strike to the heart of the matter. Whether Harry dies or not is, in his mind, not the reader's prerogative—it's the writer's. What readers don't want to see is a last minute escape or reprieve for Harry just for its own sake—deus ex machina. That's cheating the reader. So King is right: Whether Harry dies or not is a secondary issue, but Rowling must be fair to the reader and let the plot play out no matter what the cost.

10. Rowling's prolonged absence from the U.S. was not, as she made clear, a matter of prejudice or personal choice: Time and circumstance never favored her, restricting her public appearances to England—a source of frustration for U.S. fans, who comprise her largest readership. Times have changed, though, and since her children are all old enough to travel and she's nearing the end of the Harry Potter novels, she'll have more time to travel abroad, including perhaps a return trip to the U.S. when the authorial commitments of the seventh Harry Potter novel are behind her. (She'll still get asked, "What is your next book about?") Perhaps she ought to take a page from Stephen King, who published as Richard Bachman until a fan blew his cover.

11. After taking pains not to identify the major character who dies in book 6, when the question arose earlier in the press conference, the child reporter cited the character's name, which I've deleted because it's a major plot point. Rowling's response is correct: She's writing an epic and, in the end, the hero must stand alone to confront his adversary. Everything in the book series points to a final showdown with Lord Voldemort, and it's Harry Potter that must do so—not his friends, the faculty of Hogwarts, or his mentors. Harry alone must confront and defeat the villain. That's just the way it's got to be.

12. Typically, writers read from new or forthcoming works, but in this case, all three read from previously published works. Considering the fact that most of the attendees were in their early to mid-teens, King could have read from *The Eyes of the Dragon*, with a chapter in which Randall Flagg (think Voldemort) figures prominently; instead, King chose to tell (literally) a campfire story, actually a story-within-a-story, as author Gordon LaChance tells about a pie-eating contest in a novella, "The Body," which appeared in a collection, *Different Seasons*. ("The Body" is better known as its film adaptation, *Stand by Me*, directed by Rob Reiner.) In Irving's case, the choice was inspired: a pivotal chapter from *A Prayer for Owen Meany*, the humorous piece was meant to be read aloud, which he did to great effect—the best reading of both nights. Rowling, who professes a reluctance to

read in public, chose wisely, as well; the chapter from *Harry Potter and the Half-Blood Prince* is pivotal and sheds light on Lord Voldemort when he was just an unsure child at an orphanage—a scene mirrored in book one in which Hagrid tells Harry he's a wizard; this time, Dumbledore tells a young Tom Riddle that he's a wizard, too.

13. Rowling doesn't give herself enough credit. She's a fine reader of her own work, and fans always prefer to hear a story told by the original storyteller over a professional reader. But she does have a point about the questions trumping her readings: There are still many unanswered questions that fans have of the Harry Potter series, but few opportunities to get them answered. Most, if not all, will necessarily be answered in book seven, but in the interim, inquiring minds want to know. . . .

14. Though Rowling is ending the Harry Potter series, she has talked about writing an eighth book about the wizarding world, though it'll be nonfiction; the print equivalent of bonus features on a movie DVD, this book will use her notes and back stories to shed light on Harry, the wizarding world, and the Muggle world as well. This book will be published as a charity book, as were two earlier books, *Quidditch Through the Ages* and *Fantastic Beasts & Where to Find Them,* both published under pen names. There's no title yet, of course, but my suggestion is *J. K. Rowling's Harry Potter Encyclopedia.*

The Haven Foundation and Doctors Without Borders

The Haven Foundation

www.thehavenfdn.org
www.thehavenfdn.org/store

"In the summer of 1999, I was struck by a careless driver and nearly killed while taking my daily walk," King wrote on The Haven Foundation website. King also observed that audiobook reader Frank Muller, who suffered head injuries in a motorcycle accident, would never work professionally again. Those accidents, he said, got him thinking about "the uniquely perilous situation of many freelance artists. The majority of mid-list writers, audio readers, and freelancers in the book and publishing industry have little or no financial cushion in the event of a sudden catastrophic accident such as that suffered by Muller and myself."

King's answer: The Haven Foundation, which accepts donations payable via PayPal, Visa, and MasterCard. In the website's store, King is selling (one per family) signed copies of his books and books signed by his friends, notably John Irving. Because King no longer supports bookstore signings, this is the best way to not only help a very worthy cause but to guarantee that you're getting an authentic signature.

Please check out The Haven Foundation's website and register so you can donate and buy books. Know that every dollar will help mid-list artists in the book industry, who will be touched by your generosity and grateful for your concern. These are the creators who have spent their lifetimes giving us the fruits of their labors; now, you have an opportunity to make a difference in their lives. As a mid-list writer myself, I stand up, applaud, and gladly support King's Haven Foundation; I hope you do, too.

For those of you who blog, have websites, or participate on message boards, please spread the word; it costs nothing but your time.

Doctors Without Borders

www.doctorswithoutborders.org

When J. K. Rowling was asked by King which charity she wanted to support with the proceeds earmarked from the reading event, she didn't hesitate: Doctors Without Borders, she replied.

Rowling, who once worked at Amnesty International, knew the good work that this organization does, often in third world countries where they are at as much risk as the combatants; regardless, they are there to help.

From its website:

> Doctors Without Borders/Médecines Sans Frontières (MSF) is an independent international medical humanitarian organization that delivers emergency aid to people affected by armed conflict, epidemics, natural or man-made disasters, or exclusion from health care in more than 70 countries.
>
> Each year, MSF doctors, nurses, logisticians, water-and-sanitation experts, administrators, and other medical and non-medical professionals depart on more than 3,800 field assignments. They work alongside more than 22,500 locally hired staff to provide medical care.
>
> In emergencies and their aftermath, MSF provides health care, rehabilitates and runs hospitals and clinics, performs surgery, battles epidemics, carries out vaccination campaigns, operates feeding centers for malnourished children, and offers mental health care.

There are several ways you can contribute: On the home page, click "Donations" to explore your options. According to an independent audit, 85.74 of the money received goes "to our programs and public education activities." In other words, this is a lean-and-mean organization in terms of overhead, because they want (and you want) your money to go where it will make the most difference: to the person in need. (Full disclosure here: a miniscule 1.35 percent goes to management and general expenses, and 12.94 percent goes to fundraising.)

When you contribute to Doctors Without Borders, you are not only helping others in great need, but you're supporting Joanne Rowling in a cause that's near and dear to her heart. Over the years, she has lent her good name and invaluable time in support of worthwhile charities, and has dug into her purse and made substantial contributions as well. Now that she has added Doctors Without Borders to her list of organizations to support, why not add it to your list, as well?

And, as with the Haven Foundation, please get involved online and pass the word by any means possible. If by your efforts someone else is touched enough to donate, you not only earn points toward your favorite Hogwarts house but can consider yourself a card-carrying member of S.P.E.W.—the Society Promoting Extraordinary Works.

The word "magic" has many definitions, but the one that pertains here is "any extraordinary . . . influence." By donating to this worthwhile organization, even Muggles can conjure up magic of the best kind.

August 1, 2006: The First Night's Reading

"My readings in New York with Stephen King and John Irving were so much fun. It's not often that I do something like that and wish I could do it all over again, but I would have happily done a third night. If you were there, and yelling, thank you; the crowds, both nights, could not have been more wonderful."

—*J. K. Rowling from her official website*

Radio City Music Hall has, over its 60-year history, hosted some of the biggest names in show business, from Frank Sinatra to Billy Crystal. Best known for its Rockettes and its annual Christmas show, which draws a million people during its eight-week run, Radio City Music Hall is a haven for brand-name singers and heaven for its fans, who could not ask for a better venue. According to its website, it is "the largest indoor theatre in the world. Its marquee is a full city-block long." Moreover, its careful design insures that "every seat in Radio City Music Hall is a good seat."

Tonight, August 1, at 7:30 P.M., Radio City Music Hall would host some of the biggest names in entertainment—comedienne and film star Whoopi Goldberg, actress Kathy Bates, TV star Andre Brauer, comedian and TV star Jon Stewart, and reporter Soledad O'Brien. These names, however, would not be showcasing themselves and their talents; instead, they would be introducing and setting the stage for three writers reading from their works: in order of appearance, Stephen King, John Irving, and J. K. Rowling.

It's a half hour before the show is scheduled to start, and after a six-block walk from my hotel to Radio City Music Hall, I'm tired and hot, and no wonder: New York City is in a record heat wave, with temperatures hovering near 100 degrees. Concerned about power outages, New York City's mayor has asked residents to conserve, to turn up their thermostats, as the city officials dim the lights at public attractions like the Statue of Liberty and the Empire State Building. After a prolonged power outage in Queens, the mayor wasn't taking any chances.

In the back of my mind I'm wondering if the power grid will hold this evening. Broadway is lit up to the max—the show, after all, must go on—and storeowners, in an effort to entice customers, have left front doors wide open, as air-conditioners push themselves to their cooling limits.

As Muggles—non-magical folk in Rowling lingo—rushed around the streets of the city, I wondered how many of them knew that three of the most famous and most successful authors of our time were in their midst tonight, preparing to read to a collective audience of 6,000 fans, some of whom had traveled from Europe to attend the event.

I expected a long line at Radio City Music Hall, but the length of the actual line surprises me. It stretches down one city block and doubles back on itself. Even though it's early evening, it's unspeakably hot, muggy, and very uncomfortable. But the weather wasn't foremost on the minds of those standing patiently in line as it snaked around metal stalls where security checked bags, purses, and backpacks for cameras and recording devices, which were forbidden.

My first thought was that no matter how hard security screens the seemingly never-ending line of people, the die-hard fans are not going to leave without a memento: if nothing else, a photograph or possibly an audio recording. They will want, and get, a tangible souvenir from tonight's event.

Additionally, some people—mostly younger readers—have brought books that they hope to get signed. The opportunity would likely not come, but just in case. . . .

After a 20-minute wait, I make my way from the end of the line through the ticket and security checkpoints, and gratefully walk inside where the air conditioning is cranked up. With a full house of 6,000 people, the air conditioning would need to be functioning at full capacity.

As I head upstairs, my first concern is that my balcony ticket, with a face value of $100, is not going to afford the best view—a groundless concern. Located in the center section on the first mezzanine, I could see the stage clearly. Unlike a sports stadium where columns often obscure views of the playing field, Radio City Music Hall has no columns to obstruct a view of the stage.

I had expected a sell-out crowd and wall-to-wall people, but entire seat sections were empty. Were these tickets still available, or did people simply not show up?

It was clear, too, that most of the audience was comprised of young adults. This wasn't a literary crowd—in other words, not a John Irving crowd—and, given the lack of older readers in their thirties and forties, it wasn't a Stephen King crowd, either. It was clearly a J. K. Rowling crowd: not a Muggle in sight.

At 7:35 P.M., the lights dim and, to introduce all three writers, a short montage, a film clip, plays to the accompaniment of rock and roll music.

On four oversized, backlit screens, we get a quick visual and audio overview of the careers of King, Irving, and Rowling who, collectively, have sold 400-plus million copies of their books worldwide, in dozens of languages.

In the book industry, this kind of celebration is as big as it gets. In a world-class city on a world-class stage with thousands of fans paying rapt attention, it's a world apart from the one that these writers inhabit when they work and produce the stuff of nightmares . . . and dreams: a small room in which the writer sits alone, dreaming, imagining, creating something out of nothing. It's what writers *really* do most of the time.

The clip plays and we see King walking through a forest. Rowling in an open, wind-swept field. Irving walking down a country road. Rowling amidst a large crowd of fans. A close-up of King in Durham, Maine; a black-and-white photo of him taken by his brother Dave, showing a copy of *Startling Mystery Stories* propped up against the black platen of his manual Underwood typewriter, open to the page featuring his first pro sale, "The Glass Floor." A young Irving looking up at a fan at a book signing. King laughing as he's being strapped down in an electric chair on the set of *The Green Mile*, with director Frank Darabont looking on. Rowling at home, holding up *Harry Potter and the Goblet of Fire*. Irving working out, punching, swaying, boxing. A close-up of Irving's signature book, *The World According to Garp*. A close-up of King's first published novel, *Carrie*, the book and movie that launched his career, like a fighter jet catapulted off an aircraft carrier. Rowling in her home office, holding a British edition of a Harry Potter novel. Irving casually dressed, seated in front of an IBM Selectric II typewriter, pecking away with two fingers. Rowling in an Edinburgh café (formerly Nicolson's Restaurant, now a Chinese restaurant, King's Buffet), writing longhand, with a picture window in the background. King, wearing a Center Lovell (Maine) sweatshirt, at his summer home, where he's typing on a portable computer. Rowling standing up against a brick pillar as crowds of people rush past her, oblivious that a world-famous author is in their midst. From the first Harry Potter movie, actor Dan Radcliffe, in Quidditch uniform, looking skyward. A close-up of Kathy Bates in her most famous role as Annie Wilkes in King's *Misery*. Tobey Maguire in a car from Irving's *The Cider House Rules*. King walking down a country road in Center Lovell as he's reading a book with his Welsh corgi walking by his side. Rowling coming on stage at the Royal Albert Hall in England. Quick shots of all three authors. Irving boxing.

The lights come up and the audience bursts into applause and cheers as a casually dressed Whoopi Goldberg heads stage right to a podium with a facade of upright books bearing tonight's authors' names: Stephen King, John Irving, and J. K. Rowling.

"Ladies and gentlemen and readers of all ages," the professional announcer cheerfully begins, "please welcome Oscar, Emmy, Tony, and Grammy winner, a star of movies based on well-known books such as *The Color Purple, Sister Act,* and *Sister Act 2* . . . Whoopi Goldberg!"

The crowd screams and whoops it up as Goldberg informally greets the audience.

"Hey!" she says, waving. "Hey!" she says again, as the crowd finally settles in to listen to what she has to say.

"Good evening! Thank you for that! Oh, my goodness."

Whoopi starts reading from her text:

Welcome to "An Evening with Harry, Carrie, and Garp." This evening, on the great stage of the Radio City Music Hall, this legendary showplace of the nation, we are bringing you three of the world's most legendary writers: Stephen King, J. K. Rowling, and John Irving. Three fantastic writers, three unmatched storytellers, three distinct phenomenons, each an industry unto him or herself. These three writers are forces of nature equal to or greater than any of the supernatural events you can find in any of their books.

I have read every book by all three of these writers, and I can't tell you how much all of this means to me, because with a book your mind takes you on the adventure, and the writer shows you the path.

I can hear a lot of kids in the audience. And I am just so glad that you're here. I am just so glad that kids are involved in hearing writers read. It's so *cool*. And your parents are okay, too.

Harry, Carrie, and Garp. Somebody maybe should have put them all together a long time ago. Did you know, if one of those boys from the Hogwarts school had asked that poor girl at the prom out for a date, a lot of people would have been saved a lot of grief.

Now, this night is historic. Never before has such a group of literary stars assembled on a single stage. In fact, they were all just backstage, all just chitchatting quietly. I was trying to listen, but I couldn't hear anything.

But what I ascertained by just all of the hand movements and stuff is that I think they're working on a collaboration.

I don't do gossip, so don't listen to me, but I think that young Harry Potter casts a love spell on his teacher, who is a middle-aged gnome, and they have this really hot affair and relationship. On their way back to Exeter, they get lost and stumble on the lip of Hell, only to be chased down by a whole group of telepathic wolves. And I don't want to give away the ending, but it will make you laugh and cry and tingle with enchantment and finally just expunge your body. It will just blow your minds.

This intimate evening with these writers would not be possible without you, their closest fans. Six thousand of you are here tonight. We have three active fan clubs assembled under this one roof. It's quite amazing. There are plenty of fans of J. K. Rowling. And I think I know why all of the Potter fans are screaming: It's because all of the Stephen King fans are whispering to them that Harry's going to bite it.

And it's just amazing how many Stephen King fans are here tonight. And you know what, there are millions of us all over the world, but we hardly ever get together because so many of us are angry loners.

And the John Irving fans are here in full force. John is famous for writing about strong women, and maybe that's why women love him so much. He doesn't have a lot of black women yet, but I'm going to work on that. But the last time I saw him, ten minutes ago backstage, he was really talking to those Rockettes.

But the truth is that this evening is really a tribute to you all. So put your paper-cut fingers and carpal tunneled hands together and give yourselves a round of loving applause. Because in this room are the best readers in the world. And if this evening proves nothing else, it does prove that reading is alive and well.

We proved that when great books fall into the hands of great readers, what happens is that we all want to talk about it. Reading is alive and well because of the price of gas pushing four dollars a gallon. Reading a fantastic book is just about the only way most people can afford to travel right now. Reading is alive and well because due to this week's heat wave more people than ever are sitting on beaches, burning through best-sellers. And thanks to global warming [Whoopi looks as if she can't believe what she's reading] . . . sometimes you just have to skip over stuff—you know what I mean?

Finally, reading is alive and well because tonight we're harnessing its awesome power for the benefit of two brilliant causes—causes so close to the hearts of this evening's authors. The first is the Haven Foundation, established to support writers and artists who've suffered a serious illness or accident and can no longer support themselves.

And the other is Doctors Without Borders. This is a medical humanitarian organization that delivers emergency healthcare and aid to places where people are in urgent need. You can be proud of the fact that the proceeds from the purchase of your ticket will be put to good use in the pursuit of these missions. Because they're so important, even the ticket scalpers on Sixth Avenue have decided to donate a couple of dollars.

So with great authors and fantastic readers and worthy causes, we bring you this very first "Evening with Harry, Carrie, and Garp."

Introducing each of tonight's biggest stars is a collection of artists that bring us special appreciation of their work. And to introduce tonight's first author, a brilliant actress, an amazing woman, Academy Award winner, Kathy Bates.

That Kathy Bates would be introducing the first writer suggested to me that Stephen King would be the first of the three writers onstage, and I was right.

Bates, best known for her interpretation of Annie Wilkes in King's *Misery*, is no stranger to his work. She would later play Dolores Claiborne in the movie of the same name, one of King's better novels.

Bates, elegantly dressed, takes the podium positioned at stage left to loud and sustained applause, with an anecdotal introduction that garners a lot of well-deserved laughs, talking about how she came to the role of Annie Wilkes and how King excels as a writer who has the gift of "gotta": "He writes stories that cut through the shower of blood. That makes it human. Sharp insights that dig into our innermost secrets. But most of all, Stephen has the gift of 'gotta.' You know? I *gotta* turn the page. I *gotta* see what happens next. I know I *gotta* get up early tomorrow morning to go to work but I *gotta* keep reading this book."

The short film clip that follows covers King's varied book and movie career, with clips from his movies and clips of interviews with King and observations from Kathy Bates and film director Frank Darabont.

The clip sets the stage for King. Dirgelike music from *The Green Mile* rises in volume as the lights come up slowly, very slowly. Everything is back-lit in blue as a tall, shadowy man walks out of the swirling mists. King is walking toward the audience, backlit, outlined; then we see him in full, clearly illuminated as he walks, rolled manuscript in hand, toward the stage design made just for him: a curious combination of a rustic setting and an electric chair, visually crossing his Maine stories with what King calls "Old Sparky" in *The Green Mile*, the sturdy oak chair to which condemned inmates are strapped.

King looks downright folksy. Casually dressed in t-shirt and jeans, King takes a seat in the electric chair. After his introductory remarks, he reads a campfire story, "The Revenge of Lardass Hogan," which he selected because he knew the audience would mostly be teens, and he was right: This was a

J. K. Rowling crowd, not predominantly a crowd of King fans whose ages tend to be in their twenties through fifties.

Though I would have preferred to see him read a selection from *The Eyes of the Dragon,* I think his spirited reading struck just the right note with this audience, who laughed appreciatively at all the right places.

Next up: Andre Brauer, who gives a short introduction to the career of John Irving, concluding that "his novels are unusually eventful, intricately plotted, and laced with symbols, metaphors, subplots, and refrains. Novel after novel, he asks his readers to explore with him the rules and manners and the consequences of breaking social code."

Like the King film clip that preceded his talk, Irving's film clip artfully blends film clips from *The World According to Garp* and *The Cider House Rules* with observations from author Susan Cheever and from Irving, as well.

The clip ends with a shot of actor Michael Caine (in *The Cider House Rules*) closing the door to a room at the orphanage. "Good night, you princes of Maine, you kings of New England."

On the darkened stage, a casually dressed Irving strides across, waving to the audience, as he bows to them, and takes a seat in a professorial set, an uphol-stered leather chair book-ended by a table with a reading lamp and a fireplace.

Irving makes himself comfortable and explains the back story to the piece he's going to read, about a Christmas pageant play. From chapter four ("The Little Lord Jesus") from *A Prayer for Owen Meany,* Irving's reading would prove to be the best reading of the night. Using a high-pitched voice to denote Owen Meany, Irving's spirited reading of this humorous portion of *A Prayer for Owen Meany* gets the laughs from the audience in all the right places.

Irving chose wisely and well and, after the event, I spoke to a number of people who said that they had never read an Irving book, but they were

John Irving prepares to read a selection from his novel *A Prayer for Owen Meany.*

going out to the bookstore tomorrow to pick up *The World According to Garp* or *A Prayer for Owen Meany.*

Irving leaves the stage to a loud round of applause.

Two writers down, one to go. Predictably, Rowling would close out the evening.

I wondered who would introduce her and, as it turned out, the introducer would draw the biggest rounds of applause of the night. Comedian Jon Stewart *(The Daily Show)* took the podium, stage left, as loud and sustained clapping and cheering, accompanied by the unmistakable high-pitched sound of teenage girls squealing, filled Radio City Music Hall.

From start to finish, Stewart has the appreciative audience in his hands. He thanks the audience for the overwhelming welcome and begins reading:

> I was just wondering, how much do you think I could get for that chair [Irving's] on eBay?
>
> What an exciting night! And thank you all for coming down. It is my absolute honor to introduce the final author of the evening. I hope you're having a pleasant time. This is truly amazing.
>
> I was running a little late and I was talking to my friend Mel Gibson on the phone—he just wanted to make sure I wished everyone here tonight *nachas* [Jewish word for pride]. And he hopes that tonight's *mishegoss* [crazy, senseless behavior] puts a smile on your *punim* [face]. He's heading to rehab: the Betty Ford Clinic to battle alcoholism, and the Henry Ford Clinic to battle anti-Semitism.
>
> Why am I here? I am a television personality. Books are *killing* my profession. I came here tonight to make one final appeal for TV over books. Books make you provide your own imagination, but we provide the pictures for you—you don't even have to turn the page, you just sit there and stare.
>
> I'm actually here because I am an absolute great fan of each and every author here tonight. Stephen King, John Irving, J. K. Rowling. I have the honor of introducing the video for J. K. Rowling—from the audience, correcting his pronunciation of her name: "Rowling like bowling!"—You pronounce it however you want. I was talking to her backstage and she said to me, "Say Rowling [rhymes with scowling] because my crowd will yell Rowling [rhymes with bowling]."
>
> Why am I here? I have kids, two of them. And my youngest is a little girl who is five months old. And she has been in line for the latest Harry Potter book now for over three months. We miss her terribly. But I want that damn book. My son is two and he was born with a lightning bolt [on his forehead]. Actually, he wasn't, but you'd be amazed that every night if you just do this with your thumbnail [he makes slashing

marks with his fingernail], after a while he looks like he was born with a lightning bolt.

What's remarkable about Jo is her ability to just transport people into a universe of hers that is at many levels universal and yet also absolutely unique. I admire it. I look forward to each and every installment.

I should be sitting out there with you.

So please, if you can, take a look at this video.

A short video runs.

Rowling in her home office. Her voiceover: "The idea came out of nowhere. I could see Harry very clearly and it was the most physical rush of excitement. I've never felt that excited about anything."

Shots of children dressed in wizard clothes with Harry Potter books in hand. Narrator voice-over: "In this world of videogames and DVDs, many people have asked, 'What would it take to get kids to reading again?' It took . . . a wizard." Shots of kids reading Harry Potter in bed.

Shots of the British and U.S. cover art to the Harry Potter book series. Film clip of Daniel Radcliffe as Harry Potter from the first film.

Potter novels stacked at a book printing plant in England, rolling off the assembly line.

Rowling being introduced at a U.K. reading. Rowling signing copies of her books outside the Royal Albert Hall.

Profile shot of a young girl with "I Love Harry Potter" and a red heart painted on her cheek. Shots of media coverage in print about Rowling. Shots of young girls with wizard hats and a profile of one girl's cheek.

Shots of the hardback U.S. edition rolling off the printing presses. Narrator voice-over: "*Harry Potter and the Half-Blood Prince* sold 6.9 million copies in just the first 24 hours." Shots of jubilant children holding their copies of the U.S. edition of the latest novel, including one girl literally jumping with joy.

Richard from the U.K. television show, *Richard and Judy:* "This is unprecedented. It's been said that if you put all the books bought that you've written about Harry Potter end to end, they would go around the equator one-and-a-half times, and we ain't finished yet. This isn't just a best-seller—this is historic." Foreign book covers. Children behind a barrier, books and cameras in hand.

Rowling: "You pick up a paper and there are casual references to Harry Potter. That's the freakiest thing, that it permeates odd stories, and that's more of an indication how big it's become than anything else."

Clip from *Saturday Night Live* with the news announcer apologizing: "We're sorry, we didn't realize that you're under so much pressure." A teary-eyed comedienne playing a nervous Harry Potter opines, "One hundred and twenty-five million kids have read my [first] book and if the movie isn't good, they're going to rip me a new one that no magic wand can repair!" The announcer cheerily responds, "Harry, good luck!"

Shot of a train speeding on its tracks in the English countryside, puffing white cotton balls from its black stack. Rowling inside the train, surrounded by stacks of books, which she's signing. She says, "I have no idea how many books I've signed, but it's got to be in the tens of thousands now. So if anyone wants to own the very last unsigned Harry Potter in existence, I sometimes feel like I should stop signing sometime. It will be valuable one day."

"This is an old notebook in which I worked out—and then again, I don't want you to look too close—the history of the Death Eaters."

Film clip from the first movie, showing Harry, Hermione, and Ron in the train going to Hogwarts for the first time. Hermione repairs Harry's broken eyeglass frame.

"Holy cricket," Hermione says, "you're Harry Potter!"

From the *Today Show*, Katie Couric asks: "Are any of the characters you write about based on anyone you know in real life?"

Rowling replies, "Yes, but obviously I have to be careful because some of my characters are pretty unpleasant."

Film clip of Severus Snape, telling Harry Potter, "People will think you're . . . up to something."

In her office, Rowling holding a yellow folder. "This is the thing I was really dubious about showing you. I don't really know why because what does this give away? But this is the final chapter to book seven. Which I'm still dubious about showing you. I don't know why I feel like the camera is going to be able to see through the folder."

From the *George and Judy* show, Rowling says: "I wrote the final chapter in 1990."

From *News Night*: "Why stop when they grow up? It might be interesting to know what becomes of Harry as an adult?"

Rowling: "How do you know he'll still be alive?"

Interviewer: "Oh."

Ending of movie #1 in which Hermione tells Harry he's going to be a great wizard, after his battle with Voldemort.

George and Judy: "Why not extend it to nine [books]? Seriously, why stick to the seven? Is it just too much to ask?"

Rowling: "Because I think that you have to go out when you've done it. I admire the people who go out when people still want more. I don't think I'm ever going to have anything like Harry again. I think you just get one [book series] like Harry. And every day I think how lucky I am."

This is the moment fans have been waiting for. The signature theme music from the movie series plays as Rowling, wearing an elegant black dress and shoes with a unique design (snake straps), walks across the stage with a U.S. paperback edition of *Harry Potter and the Half-Blood Prince*.

The crowd goes wild. Flash-guns go off like popcorn. Fans are screaming. Rowling is smiling, clearly happy but overwhelmed by the reception.

Rowling addresses the crowd: "The great thing about tonight is . . . no pressure. You know, it was great of Stephen and John to warm up for me.

"I do have the best shoes though," she says, as the camera zooms in for a close-up and shows her open-toed shoes: a pair of custom-made, silver-colored shoes with a snake strapping sinuously twisting around her ankles.

An enthroned J. K. Rowling prepares to read from *Harry Potter and the Half-Blood Prince*.

"I'm going to be reading for you from the latest Harry Potter book. And at the end of my reading I'm going to be taking a few questions. My experience of my readers is that they want to torture me for information. But Radio City Hall didn't feel that would be allowable. So I'm just going to ask a couple of people to put out their questions for answers.

"But before that, I'm going to read a short piece in which Harry Potter goes back in time and sees another famous pupil of Hogwarts school who discovers that he, too, is a wizard.

"So Harry and present-day Dumbledore follow a much younger Dumbledore as he walks to an orphanage to tell a particular pupil that he has a place at Hogwarts," she says, setting the stage for her reading.

Rowling reads from chapter 13 of *Harry Potter and the Half-Blood Prince*, "The Secret Riddle," page 263, starting with the line, "They passed through a set of iron gates into a bare courtyard that fronted a rather grim, square building" and ending with the line from Dumbledore, "All new wizards must accept that, in entering our world, they abide by our rules."

J. K. Rowling reads from *Harry Potter and the Half-Blood Prince.*

To which Rowling added, "But as you know, he didn't."

Hers is a very good reading, with her voice changing to suit different characters. Though she expressed misgivings earlier that she wasn't a very good reader, she doesn't give herself enough credit. Though not a professionally trained reader like Frank Muller, who read many of Stephen King's books, Rowling brings a warmth to her readings that is intimate and invites a careful listening by the audience. She's charmed everyone and, with the reading behind her, she fields questions from the audience, culled from the hundreds that Scholastic has screened.

Seated upfront near the microphones positioned in the aisle for easy access, she confidently begins answering questions.

What would Hermione see if she looked into the Mirror of Erised?

Rowling: Well, at the moment, as you know, Harry, Ron, and Hermione have just finished their penultimate year at Hogwarts; and Hermione and Ron have told Harry that they're going to go with him wherever he goes next.

So, at the moment, I think that Hermione would see most likely the three of them alive and unscathed, and Voldemort finished.

But I think that Hermione would also see herself closely entwined with another person. I think you can probably guess.

If they follow the exact instructions and they have all of the ingredients, can Muggles brew potions?

Rowling: Well, I'd have to say no, because there is always a magical component in the potion; it's not just the ingredients, so at some point they will have to use a wand. I've been asked what would happen if a Muggle picked up a magic wand in my world, and the answer would probably be: something accidental and probably quite violent because the wand in my world is merely a vehicle or a vessel of sorts, and there is a very close relationship, as you know, between the wand that each wizard uses and themselves. And you'll find out more about that in book seven.

311

For a Muggle you need the ability to make these things work properly.

Potions seems on the face of it to be the most Muggle-friendly subject, but there's normally a point in which you need to use magic.

You said in a recent interview that Snape had a redemptive quality about him. I was wondering if there was any chance that Draco Malfoy might redeem himself?

Rowling: All you girls and Draco Malfoy. You've got to get past this.

And if any other characters might redeem themselves?

Rowling: I believe that *almost* anyone can redeem himself. However, if a psychologist were ever able to get Voldemort in a room, tape him down, and take his wand away, I think he would be classified as a psychopath. So there are people for whom redemption is not possible.

So I'd say for my main characters, yes, there's the possibility for redemption for all of them.

Draco . . . Harry's view is that even given unlimited time he would not have killed. I'm assuming you all have read book six by now because I don't want to hear a child cry that he was five pages away from the end. Let's just say that Draco would not have murdered the person in question. As to what that means for Draco's future, you will have to wait.

In the wizarding world, there are many wand makers, Ollivander's being the one we're most familiar with. How come Ollivander chose the three magical cores for the wands he makes to be phoenix feather, unicorn hair, and dragon heartstring? And how come he decided that these are the three most powerful cores as opposed to others such as veela hair?

Rowling: Well, it is true that there are several wand makers, and in my notes about Harry I have many different cores for wands. Essentially, I decided Ollivander was going to use my three favorites, that those are the three most powerful substances. Other wand makers might choose things that are particular to their country, because countries in my world have their own particular indigenous magical species, so veela hair was kind of obvious for Fleur's wand.

You mentioned before that you had written the final chapter, but how do you know when to stop writing an ending?

Rowling: I think some of the reviews of *Phoenix* suggest that I *didn't* know when to stop.

I decided 16 years ago where I was going. And I will say, I'm quite a long way into writing book seven now. And there's a lot still to explain and a lot to figure out. I'll probably leave some loose ends hanging and you'll be able to say, "Oh, well, in book eight, she'll explain why." But I really do know where I'm going. I'm really going to miss writing Harry Potter. I will miss it fiendishly.

TV reporter Soledad O'Brien comes on stage and reads the questions posed to all three writers.

The questions for Rowling follow.

As one of the first authors to become famous during the Internet age, how have online communication and fan interaction influenced your experience as a writer compared to authors of the past?

Rowling: You really have to resist when you're struggling for ideas to go onto Amazon and read your bad reviews. It's kind of masochistic. You scroll down past all the people who say nice things about you until you see one star.

For a long time, I never looked. People used to say to me, "Do you ever look at the fan sites or see what people have said online?" I was truthful and said I didn't. Then one bored afternoon I Googled "Harry Potter." Oh, my God. I had no idea. The shipping wars?

For people who are over 18 who may not know about this—because I certainly didn't—it's like cybergang warfare. People who wanted Harry and Hermione to end up together . . . they're still out there! And other people who wanted Hermione and Ron. And there are very weird couplings as well, but we will not go anywhere *near* there.

From the crowd: **Harry and Voldemort!**

Rowling: Yeah, exactly. So I would imagine that Jane Austen would have a little less feedback on that topic.

Overall, I think it's an exciting thing. I think that readers being able to share, in cyber book groups, is an interesting, exciting thing, if used wisely.

The last question of the night is from a father and daughter. The father's poignant comment strikes a responsive chord not only with the audience but with Rowling as well, who visibly tears up. The father's heartfelt words say what a lot of Rowling fans in the audience would say if they had the opportunity to address her and the assembled crowd.

The father's comment: "I can remember back in 1998, when my daughter was first learning how to read and becoming aware of the world around her, that the prevailing cultural phenomenon sweeping America and captivating its children were the Spice Girls and Teenage Mutant Ninja Turtles. Then Harry Potter came along and a whole generation, including my daughter, learned to love reading, learned to love the characters you created, learned to love imagination, and learned to appreciate great writing.

"In addition you handed her a tremendous role model in Hermione: intelligent, studious, humane, and compassionate.

"So for all the great characters and role models you've created, and for all the love of reading you've encouraged, and for all of the imagination you've inspired, a whole bunch of other parents, including myself, owe you a tremendous debt of gratitude. So, as a parent, I just wanted to say thank you."

His daughter's question: When you started writing and faced rejection, did you ever think of giving up? And if you had, what do you think you'd be doing now?

Rowling: There was quite a lot of rejection, although it was squeezed into a relatively short period of time.

I got an agent on my second attempt, which is pretty amazing, but then it was a couple of years before I actually faced a publisher.

During that time, did I ever feel like giving up? Truthfully, no, I didn't, because I really believed in the story, and I really loved the story.

Iris Murdoch[1] once said, "Writing a novel is a lot like getting married. You should never commit yourself until you can't believe your luck."

And I really couldn't believe my luck, having had this idea. I was determined to press on with it until the last publisher had rejected it, which at one point looked likely.

Would I have stopped writing? Definitely not. But if I'd never been published in the 16 years between having the idea of Harry and now, I think I probably would have accepted that.

Do we know of a writer who made it after 16 years of rejection? There probably is one, but I think you'd have to have a lot of self-belief after 16 years. I'm sure I would still be writing, but I might have stopped sending the manuscripts at this point. And what would I be doing? I'd be teaching. That's what I'd be doing.

That's it for the first night. King addresses the audience and says, "On behalf of my colleagues, I want to tell you that this was a magic night for us, to be able to fill Radio City Music Hall on behalf of two wonderful charities, not with guitars but with book readers."

King, who plays the guitar in a band of best-selling writers called The Rock Bottom Remainders, does not make the comparison lightly. He knows that in our celebrity-driven, media-centric world, the written word gets the

King, Rowling, and Irving clap at the end of the
first night's reading at Radio City Music Hall.

least amount of press. In *Entertainment Weekly,* for which he's a columnist, books are in the back of the bus, so to speak, and get just a few seats. Film and television stars get far more attention.

Tonight, though, the written word took center stage, and King, more than most, realizes it's been a very special night.

Notes

1. Murdoch is best known for her first novel, *Under the Net.* In 1987, she was named a Dame Commander (DBE) of the British Empire.

August 2, 2006: The Second Night's Reading

It promises to be another sweltering night, especially for Rowling fans anxious to catch a glimpse of her before the reading. Some fans position themselves hours before show time with the fond hope that a J. K. Rowling sighting—or, if they're lucky, a Rowling signature—may be possible.

Tonight, the fans are in luck. Showing up one-and-a-half hours before show time, emerging from a black limo with tinted windows, Rowling, wearing a casual shirt and slacks, emerges, flanked by security. Fans immediately pull out their digital cameras to record a genuine Kodak moment.

Some fans are lucky enough to get her to exchange a few words and get their books signed. Then she makes her way into Radio City Music Hall to prepare for this final night of readings.

This evening will essentially be the same as the first night's readings. The authors will read from the same texts, the same introductory movie clip and author clips will run, and Whoopi Goldberg will introduce the three authors; but the line-up to introduce the authors has changed: actor Tim Robbins introduces King, actor Stanley Tucci introduces Irving, and Kathy Bates introduces Rowling.

The real surprise of the night—to the audience and to the three writers assembled on stage—is the unexpected but welcome appearance of writer Salman Rushdie, the author of *The Satanic Verses* (published in 1988), which so enraged the Muslim community that in 1989 Ayatollah Ruhollah Khomeini issued a fatwa, calling for his death, forcing him to go underground for several years.

It was that kind of night, one in which anything could, and did, happen: a magical night.

Whoopi Goldberg runs through her introduction, though this time she reads the text closely with no major diversions, and then proudly introduces the next guest, "an actor, director, and an Oscar winner, and he's also a pretty damn good guy. Ladies and gentlemen, to introduce Mr. Stephen King, Tim Robbins."

Tim Robbins takes the stage to loud applause and reads from his text, which turns out to be humorous because of his deliberate misstatings of the movie's name. Tim comes across as a warm, likable kind of guy and wins over the audience. It's clear that he's not only a big fan of King's film, *Shawshank Redemption,* but a big fan of the big man himself. "Stephen King matters, not only for his prolific skill, but for his extraordinary ability to create characters that define in their unique way who we are. And now, it's time to hear the thoughts of a few others, on the subject of Stephen King."

The previously screened King film clip rolls and, after he emerges from the back of the darkened stage, King takes his seat in the mock electric chair.

"Thank you. You guys are too much. I think all the Muggles are home tonight watching TV. The real people are here. You don't think this thing's [the chair] electrified do you?"

King reads "The Revenge of Lardass Hogan" and gets a loud round of applause.

Not surprisingly, vomit—the subject of King's story—becomes the linchpin for jokes from everyone who takes the stage and has a microphone in front of him or her.

When Stanley Tucci (star of *The Devil Wears Prada*) comes on stage to introduce John Irving, Tucci can't resist commenting on King's vomit tale. "I'm not going to eat for a week," he deadpans.

John Irving reads with brio from *A Prayer for Owen Meany.*

Tucci's introduction for John Irving is illuminating and sets the right tone for Irving's appearance. As expected, Irving's reading the second time around is more spirited and more animated, with lots of hand gestures, as Irving looks directly at the audience as much as possible. It's the best reading of the night and, indeed, the two nights: Irving's high-pitched interpretation of Owen Meany's voice is dead-on, just as he "sounds" in the novel, and Irving has the audience in his hands from start to finish.

To my great surprise and delight, the

next guest introducer is a repeat from the previous night. The narrator introduces Kathy Bates, who gets a wild round of applause. She is elegantly dressed, as she was the night before, and instead of King, she's going to introduce the remaining writer for the evening, J. K. Rowling. Bates's arms are outstretched and she's beaming to the audience, taking in the moment. The assembled fans love her and she responds in kind.

> Thank you. Thank you very much. Thank you and good evening. Tonight, our next author makes her much-anticipated return to the United States, the first visit in six years. And that may explain why at this moment I feel like Ed Sullivan as he was about to introduce the Beatles. Some of you kids, be sure to ask your parents what I'm talking about on the way home. The Beatles were in a band called Wings. Anyway, but this moment seems somehow bigger because with Pottermania, J. K. Rowling has managed to pull off a feat that no one ever thought possible: transforming an entire generation of children into wild, screaming, frenzied fans of books.
>
> Let's not forget that Harry Potter arrived on our shores at a perilous moment in time: Just when it seemed that technology had infiltrated every last aspect of our lives, most at risk were our children. Between PCs and PlayStations, modems and multiplexes, we were in danger of losing an entire generation to the ravages of Attention Deficit Disorder (ADD).
>
> Then, along came an author who tamed the cacophony with a whisper. With words on a page, J. K. Rowling lured kids away from the screens and into the quiet of their rooms and took them to places where Google does not go. With each thick book that they conquered, children gained the confidence to take on the next. The Harry Potter books that collected on shelves were showcased like trophies. And in the months they awaited the publications of the next installments, something else amazing happened to these new readers: They became re-readers, devouring again and again the same book for pleasure they had rushed through the first time just for plot.
>
> Of course in our entertainment age it was inevitable that a book and a hero as popular as Harry would make his way from the book back to one of those screens. There were those who feared that the special effects of a movie would put an end to the reign of the book, and that children would rather watch a preimagined world of wizards than conjure up their own from a page. Instead, Harry's legions went eagerly to the movies and *then* faithfully back for their books.
>
> That's how we know that J. K. Rowling's spell was not so easily broken, that the magic she conjures turns children into readers for life. What are her secrets? Let's take a look.

The Rowling video rolls and fans are cheering and laughing as an elegantly dressed Rowling comes on stage, wearing a black dress and, from the

Rowling laughs at a humorous comment made by Stephen King.

previous night, a smart pair of distinctive high heels.

"No pressure then," she says. "No pressure. Like I wasn't feeling pressured enough already. You talk about Beatlemania, I feel slightly like I'm Herman's Hermits having to go on after the Stones and the Beatles. My consolation is I have the most interesting shoes. Snakes. Thank you for that. I noticed you like Snape. Just never give up hope you people, do you? Anyway, I'm going to do a short reading from *Harry Potter and the Half-Blood Prince*."

Rowling begins reading and a hush falls across the crowd, punctuated by hundreds of flash guns firing from point-and-shoot cameras from the main orchestra area and all three mezzanines, to the distraction of those around them. Apparently, the admonishment that no flash photography was allowed had been deliberately ignored by the Rowling fans who were hell-bent on getting a photographic souvenir. (It would have been better to have each author clearly state "no photographs, please" and hold a photo opportunity at the end of the event.)

The reading finished, Rowling takes pre-selected questions from the audience.

Rowling: "Thank you. You may have noticed, nobody told me the theme of the readings was to be vomit. So, I could have done something with the Puking Pastilles, but I didn't know. Anyway, we have some questions now."

If you could bring one Harry Potter character to life, other than Harry, who would it be?

Rowling: Other than Harry. Personally, although it's a really tricky one, Hagrid, if I could have anyone, because I think we'd all like a Hagrid in our life, liability though he often is. It would be really great if I met a fundamentalist Christian and asked, "Would you like to discuss the matter with Hagrid?"

In *The Half-Blood Prince*, Aunt Petunia is said to be oddly flushed when Dumbledore announces that Harry will be returning only once more to Privet Drive. Does this mean that Aunt Petunia harbors a hidden love or fondness for Harry, and the connection he provides her to the wizarding world?

Rowling: That's an excellent question. And like all the best and most penetrating questions, it's difficult to answer, but I will say this: There is a little more to Aunt Petunia than meets the eye, and you will find out what that is in book seven.

In a recent interview, you hinted at two main characters dying and possibly Harry Potter, too. Was Dumbledore considered one of the main characters or will we have the chance to see him in action once again? Since he is the most powerful wizard of all time and Harry Potter is so loyal to him, how could he really be dead?

After her reading, Rowling listens to a member of the audience pose a question to her.

Rowling: I feel terrible! The British writer Graham Green once said that every writer had to have a chip of ice in their heart. I think you may just have ruined my career. I really can't answer that question because the answer is in book seven, but you shouldn't expect Dumbledore to do a Gandalf. Let me just put it that way. I'm sorry!

Salman and Milan Rushdie: Hello, we are Salman and Milan Rushdie—

Rowling: I'm not that sure this is fair. I think you might be better at guessing plots than most. But anyway, off you go.

Salman and Milan Rushdie: We are 59 and 9. And one of us is good at guessing plots, not me. And this is really Milan's question, a kind of a follow-up to the previous one.
  Until the events of volume six, it was always made plain that Snape might be an unlikable fellow but he was essentially one of the good guys.

Rowling: I can see this is the question you all really want answered.

Salman and Milan Rushdie: Dumbledore himself had always vouched for him. Now, we are suddenly told that Snape is in fact a villain and Dumbledore's killer. We cannot or don't want to believe this. Our theory is that Snape is in fact still a good guy, from which it follows that Dumbledore can't really be dead, and that the death is a ruse cooked up between Dumbledore and Snape to put Voldemort off his guard so that when Harry and Voldemort come face to face, Harry may have more allies than he or Voldemort suspects. So . . . is Snape good or bad? In our opinion, everything follows from it.

Rowling: Well, Salman, your opinion I would say is . . . right, but I see that I need to be a little more explicit and say that Dumbledore is definitely dead.

I do know that there is an entire website out there, www.Dumbledore IsNotDead.com, so I'd imagine they're not happy right now.

But I think all of you need to move through the five stages of grief, and I'm just helping you get past denial. I can't remember what's next—it may be anger—so I think we should stop it here. Thank you.

So it is now my privilege to invite my fellow authors back onto the stage. I don't feel worthy. So here, Stephen King and John Irving.

King and Irving join Rowling on stage and, as with the previous night, Soledad O'Brien fields preselected questions for all three.

A few of the questions posed follow:

Question for Rowling: As a librarian, I would like to first thank you for attracting so many students and adults, as well, to reading. Since the Harry Potter series will unfortunately be ending, what does the future for you and for your readers hold? Do you have something planned to keep the anxious students and adults waiting to be released?

Rowling: I thought you were going to attack me for Madam Pince and I would like to apologize to you and any other librarians present here today.

My get-out clause on this is always if they'd had a pleasant, helpful librarian, half my plots would be gone because the answer invariably is in a book, but Hermione has to go and find it. If they'd had a good librarian, that would have been that problem solved. So, sorry.

I have, mercifully, a shorter book for slightly younger children that's half-written, so I may well go back to that when Harry's done.

I think I'll need a short mourning period, though. You have to allow me to get past Harry.

Question for King: The Tommyknockers is by far the most terrifying book I've ever read to the point where I have actually never finished reading it, because I am so afraid of it that I have to bury it and then try to bring it out again and then bury it again because it's so terrifying. So, I'm just wondering, what kinds of scary stories keep you up at night? Maybe your own? Maybe another author's?

King: Dig that book up, girl, and finish it!

Comment: I know. I actually tried digging it up before I came here, and I couldn't find it, so I think I'm going to have to buy a new copy.

King: That's a good idea.

I'll tell you what, I think our idea of what scares us changes as we get older. As a young person, one of the scariest things that I ever read was *Lord of the Flies* because the idea of those kids turning feral just scared the dickens out of me. Sometimes you get surprised into fright.

When I picked up the Harry Potter books, I was not prepared for the depth of some of the frightening passages in there. Frankly, I was surprised by how scary the Death Eaters were. So there was plenty of scary stuff there. I've read a range of modern scary stuff. I try to keep up with the competitors.

Rowling: I scared Stephen King!

King: You scared Stephen King. Yeah. I hope you're proud of yourself!

Rowling: Oh, I'm *very* proud of myself! Thank you, yes I am!

Question for Rowling: What is the one question your fans have never asked you, but should have?

Rowling: How can I answer that?

I can think of a couple of things that give away the ending of book seven. Having got this far, 16 years down the line, I feel that would throw it away—for me, anyway, having put the effort in.

I think that I've been asked excellent questions. It's just that the final book contains a couple of pieces of information that I don't think you could guess at. So . . . I'm sorry.

People think that it's all so fixed in my head, but it's not that obsessively plotted out. For example, this afternoon I believe I changed my mind on the title of book seven. Having been quite convinced that I had the title, I suddenly thought, "No, that would be better, wouldn't it?" in the shower just before coming out here, so . . .

But you know what, I'm not going to tell you either version, because I don't . . . oh, come on! Now really! Have I not given you enough? I gave you Aunt Petunia, I told you Dumbledore is really dead. So I am trying to give something to you.

Anyway, I'm sorry. I suppose it's *that* question. Everyone's really pleased you asked that question. It's me who's let everyone down, not you.

Soledad O'Brien: I'm going to pose the final question and I'd like all three of you to take a stab at it. You can do it in any order that you would like: If you were to have dinner with any five characters from any of your books, take a moment to think about it, who would you invite, and why would they be on your list? Any order.

King: [incredulously] Any five characters from any of *my* books? Honey, I'm eating alone. *You* answer. [He points to Rowling.]

Irving: You could just invite all the dead ones and then they wouldn't come.

King: I would eat with Harry, Hermione, and Ron.

Soledad O'Brien: No. Your own books.

King: And Owen. I don't know. I can think of other people's characters that I'd eat *with*. And I can think of other people's characters I'd *eat*. Somebody else answer that.

Irving: *You* go [looks at Rowling].

Rowling: Well, I'd take Harry to apologize to him. I'd have to take Harry, Ron, and Hermione.

Irving: Sure.

King: Hagrid, take Hagrid.

Rowling: See, I know who's actually dead.

King: Pretend you can take them anyway.

Rowling: Pretend I can take anyone? Well, then I would definitely take Dumbledore. I'd take Dumbledore, Harry, Ron, Hermione, and Hagrid. And Owen because he wouldn't take up much space.

Irving: Well, I might invite Dr. Larch because he wouldn't eat much. He's too into Ether, you know. He'd be safe. I'd also invite Owen Meany, no question—two characters are related in ways that even those of you who have read their books might not entirely understand.

I interrupted *Until I Find You* to write a much shorter and easier novel, *The Fourth Hand,* and I was aware even as I was writing it that Patrick Wallingford, the journalist who has his left hand bitten off by a lion at the beginning of the

book, was the kind of lightweight, less-harmful brother of Jack Burns. He was an easier-to-take Jack Burns, the main character of *Until I Find You.*

The difference between Patrick and Jack is that I gave Jack the worst childhood I

could think of, and I didn't give
Wallingford any childhood at all. So I
would not *not* want to have dinner with
Jack Burns, but Wallingford would be
amusing, if only to watch him eat with
one hand.

And then I would have to include
those three women I mentioned earlier—
Melanie, Hester, and Emma, who would
probably burn the house down but I'd
be interested in meeting them.

King: And before you go, thanks also on
behalf of Doctors Without Borders and
on behalf of the Haven Foundation and
on behalf of you guys who made this
evening magic for us. Thank you so much . . . and good night.

Outside Radio City Music Hall on the second night, Stephen King is surrounded by fans seeking autographs.

The audience gives the writers a standing ovation, as all three stand and
clap. They exit stage right and wave to everyone as dozens of camera flashes
go off.

Two days of magic are over and all three hang around briefly backstage.
Outside, it's hot and muggy, but fans have positioned themselves around all
the exits, hoping they'll be lucky and, perhaps, get a book or a show program
signed.

I'm lucky enough to see Stephen King emerge from the building, headed
to a black limo. Fans immediately converge on him, waving show programs,
hoping to get a signature. He signs three or four of them and then waves to
the crowd and gets in the limo that whisks him off. Rowling, we are told, has
already left the building. Presumably, so has John Irving.

It's time for things to get back to normal for all three writers and the
fans, some of whom had rushed to get to New York City after attending
Lumos 2006 in Las Vegas, which ended on July 31.

As King explained to the audience, he was staying over Friday and leaving on Saturday. Rowling likely stayed the night, then headed off with her
husband and their three children (Mackenzie, Jessica, and David) to a nearby
Hamptons hideaway on Long Island, where the rich and famous go to get
away from the crush of crowds. And Irving likely spent the night and left on
Friday or Saturday to go back home to New Hampshire.

For King and Irving, who have appeared at public readings on numerous occasions, this was surely a high point in their careers. After all, you can't

have a bigger venue than Radio City Music Hall. For Rowling, it's the last public appearance before the publication of the seventh, and last, Harry Potter novel, which she brought with her in manuscript form.

Experiencing a Stephen King-like moment of fear when passing through an airport security gate in New York City, Rowling's bulky manuscript was begrudgingly allowed to pass through as a carry-on item. Rowling, who understandably refused to be parted with the manuscript, was prepared to take a long transatlantic cruise in order to maintain custody, but the priceless manuscript was allowed through, at which point Rowling undoubtedly gave a big sigh of relief.

Rowling, her family, and the final Harry Potter novel, currently a work in progress, are headed off to Scotland where she makes her home.

The next time Rowling surfaces will be when her story, ten years in the telling, finally reveals the outcome of the prophecy imparted by Hogwarts professor and seer Sybill Trelawney, a prophecy in which it's clear that either Harry Potter or Lord Voldemort will die.

And with book seven's publication, Rowling's spellbinding story about the life and times of Harry Potter will come to its predestined end. She will regretfully put him behind her forever and turn her powerful imagination to other stories.

We will, alas, read no more from Rowling about the boy with a distinctive scar on his forehead who modestly set out to find his rightful place in the wizarding world and, by doing so, found a permanent place in the hearts of millions of Muggle readers worldwide.

A well-worn copy of *Half-Blood Prince* belonging to a fan, who had literally read the book to pieces, waiting outside Radio City Music Hall on the second night, hoping to catch Rowling's attention

Part Six:
Harry Potter Websites

Tim Kirk

The Official J. K. Rowling Site

www.jkrowling.com

Given the nature of the web, in which anyone can publish anything without any editorial control, Rowling found it necessary to have an official site to dispel not only rumors but plain "rubbish," which she categorizes as: starting to smell, excessive additives, recycled, moldy, pure garbage, and toxic.

Obviously, this is the first stop on the web for anyone wanting authoritative information by and about Rowling.

The Official U.K. Book Publishing Site

www.bloomsbury.com/harrypotter

This offers basic information about the author, her books, events (past and upcoming), fans, FAQs, news, and video clips of her appearances in the U.K. (all too short, alas!).

The Official U.S. Book Publishing Site

www.scholastic.com/harrypotter

In Flash animation, this site is principally geared toward kids, with information about the books, a need-to-know guide, a discussion chamber, a wizard challenge, fun stuff, and a special area specific to the most recent book (*Harry Potter and the Half-Blood Prince*), which includes a pronunciation guide, a glossary, a screensaver, printable bookmarks, an exclusive poster, and more.

The Official Film Site

www.harrypotter.warnerbros.com

In Flash animation, this site typically features the most recently released film, which means that *Harry Potter and the Goblet of Fire* dominates this website. Contents include: a trailer preview of *Goblet of Fire*, a news section (The

Daily Prophet), a store (Wizard Shop), an interactive games section (delightful!), Magical Trading Cards (register online and trade among fans worldwide), downloads (wallpapers, screensavers, buddy icons, and PSP), Triwizard Challenges (top scorers can record their initials—hey, glory and eternal fame), a special section on the most colorful and eccentric person in *Goblet of Fire* ("Mad-Eye" Moody), the Yule Ball, and—most ominous of all—a dark and moody section called The Dark Mark, devoted to You-Know-Who.

The most interactive Harry Potter site on the web, it's mostly plain fun and whets your appetite for the film version of *Harry Potter and the Order of the Phoenix*, due out July 13, 2007.

Rowling's Literary Agent

www.christopherlittle.net

For aspiring writers, this is a handy site to check out. The next J. K. Rowling is out there, somewhere, and like any good agency, the Christopher Little Agency is always looking for good, new talent. (The emphasis is on the word "good.")

Aspiring authors should follow the guidelines listed on the site and provide a synopsis and the first three chapters (double-spaced, of course).

Official Merchandise

www.noblecollection.com

Officially licensed film-related merchandise is offered by this company in addition to merchandise inspired by the films. The prices range from the affordable to the expensive, so there's something for everyone.

If you want an authentic replica of the wands used in the movies, or specific artifacts, this is the place to buy them.

Products include: an illuminating wand belonging to Harry Potter, Harry Potter's wand, Hogwarts bookmarks, a sculpture of Hogwarts ($295), a replica of the Time-Turner used by Hermione Granger, Hermione Granger's Wand, a chess set ($295) with figurines from the film, Dumbledore's Wand, Voldemort's Wand, a replica of the Triwizard Cup, Lucius Malfoy's Walking Stick, Hermione's Yule Ball Earrings, a bronze dragon sculpture of the first task in the Triwizard Tournament ($495), a small replica of The Mirror of Erised, etc.

As each new movie comes out, new merchandise is added to the inventory.

As well as its website, the company issues a full color catalog, which is your best bet if you want to get a good look at the merchandise. Since it's a proprietary line, it's only available online; none of the products are available in brick-and-mortar stores.

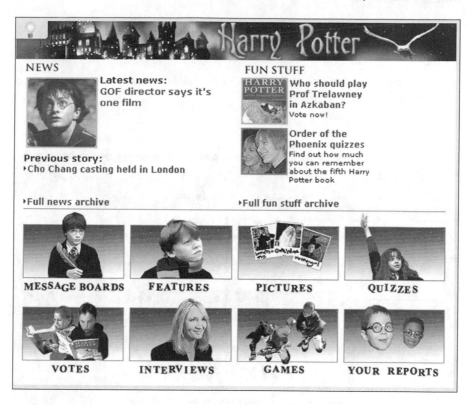

The British Broadcasting Corporation (BBC)

www.bbc.co.uk

An outstanding source for information on Rowling, it's got all the news fit to print. Type "Harry Potter" or "Rowling" in the search engine and you'll harvest a wealth of useful and interesting information, including audio-only interviews conducted by British journalists.

Publishers Weekly

www.publishersweekly.com

The electronic version of the print publication, the trade journal for the book industry worldwide, with an emphasis on U.S. books.

USA Today Newspaper

www.usatoday.com

The electronic version of a daily national newspaper, *USA Today*. It's especially useful with coverage of the latest book or film as they are released.

Graphic-friendly with accessible prose, this is also a good source of information about popular culture in general, covering the Harry Potter phenomenon.

The following websites have been personally recommended by Rowling on her website and in interviews.

The Harry Potter Lexicon

www.hp-lexicon.org

The brainchild of Steve Vander Ark, a reference librarian, this is the most detailed and authoritative source of information about the fictional world of Hogwarts. In fact, it's so good that Rowling herself consults it when she needs to double-check a fact.

I've had the pleasure of sitting on a panel with Steve, whose sly humor has won him legions of fans in the Harry Potter community.

One of the world's experts on Harry Potter and J. K. Rowling, Steve is not only a walking encyclopedia to all things in the wizarding world but an outstanding speaker, who is frequently asked to be a guest at Potter conferences worldwide.

HPANA

www.hpana.com

This site is an automatic news aggregator that pulls information from all sorts of sources. The result is that it's jam-packed with information not only about Rowling but the Harry Potter books, the films, and the Harry Potter phenomenon, as well.

It's easy to start wandering around on this site, and suddenly realize that you've spent an hour exploring the endless links.

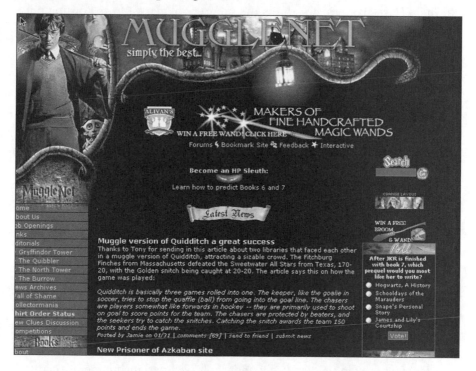

Mugglenet

www.mugglenet.com

Created in 1999 by Emerson Spartz, then 12 years old, this is generally regarded as *the* most trafficked and authoritative Harry Potter website bar none. Now in college, Spartz relies on an army of volunteers (Spartz's Army) to help collect, analyze, write, illustrate, compile, and cover every nook and cranny of the wizarding and Muggle worlds.

An estimated 20 million fans worldwide visit this site, which explains why he and his young cohorts (all in their teens) are instantly recognizable by fans at Harry Potter conferences and podcasts.

Along with the Leaky Cauldron website founder Melissa Anelli, Spartz went on a tour in the U.S., under the auspices of Scholastic Books, to promote the paperback release of *Harry Potter and the Half-Blood Prince*. And, like Anelli, Spartz was personally invited to Scotland to visit Rowling at her home and conduct a personal interview—a wise choice on Rowling's part, since Anelli and Spartz came armed with specific questions that the more general journalist would not have known enough about the Harry Potter world to ask.

If you're a Muggle who absolutely, positively needs to get a daily fix of Rowling/Harry Potter news, this is the site to bookmark. Or, as Rowling put it on her website, "It's high time I paid homage to the mighty Mugglenet. . . . I salute you."

Immeritus: The Sirius Black Fan Club

www.immeritus.org

For those fans who are serious about one of the most popular Harry Potter characters, this is where you can get your fill . . . and then some. From fanfic to an art gallery, from its active message board to glossaries and summaries, this site shows the extraordinary lengths to which fans will go to thoroughly explore one of the most fully realized characters in the Harry Potter canon.

The Leaky Cauldron

www.the-leaky-cauldron.org
www.leakynews.com
Says Anelli about her site and Rowling's reactions to it:

> J. K. Rowling, author of the Harry Potter books, has called Leaky "my favorite fan site" and "a wonderfully well-designed mine of accurate information on all things Harry Potter" that "attracts a lot of knowledgeable and entertaining debate." She said it is about "the worst-kept secret on this website that I am a huge fan." (We're still grinning.) Leaky has been recognized in several ways over the years, but received its highest honor to date, J. K. Rowling's Fan Site Award, on May 23, 2005.

The brainchild of Melissa Anelli, who is a full-time newspaper journalist, this website accurately bills itself as "an all-purpose site for the Harry Potter enthusiast. It started in 2000 as a badly designed one-page roll of news; it has turned into a destination for fan entertainment and discussion, and has

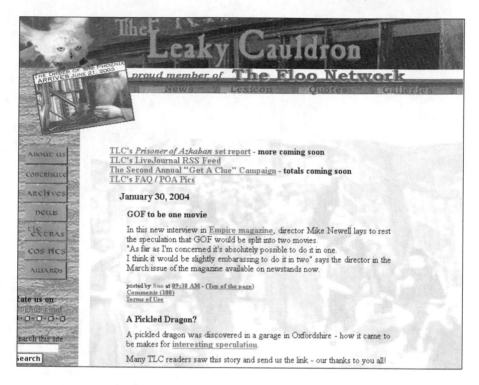

become the Harry Potter site of record, hosting the oldest and most comprehensive Potter news archive on the web." Like Mugglenet.com, this is an indispensable website.

The Scotsman

www.scotsman.com

This newspaper is Rowling's hometown newspaper and, as such, is first in reportage of news about her comings and goings.

Appendices

Tim Kirk

Appendix A
Books by J. K. Rowling: In Print and Audio

Note: In the U.S., Scholastic publishes the Harry Potter novels; in the U.K., Bloomsbury is the publisher. All other publishers are duly noted. The prices are the suggested retail prices.

U.S. Editions

Harry Potter and the Sorcerer's Stone
1. Hardback, $19.95

2. Paperback, $6.99

3. Audiocassette (unabridged) read by Jim Dale, $35

4. Compact disc (unabridged) read by Jim Dale, $49.95

5. Gift edition, out of print

Harry Potter and the Chamber of Secrets
1. Hardback, $19.95

2. Paperback, $6.99

3. Audiocassette (unabridged) read by Jim Dale, $35

4. Compact disc (unabridged) read by Jim Dale, $49.95

5. Gift edition, out of print

Harry Potter and the Prisoner of Azkaban

1. Hardback, $19.95

2. Paperback, $6.99

3. Audiocassette (unabridged) read by Jim Dale, $35

4. Compact disc (unabridged) read by Jim Dale, $49.95

5. Gift edition, out of print

Harry Potter and the Goblet of Fire

1. Hardback, $25.95

2. Paperback, $8.99

3. Audiocassette (unabridged) read by Jim Dale, $25.95

4. Compact disc (unabridged) read by Jim Dale, $69.95

5. Gift edition, out of print

6. Large print (Thorndike Press), $25.95

Harry Potter and the Order of the Phoenix

1. Hardback, $29.99

2. Paperback, $9.99

3. Audiocassette (unabridged) read by Jim Dale, $45

4. Compact disc (unabridged) read by Jim Dale, $75

5. Deluxe edition, slipcased: $60. (Note: The dust jacket features new art by Mary GrandPré; the art used for the dust jacket of the trade hardback is printed in color as its endpapers.)

Harry Potter and the Half-Blood Prince

1. Hardback, $29.99

2. Library binding: $34.99

3. Paperback: $9.99

4. Audiocassette (unabridged) read by Jim Dale, $50

5. Compact disc (unabridged) read by Jim Dale, $75

6. Deluxe edition, slipcased: $60. The slipcase and dust jacket sport a new illustration by Mary GrandPré; also, in the back of the book, all the interior art by GrandPré from this book is reprinted in the "Illustration Showcase" at nearly 100 percent of the size of the original art. The full color endpapers repeat the art from the trade edition's dust jacket.

Boxed Sets

1. In hardback, books 1–6 in a cardboard slipcase, $158.94

2. In trade paperback, books 1–6 in a cardboard slipcase, $50.94

3. Harry Potter Schoolbooks Boxed Set: Two Classic Books from the Library of Hogwarts School of Witchcraft and Wizardry; cardboard slipcase containing two "BT bound" (hardback) books written under Rowling's pen names: *Quidditch Through the Ages,* by Kennilworthy Whisp, and *Fantastic Beasts and Where to Find Them,* by Newt Scamander, $12.95.

U.K. Editions

Note: In the U.K., two editions of the books and audiotapes were published: one edition for children, and one edition for adults. There is no difference in the texts; however, the cover art is changed to reflect the age difference.

On the Bloomsbury website, it lists the print runs for the first editions in hardback: *Philospher's Stone,* 500; *Chamber of Secrets,* 10,150; *Azkaban,* 10,100; *Goblet of Fire,* 1 million. (No figures are available for *Order of the Phoenix* and *Half-Blood Prince.*)

Harry Potter and the Philosopher's Stone

1. Hardback
   a. Children's edition, £11.99
   b. Adult edition, out of print

2. Paperback
   a. Children's edition, £5.99
   b. Adult edition, £6.99

3. Unabridged audiocassette read by Stephen Fry
   a. Children's edition, £21.99
   b. Adult edition, £21.99
   c. Cassettes and travel bag, £23.99

4. Unabridged compact disc read by Stephen Fry
    a. Children's edition, £25.99
    b. Adult edition, £49.99
    c. CD and travel bag, £39.99

5. Special edition in hardback, £10

Harry Potter and the Chamber of Secrets

1. Hardback
    a. Children's edition, £11.99
    b. Adult edition, out of print

2. Paperback
    a. Children's edition, £5.99
    b. Adult edition, £6.99

3. Unabridged audiocassette read by Stephen Fry
    a. Children's edition, £21.99
    b. Adult edition, £21.99

4. Unabridged compact disc read by Stephen Fry
    a. Children's edition, £25.99
    b. Adult edition, none

5. Special edition, £10

6. Large-print edition, £13.95

Harry Potter and the Prisoner of Azkaban

1. Hardback
    a. Children's edition, £11.99
    b. Adult edition, out of print

2. Paperback
    a. Children's edition, £5.99
    b. Adult edition, £6.99

3. Unabridged audiocassette read by Stephen Fry
    a. Children's edition, £26.99
    b. Adult edition, £26.99

4. Unabridged compact disc read by Stephen Fry
    a. Children's edition, £31.99
    b. Adult edition, no information available

5. Special edition, £10

6. Large-print trade paperback, £13.95

Harry Potter and the Goblet of Fire

1. Hardback
    a. Children's edition, £14.99
    b. Adult edition, not available

2. Paperback
    a. Children's edition, £6.99
    b. Adult edition, £6.99

3. Unabridged audiocassette read by Stephen Fry
    a. Children's edition, £49.99
    b. Adult edition, no information available

4. Unabridged compact disc read by Stephen Fry
    a. Children's edition, £59.99
    b. Adult edition, no information available

5. Special edition, £25

Harry Potter and the Order of the Phoenix

1. Hardback
    a. Children's edition, £16.99
    b. Adult edition, £16.99

2. Paperback
    a. Children's edition, £7.99
    b. Adult edition, £7.99

3. Unabridged audiocassette read by Stephen Fry
    a. Children's edition, £65
    b. Adult edition, £65

4. Unabridged compact disc read by Stephen Fry
    a. Children's edition, £75
    b. Adult edition, £75

5. Special edition, £30

Harry Potter and the Half-Blood Prince

1. Hardback
    a. Children's edition, £16.99
    b. Adult edition, £16.99

2. Paperback
    a. Children's edition, £7.99
    b. Adult edition, £7.99

343

3. Unabridged audiocassette read by Stephen Fry
   a. Children's edition, £55
   b. Adult edition, £55

4. Unabridged compact disc read by Stephen Fry
   a. Children's edition, £65
   b. Adult edition, £65

5. Special edition, £30

Boxed Sets

1. Adult edition, hardback, books 1–6 in a cardboard slipcase, £85.

2. Children's edition, trade paperback, books 1–6 in a cardboard slipcase, £41.

Appendix B
Filmography and Videography

DVDs

Discovering the Real World of Harry Potter, $15, from Questar, May 2002. Running time, 74 minutes.

An authorized profile narrated by British actor Hugh Laurie, this is a professionally produced documentary that aired on PBS. It focuses on real-world places associated with Rowling, supplemented by interviews with David Colbert (producer of the Harry Potter films) and Lindsey Fraser (author of *Conversations with J. K. Rowling*). Recommended.

The Magical World of Harry Potter: The Unauthorized Story of J. K. Rowling, out-of-print, from Eaton Entertainment, August 2000. Running time, 30 minutes. An unauthorized profile.

The coverage of Rowling is limited to two public appearances; the bulk of the footage focuses on interviews with booksellers and children. The most interesting footage is an interview with members of the Potter family, whom Rowling knew in her early years.

Harry Potter Film Adaptations

Note: DVD has replaced VHS as the preferred home entertainment format. Offering a better picture, clearer sound, and more storage capacity, the DVD format is clearly superior in every way.

Two DVD formats are available: widescreen, sometimes called letterboxing, in which you see the same proportions as seen at the theater; and fullscreen, in which the left and right sides of the frame are chopped off to fit a conventional television screen.

Harry Potter and the Sorcerer's Stone [#1], $26.99, from Warner Home Video, 2002. Available in VHS and in two DVD formats: widescreen and fullscreen. (The DVD set is comprised of two discs: #1 is the movie itself, with 34 scenes, end credits, and theatrical trailers; and #2 is comprised of supplementary material.)

For Potter fans, the bonus disk is packed with material especially designed for younger fans:

Additional Scenes: There are deleted scenes from the theatrical release available on the disk, but they are hidden. You must find the clues in the areas below to access the hidden scenes.

Diagon Alley: In a courtyard behind the Leaky Cauldron, a brick wall bars the way to Diagon Alley. But if you choose the right bricks in the right order, the brick wall reshuffles itself, so you can enter Diagon Alley, where you'll need to shop for school supplies. You'll need a wand, so be sure to stop at Ollivanders; you won't have to choose a wand, for the wand will choose *you*. The Owl Emporium is your next stop and, as the narrator suggests, an owl is air mail, whereas only a Muggle would want to use the slower, and less reliable, Muggle Mail for delivery. The third stop is, of course, Gringotts Bank, where you'll need to go to get money to buy the wand and owl. (Hint: Go to the bank first.)

Common Room, Great Hall, Harry's Room: These are self-navigated tours using Apple's Quicktime to provide a 360-degree view of these rooms as seen in the films.

Library: This is like no other library you've ever seen. Pull a book off the shelf, open it, and be prepared for anything. See pictures talk on the walls and watch ghosts walk.

Classes: As a student you'll be expected to learn how to prepare potions and cast spells. Here's where you get a little hands-on experience.

Quidditch: Learn more about wizards' favorite sport and see if you, like Harry Potter, can catch the Golden Snitch. (It's harder than it looks!) You can also look for the Mirror of Erised, where you may be able to find your heart's desire.

Bonus: If you have a CD-ROM drive on your PC-compatible computer (there's no Mac version available), you can access special features. "Be Sorted. Receive owl messages. Collect Wizard cards. Enhance your Hogwarts tour. Transform your computer with downloadable features. Sample Harry Potter games, and more."

Harry Potter and the Chamber of Secrets [#2], $29.95, from Warner Home Video, 2003. Available in VHS and in two DVD formats: widescreen and fullscreen. (The DVD set is comprised of two discs: #1 is the movie itself, with 36 scenes and end credits, and some special features, such as cast and crew, year one at Hogwarts, and the theatrical trailer; and #2 is comprised of bonus material, with more elaborate [and imaginative] fare than on the first DVD.)

Behind Hogwarts: An in-depth interview with Rowling, conducted by Steve Kloves, opens this section, followed by interviews with the principal cast. Also in this section, an extensive gallery of production sketches and a look at Professor Dumbledore's office, where you can simply take a tour or, alternately, build a scene.

Activities: Tour the Chamber of Secrets and take the Chamber Challenge, if you're up to it. After screwing your courage to the sticking place, ask yourself if you're up to Forbidden Forest Challenge. For weaker hearts, stick to a tour of Colin's photographic Darkroom, or tour Diagon Alley with your fellow wizards.

Gilderoy Lockhart's Classroom: Check out his list of required reading, see Certificates, and view a photo gallery.

Spellcaster Knowledge: Think you know your spells? Test your knowledge in this section.

The second disc also has a demo of the EA Game based on the movie and, unlike the first DVD *(Harry Potter and the Sorcerer's Stone),* readily available additional scenes, which can be played individually or collectively.

Harry Potter and the Prisoner of Azkaban [#3], $19.98, from Warner Home Video, 2004. Available in VHS and in two DVD formats: widescreen and fullscreen. (The DVD set is comprised of two discs: #1 is the movie itself, and #2 is comprised of supplementary material.)
Supplementary material:

1. "Creating the Vision" interview with J. K. Rowling and the filmmakers
2. Interviews with the cast lead by Johnny Vaughan and the Shrunken Head
3. Three "challenge" games
4. "Conjuring a Scene" making-of featurette
5. "Care of Magical Creatures" animal trainer featurette
6. Self-guided iPIX tours into Honeydukes and Professor Lupin's classroom
7. Choir Practice: sing along with the Hogwarts choir
8. Hogwarts Portrait Gallery
9. Hogwarts Timeline
10. Electronic Arts game preview
11. DVD-ROM Features: Wizard Trading Cards
12. Theatrical Trailers

Harry Potter and the Goblet of Fire [#4], $23.99, from Warner Home Video, 2006. Available in VHS and in two DVD formats: widescreen and fullscreen. (The DVD set is comprised of two discs: #1 is the movie itself, and #2 is comprised of supplementary material.)

Supplementary material:

1. Conversations with the cast: Daniel Radcliffe, Emma Watson, and Rupert Grint
2. Preparing for the Yule Ball
3. Reflections on the Fourth Film
4. Triwizard Tournament, Dragon Arena: Dragon Challenge, Harry vs. the Horntail: The First Task, Meet the Champions
5. Triwizard Tournament, Lake: Lake Challenge, In Too Deep: The Second Task
6. Triwizard Tournament, Maze: Maze Challenge, To the Graveyard and Back Challenge, The Maze: The Third Task, He Who Must Not Be Named
7. Theatrical trailer
8. DVD-ROM features: EA Game Demo, Hogwarts Timeline, Web Interactivity

Appendix C
Key Collectibles: Books

A friend of mine who has a fortune invested in his Stephen King collection saw a book he wanted on eBay. He ordered it and was surprised to discover that it was unsigned. He contacted the seller, who apologized profusely and said, "I must have accidentally sent the unsigned copy I had." The skeptical collector surreptitiously marked in light pencil a page picked at random, and then returned it. A week later, the promised replacement book was sent with the promised signature; however, it was the same copy that the buyer had returned. In other words, the seller simply forged King's signature on the returned book!

That's the problem with online bid sites, unless they are bona fide auction houses like Sotheby's or Bloomsbury Auctions of London. How are you, as the buyer, to know that what you're buying is in fact a legitimately signed copy?

As Rowling pointed out on her website, in an initial visit to eBay, of every six or seven books purportedly signed by her, only one was in fact genuine; the rest were forgeries. More recently, she said that she could only find *one* genuinely signed book.

Clearly, eBay needs to do more—a *lot* more—to police itself, or at least have mechanisms in place to allow the copyright holder to comment.

My recommendation to eBay is twofold: First, to add a prominent buyer's advisory that appears on the auction page of the item in question, in which Rowling's comments are prominently posted. That way, you at least have been forewarned. Second, every signed item should have a section in which the copyright holder can check off an opinion on whether or not the signature is genuine:

1. The signature is mine.
2. The signature is definitely *not* mine.
3. I'm not sure if the signature is mine.

There should also be a mechanism in which the copyright holder can make specific comments about the item in question.

Those two steps would go a long way toward minimizing the sale of fraudulent goods on eBay.

The unfortunate thing is that there *are* legitimately signed Rowling books on eBay, but how can you be sure? And do you want to spend hundreds (or perhaps thousands) of dollars based merely on what the seller has stated?

Until eBay and other online sellers institute some commonsense policies that protect the copyright holder and prospective customers, I advise you to buy from either auction houses or a rare book dealer.

1. www.abebooks.com, a community of more than 13,500 independent booksellers worldwide, is a recommended place to buy signed Rowling books. Use the advanced search feature to look for signed books. Also, specializing in booksellers from the United Kingdom: www.aba.org.uk.

2. www.bloomsburyauctions.com lists Rowling books at its auctions labeled Modern First Editions, General Books, and Children's and Illustrated Books. Typically, the price is within the range the auction house estimates.

3. www.sothebys.com is a highly regarded auction house that deals in signed Rowling books.

Here are some general guidelines:

The Commonsense Rule

If the item in question seems too good to be true—i.e., its price seems to be exceptionally low—then you should be properly skeptical.

Prices

Because prices vary considerably, it's best to consult the current market value at www.abebooks.com or the final sales price realized at an auction house.

Original Manuscripts

To my knowledge, there has only been one holographic (i.e., handwritten) manuscript that's surfaced, and that was for a charity auction. A brief outline by Rowling, expected to fetch $9,400, sold for an astonishing $45,314.

Don't expect to see a manuscript for sale from any source other than an auction house to raise money for charity, and expect it to cost tens of thousands of dollars—well beyond the reach of most fans.

Signed Postcards and Letters

Rowling does occasionally answer fan letters, but few have surfaced on the marketplace. Clearly, most of the recipients would rather not sell at any price, though eventually some of these letters will surface.

Signed Books

Rowling has estimated that she's signed tens of thousands of books, but the days of bookstore signings are, unfortunately, over. Early on in her career, Rowling supported signings on both sides of the pond for books one through three, but with *The Goblet of Fire*, it was obviously impossible to do so, and Rowling's public appearances were subsequently limited to large venues where signings were impossible.

In recent years, Rowling has signed few copies of her novels, and those few have been offered through auction houses. However, 400 copies of *The Goblet of Fire* were signed for the 21st Annual International Festival of Authors (Toronto, Canada, Oct. 24, 2000); more recently, 500 copies of *The Half-Blood Prince* were signed for the Harry, Carrie, and Garp readings (New York City, August 1–2, 2006).

In both instances, copies have surfaced on eBay, but the discerning buyer should ask for incontrovertible proof: for *Goblet,* ask for the hand-signed certificate of authenticity on letterhead from the Administrative Director of the Centre. (Be dubious if you are offered a mere photocopy.) And for *Half-Blood Prince,* ask to see a photocopied or scanned receipt of the four tickets purchased ($250 each) and a photocopy of the mailing label *addressed to the seller.* (To be on the safe side, ask for the original copy of the mailing label, so you can assure yourself that it is genuine.)

The importance of documentation cannot be overstated. *You can no longer take a stranger's word as to the authenticity of a signed book,* unless you personally know the seller or are buying from a reputable rare book dealer or an auction house.

General Considerations Affecting a Book's Price

Condition. In the book world, the highest grade is fine, which means like new. (As a general rule, booksellers do not use the word "mint" to describe books.) The better the condition of the book, the higher the price.

Signature. A legimate signature by Rowling greatly increases the value of the book. It may be flat-signed (signature only) or, if she has the time, it may be inscribed.

Of course, if the book is signed to someone important to Rowling, it's an associational copy, which makes it more valuable than a flat-signed book. (One inscribed copy of *Goblet of Fire*, auctioned off by Sotheby's, fetched $48,000. It had been signed by Rowling to her father.)

Bookplates. If Rowling has a bookplate (and I don't know that she does), it would show that the book is from her personal collection, and thus of great interest. If it's a bookplate by someone who is not recognizable, it detracts from its value.

Markings. The author is the *only* person who should sign the book. If the book's owner signs it, or otherwise marks the book, it detracts from the book's value.

Clipped price. This is usually done by someone who is giving the book as a gift and doesn't want the recipient to know how much was paid for it, but it detracts from the book's value.

Book jacket. The most fragile component of the book, the dust jacket is very susceptible to tears, cuts, and disfiguring. Even if the book is in fine condition, unless the jacket is also in fine condition, the value of the book is diminished.

U.K. Editions

First editions for all the U.K. Potter novels are marked by a row of descending numbers to indicate their printing: 10 9 8 7 6 5 4 3 2 1. The *lowest* number indicates its printing. (The other popular alternative is to simply state First Edition on the legal page.)

The Deluxe Editions do *not* have dust jackets.

The prices below are from Bloomsbury Auctions reflecting the estimated range before the auction and, after the auction, the hammer price (which does not include the buyer's premium). These are first editions in fine condition.

Note to U.S. readers: Exchange rates fluctuate, so it's best to go to an online currency converter website to determine the equivalent in USD (U.S. dollars). One such site is www.oanda.com/convert/classic.

Note to all readers: The prices below are approximate values only, and as is the case with collectibles, market value will dictate *current* prices.

Year 1 at Hogwarts: *Harry Potter and the Philosopher's Stone* went to print with a very small 500-copy edition in hardback (with a laminated cover) and 200 proof copies.

The first Harry Potter book, this is the cornerstone of any Potter book collection.

Of the 500-copy edition: £15,000 to £20,000. Final: £17,000.

Of the 200-copy edition: £2,000 to £3,000. Final: £4,200. (Note: the proof copy has Rowling's name misspelled: J. A. Rowling.)

Year 2 at Hogwarts: *Harry Potter and the Chamber of Secrets*. In hardback with dust jacket. First printing: 10,150 copies.

A presentation copy: £1,000 to £1,500. Final: £3,000.

An uncorrected proof copy: £1,500 to £2,500. Final: £1,500.

First edition: £750 to £1,000. Final: £1,400.

Year 3 at Hogwarts: *Harry Potter and the Prisoner of Azkaban*. In hardback with dust jacket, there are two states: (1) on page 7, a misaligned text block; also, the copyright page states Copyright Joanne Rowling, and (2) on page 7, the text block is properly aligned, and the copyright page states J. K. Rowling. First printing: 10,000 copies.

A proof copy (one of 50 copies): £800 to £1,000. Final: £1,200.

A proof copy, second state: £300 to £400. Final: £650.

First deluxe edition (with signed bookplate laid in): £750 to £1,000. Final: £900.

First deluxe edition (without bookplate): £700 to £900. Final: £800.

First edition, first state (see note 1 above): £800 to £1,000. Final: £800.

First edition: £100 to £150. Final: £180.

Year 4 at Hogwarts: *Harry Potter and the Goblet of Fire*. In hardback with dust jacket. First printing, one million copies.

First deluxe edition (with signed bookplate laid in): £100 to £150. Final: £60.

First edition signed by author: £120 to £180. Final: £250.

First edition without corrections: £60 to £80.

First edition: £40 to £60.

Year 5 at Hogwarts: *Harry Potter and the Order of the Phoenix*. In hardback with dust jacket.

First edition signed by author: £1,500 to £2,000. Final: £2,700. (This copy came with a letter of authentication from Rowling's personal assistant.)

Rowling in Dough: Peter J. Rowling Sells His Harry Potter Novels

It's not unusual to see first editions of the Harry Potter novels up for auction at the prestigious Sotheby's, but four copies that sold in December 2003 stood out; in fact, they were unique: presentation copies from Joanne Rowling to her father, Peter. Of the seven offered for sale, four sold for a total of $87,600:

Book 1: *Harry Potter and the Philosopher's Stone* (U.K., paperback, first edition), for $9,600.

Book 2: *Harry Potter and the Chamber of Secrets* (U.K., hardback, first edition), for $10,800.

Book 3: *Harry Potter and the Prisoner of Azkaban* (U.K., hardback, first edition), for $19,200. (On the copyright page, Rowling circled the number "one" to indicate it is a first edition copy, with a pointing arrow highlighting a cautionary comment, "Guard it with your lives!!!")

Book 4: *Harry Potter and the Goblet of Fire* (U.K., hardback, first edition), for $48,000. What made this copy unusual was a lengthy handwritten note by Joanne in which she talked about the origins of a fictional character, Ron Weasley, with cartoons drawn on the bottom of the page.

Collector's note: By this time Rowling no longer supported bookstore signings because of logistical concerns: It simply was impossible to sign copies for all the people who showed up. From this point forward, Rowling's public appearances would be limited to large venues where it was impossible to get books signed, unless other provisions were made.

In the case of this book, the Canadian publisher arranged for 400 copies to be signed for her appearance in October 2000 in Toronto at the Harbourfront Centres International Festival of Authors, which drew 20,264 people.

Very few authenticated U.K. or U.S. copies have surfaced, though most signed copies of this book have come from her appearance at the Festival of Authors.

Year 6 at Hogwarts: *Harry Potter and the Half-Blood Prince.* In hardback with dust jacket.

First edition signed by the author, with a letter from Rowling's personal assistant laid in: £2,000 to £2,500. Final: £2,400.

Collector's note: To support a joint reading with Stephen King and John Irving (August 1–2, 2006, Radio City Music Hall, New York City), Rowling agreed to sign copies of the American hardback edition of this book. I have not been able to confirm the actual number of copies signed, but since King and Irving also signed copies of their books, and the books were sold as sets, it's likely that Rowling signed 250 copies for each night, for a total of 500 signed copies, as King reportedly signed that number. In order to get the set of signed books, the customer had to buy a family pack of seats (four seats at $250 each, with a minimum of $1,000); the set of signed books was shipped after the event.

Few copies have surfaced on eBay, where I've seen it offered for $2,000-plus. On other online book sites, I've seen it offered for $3,000.

Before you buy, ask for a scan of the receipt showing the $1,000 paid for the four tickets, a copy of the letterhead addressed to the recipient (sent with the signed book), and the original shipping box in which the books were sent. That, to me, is sufficient provenance in this case. (Furthermore, if you had a mind to do so, surely this information could be verified by Scholastic, which probably kept records of to whom they sent books.)

U.S. Editions

All U.S. editions were published in hardback with dust jacket, including the special editions. The text varies from the U.K. editions because it was thought some British words would be confusing to U.S. readers; e.g., in the U.K., the word for "sweater" is jumper.

The prices below are drawn from www.abebooks.com.

Year One at Hogwarts: *Harry Potter and the Sorcerer's Stone*. In hardback with dust jacket.
First edition, first state: $6,889. (Among its identifying points: The review on the dust jacket is from the British newspaper, *The Guardian*.)
First edition, second state: $5,500.
Proof copy: $3,500.

Year Two at Hogwarts: *Harry Potter and the Chamber of Secrets*. In hardback with dust jacket. Announced first printing: 250,000 copies.
First edition, a signed copy: $1,000 to $2,749
Proof copy: $600 to $1,489
First edition: $650 to $700

Year Three at Hogwarts: *Harry Potter and the Prisoner of Azkaban*. In hardback with dust jacket.
First edition, a signed copy: $889 to $2,449
Proof copy: $600 to $995
First edition: $390

Year Four at Hogwarts: *Harry Potter and the Goblet of Fire*. In hardback with dust jacket.

First edition, signed by illustrator Mary GrandPré, with an original full-page drawing; an edition of 25 copies: $3,500.

First edition, signed by Rowling: $760.

First edition: $45 to $150.

Year Five at Hogwarts: *Harry Potter and the Order of the Phoenix*. In hardback with dust jacket.

First edition: $30 to $50.

Year Six at Hogwarts: *Harry Potter and the Half-Blood Prince*. In hardback with dust jacket.

First edition: $10 to $30.

First edition signed by Mary GrandPré: $200.

First edition signed by J. K. Rowling: $3,000.

Special deluxe collector's edition: $200.

Recommended Dealers

On her website, J. K. Rowling has repeatedly expressed her concerns about signed books offered on eBay (and, by extension, photos as well), and for good reason. Case in point: I was recently contacted about an alleged signature of Rowling's in an unauthorized biography about her. After examining the signature, I determined it was a fake, especially after reading Rowling's postings in the news section of her website.

In this particular case, the forgery was rather blatant. Rowling, on her website, stated that there was ". . . in one case, an unauthorised biography that I would never, and have never, put my signature to."

Unfortunately, the eBay seller had originally paid more than $400 for the book and was trying to resell it but discovered there were no takers. Though she's trying to press her case with eBay and the original buyer, it's probably too late. Prevention, not a cure, is called for here.

That said, the fact remains that authentic Rowling signatures do crop up on eBay from time to time, but they are almost always offered not from private parties but well-established rare book dealers or auction houses, which can provide provenance: indisputable proof of previous ownership. For instance, Bloomsbury Auctions (www.bloomsburyauctions.com) is a London-based auction house that offers signed Rowling books, some accompanied by a letter from Rowling's personal assistant attesting that the signature is genuine.

Bloomsbury Auctions does publish online the auction results, so you'll have a pretty good idea of what you should expect to pay for a verifiably signed copy of a Rowling novel (British edition).

If you don't want to go the auction route, Bloomsbury recommends a British bookseller, Adrian Harrington Rare Books (www.harrington books.co.uk) on Kensington Church Street in Kensington, London.

As expected, you'll find no bargains at Harrington Rare Books, but you will get what you pay for: an authentic signature, as opposed to eBay where the signature is questionable.

Of course, there are numerous other antiquarian booksellers, all of whom can be found on www.abebooks.com, who also provide signed copies of Rowling's books, but in the end—whether you buy online or at a brick-and-mortar store, whether you buy from a U.S. dealer or one in the U.K.— it comes down to this: **Do you trust the source from whom you are buying?**

As always, if the deal sounds too good to be true, it usually is, and for good reason: It's likely a fake. Though many things change in the collectibles market, one thing remains true: You need to know how to identify the real goods from the fool's gold (the real signature as opposed to the fake one), and your best insurance is to buy from a reputable dealer.

Appendix D
Harry Potter Collectibles

I knew about the alarm clock. How do I feel about it? Honestly, I think it's pretty well known, if I could have stopped all merchandising I would have done [so]. And twice a year I sit down with Warner Brothers and we have conversations about merchandising and I can only say you should have seen some of the stuff that was stopped: Moaning Myrtle lavatory seat alarms and worse.

—*Rowling on merchandising from BBC News online*

I have a friend who was a Disney Imagineer. One of the projects he worked on, for a fellow Imagineer, was designing a haunted bathroom. One of its features was a mirror that, when you look into it, revealed a skeletal face staring back. Just the thing to get your attention in the morning, I think.

I *love* the idea of a haunted bathroom, so I have no problem with a Moaning Myrtle toilet seat. I imagine that when the lid is up, the toilet would emit a mournful wail; or, possibly, when you flush it, you could hear Myrtle moaning or diving into the water.

A missed opportunity for merchandising, I think, but Rowling obviously has input, so we've not seen anything that would truly offend anyone's sensibilities. (I doubt she has veto power, but if she's against a specific idea for a merchandised item, I can't see that Warner Bros. would go ahead over her strenuous objections.)

Mugglenet.com used to keep track of all the toys and merchandising, but the list changed so frequently that it was impossible to keep it current. In fact, a collector's guide to Harry Potter material would run hundreds of pages, since there are dozens of licensees that produce everything from candy to high-end collectibles.

The big news in the Harry Potter community is that Warner Bros. Consumer Products, in July 2006, put into place a multi-year licensing agreement with NECA, Inc., for North America, Latin America, and Asia Pacific. According to a press release from Warner Bros., NECA will "develop a range of gifts, toys, and specialty products including collectible action figures, plush dolls, mugs, wall décor, and more, all inspired by the characters, creatures, and themes from the Harry Potter stories. As the Harry Potter series has matured with each subsequent film, so has its audience. The assortment of products being created by NECA will therefore be geared to appeal to older, loyal fans that have followed the stories over the years, while still offering something for younger fans that are new to the series."

Harry Potter™ as Gryffindor™ Seeker
(Courtesy Tonner Doll Company, Inc.)

NECA already sells toys from *The Lord of the Rings* and *Pirates of the Caribbean,* among other film-related properties, so it's well positioned and experienced to sell film-related Harry Potter products. New Potter films will be released in 2007 (*Order of the Phoenix*), in 2008 (*Half-Blood Prince*), and in 2009 (*Deathly Hallows*).

In the meantime, as we wait for NECA to roll out its new Harry Potter line, here are my recommendations.

The Tonner Doll Company

The Tonner Doll Company (www.tonnerdoll.com) has a high-quality line of dolls based on the principal characters from the Harry Potter novels. The likenesses are quite good and the prices, considering the quality of the work and the size of the dolls, strike me as very reasonable.

The quality of the work can best be seen in larger photos, so here and in the color section I've placed photos of some of the dolls below:

a. Hedwig on a tree stand (eight inches tall, $49.99)
b. A Firebolt (16 inches tall, $49.99)
c. A Triwizard Cup (4.5 inches tall, $39.99)
d. Crookshanks (4 inches tall, $29.99)
e. A set of Quidditch accessories (8 inches long, $99.99)
f. Harry Potter as a Gryffindor Seeker ($159.99)
g. Harry Potter in Muggle street clothes ($79)
h. Ron Weasley in Muggle street clothes ($74.99)
i. Hermione Granger in Muggle street clothes ($79.99)
j. Harry Potter in Hogwarts school robes ($124.99)
k. Harry Potter at the Yule Ball ($149.99)
l. Ron Weasley in Hogwarts school robes ($124.99)
m. Ron Weasley at the Yule Ball ($149.99)
n. Hermione Granger in Hogwarts school robes ($124.99)
o. Hermione Granger at the Yule Ball ($149.99)

Hedwig™ (left), Hermione Granger™, and Crookshanks™ (Courtesy Tonner Doll Company, Inc.)

Giclee Prints

A line of artwork printed by the giclee process features the talents of Jim Salvati, Fred Bode, and U.S. illustrator of the Harry Potter books, Mary GrandPré. Issued in limited editions (a few hundred, at most), these high-quality, full color prints have a high fidelity to the original art. (As the original art is owned by Warner Bros. and is not for sale, these prints are the best way to own affordable reproductions of the commissioned pieces, which were used for calendars and prints.)

Because these are limited editions and signed by the artists in question, they have investment potential. These are usually available from art dealers who specialize in cartoon or animation art, both online and at brick-and-mortar stores.

The prints, sold unframed, include:

1. Harry Potter: Battle with the Dragon. Mary GrandPré. Print size, 11 x 14 inches. Edition run of 250 copies. $150.

2. Harry Potter and the Sorcerer's Stone: Quidditch. Mary GrandPré. Print size, 11 x 14 inches. Edition run of 250 copies. $150.

3. Harry Potter and the Sorcerer's Stone. Mary GrandPré. Print size, 21.5 x 26 inches. Edition run of 250 copies. $325.

4. Harry Potter and the Prisoner of Azkaban. Mary GrandPré. Print size, 11 x 14 inches. Edition run of 250 copies. $150. (A larger version, 21.5 x 26 inches, is $350.)

5. Harry Potter: Christmas in the Great Hall. Mary GrandPré. Print size, 11 x 14 inches. Edition run of 250 copies. $150.

6. Harry Potter: The Enchanted Car. Mary GrandPré. Print size, 11 x 14 inches. Edition run of 250 copies. $150.

7. Harry Potter Portfolio. Mary GrandPré. A numbered edition of 100 sets, this includes six prints and a bonus print (Harry Potter: The Flying Keys). Print size, 11 x 14 inches. $1,050.

8. Harry Potter: Dueling Wizards. Mary GrandPré. Print size, 11 x 14 inches. Edition run of 250 copies. $150.

9. Harry Potter: Counting the Days. Mary GrandPré. Print size, 11 x 14 inches. Edition run of 250 copies. $150.

10. Harry Potter: Three Broomsticks. Mary GrandPré. Print size, 11 x 14 inches. Edition run of 250 copies. $200.

11. Harry Potter and the Sorcerer's Stone: In Potions Class. Fred Bode. Print size, 21 x 29 inches. Edition run of 100 copies. $595.

12. Harry Potter and the Sorcerer's Stone: Harry's Key Flight. Fred Bode. Edition run of 250 copies. $250.

13. Harry Potter: The Maze. Jim Salvati. Print size, 17 x 22.25 inches. Edition run of 250 copies. $225. (On canvas, 21.75 x 28.5 inches, $550.)

14. Harry Potter: Full Moon at Hogwarts. Jim Salvati. Print size, 17 x 20.5 inches. Edition run of 250 copies. $225. (On canvas, 21.75 x 25.75 inches, $550.)

Some tips: Prints are very fragile and require careful handling, especially since fingers are naturally oily and can mar the print's surface. Likewise, prints are very susceptible to denting.

When storing prints, either store them flat or in an oversized mailing tube. The storage room should be air-conditioned and have low humidity; otherwise, the paper can absorb the moisture content in the air and the paper will warp.

When framing, under *no* circumstances allow the framer to permanently affix the print to the back of a matte board. The print should hang freely, secured by a single acid-free adhesive tape, and the matte board should be acid-free, as well.

Whirlwood Magick Wands

"I bought a wand from another wand maker and I had nothing but problems. I started to bark or neigh or meow at the most embarrassing moments. I even had weeds sprouting from my nose every time I sneezed. But once I bought a Whirlwood Wand, all those problems cleared up. The only side effect I've noticed with your wand is that I tend to levitate a little every time I use it. Well, it's either the wand or the Snorkblains hoisting me up by my armpits, but I don't care. I enjoy the sensation."

—"Ever So Grateful" in
Belgium, Ms. Zelladora

For the well-heeled wizard, Whirlwood Magick Wands (www.whirlwood.com) offers an outstanding selection, from the moderately priced to the very pricey. Designed, hand-manufactured, and finished by artisan Gary Hall, his line of wands are constructed from durable hardwoods, with each wand encased in a two-piece box lined with purple paper, and a gold-tasseled velvet sleeve.

Prices range from those who can only afford a few Knuts or Sickles to those who can shell out Galleons, so there's something for everyone. (My favorite is the L-Dragoo, a wand with a hidden chamber in which you can insert what you want in its core.)

An artisan of the first order, Gary Hall's wands are works of art.

For any Harry Potter fan who wants to complete his wardrobe, a wand from Whirlwood is a must.

Though framing is a preference, choose wooden frames instead of metal ones, since a wooden frame allows for a dust cover to be installed. (A metal one does not allow a dust cover to be installed, and is thus more prone to print warpage.)

Although there are many sources online for children's art, I recommend Art-cade, a cozy gallery located in southeast Virginia. The gallery has an excellent line of originals, giclees, paper prints, sculpture, and books that cater to cartoon and animation fans. Among the lines it carries: Dr. Seuss Fine Art, Greenwich Workshop, Disney Fine Art, Mill Pond Press, Bethany Lowe Designs, and sculpture by Richard Masioski and Mark Hopkins.

Storeowners Mickey and Arlene Sego have chosen wisely and well, and their inventory reflects their sensibilities: affordable art that tells a story.

If you can't make the trip to Williamsburg, Virginia, then check out the store's website at www.artcadeonline.com.

The Noble Collection

Well known for its movie tie-in products (*The Lord of the Rings* and *The Da Vinci Code*), the Noble Collection sells exclusively through its website and print catalog; it does not sell through retailers or big-box stores.

The web address is www.noblecollection.com.

The line of Harry Potter products is diverse. Unlike the giclee prints, which are limited in number and signed, the Noble Collection line of products is issued in an open edition and thus does not have investment potential, until the line stops and availability dries up.

The Noble Collection's Harry Potter line includes wands, sculptures, jewelry, writing implements, coins, pendants, and film artifacts.

After looking at several catalogs from the Noble Collection, I have mixed feelings about its line of merchandise. On one hand, I think the jewelry, sculptures, specific artifacts, and wand replicas are especially well done, but products like "Hagrid's Cottage Candle Holder" ($45) strike a dissonant chord with me: Although it's hand-painted porcelain, the idea of sticking a candle inside a hut, which looks like something out of a Thomas Kinkaide painting, doesn't work for me. The end result is simply movie kitsch. (Hey, kids, what about a Lord Voldemort Candle Holder with the candle being inserted in the Dark Lord's . . . oh, never mind!)

Another example: the "Sorting Hat Display" ($25), which has an ornate base topped with the weathered Sorting Hat, and four insets where pens can be inserted. In other words, it doesn't really capture the whimsical quality of the Sorting Hat (as does the full-size reproduction, which can be worn). Again, what we have here is kitsch.

One complaint about the website's main page: The initial pictures are too small to show the detail work. For instance, there's a sculpture of Fawkes the Phoenix ($125), but we get a head shot, although the piece stands 14 inches high.

Similarly, a 34-inch replica of the Godric Gryffindor Sword shows a photo of the handle only—not enough (to my mind) to give you an idea of what you're buying, especially since you cannot buy the products in a brick-and-mortar store.

So be sure to turn off your pop-up blocker so you can open enlarged windows of the items.

Appendix E
Whimsic Alley

If you're a Harry Potter fan, the name of this retail store sounds familiar, doesn't it? Does it make you think of . . . Diagon Alley?

If so, then you've hit upon the obvious connection of Stan Goldin's inspired store, Whimsic Alley, which is located in southern California in Santa Monica, sandwiched in between rather ordinary retail stores.

But there's nothing ordinary about Whimsic Alley beyond its rather ordinary facade . . . like the mundane row of bricks behind an English pub called the Leaky Cauldron, which opens up to Diagon Alley.

Muggles—nonmagic folk like you and me—will never

The entrance to Whimsic Alley

Stan Goldin:
A Wizard at Words

To have a book published is a common dream. For most aspiring wordsmiths, however, it remains a dream; for a select few, it becomes a reality. Case in point: Stan Goldin, whose customers frequent Whimsic Alley, his retail store in Santa Monica, California.

The idea for the book came from his customers, who wanted a book of imaginary spells. (All of the current books are for Wiccans.) The idea came to fruition when I was at his store to support a book signing, in the company of Tim Kirk and Britton McDaniel, two artists who contributed to *Fact, Fiction, and Folklore in Harry Potter's World: An Unofficial Guide.*

Stan solicited spells from his customers worldwide and, after he made the initial cut, I made the final selection for publication. Stan then chose the best and awarded prizes from his store's inventory.

I've had a few books published, but this is Stan's first book, so I'm happy to welcome him to the fraternity of writers. I'm sure you can expect to see many more books from him in the future.

The book is titled *The Whimsic Alley Book of Spells: Mythical Incantations for Wizards of All Ages* (trade paperback, $14.95, Hampton Roads Publishing).

see Diagon Alley, except through the magic of movies, so Whimsic Alley is the next best thing, especially since cash, checks, and credit cards are accepted: no Knuts, Sickles, or Galleons are needed here.

Though the store obviously carries a lot more than just Harry Potter–related products, the wizarding world is really front and center. Just take a good look around and you'll find that any Muggle with magical interests will find much of interest.

Need a wand? Visit the Phoenix Wands, where a wide assortment of wands are available for sale.

What about clothing for school? What should the well-dressed Muggle wear? Visit Habber & Dasher to deck yourself out in sartorial splendor.

The wand room at Whimsic Alley

Candy? Take your pick from Pilcher & Botts, which has everything you can imagine, and some things you'd never imagine—troll boogers, anyone? Hmmm, you say it's not to your taste? What about messenger-owl eggs?

Need books? A wide selection of journals, spellbooks, fantasy novels, and all the Harry Potter novels can be found here.

Finally, at the back of the store, the Harry Potter Wizard store has a full line of licensed products, from backpacks to hats, Harry Potter bookends to mouse pads—you name it, and Whimsic Alley's got it.

Interior shot of Whimsic Alley

Obviously, not everyone will make it to southern California, though a surprising number of tourists *do* make a special pilgrimage just to seek out the rare, the unusual, and the uniquely different at Whimsic Alley.

Most people, however, visit the cyberstore version (www.whimsicalley.com), which caters to Muggles worldwide.

The storefront to Whimsic Alley

I really don't believe in magic. I believe in some kinds—the magic of imagination and the magic of love.

—*Joanne Rowling, during a Q&A*
at the Royal Albert Hall in London,
June 2003

The Prophecy Fulfilled

> "I cannot complain at all, what a fantastic thing Harry Potter has given me. But one of my regrets would be that I will never again have the pleasure of sneaking into any café I like, sitting down and diving into my world and no one knowing what I am doing and no one bothering me and being totally anonymous."
>
> —*J. K. Rowling quoted in "Newsround" online*

Harry Potter fandom is already gearing up for what will be a day of mixed emotions: the publication date of the seventh, and last, Harry Potter novel.

On one hand, it's the book that fans have been waiting for since a decade ago, when the first book appeared in England in a miniscule run of 500 copies. On the other hand, it marks the end of the series, after which point the Rowling fans will, like Tolkien's fans, find other aspects of their phenomenon to sustain their enthusiasm.

Yes, I know that Rowling is planning a nonfiction book, an encyclopedia, that gives the back story about Hogwarts and the wizarding world, but that's not the same thing as a novel. And, yes, I know that we will learn the fates of all the characters in an epilogue that will be published in the seventh book, but . . . we want more.

Just *one* more novel—perhaps Harry in his first assignment as a junior Auror (assuming he lives), teamed up with Tonks and Lupin, who help him hunt down members of a new group that took its inspiration from the Death Eaters.

Or perhaps a novel in which the Ministry of Magic is under attack—from within—and Harry is implicated and must defend himself against what is clearly a witch hunt.

But these are fantasies, mere flights of imagination, that will see the light of day as subjects of fan fiction because there's only one guarantee: Rowling will *not* be writing an eighth novel, no matter how many millions of fans demand it.

This is as it should be. As Stephen King put it, when asked at a press conference for a joint reading in New York City with J. K. Rowling and John Irving, "Should Harry Potter die?", he responded: "Just be true to the story." Meaning, if the story dictates it, then so be it. The story is boss. Honest storytelling isn't about the readers' wishes or, from the author's point of view, the politically correct thing to do. It's about understanding that the story imposes its own rules, no matter what.

Book number six, *The Half-Blood Prince*, went to press with 10.8 million copies, with an immediate reorder of 2.7 million copies.

Book number seven will likely go to press with 13 million copies. I suspect that even some of the Muggles who haven't kept up with the series will buy the last one, just to be a small part of book publishing history. The best-selling book of all time will undoubtedly be ushered in by a book promotion that will insure virtually every Muggle on the planet will know the book is out.

That, I think, will be a good thing. It's good to see books—instead of movies or rock stars or television stars—get the limelight. It's good to see people get excited about reading. It's especially good to see children put away their electronic gadgets and pick up *Half-Blood Prince*, a 652-page book—more than good, it's *wonderful*.

Most of all, it's good that millions of people have rediscovered the magic of the written word, which engages the imagination in a way that the visual media cannot: Movies and television are passive entertainments, but a book is a private theater in which one's imagination is actively engaged—it's *real* magic.

And after that last book is out, the entry point to the wizarding world, Platform Nine and Three-Quarters, will be closed forever, and two prophecies will be fulfilled: first, the prophecy at the heart of the series, the fact that a final confrontation is in the stars between Lord Voldemort and Harry Potter; and, second, the observation that Professor McGonagall made in the first chapter of the first Harry Potter book: "He'll be famous—a legend—I wouldn't be surprised if today was known as Harry Potter day in the future—there will be books written about Harry—every child in our world will know his name!"

When book one was published, it had a tiny first printing. The author, her agent, and her publisher hoped for the best but braced for the worst: In those days, a children's book would earn, at best, a modest return.

But who could have imagined that Rowling, in time, would become the best-selling author in the history of book publishing? Rowling was understandably gobsmacked; in other words, totally and completely stunned.

From a first printing of 500 copies (for the first book) to a first printing of 13–15 million copies in the U.S. alone (for the seventh book), Rowling's Harry Potter novels have produced a renewed interest in children's books, which are now enjoying a resurgence, appealing not only to children but to adults, as well.

But in all of this, it's important to remember that in the end, the dollars don't matter, the fame doesn't matter, and the print runs don't matter—not to the reader.

In the end, not even the storyteller matters, as Stephen King pointed out: "It's the tale, not he who tells it."

In the end, the *story* matters.

Harry Potter has earned his place on the same shelf with Alice and Dorothy, Mr. Toad and Pooh Bear and Mowgli, Tom Sawyer and Huck Finn, Superman and Tarzan, Frodo and Sherlock Holmes.

No matter what Rowling writes after the Harry Potter novels, nothing for her is likely to be a success on the same scale. But that really doesn't matter, does it? Because Harry Potter has made his indelible mark around the world—the Harry Potter phenomenon is firmly entrenched as part of the world's popular culture—and so, too, has his creator, Joanne Rowling, who through the magic of storytelling changed her world, and ours, for the better. That's *real* magic.

What writer could ask for anything more?

That this book changed something, and changed it for the better, is beyond all doubt. It gave to those who otherwise might not be great readers an insight into what the joy of reading can be. It gave to those whose imagination had not been given room to flourish the opportunity to enter a world of imaginative fantasy. It brought great happiness and excitement, just that, into countless young lives. No other book in history has done this to the same extent, and probably no other book will. That is why this book will not be forgotten.

—*Alexander McCall Smith, in his introduction to a special edition of* Harry Potter and the Philosopher's Stone, *part of Bloomsbury's "21 Great Reads for the 21st Century" collection*

About the Author

George Beahm has published 27 books, among them *The Essential J. R. R. Tolkien Sourcebook, The Stephen King Companion, The Unauthorized Anne Rice Companion, The Unofficial Patricia Cornwell Companion, Stephen King from A to Z: An Encyclopedia of His Life and Work,* and *War of Words: The Censorship Debate.*

Actively involved in the book industry since 1975, Beahm has also been a self-publisher, regional publisher, book marketing director, book publishing consultant, and book packager.

George Beahm lives with his wife Mary in Williamsburg, Virginia. His website is at www.georgebeahm.com.

About the Contributors

Catherine Collins is a huge Harry Potter fan who has worked at online fan sites TheQuidditchPitch.net (formerly TheDarkLord.net), HarryPotter FanZone.com, and MuggleNet.com, and reported on HP Fan Trip 2004 and Spellbound! 2005.

Tim Kirk is a design director for Kirk Design, an enterprise that draws on his vast experience in conceptualization, content creation, and art direction for Walt Disney Imagineering, where he worked for twenty-two years. Among his many credits at Disney, Kirk was the overall senior designer for Tokyo DisneySea, a three-billion-dollar theme park. He also played a key role in conceptualizing the popular Disney MGM Studio Tour Park in the Walt Disney World Resort. A five-time Hugo award winner for best art in the fantasy and science fiction field, Kirk has illustrated fanzines, calendars, limited edition books, and trade books for numerous publishers, including Ballantine Books, which issued his Tolkien illustrations, done for his master's degree in illustration, as the 1975 *Tolkien Calendar*. A former artist for both Hallmark Cards and Current, Kirk has designed greeting cards, jigsaw puzzles, wrapping paper, stationary, and books. In June 2004, one of Kirk Design's projects made its debut: The Science Fiction Museum and Hall of Fame in Seattle, Washington. Kirk Design's website is www.kirkdesign inc.com.

Stephen McGinty is a senior feature writer with the *Scotsman* newspaper and author of *This Turbulent Priest: A Life of Cardinal Thomas Winning*, a critically acclaimed biography published in 2003 by HarperCollins.

The Whimsic Alley Book of Spells

Mythical Incantations for Wizards of All Ages

Edited by George Beahm and Stan Goldin

Illustrated by Tim Kirk

Available in trade paperback,
192 pages, $14.95

It was only after attending Lumos 2006 (a Harry Potter conference in Las Vegas) that I understood the scope of Harry Potter fandom. In many ways, it's similar to fandoms of other popular culture fixtures, such as *Star Trek*. The key difference between the *Star Trek* and Harry Potter fandoms, as Megan and Mallory Schuyler pointed out on their Wizard Rockumentary website, is that Harry Potter fandom is *cool.*

Lumos 2006 was a blast for me. Even if I had not been one of the guests of honor who enjoyed all the privileges, I would have come away from the experience enriched, invigorated, and inspired by the enthusiasm of the fans. They showed their great love for Harry Potter and everything in the wizarding world by singing songs, dressing up in costume, creating art, and simply hanging out in the halls and doorways to talk about anything and everything in the Harry Potter world.

This book is yet another example of how Rowling's works have inspired her fans. In this case, fans contributed—at the request of Whimsic Alley storeowner Stan Goldin—spells, with the understanding that the best would be published in this book, and the best of the best would be awarded prizes from the inventory of Whimsic Alley.

The result is a collection of fanciful spells from fans worldwide, each offering a fictional wizarding biography that in many cases was as imaginative as the spells themselves!

The original plan was for me and Stan to write a lot of supplementary essays about wands, dark wizards, spell casting, etc., but Stan and I went overboard and wrote with wild abandon, resulting in a wordage that exceeded the boundaries of common sense—and the page count allocated to this book project. The (sad) result is that I made some ruthless cuts and trimmed the book down, which resulted in a more compact book.

Again, I turned to Tim Kirk to provide the illustrations. He did a wonderful full-color cover and interior art, too. I've come to associate his whimsical touch with Rowling's wizarding world and, as always, I appreciate his presence in the book.

In any event, this book project was a rare opportunity for me to hobnob with a fellow wizard, and to contribute a spell of my own making, as well.

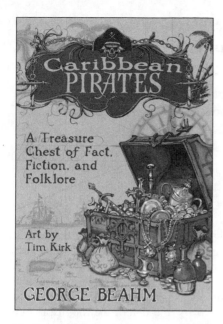

Caribbean Pirates

A Treasure Chest of Fact, Fiction, and Folklore

By George Beahm

Introduction and illustrations by Tim Kirk

Additional art by Britton McDaniel

Available in full-color trade paperback, 256 pages, $16.95.

Chances are pretty good that if you know anything about pirates, you have seen Disney's wonderful *Pirates of the Caribbean* movies. Though pirates have been a staple of popular culture since the turn of the century, when N. C. Wyeth sumptuously illustrated Robert Louis Stevenson's *Treasure Island*, their appeal skyrocketed when Johnny Depp as Captain Jack Sparrow made his dramatic entry in this new film franchise.

Unfortunately, most of the books that have been published have pirated art and text from other books about pirates, with the result that there's a dreary sameness about pirate books: the same ground, covered again, with the same public domain photos and artwork.

Though there are several great books about pirates (and I take care to recommend them to you in this book), I wanted to take a completely different approach: to discuss what's historically correct about pirates in light of what we see in *Pirates of the Caribbean,* and to discuss instances in which Disney took a few liberties with the history.

The first part of the book, then, is a thorough discussion about the history of pirates as interpreted through Disney's lens, along with an extensive write-up about the film franchise and the theme park ride on which it is based; the second section focuses on how to talk and dress like a pirate, where to go to be a pirate (pirate festivals and cruises), and where to go to find out more about pirates (museums and the like).

Because the world of pirates is all about color, about flamboyance, about piratitude, this book is amply illustrated with full-color photos throughout. "Long John" Tim Kirk—a huge pirate fan and the scourge and terror of Long Beach, California, with his brother Steve when they were kids—provides a full-color treasure chest on the cover and numerous black-and-white illustrations done especially for this book.

This book is a combination history book and resource guide, which makes it an unusual and distinctive addition to the existing books on the subject.

So climb aboard, find yourself a comfortable perch in the crow's nest, and let's cast off to the Caribbean islands in search of buried treasure, adventure, and glory!

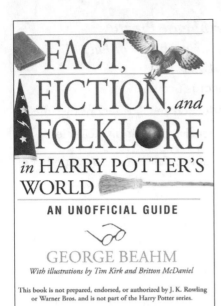

This book is not prepared, endorsed, or authorized by J. K. Rowling or Warner Bros. and is not part of the Harry Potter series.

Fact, Fiction, and Folklore in Harry Potter's World
An Unofficial Guide
By George Beahm

Illustrated by Tim Kirk and Britton McDaniel

Available in trade paperback,
280 pages, $16.95

This book was a lot of fun for me to write because it allowed me to talk about not only the wizarding world but our Muggle world as well. The book is arranged in four sections: fabulous beasts, prominent wizards, magical artifacts, and magical places.

Within each section, I wrote about Rowling's universe, and then looked in our world to try and determine the inspiration for the wizard counterpart. The result is a fun-to-read book that covers a lot of history, science, myth, and folklore. My hope is that the book's approach will inspire curious readers to go out and find on their own some of the subjects I've written about.

For instance, in *Fantastic Beasts & Where to Find Them*, Rowling has an entry for "Yeti," better known as the Abominable Snowman. His North American cousin is Sasquatch ("Bigfoot") and there's a whole field of exploration called Cryptozoology.

Sometimes the books I write are heavy on reference, which requires a lot of slogging through dull texts. In this case, it was pure joy. I found my curiosity sparked by trying to imagine where Rowling had gotten her inspiration for the various critters, beasties, people, and places that populate her fully realized world.

Because the book practically cried out for illustrations, I asked Tim Kirk for art. Tim is one of the world's most imaginative artists—he's done everything from fanzine work to greeting cards and book illustration to calendar work—and his time at Disney Imagineering served him in good stead when he, his brother Steve (another Disney Imagineer), and his sister-in-law Kathy started Kirk Design Inc., which carries their imaginative visions to new heights.

I also asked Britton McDaniel—a young artist fresh out of college—to contribute, since I like her art a lot, too. She's talented, fun to be with, and has unbridled enthusiasm. I hope you like her art as much as I do.

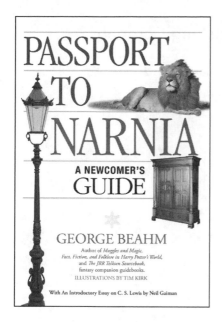

Passport to Narnia
A Newcomer's Guide
By George Beahm

Illustrated by Tim Kirk

Available in trade paperback,
200 pages, $12.95

Although C. S. Lewis's Narnia books have been around for a half century, it struck me that for many people—especially young readers—the world of Narnia would have to be explained in a very basic framework because the first film adaptation would likely be their first exposure to the enchanting world of Narnia. This book was the result.

An accessible book written especially for newcomers, it covers a lot of ground: a biography of C. S. Lewis, background information, the world of Narnia, a book-by-book look, the merchandising surrounding the first movie, and resources for the curious reader wanting to do a little exploration on his own.

My hope with this book is to get you sufficiently grounded in the real and imaginative worlds of C. S. Lewis to seek out, perhaps, a biography or a critical study, after reading *The Chronicles of Narnia*.

The Narnia books have stood the test of time and are classics in the field of children books. My hope was that, with this book, I could share some of my enthusiasm for the man and his work with you, and perhaps you, too, will go out and share your newfound enthusiasm with others.

Narnia is a big place, so when you take your first step through the enchanted wardrobe and make your way past Lantern Waste, you'll soar on Lewis's flights of imagination into the beautiful, and treacherous, world of Narnia.

The art is by Tim Kirk, who knows Lewis's work and Narnia much better than I do. I think you will agree with me that his art lends just the right touch.

Hampton Roads Publishing Company

. . . for the evolving human spirit

HAMPTON ROADS PUBLISHING COMPANY publishes books
on a variety of subjects, including metaphysics, spirituality,
health, visionary fiction, and other related topics.

For a copy of our latest trade catalog, call toll-free,
800-766-8009, or send your name and address to:

HAMPTON ROADS PUBLISHING COMPANY, INC.
1125 STONEY RIDGE ROAD • CHARLOTTESVILLE, VA 22902
e-mail: hrpc@hrpub.com • www.hrpub.com